A Social and Economic History
of Twentieth-Century Europe

A Social and Economic History
of Twentieth-Century Europe

Gerold Ambrosius
William H. Hubbard

*Translated by Keith Tribe
and William H. Hubbard*

Harvard University Press
Cambridge, Massachusetts
London, England
1989

Originally published as *Sozial- und Wirtschaftsgeschichte Europas im
20. Jahrhundert;* copyright © 1986 by C. H. Beck'sche Verlagsbuchhandlung
(Oscar Beck), Munich.

This book is printed on acid-free paper, and its binding materials
have been chosen for strength and durability.

Library of Congress Cataloging-in-Publication Data
Ambrosius, Gerold.
    [Sozial- und Wirtschaftsgeschichte Europas im 20. Jahrhundert.
English]
    A social and economic history of twentieth-century Europe / Gerold
Ambrosius, William H. Hubbard ; translated by Keith Tribe and
William H. Hubbard.
        p.   cm.
    Translation: of Sozial- und Wirtschaftsgeschichte Europas im
20. Jahrhundert.
    Bibliography: p.
    Includes index.
    ISBN 0-674-81340-5.—ISBN 0-674-81341-3 (pbk.)
    1. Europe—Social conditions—20th century. 2. Europe—Economic
conditions—20th century. 3. Europe—Industries—History—20th
century. I. Hubbard, William H. II. Title.
HN373.5.A5913   1989
306'.094—dc19   89-1750

Preface

Several institutions and persons deserve thanks for assisting the writing of the original German edition. I am grateful to Concordia University for granting me research leave in Paris, where the Institut National d'Etudes Démographiques and the Fondation Nationale des Sciences Politiques gave generous access to their libraries. The greater part of the sources and literature was provided by the libraries of the universities of Marburg and Bremen, the Free University of Berlin, and McGill and Concordia universities in Montreal. My coauthor and I are grateful to the following persons for their support and advice: R. Ambrosius, C. Bertrand, S. Bornstein, W. Fischer, G. Hardach, I. Henke, B. Hubbard, H. Kaelble, D. Räuchle, R. Rudin, H. Siegrist, L. Sprecher, M. Vipond, and H. Volkmann. We would also like to thank our editor at C. H. Beck, Christine Zeile, to whose enthusiasm and support our work owes much.

The publication of an American edition has given me the opportunity to review the manuscript and smooth out some rough spots, to revise it to accommodate a different audience, and to append a postscript referring to some key developments of the last three years. It has also meant incurring new debts of gratitude, which I wish to redeem with thanks. The Ludwig-Boltzmann-Institut für Historische Sozialforschung in Salzburg, directed by Gerhard Botz, provided me with a congenial academic home abroad during much of this time. A generous grant from the Inter-Nationes Foundation in Bonn financed the translation. Stephen Bornstein and Ronald Rudin patiently responded to queries about style and substance, and Mary Vipond's critical reading of the entire manuscript removed a number of infelicities. I am also very grateful to the book's editors at Harvard University Press—Patricia Williams, Elizabeth Suttell, and Jennifer Snodgrass—for their encouragement, friendliness, and competence.

Finally, to Berit, kjaere livsledsagerske, I simply owe much, very much.

William H. Hubbard

Contents

Tables

Figures

Europe 1918–19

Europe 1980s

European Countries by Region

Western Europe

Austria
Belgium
Britain or United Kingdom (UK)
Germany; after 1945, Federal Republic of Germany (FRG)
   or West Germany
France
Ireland
The Netherlands
Switzerland

Northern Europe

Denmark
Finland
Norway
Sweden

Eastern Europe

Bulgaria
Czechoslovakia (CSSR)
German Democratic Republic (GDR) or East Germany
Hungary
Poland
Rumania
Yugoslavia

Southern Europe

Greece
Italy
Portugal
Spain

Introduction

This book is intended to be introductory. It has to remain introductory, for comparative European social and economic history is still in its early stages—the available literature permits only a limited tentative survey since it either deals with quite specific social problems or takes the form of voluminous reference works. But this book is also meant to remain introductory, since it is not primarily written for specialists in social and economic history. The orientation of modern social and economic history is towards contemporary sociology and economics. It uses the specialist terminology of these academic disciplines and seeks to verify its hypotheses empirically. Our book follows this orientation in social and economic history without, however, allowing general accessibility to suffer. That sums up the didactic and methodological intention behind this text. We attempt to present and analyze relationships and contexts in a language as direct and clear as possible. We explain, when necessary, specialist sociological and economic terminology and interpret statistical material for the non-expert. Tables are kept to a minimum; we believe that graphics are more accessible to the reader. We must note that the database for this material is sometimes problematic and that numerous methodological problems occur in the construction of long time-series. These problems are repeatedly referred to in the text, so that the reader might more easily maintain a proper critical distance from the statistical data.

The book is organized so that individual themes are dealt with longitudinally over the whole of the century. This procedure has its difficulties, for it runs counter to the common chronological presentation of history. Complex and comprehensive social and economic structures within different historical periods are wrenched apart in such a systematic longitudinal analysis. We believe that this presentation is nonetheless clearer and more comprehensible than a chronological survey for those who seek an introductory overview.

Maintaining a clear general picture despite the number of different countries involved is an additional problem. On the one hand, we wish to identify typical developmental processes and to categorize individual countries according to special criteria; on the other, we do not want to push the pan-European perspective so far that differences between countries or regions become completely obscured. We have sought a middle way, but because of our longitudinal approach we are forced to treat specific events and issues in individual countries mainly in passing. The book's comparative European perspective also downplays the need of particular periods and countries, despite their numerous common features, for their own explanatory models of socioeconomic development. In spite of this caveat, inevitably some readers will be disappointed or surprised at the paucity of specific information on individual countries in the following account. Those who seek more detailed information are referred to the Suggestions for Further Reading.

The presentation that follows is more descriptive than analytical. Our thematic approach and methodological procedure dictated this in part. The book traces the social and economic development of European countries primarily by means of key indicators. Naturally this approach does not exclude an explanation of the developmental process, although more detailed analysis is hindered by the current state of research. Complete, complex explanatory models for comparative social and economic history are as yet in their early stages. To construct transnational development models within the framework of international comparative research is no simple matter; such models as do exist are mostly limited to very general interpretive approaches or to a few factors and relations with whose aid socioeconomic processes might be analyzed.

A topic as broad as the social and economic history of an entire century for an entire continent, which itself consists of many countries each with its own pattern of development, necessitates some restriction of subject matter, time, and geographic scope. Making a selection inevitably involves a degree of arbitrariness; some will question why one topic is dealt with and another, deemed equally important, is omitted. We can respond only that our selection treats those topics customarily present in modern introductory texts of social and economic history and that we also believe this selection meaningful and workable.

We have treated chronological boundaries flexibly. To demonstrate some long-term developmental trends, we have occasionally gone back into the nineteenth century. For other topics we have begun our coverage with the First World War. In a few cases we have restricted our account to the period after the Second World War, especially when relevant statistical data are unavailable for the prewar years. Nevertheless, we have sought to provide a general impression of European social and economic development over the last one hundred years.

Apart from Albania, Cyprus, Iceland, Luxembourg, Malta, and Turkey, all sovereign states in Europe are included. Russia, or rather the Soviet Union, represents a special case. It is generally excluded, although its great importance for Europe—in particular, for the development of the eastern European states after the Second World War—means that it cannot be disregarded entirely. The regional division used in the following account distinguishes between northern, western, southern, and eastern Europe (see the listing opposite page 1). This division is primarily geographical, but it does also serve to indicate socioeconomic differences. In contrast to the customary geographical division used in the publications of the United Nations, we include Great Britain and the Irish Republic in western Europe rather than northern Europe, and Yugoslavia in eastern Europe rather than southern Europe. Maintaining a geographically identical delimitation of eastern Europe over the entire century is not possible; after each world war the frontiers, especially those bordering the Soviet Union, were substantially altered, and since the Second World War the eastern part of the German state—now the German Democratic Republic—has been incorporated into this region. The designations Western Europe and Eastern Europe are used occasionally to refer to the areas bounded respectively by the capitalist market economies of northern, western and southern Europe and by the state socialist economies of eastern Europe.

CHAPTER 1

Demographic Foundations of
Social and Economic Development

General Trends

Often taken for granted, a country's own population is its most fundamental and important natural resource. Population comprehends not only the laborers who produce goods and services but also the consumers who purchase or use those products. In other words, population is the central element of both supply and demand in the economy. All things being equal, a country with a large population will produce and consume more than one with a small population. In reality, the relationship between population and economic performance is much more complex. Production is not simply a function of mere numbers; it also depends on, among other things, the proportion of the population employed, the length of time worked, and the skills of the work force, as well as on managerial organization and technological development. Likewise, consumption is determined by more than mere numbers of heads; age structure, sex ratio, distribution of income, taste, and custom play decisive roles. Thus, the number of variables to be considered is large, and their interplay is difficult to unravel even on the theoretical plane. The concrete historical reality is extremely diverse, differentiated by nation as well as by region.

Population change is the product of three factors: births, deaths, and migration. A given constellation of births and deaths in a population, its reproductive structure or *régime démographique,* reflects not only economic conditions but also social and moral attitudes towards the position of women and children, the role of the family, the institution of marriage, and the practice of sexual relations. In order to compare reproductive structures over time and space, births and deaths are expressed not as absolute numbers but as rates in a given standard base population. Thus, the crude birthrate is the number of live births in a given year per thousand of the total population in that year; similarly, the crude death rate is the number of deaths per thousand of the total population. When making comparisons, however, a word of warning is in order: the aforementioned rates do not take the age structure of the population into account. If populations have markedly different distributions of age-groups—for example, skewed either towards youth or towards the aged—comparison of their respective crude birth and death rates can be misleading. Age-specific rates, which use a uniform age-group as the base population, are more accurate for comparative purposes, but their calculation is not always possible. The most commonly utilized age-specific demographic rate is the number of births per thousand women of childbearing age (internationally defined as 15–44).

Population Growth

Notwithstanding two terrible periods of enormous bloodletting, Europe's population in the twentieth century has increased at an historically rapid rate. In the 72 years between 1913 and 1985 the total population grew by over 44 percent from 341 million to over 492 million. This substantial growth is often overlooked, for two reasons. First, the European rate of increase seems modest compared with recent world rates, especially the rate of growth experienced by Africa, Asia, and South America since the 1950s. As a result, Europe's population declined to barely 11 percent of the world's in 1980. Throughout the nineteenth century, by contrast, Europe's population grew more quickly than the world average, thereby raising its share of the world population from about one fifth in 1800 to over one fourth in 1913. Second, whereas between 1850 and 1914 population increased steadily almost everywhere in Europe, the pattern of growth since then has been more varied, with a number of countries experiencing periods of contraction as well as expansion.

Periodization

In general, the demographic history of twentieth-century Europe divides into two distinct periods: from 1914 to 1945, and from 1945 to the present. The first of these two periods was dominated by the effects of war, both international and civil. The demographic consequences of these wars cannot be calculated fully, but they were clearly profound. The bloody trench battles of the First World War cost the belligerents (excluding Russia) some six million soldiers. Expressing these direct military losses in relation to the labor supply illustrates their enormity. France and Germany each lost about 10 percent of their male work force, Austria-Hungary and Italy over 6 percent, and Britain roughly 5 percent. Civilian deaths from undernourishment and disease—especially the Spanish flu epidemic of 1918-1919—were almost as numerous. The total estimated losses of eleven million persons amounted to over 3 percent of Europe's prewar population. As can be seen in table 1.1, ten countries had smaller populations in 1920 than in 1913. The largest individual loser was France, which even after the reacquisition of Alsace-Lorraine had almost two million fewer inhabitants in 1920 than in 1913. The war also disrupted enormously the pattern of marriages and births, resulting in four greatly diminished birth cohorts, the well-known *classes creuses* of French demography, and leaving a legacy of late marriage, premature widowhood, and enforced celibacy that has affected not only population growth but also the structure of European society and economy throughout the twentieth century.

Tragically, the far-reaching demographic costs of the First World War were exceeded by those incurred in the Second World War. Actual military losses were substantially less for many belligerents than in 1914–1918—France, for example, lost "only" 167,000 soldiers, although the German army lost roughly four million men and the Soviet military losses have been estimated at eighteen million. However, the geographic scope of the military campaigns, the widespread use of aerial bombardment, and the campaign of genocide conducted by National Socialist Germany raised the number of civilian victims to double that in 1914–1918, or roughly twelve million. Civilian and military losses (excluding the Soviet Union) together amounted to about seventeen million: over 4 percent of the prewar population.

This figure omits the tens of thousands of deaths caused by malnutrition and exposure in the years of social and economic dislocation immediately following the war. Leaving aside the Soviet Union, whose nonmilitary deaths numbered more than fifteen million, the most heavily afflicted areas were in central and east-central Europe. All told, Poland suffered the most, losing at least 13 percent of its prewar population; Yugoslavia lost 11 percent, and Germany lost some 9 percent. The overall demographic balance sheet of these terrible years

Table 1.1. Population by Country, 1913–2000 (in millions)

	1913	1920	1930	1940	1950	1960	1970	1980	2000[a]
Northern Europe[b]	14.6	15.1	16.2	17.2	19	20.5	22.1	22.6	22.8
Sweden	5.6	5.8	6.1	6.3	7	7.5	8.1	8.3	8.4
Denmark	2.9	3	3.5	3.8	4.3	4.6	4.9	5.1	5.4
Finland	3.2	3.1	3.4	3.7	4	4.4	4.6	4.8	4.6
Norway	2.5	2.7	2.8	3	3.3	3.6	3.9	4.1	4.4
Western Europe[c]	170.8	170.2	181	189.9	175.6	189.8	207.6	212.8	227
Germany	58.5	59.9	64.7	69.3	—	—	—	—	—
FRG[d]	—	—	—	—	49.9	55.3	60.7	61.6	58.7
United Kingdom	43	43.5	45.7	47.8	50.6	52.5	55.4	55.9	64.1
France	41.7	39	40.8	41.3	41.7	45.7	50.8	53.7	59.6
Netherlands	6.3	6.8	7.8	8.9	10.1	11.5	13	14.1	16
Belgium	7.7	7.6	8.1	8.4	8.6	9.2	9.7	9.9	10
Austria	6.6	6.4	6.7	6.7	6.9	7.1	7.4	7.5	7.5
Switzerland	3.9	3.9	4	4.2	4.7	5.4	6.3	6.4	6.8
Ireland	2.9	2.9	2.9	2.9	2.9	2.8	2.9	3.4	4.3
Eastern Europe	86.4	84.4	92.7	102.4	105.9	115.6	125.8	134.4	148.4
Poland	30.7	29.4	31.1	34.9	24.8	29.7	32.6	35.6	38.5
Yugoslavia	12.3	11.7	13.5	15.6	16.3	18.4	20.4	22.3	25.6
Rumania	16.2	15.9	18.2	20	16.3	18.4	20.2	22.2	25.6
GDR[e]	—	—	—	—	18.9	17.9	17.1	16.7	18.2
Czechoslovakia	13.6	13.5	14.6	15.3	12.4	13.6	14.3	15.3	15.8
Hungary	7.9	7.9	8.6	9.2	9.3	10	10.3	10.7	10.8
Bulgaria	4.9	5.2	5.7	6.3	7.3	7.9	8.5	8.9	9.6
Albania	0.8	0.8	1	1.1	1.2	1.6	2.2	2.7	4.3
Southern Europe[f]	68.8	68.6	77.2	84.9	90.9	97.5	106.9	114.4	128
Italy	36.2	35.9	40.7	44.3	46.6	49.4	53.6	57.1	61.4
Spain	20.3	21	23.2	25.5	27.9	30.3	33.8	37.4	45.4
Portugal	6	6.4	6.7	7.6	8.4	8.8	9.6	9.9	11.2
Greece	6	5	6.3	7.2	7.6	8.3	8.8	9.6	10
Total Europe	340.6	338.3	367.1	394.4	391.7	423.4	462.4	484.2	525.5

Sources: Brian R. Mitchell, *European Historical Statistics 1750–1970* (London, 1975), pp. 19–24; United Nations, *Demographic Yearbook 1963* (New York, 1964), pp. 156–59; *1978* (New York, 1979), pp. 119–20, 133–34; *1981* (New York, 1982), p. 186; UN (ECE), *Economic Survey of Europe in 1974,* Part II: *Post-War Demographic Trends in Europe and the Outlook until the Year 2000* (New York, 1975), p. 176.

Note: The years 1913–1940 refer to 1923 frontiers, 1950–2000 to 1950 frontiers.

[a] UN projection based on vital rates prevailing in the early 1970s.

[b] Including Iceland and the North Sea Islands.

[c] Including Monaco, Liechtenstein, and Luxembourg.

[d] Including West Berlin.

[e] Including East Berlin.

[f] Including Gibraltar, San Marino, Andorra, Malta, and the Vatican.

is sobering: each of the great wars eliminated a full decade of European population growth.

By contrast, the second period has experienced no such catastrophic shocks of mass slaughter. Moreover, the prolonged economic prosperity after 1950 established a more propitious climate for demographic growth than had prevailed in the interwar years. In the 1950s and 1960s the population of all European countries (except East Germany) expanded rapidly. The European decennial growth between 1961 and 1970 was the highest since 1913: 9.2 percent. Since then expansion has slacked off markedly, especially in western and northern Europe. In recent years natural population growth—the excess of births over deaths—has virtually ceased in Sweden, Denmark, Britain, and Belgium; in three countries—West Germany, East Germany, and Austria—it has even been negative.

National and Regional Variations
Changes in national borders between 1913 and 1980 make close comparison of national and regional growth rates difficult. As the maps at the beginning of the volume show, the westward shift of Polish borders, the division of Germany, and the transfer of eastern portions of Czechoslovakia and Rumania to the Soviet Union alter the geographic definition not only of individual countries but also of the defined socioeconomic regions of western and eastern Europe.

The picture of twentieth-century European demographic developments in table 1.1 shows at once relatively constant regional differentials and a great variety of national experiences. Throughout the entire period 1913–1980 population in northern, eastern, and southern Europe grew faster than the European average; in western Europe, by contrast, expansion was slower than average. In addition, the rate of growth in northern and southern Europe remained stable, whereas eastern and western Europe, as a direct result of the two major wars, experienced significantly faster growth in 1950–1980 than in 1913–1940; in the case of western Europe the rate of growth doubled between the first period and the second.

The records of individual countries are more diverse and reflect not only differences in war losses but also different constellations of births, deaths, and migration. Again western and eastern Europe contain the greatest variety. Austria registered the lowest rate of growth between 1913 and 1980: a mere 14 percent. Similarly low rates are found in Ireland, Poland, and Czechoslovakia; in the case of the last two, however, border changes and war losses obscure the actual trend, which was considerably higher. At the other end of the spectrum, the population of the Netherlands has more than doubled since 1913. Among the larger states France is the most striking example of changes in rate of population growth. Between 1913 and 1940 heavy war losses and the lowest birthrate in Europe combined to reduce the French population by almost half a million. The number of deaths exceeded that of births not only in 1914–1918 but also in 1919, 1929, and 1935–1944. This situation was reversed with startling rapidity after 1945; since then France has sustained a high natural growth rate. During the 1960s its population increase, including migration, was the fourth highest in Europe at 11.2 percent. In 1985 its birthrate was among the highest in Europe, exceeded only by that in Portugal, Greece, the Irish Republic, Spain, and the eastern European countries (except Hungary and East Germany).

Geographic Distribution
As a result of this demographic growth, population density in twentieth-century Europe increased from 66 persons per square kilometer in 1920 to 101 in 1985. The distribution of settlement, however, has remained remarkably stable. The Netherlands, Belgium, and England/Wales, each with a density in 1985 of over 330 persons per square kilometer, were by far the most densely settled countries in Europe in 1920, with over 250 persons per square kilometer. The fourth and fifth in line in 1985, West Germany and Italy, had densities of 245 and 191 persons per square kilometer respectively. Virtually all other countries had population densities between one fourth and one third of that in the Netherlands. At the bottom came Norway, Finland, and Sweden, with densities in 1985 of eighteen and below. The regional variation in population density also indicates differences in socioeconomic structure. As a comparison of the maps in figures 1.1 and 3.5 clearly shows, concentrations of population correspond roughly with the most developed, and often the most wealthy, areas of the European capitalist economy, although certain areas of northern Europe constitute an exception.

The regional and national rankings by population have also changed little throughout the century notwithstanding the differential growth rates. The slide of western Europe's proportion of the European total from 50 percent in 1913 to 44 percent in 1980 is primarily attributable to the division of Germany in 1945. In return, both eastern and south-

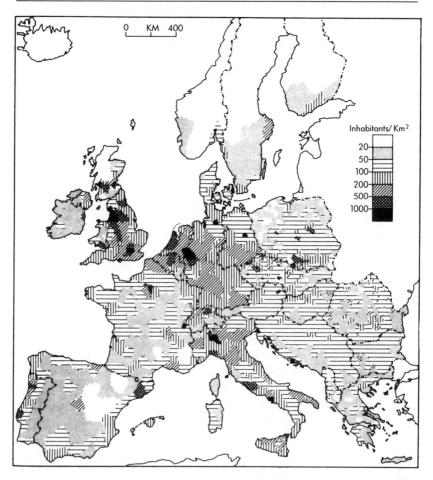

Figure 1.1. Population Density, c. 1970 (inhabitants per square kilometer). *Source:* John Salt and Hugh Clout, eds., *Migration in Post-War Europe: Geographical Essays* (Oxford, 1976), p. 11.

ern Europe increased their proportions by roughly 3 percent and in 1980 contained 28 percent and 24 percent of Europe's total population respectively. Northern Europe accounted for the remaining 4 to 5 percent. The ranking of individual countries has likewise stayed approximately the same; the six most populous states in 1913 were also those with the largest populations in 1985. Their order, however, has shifted slightly: Italy is now second instead of fourth, and Spain has moved ahead of Poland to fifth place. In general, though, the gap between large and small states has shrunk. In 1913 the population of the tenth-ranking country amounted to only 13 percent of the largest state's population; in 1980, it was 25 percent.

The Demographic Transition

Behind the variety of growth lies a transformation of the biological and cultural behavior of Europeans. Dubbed initially the "demographic revolution" by the French demographer Adolphe Landry, this transformation is now called more prosaically the "demographic transition," referring to the transition from high vital rates to low ones. According to this simple model of demographic change, fertility and mortality are inversely related to the degree of modernization obtaining in a given society, defined in terms of the extent of urbanization, the level of education, the degree of industrialization, and so forth. Four ideal-type phases constitute the complete process:

1. Pre-transitional or pre-industrial populations typically have high birthrates (35–40 per mil, or thousand population) as well as high death rates (25–30 per mil and in crisis years over 40 per mil) resulting in a modest and unsteady rate of natural population growth.
2. The actual transition begins when improvements in sanitation, health care, nourishment, and general living standards bring about a fall in mortality to below 20 per mil, while fertility remains relatively high (30–35 per mil). This constellation produces high rates of natural growth in the neighborhood of 1.5 percent per annum.
3. Increasing modernization leads to the adoption of birth control practices, and the birthrate falls to 15–20 per mil. Since death rates are below 15 per mil and continue to fall, natural population growth occurs but at a slow pace of 0.5–1.0 percent per annum.
4. The final phase is the modern reproductive structure in which mortality hovers around 10 per mil, while widespread contraception stabilizes the number of births in the neighborhood of 12–14 per mil. The result is very slow growth of under 0.5 percent per annum or even zero growth.

The onset and pace of the demographic transition in Europe were not uniform in either time or space. Starting first in France and northwest Europe in the nineteenth century, it has in the course of the twentieth century both progressed in northern and western Europe and expanded to eastern and southern Europe. The curves of birth and death rates presented in figures 1.3 and 1.6 show the geographic variations. In many countries of western and northern Europe mortality and fertility were already at rates typical of Phase 3 at the beginning of the century and declined rapidly to Phase 4 rates in the interwar years. Populations in eastern and southern Europe, on the other hand, were still in Phase 2 of the transition in 1913, with birthrates above 30 per mil and death rates over 20 per mil. During the interwar period vital rates declined in these regions, but, except for Czechoslovakia, Hungary, and to a lesser extent Italy, they remained in the upper reaches of Phase 3. The fourth phase of the demographic transition did not occur in eastern and southern Europe until after 1945. A comparison of the data in figures 1.2 and 1.4 reveals the consequences of the differential pace of the demographic transition in twentieth-century Europe. Throughout the entire century eastern and southern Europe have sustained substantially higher natural growth rates than northern and, especially, western Europe. Given the less-developed state of the economies in the former regions, this above-average population growth was, especially in the interwar years, a major source of grave social and economic difficulties, hampering economic expansion and promoting emigration.

Reproduction

Mortality

The seventeenth-century English political philosopher Thomas Hobbes once described life as "nasty, brutish, and short." At least with respect to the latter characteristic, twentieth-century Europe has experienced a dramatic change. Improved nutrition, more sanitary housing and living conditions, and better medical care have lowered mortality in all European societies to close to its biological limits. As the curves in figure 1.2 show, the wide variation in death rates prevailing at the beginning of the century narrowed substantially in the interwar years. By the 1950s crude death rates in almost all European countries had fallen below 12 per mil; in the 1960s and 1970s roughly one half of European countries registered death rates under 10 per mil.

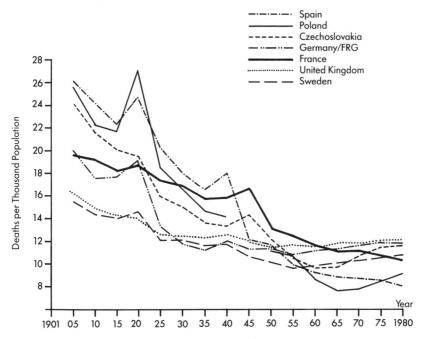

Figure 1.2. Crude Death Rates for Various Countries, 1905–1980 (number of deaths per thousand population). *Sources:* UN (ECE), *Economic Survey of Europe in 1974,* Part II: *Post-War Demographic Trends in Europe and the Outlook until the Year 2000* (New York, 1975), pp. 220–22; UN, *Demographic Yearbook 1982* (New York, 1983), pp. 334–35.

Life Expectancy

The reverse side of this fall in mortality has been an enormous rise in average life expectancy. Figure 1.3 presents data on life expectancies in selected countries representing the spectrum of socioeconomic development. In 1900 in the most advanced countries of northern and western Europe—England, the Netherlands, Sweden—a newborn child could expect to live to the age of fifty or fifty-five, whereas in countries in southern and eastern Europe thirty-five to forty years was the rule. By 1980 the situation had changed fundamentally: not only had average life expectancy generally increased by one third (in Spain it doubled), but regional variations had also become less marked. New-born males in all European countries could expect on average a life span of sixty-five years; in some countries the male life expectancy exceeded seventy years, in Sweden even seventy-six. Already in 1900 females had a longer average life expectancy than males, and this differential has persisted. Indeed, the gap between sexes within each country has become wider than the variations between countries for the same sex.

Infant Mortality

Average life expectancy is calculated by comparing the proportion surviving from one year to the following year with the known death rates for the specific age-group. The largest contributor to the rise in average life expectancy has been the fall in infant mortality. As can be seen in figure 1.4, this exceptionally sensitive indicator of the social and economic well-being of a population exhibited until very recently a sharp geographic gradient, with northern Europe in the lead followed reasonably closely by western Europe and then at considerable distance by southern and eastern Europe. At the beginning of the century, only in Sweden and Norway did fewer than 10 percent of infants die before completing their first year. In most eastern European countries, the rate of infant mortality at that time was twice as high, with close to 20 percent of newborns dying within one year. These rates fell noticeably in the interwar period almost everywhere, but not until the development of antibiotics and effective vaccines against such child-

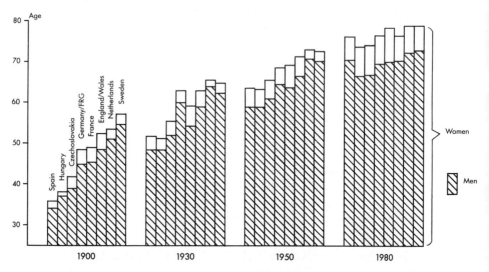

Figure 1.3. Life Expectancy in Various Countries, 1900–1980 (in years). *Sources:* UN (ECE), *Economic Survey of Europe in 1974,* Part II: *Post-War Demographic Trends in Europe and the Outlook until the Year 2000* (New York, 1975), pp. 218–19; UN, *Demographic Yearbook 1982* (New York, 1983), pp. 438–39.

hood scourges as scarlet fever, diphtheria, measles, and whooping cough in the 1940s and 1950s was the social wastage implied in infant mortality reduced substantially in all European countries.

National aggregates, of course, conceal enormous geographic differences within individual countries, such as variations between urban areas with comprehensive medical facilities and less well-served rural regions. For example, the infant mortality rate in the Italian South, the *mezzogiorno,* in the 1970s was almost twice the rate prevailing in northeastern Italy (21.8 per mil versus 36.3 per mil). Variations of a similar magnitude existed at that time between *départements* of France, with the significant difference that the highest rates of infant mortality in France were below the lowest rates in Italy. Such large regional variations also existed in other countries of southern and eastern Europe.

Differential Mortality Rates

Although death ultimately comes to everyone, it does not necessarily arrive at the same time or for the same reason. The most elemental inequality is that between the sexes. Even at the beginning of the century, women of all ages experienced a lower mortality than men, except during the more vulnerable childbearing years. Since 1945 advances in medical treatment have sharply reduced the risks encountered during those years, and hence the gender-specific differential in life expectancy has increased further. In 1980 male mortality exceeded female mortality in all age-groups; women lived on average seven to eight years longer than men, whereas in 1900 the difference was only two to three years (see fig. 1.3). The social and economic consequences of this seemingly minor development are in fact profound, ranging from effects on the relations between marital partners and between generations to the financing of social security programs and pensions.

A second persistent inequality in face of death derives from position in the socioconomic hierarchy. The general improvement in living standards in the twentieth century has decreased socioeconomic differentials but not eliminated them. A study of the mortality of 800,000 French men between 1955 and 1971, conducted by the French National Institute of Demographic Studies (INED), amply confirms this contention. At age thirty-five, engineers, middle and senior civil servants, independent professionals, and teachers had a greater than 50 percent chance of surviving to age seventy-five. By contrast, workers—both skilled and unskilled—had a less than 38 percent chance of sur-

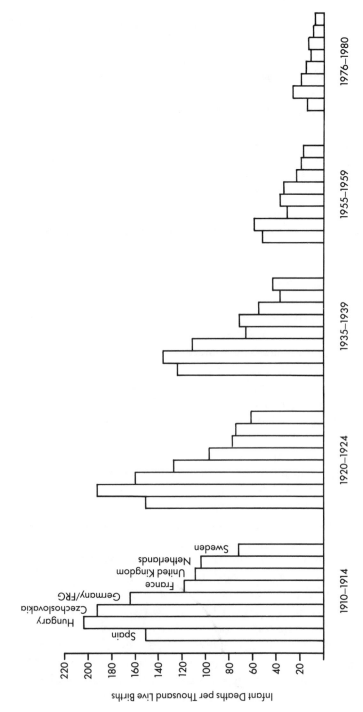

Figure 1.4. Infant Mortality in Various Countries, 1910–1980 (infant deaths per thousand live births). *Sources:* UN, *Demographic Yearbook 1966* (New York, 1967), pp. 290–93; *1982* (New York, 1983), pp. 315–16.

viving to the same ages. Infant mortality is similarly related to the social position of the parents. In France and Italy during the 1960s the incidence of infant mortality among workers' families was almost twice as high as among families headed by professionals or civil servants. As mentioned in the previous section, mortality varies according to geographic region and place of residence. At the beginning of the century higher mortality prevailed in the urban areas, largely as a consequence of unhealthy living and working conditions. Far-reaching improvements of housing, hygiene, and medical facilities have reversed the situation: in many countries mortality in urban areas is now below that prevailing in rural areas.

Fertility

Decline of the Birthrate

Whereas the fall in mortality has been relatively uniform and universally welcomed, the pattern of fertility has been more complex, and its interpretation and reception are still a matter of some controversy. The diffusion of the demographic transition has led to declining birthrates everywhere and to a gradual reduction of the differences between states (see fig. 1.5). In 1920 birthrates in all countries exceeded 21 per mil, but the gap between rates in northern and western Europe and those in southern and eastern Europe was large. In the former regions fertility lay between 21 and 25 per mil, whereas in the latter 31 per mil and above was the rule, Bulgaria having the highest rate of 39.9 per mil. During the interwar years this differential increased. The uncertain economic climate with its inflation and mass unemployment, the changing economic roles of children and women, the increased value attached to individualism, the greater availability of contraceptive information and devices (the first birth control clinics opened in Germany and England shortly after 1920) all combined to reduce births in many countries in northern and western Europe by a third or more. In southern and eastern Europe, the socioeconomic and cultural environment did not yet encourage or facilitate widespread limitation of births. Birthrates declined there, too, but only in Hungary, Czechoslovakia, and Italy was the drop comparable to that found in northern and western Europe.

Coming so close on the heels of the demographic catastrophe of the First World War, the sudden drop in fertility provoked anxious utterances about "dying populations." Sweden, Denmark, Finland, and Brit-

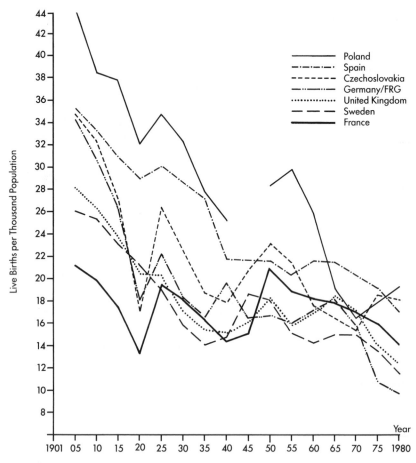

Figure 1.5. Crude Birth Rates for Various Countries, 1905–1980 (number of births per thousand population). *Sources:* UN (ECE), *Economic Survey of Europe in 1974,* Part II: *Post-War Demographic Trends in Europe and the Outlook until the Year 2000* (New York, 1975), p. 231; UN, *Demographic Yearbook 1982* (New York, 1983), pp. 270–71.

ain established parliamentary commissions to study the population problem and to recommend policy responses. In attempts to stem the decline, France and Belgium, and later Fascist Italy and National Socialist Germany, enacted legislation to limit or prohibit the dissemination of information on birth control and to curtail the widespread practice of illegal abortion. These countries also initiated various pronatalist schemes such as family allowances and marriage loans to promote larger families by reducing the attendant economic burdens. The actual demographic results of the programs were minimal.

Since 1945 fluctuations and complexity have characterized the pattern of European fertility. Confounding demographic projections, many countries in industrial northern and western Europe experienced a resurgence of fertility during the 1950s and1960s, a "baby boom" that corresponded with the postwar "economic miracle." The summit of the baby boom was attained in 1964, after which fertility in many countries collapsed to the lowest peacetime rates in European history. Such traditional laggards as the Netherlands and Italy also followed the steep downward trend, and even Spain and Portugal began from the early 1970s to show a sharp downturn in birthrates. In agrarian eastern Europe no sustained baby boom occurred; on the contrary, the drive to industrialize after 1950 was accompanied by a plummeting of the birthrate by more than one third in barely a decade. The timing and pace of the postwar decline in fertility throughout Europe have undoubtedly been affected by the invention and spread of highly effective contraceptive methods such as the hormone pill and the intrauterine device as well as by the passage of more permissive legislation on abortion in many countries—for example, all eastern European countries except East Germany (1956–1957), England/Wales (1967), France (1975–1979), West Germany (1976).

Yet the attempts by numerous conservative politicians to assign chief responsibility for the decline to these products and laws is unwarranted. The timing and near-universality of the trend indicate that sociocultural factors, although themselves hard to specify exactly, so increased the desire and will of couples to limit pregnancies that even such traditional techniques as withdrawal (coitus interruptus) became more effective than before. Surveys conducted in a number of countries at the beginning of the 1970s revealed that only in the Netherlands, Denmark, and Finland did more than one quarter of the couples use modern birth control methods; in eastern Europe the proportion was usually below one tenth. A French survey in 1978 found that barely one third of women in the primary childbearing years 20–44 used modern contraceptive devices; even among the younger women less than one half used them. According to a Dutch survey from the same year, on the other hand, some two thirds of the women married since 1963 used the birth control pill. The role of abortion has been even more controversial and also harder to determine accurately. Thus, although abortion certainly played a key role in initiating the rapid drop in births in eastern Europe after 1950, it was not the sole factor at work; a restricting of its availability in the late 1960s produced only a temporary rise in the number of births, after which the general downward trend in fertility continued.

Since the early 1980s fertility in all European populations, except for Ireland and Albania, has hovered around the rate needed to replace the number of deaths. Such a condition of zero population growth had already occurred during the crisis-ridden interwar years in several countries—France, Britain, Sweden, and Austria—but it became a generalized phenomenon during the 1970s. Between 1968 and 1975 the total fertility rate, the sum of all age-specific fertility rates in a given year, dropped in most countries outside eastern Europe below the replacement rate of 2.1 children per woman. By the early 1980s only Greece and Ireland had a rate above 2.1; elsewhere the average was 1.7, with West Germany having the lowest rate of 1.4. In eastern Europe, on the other hand, fertility has stabilized at just above the rate of replacement (2.2–2.3) except in Hungary and East Germany, where it was just below, at 1.9–2.0 children per woman.

Reproductive Behavior as Social Behavior

As already suggested, aggregated demographic data usually conceal variations generated by biological, socioeconomic, and cultural factors. The most significant variations in the structure of reproductive behavior relate to the age structure of childbearing and to the couple's social and cultural background. The most important variable is age: a woman's fecundity declines naturally with age, and consciously applied birth control can alter the timing of births as well as their number. The variations and changes in the age distribution of childbearing seen in figure 1.6 attest important social dimensions of the fall in European fertility. Clearly, birth control has been practised primarily and most effectively by women above the age of thirty. In these age-groups the frequency of childbearing has fallen drastically—often by more than 75 percent—over the course of the twentieth century. Until the 1920s in northern and western Europe and until the 1950s in eastern and southern Europe, there were roughly 150 live births per thousand women aged 30–34 and around 100 per thousand women aged 35–39. By 1980 the numbers had fallen throughout Europe to about 50 and 20 respectively. Among women under age thirty the reduction in births has been significant but proportionately considerably less.

Broadly speaking, two patterns of the timing and length of childbearing existed in 1980, reflecting differences in age at marriage, length of schooling, and age of entry into the active labor force; one pattern prevailed in eastern Europe, the other in the rest of the continent. Thus, in Bulgaria, Czechoslovakia, East Germany, Hungary, Poland, Rumania, and Yugoslavia birthrates reached their peak—at values up to one-third higher than those found in the rest of Europe—among women aged 20–24; in older age-groups they fell steeply and did not differ greatly from those prevailing in northern and western Europe. In the second pattern, of which West Germany and Spain represent opposite extremes, childbearing extended over a decade but had a clear peak in the age-group 25–29.

Social origin and cultural environment also affect reproductive behavior. One can discern on a smaller social scale the demographic transition seen in the aggregated national data. Therefore, birthrates in rural agrarian areas have been invariably higher than in urban industrial areas even within the same country. Again Italy provides a pronounced example of this dichotomy: throughout most of the twentieth century fertility in the industrialized northern provinces has been almost 50 percent lower than in the rural southern provinces. In Poland the rapid industialization since 1945 has widened the gap between the urban and rural birthrates. Such urban-rural variation is also particularly marked in Yugoslavia, where ethnic and religious factors reinforce the socioeconomic differences. Low fertility has emerged first in the more industrialized Roman Catholic provinces of Croatia and Slovenia, whereas the Muslim populations of the less-developed provinces of Bosnia and Kosovo have continued to maintain one of the highest birthrates in Europe. In many countries programs promoting regional industrialization as well as the increasing effectiveness of countrywide communications networks have reduced such dramatic variations, but substantial differences persist.

Fertility likewise continues to vary according to social background. Until 1945 a direct inverse relationship between socioeconomic standing and number of births predominated: the higher the standing, the fewer the children. The democratization of birth control has since weakened this relationship without eliminating it entirely. In most European societies the relationship has become U-shaped, with the highest fertility occurring at both extremes of the socioeconomic scale. According to the French family census of 1975, the total fertility rate for families headed by workers was 2.74 children, whereas the rate

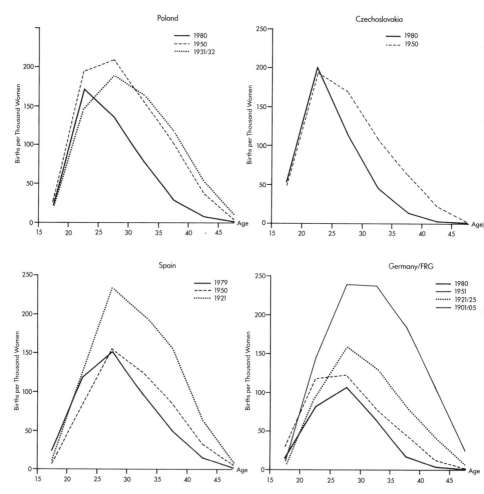

Figure 1.6. Age-Specific Fertility in Poland, Czechoslovakia, Spain, and Germany/FRG, 1901–1980 (births per thousand women of given age). *Sources:* Peter Marschalck, *Bevölkerungsgeschichte Deutschlands im 19. und 20. Jahrhundert* (Frankfurt, 1984), p. 157; Patrick Festy, *La fécondité des pays occidentaux de 1870 à 1970* (Paris, 1979), pp. 222, 281–82; Institut National d'Etudes Démographiques (INED), *Natalité et politiques de population en France et en Europe de l'Est* (Paris, 1982), pp. 277, 280; UN (ECE), *Economic Survey of Europe in 1974, Part II: Post-War Demographic Trends in Europe and the Outlook until the Year 2000* (New York, 1975), pp. 232–39; UN, *Demographic Yearbook 1982* (New York, 1983), pp. 300–303.

receded to 2.16 for middle-rank salaried employees and to 2.15 for independent small artisans and shopkeepers; senior salaried employees and professionals, on the other hand, had total fertility rates of 2.38 and 2.56 respectively.

The End of the Large Family

The drop in the birthrate has inevitably affected the composition of the family, with important consequences for the socialization of children. Contrary to a widespread impression, however, the major effect has not been a large rise in the number of married couples without children. Although the proportion of childless marriages has increased in some countries—such as England/Wales and Germany/FRG—from 10–12 percent before 1914 to 15–17 percent in the 1960s and 1970s, in others—such as France and Czechoslovakia—the reverse has occurred: a decrease from 15–17 percent to 10–12 percent over the same period.

The profound change has been rather the almost universal disappearance of the large family with four or more children. At the beginning of the century such families were very common. In Czechoslovakia their proportion among all families was over one half; even in England, where the birthrate was already falling rapidly, they amounted to over one fourth. The sharp decline of births in western European countries during the interwar years was produced, above all, by a fall in births beyond the third child. This trend intensified after 1945 in western and northern Europe and also spread to southern and eastern Europe. During the last three decades the proportion of fourth-order and above births among total births has fallen to 5–7 percent in every European country except Ireland and Albania. Likewise, again except in Ireland and Albania, the relative number of third births has fallen markedly, from 15–20 percent of all births in the 1950s to 9–12 percent by 1980. At that date West Germany and East Germany had the lowest proportions at roughly 7 percent, whereas Bulgaria, Hungary, Czechoslovakia, Poland, and Ireland had slightly above-average percentages.

The single-child family—an especially widespread phenomenon in interwar France, where it amounted to one fourth of all families—has also become rarer, or at least, as in the case of West Germany, it has not become more common. Thus, the two-child family has been since 1945 increasingly not only the statistical average but also the real practice in European family life. National surveys on ideal family size conducted in both West and East at the end of the 1970s disclosed that two thirds of those questioned considered two children ideal; about one fifth believed three children were the ideal family (in France 45 percent); and less than one tenth considered a single child or four or more children to be ideal. Only the Irish Republic constituted an exception to this European family ideal in 1980: 56 percent of Irish respondents thought a family should have four or more children. Moreover, Irish families actually approached this expressed ideal, having on average 3.6 children. Whether this European-wide congruence between ideal and real family size means that family life is now happy and psychologically healthy is obviously an extremely difficult question to answer.

Family and Household Formation

Marriages

Although strictly speaking more a social than a demographic event, marriage has historically been the formal context of reproductive behavior throughout Europe. Since it constitutes the legal and customary foundation of family life and household formation, marriage is the linchpin between population, society, and economy. Until recently the marriage rate in almost all European countries hovered around 7–9 per mil of the total population. The fluctuations reflected temporary economic or political conditions—depressions, epidemics, or wars— and did not indicate any substantial change in the moral esteem of marriage in European societies.

Leaving aside the role of attitudes, marriage is linked to reproductive behavior by two factors: age at marriage and the proportion of the population unmarried. Until the interwar years a specifically European pattern of marriage predominated in many countries. As identified by the English demographer John Hajnal, this pattern was characterized by a late age at marriage—25–26 years for females and 27–28 for males—and by high rates of lifelong celibacy, with 10–20 percent of both sexes never marrying. Much of eastern Europe, lying along a diagonal line from Leningrad to Trieste, remained outside this pattern, as did the non-European world. Thus in eastern Europe permanent celibacy has seldom exceeded 5 percent, and average age at first marriage has been close to 20 years for females and under 25 years for males. These structural differences have certainly contributed to the consistently higher fertility rates in eastern Europe.

The economic prosperity and social stability of the "thirty glorious years" (Jean Fourastié) following the Second World War encouraged fundamental alterations in the traditional European marriage pattern. Everywhere the proportion of celibates has declined, especially among women. In northern Europe, where celibacy was the most widespread, the fall has been dramatic. Between 1950 and the mid-1970s the proportion of unmarried women in the age-group 45–49 (Hajnal's definition of lifelong celibacy) dropped from 18.5 to 7.0 percent in Sweden, from 16.6 to 7.0 percent in England and from 20.5 to 5.9 percent in Norway. In France, West Germany, Italy, Spain, and Portugal the decline was less marked but nonetheless substantial: from 11–13 percent to 7–8 percent. The major exception here, as in other aspects of demographic behavior, was Ireland, where in the 1980s approximately one fifth of the men and one fourth of the women still never married. In spite of this shift a noticeable gap between eastern Europe and the rest of the continent persisted. In Bulgaria, Hungary, and Rumania, for example, the quota of permanent celibacy has been a mere 2–4 percent throughout the twentieth century.

Late marriage has also become less common. Between the early 1920s and the 1970s the average age at first marriage in northern and western Europe fell roughly 2-3 years for men and 3-4 years for women, to about 25 and 23 respectively. Such average marital ages have prevailed in southern Europe all along, whereas in eastern Europe they have been consistently even lower: in Hungary and Rumania usually at least one third of new brides have been under the age of 20. These aggregate figures of course obscure substantial variations produced by differences in social position, proportions of males and females of marrying age, and local customs, but in general marriage has since 1945 been occurring earlier and more universally than ever before in European history.

Destabilization of the Traditional System of Marriage and Family
Ironically, just as marriage has become more universal, its internal structure and interpersonal dynamics have altered, calling into question its central role as a social institution. This development has appeared in all European countries to a greater or lesser degree, depending on a complex interplay of demographic, economic, cultural, and political factors. Most obviously, earlier marriage and longer life expectancy mean that married persons live together longer, thus increasing the potential for tension and conflict. Whereas at the beginning of the century a majority of marriages lasted barely twenty years before being

dissolved by the death of one of the spouses, the average duration of marriages in 1980 was over thirty-five years. At the same time the drastic reduction in the number of births and the years of actual child-bearing, coupled with increasing female employment outside the home, has provoked changes in, or at least a questioning of, the traditional sex-specific roles within marriage, family, and household. The trans-formation of demographic and economic structures has also been ac-companied by a substantial loosening of the legal and cultural sanctions that had previously enforced the traditional patriarchal family.

The most obvious, though not the most unambiguous, indicator of destabilization is the incidence of divorce. Throughout the century the number of marriages dissolved by court ruling has risen substantially almost everywhere. The late 1960s marked the beginning of a dramatic increase in the divorce rate; by 1980 it had at least doubled in most European countries. Differences in legal systems, only partly dimin-ished by the wave of reforms in the early 1970s, make comparisons between countries and over time hazardous. Nonetheless, divorce clearly has become most widespread in northern Europe: in the early 1980s Sweden and Denmark registered almost half as many divorces each year as marriages; in 1950 the rate was 15 percent and 18 percent respectively. In a majority of countries in western and eastern Europe divorces amounted to 20–25 percent of the annual number of mar-riages in the early 1980s. Only Belgium in the West and Bulgaria, Poland, and Rumania in the East had lower rates, with Poland's the lowest at 11 percent. In southern Europe, on the other hand, divorce still scarcely existed in 1980. The legal provisions for divorce were very restrictive in Portugal, and divorce was not allowed at all in Spain (or the Irish Republic); Italian marriages have been dissoluble by civil judicial means only since 1971. Divorce, of course, does not necessarily imply rejection of the principles of marriage and family; rather, it liberates individuals from personal obligations that have become in-tolerable. Many divorced persons in fact remarry and establish new families.

Since the mid-1960s a different challenge to the traditional pattern of marriage and family has emerged in northern Europe, particularly in Sweden and Denmark. Its central indicator is the number of births out of wedlock, which has risen dramatically in these two countries. In 1965 the proportion of illegitimate births among total births was under 15 percent in Sweden and under 10 percent in Denmark; a mere decade and a half later the rates were 38 percent and 34 percent respectively. Since effective contraceptive methods and abortion have been readily obtainable in both countries for some time, this rise in births outside wedlock implies a conscious rejection of legal marriage as the predominant setting for socially acceptable fertility. The simultaneous reduction in the number of marriages and the increase in unmarried cohabitation also support this inference: a 1974 survey in the two countries found that unmarried couples outnumbered married ones in the group aged 20–29 years.

Whether this so-called Swedish model of marriage and family will become widely imitated elsewhere is uncertain; few other countries possess the combination of comprehensive social services and widespread acceptance of sexual equality in all socioeconomic roles that permits, if not promotes, such a familial model. Nevertheless, its two chief structural indicators—illegitimate births and unmarried cohabitation—have increased in several countries during the 1970s. In France, for example, the illegitimacy rate rose from about 7 percent in 1971 (its average throughout the century) to 13 percent in 1981; in the latter year 10 percent of cohabiting couples under the age of thirty in the Paris region were not married. These rates are considerably below those in Scandinavia, but they nevertheless attest the weakening of the age-old moral union of marriage, sex, and childbearing in twentieth-century European societies.

Households

Household and family are closely linked to one another; before the twentieth century they were virtually congruent, with parents and children forming the core of most households. The transformation of the demographic structure of the family has necessarily affected the size and composition of the household. The universal trend has been a steady shrinkage of the size of this group from 4.5–5 persons at the beginning of the century to about 2.5 persons in the early 1980s. Two fundamental causes of this decline were the virtual disappearance of live-in domestic servants and shop assistants and the reduced number of children.

A third decisive cause has been the increase of single-member households. Before 1950 living alone was uncommon. At the beginning of the century and in the interwar years single-member households amounted to only 7–11 percent of all households in Denmark, Britain, Germany, and Switzerland. These solitaries were predominantly older widowed persons, usually women. Since circa 1960 the situation has changed considerably. Increased prosperity, coupled with more individualistic life-style—a striving for self-realization and independence—has led to doubling of the proportion of single-member households in several northern and western European countries. By 1980 one quarter of British, Danish, French, and Swiss households contained only one person; in Austria and West Germany the proportion was one third.

Although not exclusively an urban phenomenon, this type of household prevailed above all in the large cities. In 1980 more than one half of the households in Copenhagen, Paris, West Berlin, and Vienna contained only one person; almost one in four of the residents of these cities lived alone. Elderly widows continued to constitute a large part of such solitaries, but all adult age-groups were strongly represented. Southern and eastern Europe still present a strong contrast to this trend. The continuing strength of traditional family ideology in conjunction with a chronic shortage of residential dwellings, especially in the cities, has inhibited the spread of single-member households. Thus only 15 percent of Italian and Polish households in the early 1980s were solitaries.

Redistribution

The third element of population change—migration—differs fundamentally from the first two, births and deaths, because it is not a biological phenomenon but a social and economic act. Migration, moreover, is reversible; it can be temporary, even seasonal, long-term, or permanent; the distance travelled can vary from short stretches to thousands of kilometers, from shifts between neighboring villages to moves between continents. Individuals may often have complex reasons for moving, but the general determinants are clearly political and socioeconomic. Political motivation has been particularly important in twentieth-century Europe for migration across state boundaries: the refugee fleeing from political, religious, or racial persecution has unfortunately been a frequent figure. More commonly, however, socioeconomic factors have played the key role in prompting migration, and the typical migratory flow has been from less-industrialized areas characterized by relative overpopulation, low wages, and chronic underemployment to more-industrialized areas, in which a relative labor shortage, higher wages, and diversified opportunities for work prevail. Within individual countries, this has meant normally a shift from rural agricultural areas to urban industrial zones. Internationally, such migration is typified by the flow of migrants from agrarian southern and eastern Europe to North America or to industrialized western and northern Europe.

International Migration

Overseas Emigration

European emigration to new territories overseas, especially to the "promised land" of North America, became a major social and economic phenomenon in the nineteenth century. At the beginning of the twentieth century overseas emigration attained floodtide dimensions with about 1.3 million departures annually. This emigration was predominantly economically motivated. In general the timing and national origin of the outflow were related to the high natural population growth associated with the second phase of the demographic transition as well as to the spread of industrialization. Hence the outflow shifted from western and northern Europe—Britain, Ireland, the German states, and later Scandinavia—which dominated emigration until the 1890s, to southern and eastern Europe, which provided three quarters of the some twenty million Europeans who emigrated overseas between 1900 and 1920. Italy, the quintessential country of emigration during the ninetenth century, contributed almost seven million emigrants during these years (see fig. 1.7).

The First World War sharply curtailed this enormous transatlantic movement, which did not regain its prewar numbers with the coming of peace. Not that the propensity to emigrate had weakened substantially; on the contrary, the same push produced by high birthrates and limited economic opportunities continued to exert itself throughout most of agrarian southern and eastern Europe. Overseas migration declined because the immigration laws passed by the United States in 1921 and 1924 established national quotas that deliberately discriminated against emigrants from southern and eastern Europe. Nevertheless, 700,000 Europeans, roughly half from northern and western Europe and half from southern and eastern Europe, emigrated overseas each year during the 1920s.

In the 1930s European overseas emigration fell below 130,000 annually, the lowest figure in over a century. On the one hand, mass unemployment and destitution prevented many potential emigrants from amassing the necessary money for travel and resettlement. As

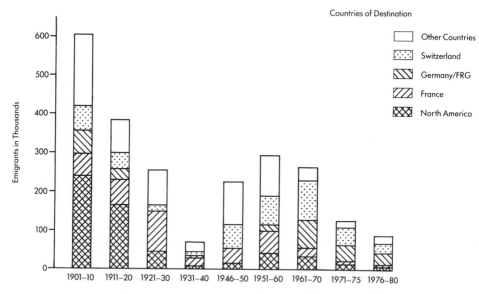

Figure 1.7. Italian Emigration, 1901–1980 (average annual number of emigrants, in thousands). *Sources:* Alain Monnier, "L'Italie, l'Espagne et le Portugal: situation démographique," *Population*, 35 (1980): 956; *The Europa Year Book 1983* (London, 1983), p. 840.

well, some European states, for example Fascist Italy, motivated by fears of slowing population growth, actively discouraged emigration. On the other hand, the collapse of the North American economy discouraged immigration and even persuaded many who had recently arrived to return to their native countries. The Great Depression thus finally broke the long-standing relationship between the emigration needs of Europe and the immigration needs of North America.

The international refugee problem after 1945, which led to the formation of special departments within the United Nations Organization, led to a resurgence of overseas migration. Between 1946 and 1960 an average of 500,000 persons left Europe every year. Several European governments, among them Italy and the Netherlands, encouraged emigration as a general means of combatting overpopulation and unemployment. Yet in spite of this apparent resurgence, the importance of overseas emigration in European society has lessened noticeably since 1945. For one thing, regular emigration from eastern Europe has virtually ceased. Additionally, the demand for labor created by the expansion of the European economy, especially after 1960, has redirected potential migrants from overseas destinations to European ones. Moreover, decolonization after 1945 provoked the repatriation of many colonists of European origin. The most dramatic movement was perhaps that of almost one million persons from Algeria to France after 1962, but the Netherlands had to absorb some 300,000 refugees from Indonesia, and Britain close to 750,000 persons from its various former colonies in Africa and Asia. In the late 1970s about 750,000 persons returned to Portugal from Mozambique and Angola. As a consequence of these changes, Europe has shown since 1960 a positive migration balance for the first time in the century (see fig. 1.8).

A country-by-country distribution of European overseas emigration can only be approximated because of incomplete data. Nonetheless, the available information demonstrates the mixture of economic and political motives as well as the caesura after 1945. Consistent with the notion of emigration as a safety valve for relative overpopulation, the

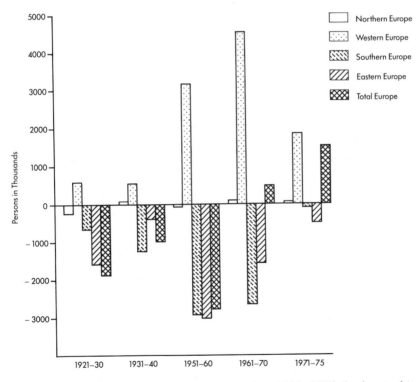

Figure 1.8. European Net Migration by Region, 1921–1975 (in thousands). *Sources:* Dudley Kirk, *Europe's Interwar Population* (Princeton, 1946), pp. 284–85; UN (ECE), *Economic Survey of Europe in 1977,* Part II: *Labour Supply and Migration in Europe* (New York, 1979), p. 299.

less-developed countries of agrarian southern and eastern Europe contributed over 60 percent of the emigrants between 1901 and 1960.
The largest single contributor was Italy with some 25 percent, followed
by the Iberian peninsula with about 15 percent. But a radical shift in
composition occurred between 1901–1939 and 1946–1960. In the
first period the share of emigrants from agrarian Europe attained
roughly 70 percent; the effective closure of eastern European emigration after 1945 halved this figure to 34 percent for the second period.
Britain and Ireland sent roughly the same proportion of emigrants as
Italy, namely 25 percent, undoubtedly reflecting historical cultural and
political ties to North America and Australia in addition to the push
exerted by domestic economic difficulties. The increased movement of
skilled professionals overseas—the "brain drain"—raised the British
proportion of European emigration in 1946–1960 to 30 percent, noticeably higher than its 20 percent in 1901–1939. The contribution
of Germany/FRG was considerably lower, roughly 8 percent in each
period. In smaller countries such as the Netherlands or the Scandinavian countries, overseas emigration played an important role in relation to the national population but was naturally small in European
terms.

Intra-European Migration
Labor migration across European borders, prompted by differentials
in income and job opportunities, has a long history. Before 1914
seasonal agricultural employment attracted hundreds of thousands of
Polish and Dutch workers into Germany as well as Italians, Belgians,
and Spaniards into France and Switzerland. Italian construction workers and Belgian, Polish, and Czech miners were also recruited in large
numbers in several countries, and hundreds of thousands of Irish
moved to the industrial cities of Scotland and England in search of
work. In 1910 Germany and France each contained over one million
foreigners; Switzerland contained 600,000.

In interwar Europe economic instability and stagnation, coupled
with an upsurge of virulent nationalism, inhibited large-scale labor
migration. France, whose work force had suffered enormous losses in
the war and whose rate of natural population growth was the lowest
in Europe, was the major exception. In the 1920s, partly under the
terms of labor recruiting agreements with Poland, Czechoslovakia, and
Italy, over two million immigrants came to France, where they worked
above all in the mining and industrial centers of the north and east.

At the high point of this migration, in 1931, foreign workers amounted to 7 percent of France's total population, and in some industries, such as mining and extractive enterprises, their proportion in the work force exceeded one third. Italians formed the largest group with 30 percent of all foreign workers, followed by Poles (19 percent), Spaniards (13 percent), and Belgians (9 percent). During the economic crisis of the mid-1930s over one million returned to their home countries; some were deliberately expelled by the French government. But many stayed and became naturalized French citizens.

Yet until the massive migration of laborers in the 1960s, the largest intra-European movements were the politically motivated transfers of populations that occurred after each world war in conjunction with the redrawing of state boundaries. Official estimates of how many persons were involved in these population "adjustments" vary, but the numbers were huge and the social and economic consequences dramatic. The largest transfers of persons following the First World War took place in the Balkan peninsula. The Treaty of Lausanne in 1923 ordered the largest single exchange: the repatriation of some 1.2 million Greeks from Turkey and 400,000 Turks from Greece. Bulgaria and Greece also traded large numbers of persons, and roughly 500,000 Hungarians moved out of Rumania, Yugoslavia, and Czechoslovakia into the smaller territory of Trianon Hungary. Furthermore, the reemergence of an independent Poland and the return of Alsace-Lorraine to France prompted over a million Germans to leave those territories. Some 1.2 million persons fled before the political upheavals in Russia, and about 300,000 refugees resulted from the Spanish Civil War.

Yet these numbers pale in comparison with those of the 1940s. Throughout that decade the population in central and east-central Europe was in turmoil. During the war itself a total of fourteen million foreigners were employed in the Third Reich. The high point of 7.5 million foreign workers was reached in 1944, 1.5 million of them being prisoners of war. During the war some 800,000 ethnic Germans living in South Tyrol, Rumania, Yugoslavia, and Hungary were repatriated, and in the last year of the war several millions fled westwards from the German eastern territories to escape advancing Soviet armies.

After 1945 Germans were the most affected by compulsory transfers across state boundaries. The Potsdam Agreement, establishing new boundaries for Poland and authorizing the expulsion to Germany of the remaining ethnic German populations in Poland, Czechoslovakia, and Hungary, caused the greatest upheaval. Roughly 7.5 million persons were transferred out of the three countries in 1945–1946. The westward shift of Polish borders also entailed the repatriation of about 1.5 million persons of Polish nationality from territories annexed by the Soviet Union. Other exchanges involving smaller numbers occurred between Czechoslovakia and Hungary, the Soviet Union and Rumania, Hungary and Yugoslavia, and Yugoslavia and Italy. In the decade after the end of the war the absorption of these refugees was a fundamental social and economic problem. This was especially true for the western zones of divided Germany. By 1950 West Germany recorded 7.8 million refugees, whereas East Germany had about 3.5 million. Moreover, between 1950 and the building of the Berlin Wall in 1961 an estimated three million persons fled from East Germany to West Germany; at the latter date refugees amounted to one fifth of the population in West Germany.

From the late 1950s economics replaced politics as the predominant cause of migration across state boundaries. The prolonged economic expansion following the postwar reconstruction of Europe has stimulated intra-European labor migration on an unprecedented scale. The migrants have typically been unskilled or semiskilled workers on short-term contracts; annual turnover has averaged about 50 percent. Bilateral agreements between worker-exporting and worker-importing countries regulated the recruitment, and in theory all parties benefited. The receiving country obtained a flexible supply of cheap labor to perform menial and routine tasks, above all in construction and assembly-line work such as in the automobile industry, thereby freeing native workers to take better-paid skilled employment in factories or offices. Being temporary, migratory labor was supposed to function in the recipient economy as an employment buffer by enabling layoffs in time of recession with a minimum of social antagonism, since the migrants would simply return whence they came. For the individual foreign worker, often faced with under- or unemployment at home, the opportunity of relatively well-paid work even in another country was compelling. For the sending country exporting workers was a quick and inexpensive means of reducing unemployment; moreover, through the remittances or savings of the migrant workers the sending country obtained substantial capital imports that promoted consumer demand and thus the expansion of its own economy. The costs of training an industrial labor force were also shifted to the receiving country.

This intra-European exchange of labor divided the continent into socioeconomic blocs: the countries demanding labor in northern and western Europe—Sweden, Switzerland, France, West Germany, and Belgium; and the suppliers of labor in Mediterranean Europe—Italy, Spain, Portugal, Greece, and Yugoslavia, as well as Turkey and North Africa. Countries in a third group, including Britain, the Netherlands, Austria, Norway, Denmark, and Finland, have alternated between being suppliers and demanders of migrant labor. Development of this European-wide labor market has been facilitated by the establishment of associations such as the Common Nordic Labor Market in 1954 and, above all, the European Economic Community (EEC) in 1957.

Eastern Europe, with the exception of Yugoslavia, has formed its own migration field since the Second World War. For both economic and political reasons the scale of movement has been much smaller, the migration being limited to the exchange of specialized technical workers. In spite of substantial labor shortages in the eastern European countries in the 1970s, only about 150,000 foreign workers have been employed at any given time; roughly one half of them were in East Germany.

On the whole, intra-European labor migration was modest through-out the 1950s in spite of generally high demand for goods and services. Only Switzerland imported substantial numbers of foreign workers in the immediate postwar years; between 1950 and 1960 the number of non-Swiss workers rose from 90,000 to 435,000. France was the second largest importer of foreign workers during this period, followed by Belgium and Britain. The Netherlands, by contrast, experienced high unemployment throughout the decade and was a net exporter of labor. West Germany also initially suffered high unemployment and did not begin to recruit foreign workers until after 1955, but by 1960 the numbers had reached over 500,000. Here and elsewhere in north-ern and western Europe economic expansion increased demands for labor at a time when the natural growth of the labor supply was slowed as a consequence of the low birthrates of the interwar years. To over-come the labor shortage either an increase in female employment or the importation of migrant laborers was needed—or both.

In the decade and a half after 1960 the dimensions of intra-European migration changed profoundly—quantitatively, geographically, and qualitatively. The sheer numbers involved became massive: an esti-mated gross annual movement of between two and three million work-ers. France and West Germany were the largest recipients, with annual entries between 250,000–300,000 and 400,000–600,000 respec-tively, but foreign workers assumed a significant role in the socioeconomic life of virtually all countries in northern and western Europe. In 1973 the International Labour Organization (ILO) estimated that the then nine EEC countries together with Austria, Norway, Sweden, and Switzerland contained 7.5 million foreign workers. Of these, 2.6 million lived in West Germany and 2.3 million in France, representing respectively 12 percent and 10 percent of each country's labor force. In Switzerland the absolute number was much smaller at 600,000, but it constituted 30 percent of the labor force. Sweden and Belgium each had some 200,000, or 6–7 percent of the labor force, whereas foreign workers made up only 2 percent of the Dutch work force. 1973 marked the high point of the labor migration. In the wake of the recession of 1965–1966 Switzerland had already restricted migration. The economic crisis of 1974–1975 led first to a general halt in formal recruiting outside the EEC and ultimately to the implementation of policies to encourage foreign workers to return to their native countries. Tens of thousands did so, but the majority remained. At the beginning of the 1980s foreign workers still constituted 7–8 percent of the total work force in France and West Germany and played a particularly important role in construction and manufacturing.

The increase in labor migration necessarily enlarged its geographical scope. Prior to 1960 Italy, above all southern Italy, was the main source. During the 1950s it supplied over two thirds of the migrant workers throughout Europe. By the early 1960s, however, the postwar boom in the Italian economy enlarged the domestic demand for labor, and the number of Italian emigrants declined sharply to less than half of the 1950s average. Other countries of Mediterranean Europe stepped in as new sources of labor supply for industrial Europe. The lifting of restrictions on emigration in Franco's Spain in 1959 enabled hundreds of thousands of impoverished Spaniards to seek work abroad, primarily in France. France also recruited large numbers from Portugal and, beginning in the early 1970s, from North Africa. West Germany continued to draw workers from Italy but shifted its recruitment first to Greece and then, in the mid-1960s, to Yugoslavia and Turkey. These last three countries plus Portugal also sent substantial numbers of workers to Belgium, the Netherlands, Sweden, and Austria. In this way the poorer societies on the periphery of industrial Europe profited from the economic boom of the 1960s and early 1970s: in 1973 the remittances and earnings of migrant workers amounted respectively to 90 percent of export earnings in Turkey, roughly 50 percent in Greece,

Portugal, and Yugoslavia, and about 25 percent in Spain, Algeria, Morocco, and Tunisia.

In the course of this expansion the social composition of the migratory stream and the position of the foreigners in their host countries also changed. Contrary to the original assumptions and policies, increasing numbers of foreign workers stayed for long periods; in 1977 one quarter of migrant workers in West Germany had been there ten or more years. Unsurprisingly, such persons had established families or, if already married before migrating, brought their families to the host country. In the course of the 1970s the number of family dependents per worker increased significantly, a consequence in part of the higher fertility of the migrants compared to that of the host population. Businesses and services catering to the emigrant groups, and largely owned by emigrants, also emerged. A situation of de facto permanent immigration has thus arisen and has transformed the recipient countries into multiracial and multicultural societies on a scale unknown in modern European history.

Internal Migration

Urbanization

The most important source of supply for the labor demands generated by industrialization has been not the importation of foreign workers but rather the internal migration of each country's domestic population. The commonest form of redistribution is the move from farm and village to town or city. Such migration has occurred throughout history, but not until the nineteenth century did the aggregate urban population show a steady and permanent increase in its proportion of the total population. This urbanization has entailed the movement of millions of persons in all European countries and has transformed the fabric of society and economy.

A complete examination and comprehensive comparison of urbanization country by country are hindered by inadequate data. Migrational movements are incompletely recorded; moreover, considerable variation exists in national definitions of "urban" and "rural." At one extreme Denmark counts all settlements of at least 250 inhabitants as urban; at the other end of the scale Italy requires 20,000. In several countries the definition is based on administrative criteria and not necessarily related to population at all. The redrawing of communal boundaries and the consolidation of small dispersed settlements into a single administrative unit, as happened in West Germany after 1968, further complicate a comparative view of urbanization. Figure 1.9 thus uses the international standard of 20,000 proposed by the United Nations; the various national definitions frequently give values for urban proportions that are markedly higher than those traced in the graph, but the trends do not differ substantially.

As the data in figure 1.9 clearly show, the extent of urbanization varied considerably at the beginning of the century, when few countries could be classified as urban societies. Only in Britain did substantially more than half of the population live in cities in 1910. Belgium, Germany,

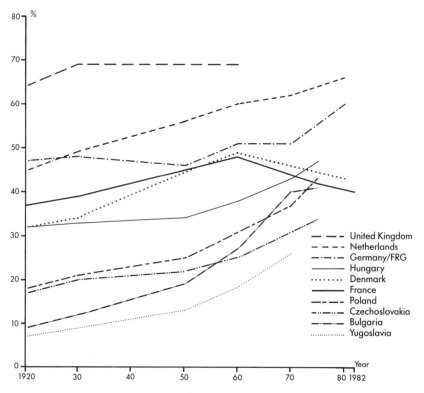

Figure 1.9. Urban Population in Various Countries, 1920–1982 (population in towns with more than 20,000 inhabitants as percent of total population). *Sources:* UN, *Growth of the World's Urban and Rural Population 1920–2000* (New York, 1969), pp. 105–106; UN, *Demographic Yearbook 1983* (New York, 1985), pp. 902–904; Paul S. Shoup, *The East European and Soviet Data Handbook* (New York, 1981), pp. 397–407.

and the Netherlands followed with urban quotas of roughly 50 percent. France, Italy, Denmark, Austria, and Hungary occupied an intermediate position with approximately one third of the population residing in cities with at least 20,000 inhabitants; in the latter two cases, however, the enormous sizes of Vienna and Budapest disguised the effective low degree of urbanization outside the metropolis. In the remaining agrarian countries in southern, eastern, and northern Europe less than one quarter of the population lived in urban communities; Bulgaria and Yugoslavia had the lowest quotas of respectively 9 percent and 7 percent.

The uneven economic growth during the interwar years did little to alter this pattern. Large cities, defined as those containing over 100,000 inhabitants, however, did increase their relative position in several countries. The proportion of the population residing in large cities grew in Germany from 21 percent in 1910 to 37 percent in 1930, and in Italy from 11 percent to 17 percent. In the latter case this surge of urban growth provoked governmental restriction of internal migration in 1928, not removed completely until 1961, in an attempt to ease pressure on housing, jobs, and social services in the urban areas. In Britain big cities enlarged their share of the country's population from about one quarter before the war to almost three quarters by the early 1930s. The pervasive cultural criticism of big cities as concrete wastelands and promoters of social anonymity could not prevent their growth as a logical consequence of industrialization.

Since 1945 the combined effect of agricultural modernization and industrial expansion has effected the transfer of the rural reserve army of labor into the cities and fundamentally altered the distribution of urban and rural populations. By 1980 at least one third of the population of all European states except Albania resided in urban agglomerations; that had been true in less than one half of the states in 1950. Moreover, the shift in relative positions entailed for the first time in most countries an absolute decline in the rural population. The more generous national definitions of urban areas would raise the degree of urbanization in all countries (again excepting Albania) to over 50 percent of the population. According to prevailing national definitions three persons out of four in Belgium, Denmark, West Germany, France, Britain, and the Netherlands lived in urban settlements at the beginning of the 1980s.

The rate of urban growth since 1945 was generally highest in those regions and countries with the lowest initial urban quota. During the

1950s and 1960s southern and eastern Europe led the pace with average annual urban growth rates of roughly 2.5 percent. In these years
in eastern Europe more than twenty million persons, encouraged by
deliberate state economic policies of higher wages and less harsh working conditions in industry, moved from agricultural villages into industrial urban communities. Likewise in Spain nearly 4.5 million left
the countryside between 1961 and 1970 to settle permanently in the
burgeoning cities, primarily Madrid, Barcelona, and Bilbao.

In northern and western Europe the rates of urban growth were
generally slower and the variation between individual countries greater.
Between 1950 and 1975 Switzerland's urban population grew at close
to 3 percent per annum, France's and Belgium's around 2 percent,
West Germany's 1 percent, and Britain's only 0.3 percent. Taking all
European countries into consideration, urban growth after 1950 was
most rapid in Bulgaria, Rumania, Yugoslavia, and Spain and least rapid
in East Germany and Britain. In the latter country the saturation point
of urban growth has evidently been reached; the rural population grew
twice as fast as the urban population after 1960, reflecting a reversal
of the usual rural-urban movement. In the 1970s this phenomenon
appeared in several other countries, most notably in France, Belgium,
Denmark, and Sweden. In West Germany the urban quota rose in the
1970s as a consequence of the redrawing of communal boundaries,
but the number residing in large cities actually declined by one million
between 1975 and 1980.

Nevertheless, one of the most evident characteristics of European
urbanization has been the growth of large cities. In 1950 seven countries had more than one quarter of their respective populations in big
cities; in 1980 this degree of concentration obtained in all but three
European countries: Ireland, Czechoslovakia, and Albania. At this latter date more than one third of the population of northern, western,
and southern Europe resided in a total of 427 large cities; in eastern
Europe, 103 large cities contained 26 percent of the region's total
population.

The epitome of modern urban life is the metropolis, a city with more
than one million inhabitants. The number of such giant cities has more
than doubled, from fifteen in the interwar period to thirty-five in 1980.
At that time they accounted for one sixth of the population in half of
all European countries. In Austria, Denmark, Finland, Greece, and
Hungary a single metropolis contained one fifth of the national population. In 1980 the two largest metropolitan conurbations, Paris and

London, had respective populations of 8.5 and 6.8 million and were thus by themselves larger than several European countries.

The geographic mobility resulting from urbanization is more than a simple transfer of residence; it involves adapting to a new physical, economic, and psychological environment with different life-styles and patterns of social relationships. The sudden acceleration of urbanization since 1950 has aggravated many social problems, especially in southern and eastern Europe, ranging from desperate housing shortages to culture shock, ghettoization, and linguistic-religious tensions such as in the cases of Sicilians in Turin, Galicians and Andalusians in Barcelona, or Kosovans in Zagreb. In many of the cities of southern and eastern Europe half of the residents in the 1970s were recently arrived migrants. In the countryside the pervasive rural exodus since 1945 has left a social legacy of aging communities, abandoned farmsteads, and even abandoned villages.

On the other hand, the contrast between city and country, an essential differentiating element in the historical development of European civilization, has been weakened by the spread of urban settlement patterns beyond the narrow boundaries of the city, together with the diffusion of urban values and urban-oriented consumer products. The socioeconomic category of "worker-peasant" devised by Marxist sociologists in Eastern Europe expresses the confluence of previously contradictory life-styles. In Western Europe the development of so-called satellite cities and bedroom suburbs characterized by a more dispersed, semirural residential style also evinces this trend. In both instances the employed persons typically leave their communities of residence to work elsewhere, a life-style made possible by the shortening of daily work hours and by modern communications and transportation. Commuting to work has become a widespread phenomenon; in countries as different as West Germany, Switzerland, Yugoslavia, and Poland at least one third of the work force in 1980 was employed outside its commune of residence.

Interregional Migration

Internal migration comprehends more than just movement from countryside to town. Since 1945, and especially since 1960, the new technological base of the European economy has encouraged, above all in the older industrial countries of northern and western Europe, a second type of migrational movement. This movement flows from one urban area to another, from regions dominated by mining or traditional industries to regions with more dynamic modern industries such as electronics, petrochemicals, or services. Often these latter regions also have environmental and recreational attractions. Good examples of this type of migration are moves from the coalfields and shipyards of Scotland, northern England, and Wales to the Midlands and southern England, or from overcrowded, expensive London to East Anglia and the Southwest. Others are the shift away from the Belgian coalfields or from North Rhine–Westphalia and the Saarland to Baden–Württemberg or areas surrounding Hamburg, Frankfurt, and Munich. France, as befits its intermediate position in European industrialization, has experienced since 1945 both types of internal migration: regions of rural decline in the northwest (Brittany and Normandy) and center (Auvergne, Limousin) together with regions of industrial decline in the northeast (Nord and Lorraine) contrasting with rapid growth in the Paris Basin, the Rhône valley (Lyon–Grenoble), and the Mediterranean sunbelt. The region around Stavanger in southwestern Norway provides a different version of this phenomenon: the traditional shipbuilding industry has been transformed into a support service for the oil industry in the North Sea, a change accompanied by an increase in international commercial ties.

Summary

The changes in tempo and structure of population growth just outlined have had far-reaching ramifications—direct and indirect—for the social and economic structures of Europe in the twentieth century.

1. The demographic transition has transformed the traditional biological and psychological dimensions of the family. Birth control makes possible a conscious choice of the timing and length of parenthood, thereby emancipating women and the family from domination by the biological function of childbearing. The reduction in the average number of childbearing years from 14–15 at the beginning of the century to 4–5 in the late 1970s has dramatically altered the role of the mother in the family and the position of married women in the labor force and in society in general. The character of relationships between parents and children, between siblings, and between the nuclear family and relatives has also been affected.

2. The decline in fertility and mortality has shifted the age pyramid of European populations towards the older age-cohorts. At the start of the century over one third of the population in every country except

France was under the age of fifteen; by the beginning of the 1980s this cohort amounted to only one fifth of the population in northern and western Europe (except in the Irish Republic) and to one quarter in southern and eastern Europe. On the other hand, the proportion of persons sixty-five and over has risen everywhere (again except in Ireland) from 6–7 percent in 1910 to 12–17 percent in northern and western Europe and 9–13 percent in southern and eastern Europe. The social and economic implications of this transformation, which has occurred mostly since 1960, have been and continue to be far-reaching, ranging from contractions in the labor supply and reduction in the demand for educational services to increases in the demand for and social costs of services to the aged, such as pensions and medical care. Ironically, this shift has taken place within the context of a popular culture emphasizing youth and youthfulness as never before.

3. The spread of the demographic transition has been aided by massive migration from the countryside into the cities and by the diffusion through modern communications of urban secular values in rural areas. By the 1970s all European societies approached total urbanization, at least in socioeconomic functional terms, if not in actual residential patterns. The suddenness and massiveness of urban growth since 1945 have disturbed long-standing social relationships in many communities, overburdened social, economic, and political facilities, and despoiled the natural surroundings through rapid, unconsidered expansion.

4. Geographical mobility has become a standard feature of modern society, promoting simultaneously integration and conflict, standardization and differentiation. The migration of workers from Mediterranean Europe to northern and western Europe embodies both dimensions. On the one hand, these workers have imbibed the secularist, individualist, rationalist values of modern capitalist society, and imported them back into their native countries. The migrants have thus played a major role in the social and economic modernization of southern Italy, Greece, Spain, Portugal, and Yugoslavia. On the other hand, the migration of foreign workers has created tensions in the receiving countries, which have been aggravated by the slowdown of economic growth and the rise of unemployment since the mid-1970s.

CHAPTER 2

Continuity and Change in Social Structures

General Trends

Social Indicators

Society consists of persons and groups interconnected by particular social orders and structures. Social orders are based upon values, norms, and institutions, and are guided and defined by socially accepted modes of behavior, which lend society a degree of internal consistency. Social structures are related more to the distribution of economic, political, and social rights and claims between individuals. The order and structure of a society are not immutable; rather, societies are characterized by a constant tension between change and continuity.

Factors motivating change and those contributing to the stabilization of existing relationships operate simultaneously and are closely interconnected. However, the analysis of the process of change and continuity demands that we must investigate each factor separately. Chapter 1 dealt with the demographic dimension of social and economic change. This chapter presents and analyzes social structures, processes, and orders, such as stratification and mobility, integration and conflict, and socialization. It also examines institutions such as church, family, and school, specific economic and political interest groups, and social organizations. Change is usually brought about through social conflict, whereas continuity is predominantly based upon social consensus. In either case, however, the central issue is the definition and control of social orders and structures, or, in other words, the question of domination in economy and society.

The normative and psychological dimensions of a social order render each society unique. This makes societal and social change difficult to grasp by means of comparative quantitative indicators such as those used to measure international economic development. Recently the Organization for Economic Cooperation and Development (OECD), the United Nations, and the World Bank have assembled "social indicators," which make it possible to compare the level of development of diverse societies. Although these indicators vary in substance from organization to organization, they do provide a considerable amount of data on population, health and nutrition, education and communication, occupation and income, patterns of consumption, and so forth. Some of these indicators have already been introduced in Chapter 1: average life expectancy, child mortality, fertility, age structure, urbanization. Others will be dealt with at least in part in the following: physicians per inhabitant; caloric consumption per head; number of pupils in primary and secondary education; cars, radios, televisions, or refrigerators per thousand inhabitants, and so on. This list could easily be extended by, for instance, data on elections, membership in political parties, churches, trade unions or other organizations, strikes and political demonstrations.

In spite of this variety of data one must avoid falling prey to a "fetishism of indicators," for such data also have their weaknesses. First, they create the impression of an exactitude greater than is in fact attainable given the varying methods of collection in the different countries concerned. Second, these data cover only quite formal relationships; although treating an important aspect of twentieth-century European social and economic history—namely, the increase and diffusion of material welfare—they neglect those qualitative dimensions of societal development not susceptible to quantitative measurement. Third, the indicators of social behavior in particular are culturally determined, and the standardized figures cannot do justice to their varying significance within diverse societies.

Nonetheless, social indicators are a useful resource for the formation of an initial impression of the varying tempos of socioeconomic change in European societies. For the majority of these countries the year 1950 represents a break in the trendlines. In the political domain substantial changes indeed occurred during the first half of the century, but in the socioeconomic domain a comparable transformation was delayed by two wars and the international economic depression. The socioeconomic, political, and "moral" reconstruction of Europe after 1945 did not immediately bring about the shift in trends, but it did encourage those forces promoting change. The changes that then occurred from 1950 onwards led to such fundamental transformation of social structures that many analysts (Daniel Bell and Alain Touraine for instance) believe that industrial society has in the recent past been displaced by the so-called post-industrial society.

Theories of Social Change

Numerous social theorists since the Enlightenment have attempted to explain social development by means of so-called single-factor theories of social change; at the center of each of the various approaches is a single (or at least dominating) factor—technology, war, "social structural malintegration and tension-management" (Talcott Parsons), cultural diffusion and cybernetic mobilization (Karl Deutsch), and so forth. The best-known explanations are those provided by materialist and idealist theories. The economic-technological approach, which is closely associated with that of Marxism, postulates that the economic mode of production, the so-called base, determines directly or indirectly social organization, the so-called superstructure. The superstructure contains not only the forms of political organization and their corresponding ideologies and social relationships, but also spiritual values— worldview, morality, aesthetics, and religion—together with their respective institutions. According to Marx, the capitalist mode of production contains an inherent fundamental contradiction, which is the motive force behind a permanent process of socioeconomic and political transformation. This contradiction is founded on the irreconcilable economic, social, and moral antagonism between the bourgeoisie (the capitalist class, which owns the means of production) and the proletariat (the working class, which possesses only its labor power and must sell this below its actual value in order to live). The relation between capitalists and workers is therefore a relation of exploitation, since the worker never receives the full value of the labor rendered and thus creates surplus value retained by the capitalist. The process of industrial capitalist development inevitably sharpens this immanent systematic contradiction. The increased investment in fixed capital demanded by technical progress leads to a falling general rate of profit; this tendency and periodic business crises produce a concentration of capital ownership, which further intensifies the exploitation and impoverishment of the proletariat. The class conflict becomes ever more severe and terminates with the abolition of capitalist relations of production; these are replaced by socialist relations of production in which exploitation and class conflict are ended because the means of production no longer belong to individuals, but to the entire society.

The idealist, or liberal, conception rejects the Marxist approach and proposes that ideas, convictions, and values are the ultimate determinants of social change. Perhaps the best-known example of this position is Max Weber's argument about the decisive role of the Protestant ethic for the emergence of the capitalist spirit. Weber's concept of charisma and his study of the role of charismatic leadership provide another variant among numerous idealist theoretical approaches.

Neither of the above approaches is by itself satisfactory as a comprehensive explanation of social change, but each is of enormous significance at the political as well as the theoretical level. The ideological gulf between them has widened since the political division of Europe in the years 1945–1948. In eastern Europe state socialist societies based upon the principles of Marxism-Leninism were created, in which state ownership of the means of production, central economic management, extreme social control, and the political monopoly of communist parties were leading features. Elsewhere in Europe, social variants of capitalism persisted, combining market economies with private ownership of the means of production and characterized by an organizational and ideological pluralism in society and polity. The division of Europe not only involved differing principles and structures in society and economy, which were bound up with considerable tensions in international relations; it also meant that the same factors were often endowed with differing meanings and were subject to differing interpretations, thus rendering a direct comparison between East and West difficult and to a certain extent always unsatisfactory. This applies most of all to such value-laden evaluative concepts as "democracy," "equality," or "class," but also to such apparently neutral terms as "national product" and "productivity." The paucity of data relating to socioeconomic development in eastern Europe and the necessity of reinterpreting them in any case because of these definitional differences further increase the difficulty of comparing the two socioeconomic and political systems. For this reason the following analysis treats eastern Europe separately, and often in a less exact fashion.

Although social analysis lacks a systematic framework comparable in rigor to that of national income accounting for economics, the structural functionalist perspective used by many sociologists and political scientists offers a substantially neutral heuristic for our work. The core of this approach is the question of social inequality and its

degree of intensity. From the variety of possible indices of social differentiation only a few—occupation, income, property, life-style—can
be dealt with here. Using occupational mobility as an indicator, we
examine the extent to which lasting social strata have formed around
these indices. As the French sociologist Emile Durkheim has pointed
out, the process of social differentiation generates inevitably its logical
opposite, social integration—that is, the establishment of superordi-
nate values and patterns of behavior that override occupational, regional, confessional, and other differences, or at least limit their
potential for conflict. This highlights the role of the political, for a key
issue in the rivalry between differentiation and integration is the role
of the state in society, a role combining that of mediator in situations
of conflict with that of manager of social development. Here again
only a limited number of themes can be presented. We take up the
question of the nation as the central social reference point, and then
examine the extension and institutionalization of participation in societal decision-making. Thereafter we look at the interaction between
individuals, groups, and institutions, in particular the reproduction of
social values in family and church, school and the public media. Finally
we consider some central aspects of sociopolitical administration and
management.

Differentiation and Stratification

Work and Occupation

One of the foundations of modern European society is the work ethic.
Work and occupation are not only economic categories, but have a
central importance to human personality as a whole. For youth, entry
into working life means independence and the transition to maturity.
Loss of job or occupation—for whatever reason—brings with it dis-
honor, which although social in origin is experienced as a personal
problem. Even the retirement from working life in old age is often felt
to be socially ambiguous, despite its being stipulated by legislation and
underwritten by state pension rights; one French sociologist has in
this connection talked of "social death." Work is therefore not merely
a factor of production in the generation of the national product; work
and occupation also constitute a significant part of the foundation upon
which social structures are built, and they are the channels through
which socially produced wealth and social recognition are distributed.

During the twentieth century the composition of the potential labor force has altered with respect to age, gender, qualification, working hours, the nature of work, and working conditions. All of these have directly affected the position and function of work and occupation in the social framework. The state has also altered its relations to labor as a factor of production—that is, to the economically active section of the population—by assuming a greater degree of social responsibility for the individual citizen and seeking to exercise greater influence on the potential supply of labor.

Participation Rate

The participation rate of a society, also called the labor force participation rate or activity rate, is a central socioeconomic indicator. It determines the volume of labor in a society and also reflects that society's demographic structure and sociocultural norms. In theory the rate is easily computed: the number of economically active (employed or temporarily unemployed) persons is divided by the total population. In practice, however, national statistics often count persons such as assisting family members or the unemployed differently and inconsistently, thus hampering accurate calculation of the rate. As with many other forms of social and economic data, geographical and chronological comparison of participation rates is not without problems. Nevertheless, one can identify some general trends.

As a whole, the number of economically active persons in Europe (excluding the Soviet Union) increased from about 147 million before the First World War to around 217 million in 1980. This increase exceeded actual population growth, and so the overall European participation rate increased over this period from 43 percent to 45 percent. As always such aggregated data conceal important regional and national differences. The growth of the labor force in northern and eastern Europe (excepting East Germany and Yugoslavia) during this period, for example, was especially strong. In three of the four southern European states, on the other hand, the increase in the labor force lagged behind that of the population. Western Europe displayed both tendencies. In France, Belgium, Ireland, and Austria the number of persons actively seeking work increased at a markedly slower rate than did the general population, bringing about a fall in prevailing participation rates of several percentage points, whereas the remaining western European states experienced a slight increase in participation rates. In fact, during the period following the Second World War three distinct groupings emerged: eastern Europe with a rate of 50 percent, western and northern Europe with 45 percent, and southern Europe with 40 percent.

The share of a population engaged in economic activity is, however, no real guide to the economic impact of such work. Later sections will examine some of the factors that determine this impact: occupational structure, unemployment, and labor productivity, among others.

Closer examination of the participation rates of individual age-groups reveals a fundamental change in the social meaning of work. At the beginning of the century practically all men worked from early

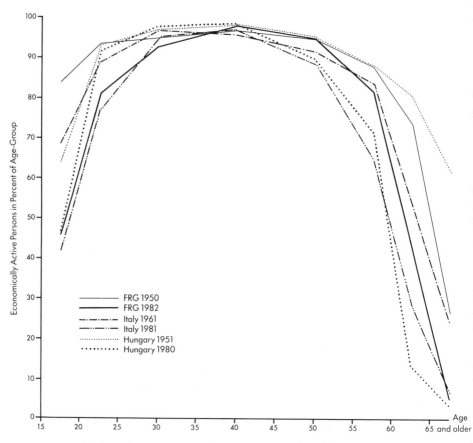

Figure 2.1. Age-Specific Male Participation Rates for Various Countries, 1950–1982 (percent economically active persons in age-group). *Sources:* UN (ECE), *Economic Survey of Europe in 1977,* Part II: *Labour Supply and Migration in Europe* (New York, 1979), pp. 18–20; ILO, *Yearbook of Labour Statistics 1984* (Geneva, 1984), pp. 33–43.

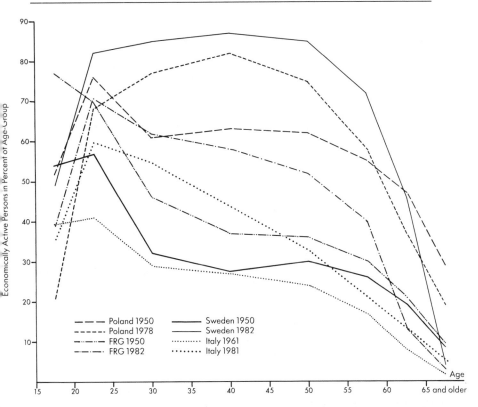

Figure 2.2. Age-Specific Female Participation Rates for Various Countries, 1950–1982 (percent economically active persons in age-group). *Sources:* UN (ECE), *Economic Survey of Europe in 1977,* Part II: *Labour Supply and Migration in Europe* (New York, 1979), pp. 18–20; ILO, *Yearbook of Labour Statistics 1984* (Geneva, 1984), pp. 33–43.

youth until their death or incapacity. The coefficient of utilization of potential male labor—the number of economically active males expressed as a percentage of the total number of men between the ages of fifteen and sixty-five—exceeded 100 percent in all countries except Finland, implying that the labor force included workers under the age of fifteen and over sixty-five. The coefficient changed little before 1945; thereafter, and especially after 1960, it began to sink in all countries. Simultaneously, regional differentiation increased. The lowest coefficients, of 80 percent or less, were typical of northern and southern Europe, whereas in eastern Europe 85 percent was the rule. The highest rate was Switzerland's 90 percent. As can be seen clearly from figure 2.1, the reductions in this statistic mean a shorter working life.

The precondition for this development was the decline in independent work and the ever greater predominance of dependent employment. On the one hand, the constantly rising level of skill required of the labor force necessitated a longer period of schooling, delaying the entry of the young into the labor force. On the other, the development of state pension rights made earlier retirement possible. During the 1920s and 1930s between 80 percent and 90 percent of males aged 15–19 were already employed. By 1960, this proportion had sunk in most countries to 60–70 percent; by 1980 it was below 50 percent, and for Czechoslovakia, Finland, France, Greece, and the Netherlands below 30 percent. For the 20–24 age-group the figure remained at 90 percent well into the 1960s, declining since that time to 80–85 percent. Since retirement from working life is closely related to state legislation on pensions, the participation rate among older age-groups diverges between countries that are otherwise at a similar level of economic development. Nonetheless, a comparison of the 60–65 age-group shows that in the wake of the Second World War, and especially since the 1960s, there has been a marked and widespread decline in the labor force participation rate of this age-group. In West Germany in 1960, 72 percent of males between the ages of sixty and sixty-four were employed, as in the interwar years, but by 1980 only 44 percent were. In the same period this age-specific participation rate declined in the Netherlands from 81 percent to 58 percent, in Italy from 54 percent to 40 percent, and in Hungary from 70 percent to 13 percent. In Switzerland, where pension legislation was not so advanced, the male participation rate among 60–65-year-olds fell only from 89 percent to 83 percent.

Not only the length of an active working life declined in the course of the century, but also the number of hours worked each day or week. Unfortunately, reliable continuous data on this process are scarce; indeed, for agriculture none exist at all. The basic pattern of development is nevertheless evident. As a rule, at the beginning of the century full employment in a productive enterprise entailed a working day of 10 hours and a working week of more than 50 hours. After the First World War several countries, following the recommendations of a conference on international labor law, introduced an eight-hour day as the legal norm for industry. Theoretically this reduced the average number of working hours to around 48 per week. The economic crisis of the 1930s brought about a further reduction of working hours. In the mid-1930s France and Italy, for example, decreed a forty-hour week as the norm, intending in this way to counter mass unemployment; during the war and in the period of reconstruction following 1945, however, this norm was no longer observed. As is evident from the data in figure 2.3, a general reduction of working hours took place in Western Europe only from the 1960s. The average number of hours worked per week declined from 40–45 hours in 1960 to around 40 in 1980, in Belgian and Scandinavian industry falling below 35 hours. In Eastern Europe the state socialist policy of forced growth and a lower level of technical capacity prevented a similar chronological pattern. Here the five-day week was generally introduced only at the end of the 1960s, and in 1980 the number of hours worked per week still stood at an average of 43.5 hours.

The annual number of hours worked was additionally reduced by holidays. In 1919 Norway was the first country to introduce two weeks' paid vacation for all industrial workers; three years later Poland introduced a similar law. During the interwar years workers in other countries negotiated paid vacations and public holidays. Towards the end of the 1930s France, Britain, and Sweden officially stipulated paid vacations varying from six to twelve days for all employees. These stipulations were then imitated by all other European countries in the period 1945–1960. At the same time several countries—Norway, Denmark, Sweden, and France—extended the minimum vacation period to three weeks; other countries did not follow suit until the 1960s. During the 1970s, then, all northern and western European countries, with the exception of Britain and Ireland, increased the minimum length of vacations to four or five weeks.

In aggregate these measures halved the number of hours worked in a normal working life over the course of the century. Since at the same time life expectancy rose ten years, the number of hours spent in paid employment in the course of a lifetime was reduced even further. Unsurprisingly, such a fundamental shift in the relation of working to leisure time has led to the questioning of traditional values and patterns of behavior in the so-called work-society.

The development of paid employment among women, that is, employment outside the home, is more complex. At the beginning of this century, relatively large differences existed between different countries, involving culture, religion, the level and structure of the productive forces, the structure and growth of the population, and the prevailing definition of employment. Nevertheless some common features emerge. Running counter to the trend for male employment, the num-

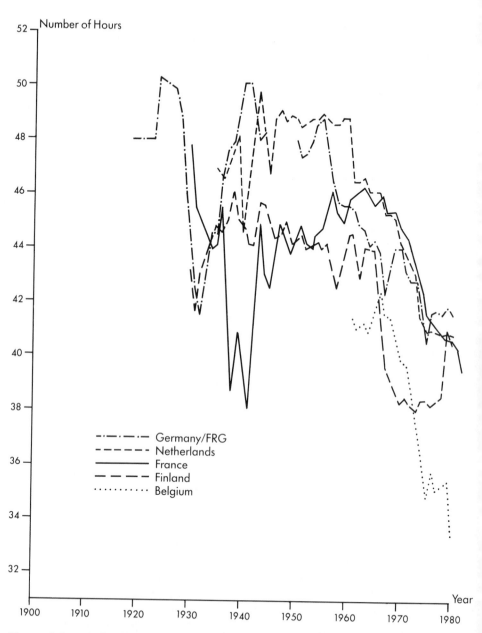

Figure 2.3. Weekly Hours Worked in Industry in Various Countries, 1920–1982 (in hours). *Sources:* ILO, *Hours of Work in Industrialized Countries,* by Archibald A. Evans (Geneva, 1975), pp. 141–42; ILO, *Yearbook of Labour Statistics 1938* (Geneva, 1938), pp. 85–87; *1956* (Geneva, 1956), pp. 164–65; *1964* (Geneva, 1964), pp. 287–88; *1974* (Geneva, 1974), pp. 442–43; *1984* (Geneva, 1984), pp. 542–44.

ber of women in paid work outside the home has risen relatively and absolutely. The coefficient of utilization of potential female labor—the number of economically active females expressed as a percentage of the total number of women between the ages of fifteen and fifty-nine—in 1920 seldom amounted to 50 percent and was more often around 40 percent. By contrast, in 1980 in ten countries this figure was 66 percent, and below 50 percent in only six. Whereas in 1920 women made up one third or more of the working population in only nine countries, by 1980 this was true of nineteen countries. The lowest coefficients, of 30 percent and below, were to be found in southern Europe and Ireland, and, at least into the 1970s, also in the Netherlands, Belgium, and Norway. Since the 1940s the highest rates have been recorded in eastern Europe, varying from 60 to 70 percent; this was as much a result of the Marxist principle of equal rights for women as of a generally tight labor market and a specific shortage of male workers. Aside from Yugoslavia, the proportion of women in the total employed populations of eastern Europe has been around 45 percent since the mid-1960s.

In all countries the rise in economic activity on the part of women is attributable in the first instance to the rise in the number of married women seeking employment. In the first half of the century the typical female worker was a young unmarried woman. Apart from southern Europe, the majority of single women were employed. Marriage meant in most cases exit from employed life; re-entry into steady employment was rare. This has changed radically in the last three decades, the most important reasons being the curtailment of childbearing years, improvements in public child care, more extensive employment opportunities (above all in part-time employment), improved education, and the wish of many women not to exist exclusively for the sake of a family. Behind all these changes is, of course, the fundamental shift in sociocultural or social norms regarding the role of women in society.

Since the Second World War a majority of married women in eastern Europe, Scandinavia, and Britain have joined the labor force. Likewise in many other countries the proportion of married women in paid employment rose considerably—in West Germany, for example, from 25 percent in 1950 to 42 percent in 1980. Paid employment came to be a permanent occupation for more and more women. As can be seen in figures 2.1 and 2.2, over time the age-specific labor force participation rates for men and women have become increasingly similar. In Poland, Sweden, and other northern and eastern European states the curves for men and women are virtually identical. By contrast, for southern European countries, Ireland, Belgium, and the Netherlands, the traditional differences remain, albeit in weaker form. The patterns in the age structure of female employment followed a middle course in West Germany, France, Austria, Switzerland, and Britain.

Sectoral Distribution of the Working Population

The distribution of labor between the primary sector (land and forestry), the secondary sector (mining, energy, manufacturing industry, and construction), and the tertiary sector (trade, communications, media, credit and insurance, health, science and education, public administration, and so on) is regarded as one of the most important indicators of a country's level of development. One speaks roughly, if not entirely accurately, of the distribution of labor between agriculture, industry, and services. The major changes with respect to the level and composition of employment noted in the previous section were directly related to sectoral shifts in occupational structure. Generally, all European countries have followed the same developmental pattern, at varying rates: the share of agriculture both as a source of paid employment and more generally as an occupation has fallen continually; that of industry first rose and then declined, and that of services has risen steadily.

This process is summarized for the principal European regions in figure 2.4. Particularly striking are the differences between northern and western Europe, and southern and eastern Europe. In western Europe in 1910 the distribution of employed persons between sectors was 30 percent in agriculture, 41 percent in industry, and 29 percent in services; in eastern Europe at that time the shares were 80 percent, 8 percent, and 12 percent respectively. By 1980 in western Europe the proportion of agricultural labor in the work force had fallen to 6 percent; that of industry rose in the 1960s to more than 45 percent, thereafter declining to 39 percent; and that of services had grown more or less continuously to reach 55 percent. In eastern Europe, on the other hand, the agricultural sector still employed 24 percent, industry 42 percent, and services only 34 percent of the work force.

Against this background Jean Fourastié, Colin Clark, and A. G. B. Fisher developed their well-known three-sector hypothesis concerning the necessary transformation of agricultural society through industrial society to a service or post-industrial society, based on the logic of the modern economic system:

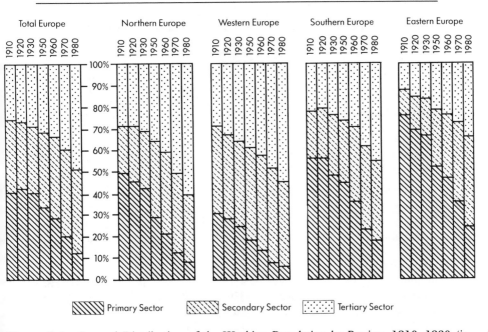

Figure 2.4. Sectoral Distribution of the Working Population by Region, 1910–1980 (in percent). *Sources:* Thomas Deldycke et al., *The Working Population and Its Structure* (Brussels, 1968), pp. 27–34; ILO, *World Labour Report*, vol. 1 (Geneva, 1984), p. 89; ILO, *Yearbook of Labour Statistics 1938* (Geneva, 1938), pp. 6–15; *1970* (Geneva, 1970), p. 126; World Bank, *World Tables*, 3rd ed., vol. 2: *Social Data* (Washington, D.C., 1983), pp. 35, 76, 100, 112; Jürgen Hartmann, *Politik und Gesellschaft in Osteuropa* (Frankfurt, 1983), p. 216.

1. The demand for foodstuffs is physically limited; as welfare increases, the structure of demand of the private household shifts to goods supplied by industry and the service sector.
2. The mechanization and centralization of industrial production prompt the extension of services supplied by the tertiary sector, for example the sales and maintenance of secondary goods.
3. Whereas technical progress raises productivity in the primary and secondary sectors, and in this way frees labor, the increase in labor productivity is much slower in the tertiary sector; a rising demand for tertiary goods brings about a rise in employment.
4. The tertiary sector is overwhelmingly oriented to the domestic market; its size and potential for expansion are determined less by world markets and foreign competition than are those of the primary and secondary sectors.

The empirical evidence seems to confirm this thesis in the case of Europe, even if the actual process of development diverges somewhat

Table 2.1. Sectoral Distribution of the Working Population by Country, 1910–1980[a] (in percent)

	1910			1930		
	A	I	S	A	I	S
Northern Europe						
Sweden	49	32	19	39	36	25
Denmark	36	28	36	30	29	41
Finland	80	12	8	71	16	13
Norway	39	25	36	36	27	37
Western Europe						
Germany	37[a]	41[a]	22[a]	29[b]	40[b]	31[b]
FRG	—	—	—	—	—	—
United Kingdom	9	52	40	6[c]	46[c]	48[c]
France	41	33	26	36	33	31
Netherlands	29	33	38	21	36	43
Belgium	23	45	32	17	48	35
Austria	32[f]	33[f]	35[f]	32[g]	33[g]	35[g]
Switzerland	27	46	28	21	45	34
Ireland	51[h]	15[h]	34[h]	48[i]	16[i]	36[i]
Eastern Europe						
Poland	77[j]	9[j]	14[j]	66	17	17
Yugoslavia	82[f]	11[f]	7[f]	78	11	11
Rumania	80	8	12	77	9	14
GDR	—	—	—	—	—	—
Czechoslovakia	40[f]	37[f]	23[f]	37	37	26
Hungary	58[f]	20[f]	22[f]	5	24	23
Bulgaria	82	8	10	80[g]	8[g]	12[g]
Southern Europe						
Italy	55	27	18	47	31	22
Spain	56	14	30[m]	—	—	—
Portugal	57	22	21	—	—	—
Greece	50[f]	16[f]	34[f]	54[n]	16[n]	30[n]

Sources: Thomas Deldycke et al., *The Working Population and its Structure* (Brussels, 1968), pp. 27–34; ILO, *World Labour Report,* vol. 1 (Geneva, 1984), p. 89; ILO, *Yearbook of Labour Statistics 1938* (Geneva, 1938), pp. 6–15; *1970* (Geneva, 1970), p. 126; World Bank, *World Tables,* 3rd ed., vol. 2: *Social Data* (Baltimore, 1983), pp. 35, 76, 100, 112; Jürgen Hartmann, *Politik und Gesellschaft in Osteuropa* (Frankfurt, 1983), p. 216.

Note: A = Agriculture, including forestry and fisheries; I = Industry, including manufacturing, construction, and energy; S = Service, including communications, banking, public administration, and so on.

[a] 1907.

[b] 1933.

[c] Excluding Northern Ireland.

Table 2.1. (Continued)

1950			1960			1980		
A	I	S	A	I	S	A	I	S
21	41	38	14	45	41	5	34	61
25	34	41	18	37	45	7	35	58
47	28	25	36	32	33	11	35	54
26	37	37	20	37	44	7	37	56
—	—	—	—	—	—	—	—	—
23	43	34	14	48	38	4	46	50
5	49	46	4	48	48	3	42	56
27[d]	36[d]	37[d]	22	39	39	8	39	53
20[e]	34[e]	46[e]	11	42	47	6	45	49
13[e]	50[e]	37[e]	8	48	45	3	41	56
33	37	30	24	46	30	9	37	54
17	47	37	11	50	39	5	46	49
40	24	35	36	25	40	18	37	45
54	26	20	48	29	23	31	39	30
71[k]	16[k]	13[k]	63	18	19	29	35	36
74	14	12	67	15	18	29	36	35
27	44	29	18	48	34	10	49	41
39	36	25	26	46	28	11	48	41
51	23	26	37	35	28	20	43	37
65[l]	19[l]	17[l]	56	25	19	37	39	24
42	32	26	31	40	29	11	45	44
50	26	25	42	31	27	14	40	46
49	25	26	44	29	27	28	35	37
51	21	28	56	20	24	37	28	35

[d] 1954.
[e] 1947.
[f] 1920.
[g] 1934.
[h] 1926.
[i] 1936.
[j] 1920, excluding Silesia and a part of Vilno.
[k] 1953.
[l] 1956.
[m] Contains a large number of unspecified occupations.
[n] 1928.

from the model. An international comparison clarifies the significance of geographical and historical structural conditions as well as national peculiarities: in all highly developed states outside Europe—the United States, Canada, Japan, Australia—the service sector has always employed a greater proportion of the work force than has the industrial sector, despite the degree of development of the latter. In these countries the transition from an agrarian to a service society occurred directly, without an intermediate stage. Even in Europe the timing and degree of this structural change varied from country to country (the relevant data can be found in table 2.1). In Britain, the country in which the Industrial Revolution was inaugurated, the transition was far advanced even before the First World War. At that time industry employed more than half of the labor force and agriculture only 10 percent. During the interwar years the pace of change was slower, accelerating once again only in the 1950s. Between 1951 and 1980 the proportion of the labor employed in agriculture sank further to 3 percent, while the proportion employed in the service sector rose from 43 percent to 59 percent, and that in the industrial sector declined from 49 percent to 38 percent. Although in the Germany of 1907 over one third of employment was still in agriculture, industrial employment accounted for a good 40 percent of the labor force. Subsequently the agricultural share fell slowly to one quarter in 1939. In 1950 agriculture still employed 22 percent of the West German labor force, but its share declined rapidly to 13 percent in 1961 and thereafter to 6 percent in 1980. Industrial employment in West Germany continued to grow in the 1950s, but it levelled out in the 1960s and began to recede in the 1970s. The majority of those leaving the agricultural sector entered the service sector (sometimes via temporary industrial employment), and this sector accordingly expanded from one third of all employment in 1950 to one half in 1980.

A third variant of the Fourastié model is provided by France, whose pattern of development is more typical of that for other countries, or at least more representative than the path followed by Britain and Germany. In 1911 French agriculture employed 40 percent of the labor force, and the industrial and the tertiary sector each employed 30 percent. This structure changed little during the interwar years; at the beginning of the 1950s each principal sector employed around one third of the labor force. The following economic boom brought about a major shift in employment structure. By the early 1980s so many workers had left agriculture that it accounted for only 8 percent of employment. During the same period both industry and services grew strongly. In 1968 the tertiary sector already employed 46 percent of the work force, the figure rising to 53 percent in 1980.

Apart from eastern Europe, service industries became the major source of employment in the three decades following the Second World War. In quite varied economies—Sweden, Belgium, Switzerland, Britain, West Germany—industrial employment fell not only relatively, but absolutely; this "deindustrialization" was caused in part at least by high unemployment in industry and not exclusively by intersectoral shifts in employment. By 1980 agriculture employed more than 10 percent of the labor force only in Ireland, Finland, and southern Europe. The postwar transformation from an agrarian to a service society took less than a generation in France, Ireland, and northern and southern Europe. For these countries the period in which industry employed the greatest proportion of labor was extremely short. The brevity of this period of industrial domination must be borne in mind when considering national variations in the development of working conditions, labor relations, and the labor movement.

Eastern Europe provides yet another variant of the three-sector hypothesis of socioeconomic development. An initially high proportion of persons employed in agriculture was reduced between 1950 and 1980 by half. This was not only a consequence of the shedding of labor through greater agricultural productivity but to a great extent a consequence of the migration of underemployed surplus rural workers into towns and cities, where they found full-time employment and better wages. The forced pace of industrialization at the same time greatly stimulated the secondary sector, so that by the early 1980s the less advanced countries had 40 percent of their labor force in this sector, and the more advanced countries (East Germany and Czechoslovakia) had almost 50 percent. On the average, therefore, the share of industrial employment was above that prevailing in the rest of Europe. Above all, it did not decline in eastern Europe; its growth merely flattened out. The tertiary sector's position in the work force strengthened in all state socialist economies, but in the mid-1980s it still remained much weaker than was typical for the market economies of the West.

Of course, in considering this structural transition one should not overlook regional variations within individual countries. Great differences continued to exist between town and countryside, for instance between the Limousin and Greater Paris, Calabria and Turin. But such differences should not be overemphasized, for the extension of modern means of communication and transport—television, telephone, the automobile—rendered the "tertiarization" of society a universal phenomenon.

Occupational Categories

The sectoral shifts in employment also entailed varied and complex consequences for the inner composition of the work force. The number of employers and self-employed greatly declined; their share in the labor force sank in the course of the century by more than one half in most countries. In Germany in 1907 they constituted 20 percent of the economically active persons; in West Germany in 1980 they made up just 9 percent. In Sweden the proportion fell from 21 percent in 1930 to 7 percent in 1980, in Belgium from 35 percent in 1900 to 12 percent in 1980, in France from 45 percent in 1926 to 15 percent in 1980, and in Italy from over 40 percent in 1931 to 21 percent in 1980. Only in Spain, Ireland, and Greece was the share in 1980 as high as that in Italy. In the majority of countries self-employment declined rapidly from the early 1950s. In Eastern Europe, aside from Yugoslavia and Poland, private enterprise was almost completely dismantled in the 1950s and 1960s. This corresponded to the Marxist ideological principle that with the abolition of private property class differences also disappeared. But private enterprise also declined in significance throughout Western Europe, with far-reaching economic and social consequences.

The shrinkage in the number of the self-employed was naturally accompanied by a decline in the employment of unpaid family labor—primarily supplied by women. In the 1930s this group made up from 10 percent to 20 percent of all labor in western Europe (including Italy); in some countries of eastern and southern Europe the figure was nearer one third. This share was halved by the 1960s. By the beginning of the 1980s the proportion of family labor in the total of employed persons had fallen to 5 percent, with the exception of Greece, Poland, and Yugoslavia where it was still at the 10 percent mark.

This decline of independent and family labor can be attributed primarily to the structural transformation of agriculture. Relinquishment of agricultural employment did not simply involve the transfer of labor from one sector to another; it also involved the decline of an independent peasantry with its associated perspective and life-style. Between 1945 and 1980 the number of independent farmers fell in France from 4 million to 1.5 million, in West Germany from 1.2 million to

533,000, and in Italy from 2.5 million to 1.4 million. During the period 1950–1979 it dropped in Spain from 2.5 million to one million and in Denmark between 1933 and 1981 from 215,000 to 100,000. The collectivization of agriculture in eastern Europe after the Second World War virtually obliterated an independent peasantry; only Poland and Yugoslavia were exceptions. Thus in little more than a generation, a social group that had hitherto molded the nature of European society declined to a very small minority in many countries. For the rural population that remained, mechanization, the commercialization of agricultural production, and increasing urbanization brought fundamental changes in everyday life, ultimately destroying peasant life-styles and customs.

Thus, the dependently employed—those whose working conditions are governed by pay agreements and whose income is composed of wages and salaries—came to be increasingly predominant in the work force. The class antagonism of capitalist and proletariat described by Marx did not, however, become intensified in the way he had supposed. Instead, corresponding to the social logic of the three-sector hypothesis, a new socioeconomic group emerged: white-collar salaried employees. The growth of this group expressed the technical and organizational changes associated with the diffusion of mass production and the expansion of the service sector. In the course of the century the number of managers, office workers, technicians, and retailing staff rose considerably. As can be seen from figure 2.5, nonmanual workers constituted the majority of the work force in most European countries by 1980. In Britain, for example, the comparatively high level of development reached in 1910 is reflected in the highest European proportion of salaried employees in the labor force, at 19 percent; the proportion climbed to 30 percent in 1951 and by 1980 had reached 40 percent. In West Germany between 1950 and 1980 this social group more than doubled its relative weight in the country's work force.

The course of development was similar in other countries. In France the proportion of salaried employees in the work force rose from 11 percent in 1906 to over 18 percent in 1954 and then to 41 percent in 1981. In Sweden it grew from 16 percent in 1930, to 27 percent in 1950, to 59 percent in 1980, this last representing the highest proportion in Europe. Different forms of classification applied in Eastern Europe hinder an exact East-West comparison, but a similar trend can be detected there too. In general the service sector, and in particular public administration, has provided the majority of positions for sal-

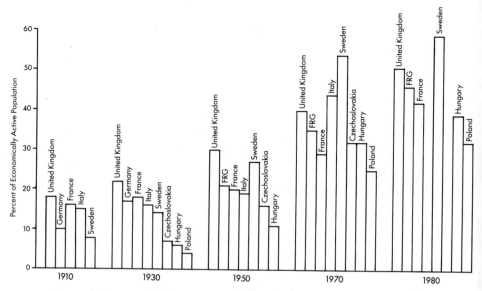

Figure 2.5. Nonmanual Employment in Various Countries, 1910–1980 (as percent of working population). *Sources:* A. H. Halsey, *Change in British Society* (Oxford, 1978), p. 26; A. W. J. Thomson and L. C. Hunter, "Great Britain," in *Labor in the Twentieth Century,* ed. John T. Dunlop and Walter Galenson (New York, 1978), p. 93; Dietmar Petzina et al., *Sozialgeschichtliches Arbeitsbuch III* (Munich, 1978), p. 55; Gerold Ambrosius, "Das Wirtschaftssystem," in *Die Bundesrepublik Deutschland,* ed. Wolfgang Benz, vol. 1 (Frankfurt, 1983), p.258; Jean-Pierre Briand and Jean-Michel Chapouli, *Les classes sociales* (Paris, 1980), p. 94; Corrado Barberis, *La Societa Italiana* (Milan, 1976), p. 353; K.-G. Hildebrand, "The New Industrial Structure—the Scandinavian Experience," in *Post-Industrial Society,* ed. Bo Gustaffson (London, 1979), p. 61; P. M. Johnson, "Changing Social Structure and the Political Role of Manual Workers," in *Blue-Collar Workers in Eastern Europe,* ed. Jan Triska and Charles Gati (London, 1981), p. 30; Iván T. Berend and György Ránki, *Underdevelopment and Economic Growth* (Budapest, 1979), p. 200; ILO, *Yearbook of Labour Statistics 1965* (Geneva, 1965), p. 210; *1977* (Geneva, 1977), p. 266; *1982* (Geneva, 1982), p. 178.

aried employees. However, such employment also rose generally in the different branches of industry, especially in those such as chemicals, machine construction, and electrical equipment that applied advanced technology, with the associated research and development costs. This increase accelerated in the wake of the Second World War, and in these branches of industry in the mid-1980s salaried employees constituted between a quarter and one third of all employees.

Salaried employees can be distinguished from other workers by education and qualification, the manner and level of remuneration (monthly salary as against daily or hourly rates of pay), labor relations, working conditions, and prospects for promotion, to name only the most important differences. Such salaried employees have always seen themselves as a distinct socioeconomic group and separate even from other workers in the same industry or in the same enterprise. In the organization and internal ranking of a particular enterprise they occupy a position between management and blue-collar worker, although they would undoubtedly associate themselves more with management than with workers. The connection between the lower and the upper levels of salaried employees was especially close in public administration, and those employed by private concerns perceived in this a model to be imitated in respect of pay, privilege, and status, an imitation implied in the now archaic term "private official." Early industrial sociologists readily classified salaried employees as a special social group—a new middle class, which differed from the older middle class of craftsmen and traders, but which like it was differentiated from the ordinary blue-collar worker.

Such an interpretation makes sense, especially for the interwar years. After the Second World War both the number of salaried employees and their internal differentiation increased, and in this way the inner coherence of a socioeconomic category occupying a particular social stratum was lost. The increasing size of enterprises led to a greater formalization of organization and hierarchy; qualifications became more specialized and with this the dividing lines between higher management, middle management, and office workers more clearly drawn. In this process gender differences became especially marked. Positions involving supervision and leadership are still today almost exclusively male prerogatives. In 1980 only in eastern Europe did women occupy a substantial portion—almost one third—of supervisory positions. Even in such "emancipated" countries as Denmark and Sweden only a quarter of all managers were women; in Spain the figure was a meagre 3 percent. Men also dominated technical and academic positions until well into the 1960s, although in these areas a fairly equal division between men and women existed in some countries by the 1980s. The sphere of office work—that is, the less-qualified, worse-paid, and less-regarded domain—remained one of women; here there were two women for every man. Spain, Greece, and the Netherlands, where female participation in the work force was generally low, were exceptions to this; there men predominated even in salaried office work.

The factors that altered the status and structure of the salariat also affected the position of skilled, semiskilled, and unskilled workers.

Their share of total employment had been receding since the 1960s; in some countries their numbers fell absolutely. Whereas 71 percent of those employed in Britain in 1910 were workers of this sort, by 1980 the proportion had fallen to 38 percent. Between 1930 and 1965 the percentage of manual workers in the Swedish labor force fell from 69 percent to 49 percent, and in West Germany it dropped from 51 percent in 1950 (the same share as had existed in prewar Germany) to 41 percent in 1980. France, which in comparison to these two countries was relatively weakly industrialized and in which agriculture played a more prominent role, saw the number of industrial workers increase between 1921 and 1975 from 7.1 million to 8.2 million; expressed as a proportion of total employment, however, this in fact represented a drop from 49 percent to 39 percent.

The composition of blue-collar employment likewise changed in the course of the century, although not to the extent foreseen by industrial sociologists in the first few decades of the century. They had anticipated that mechanization and rationalization would produce a homogeneous working population, a proletarian mass lacking occupational differentiation. This image of the undifferentiated, unqualified machine-age worker was widely propagated in films such as *Metropolis, Modern Times,* and *À nous la liberté.* This cliché not only concealed the extremely complex shifts in the composition of blue-collar work but also obscured a reality that was quite the opposite. Estimating the educational standards of various groups of workers in the past is difficult, but the available data show that in all countries the share of unskilled labor declined whereas that of skilled labor did not. One of the important reasons for a general rise in the level of qualification was the drastic decline in unskilled agricultural labor. In France, for instance, the number of unskilled rural workers fell from almost 3 million in 1921 to something over 1 million in 1954 and ultimately to 270,000 in 1982. In Italy in 1954, 2.5 million unskilled rural workers were still employed, but by 1982 the figure was less than 1 million. The decline was even more dramatic in Spain: from over 3 million in 1950 to under 700,000 in 1983.

At the same time the decline of the less technically demanding sections of manufacturing, such as the textile and clothing industries, also contributed to the reduction in the numbers of unskilled workers. On the whole, the increasing technological complexity of modern industry brought about a progressive improvement in school and vocational education in the course of the century. In France over one third of workers in 1911 had not completed elementary education; only 20 percent had attended higher schools. By 1931 these figures had altered to 15 percent and 24 percent respectively; by the early 1970s only 5 percent had failed to complete elementary school, and more than 50 percent of manual workers had gone on for two to three years to a higher school and acquired specific qualifications. In Britain the average number of years spent in school by a worker rose from six or seven years in 1910 to over ten years in 1960.

Although a direct comparison of results is hindered by variations in definition, occupational statistics confirm the implications of the school statistics. The share of qualified and trained workers in West Germany in 1980 represented around 80 percent of the male blue-collar labor force; in the Germany of 1925 it had been only 65 percent. The level of qualification rose similarly in other countries. In Italy the share of skilled workers was at the relatively low level of 58 percent in 1951, but it then expanded in the subsequent decades to 70 percent. Schooling and vocational training were developed in eastern Europe as well. In 1982 almost two thirds of all employed persons in East Germany possessed a vocational qualification, by contrast with 1971 when only one half did. The percentage of Polish blue-collar workers with vocational training increased between 1958 and 1979 from 8 percent to 24 percent. In Hungary over the same period the share of skilled workers in the industrial blue-collar work force rose from 40 percent to 50 percent and that of unskilled fell from 27 percent to 12 percent.

Neither women nor immigrants participated in this process of skill enhancement to the same extent as native male workers. In the case of women, the proportion of unskilled workers in the female manual work force remained fairly constant, as in West Germany with 55 percent and France with 35 percent, or it even rose, as in Italy from 40 percent in 1951 to 56 percent in 1971. Similar variations in the level of training of men and women existed in the eastern European economies. Thus in Hungarian industry only 22 percent of the female blue-collar workers had completed vocational training as against 65 percent of the men. The foreign workers who sought work during the 1960s and 1970s in northern and western Europe had for the most part no training at all. Rapid changes of employment and a poor knowledge of the language prevented the mass of them from completing a course of vocational training in the land to which they had emigrated. For the most part they were employed in positions that either required no skill or whose skills could be quickly picked up, and in this way gender and national distinctions among the workers were sharpened. In 1970, 55 percent of West German male blue-collar workers were skilled and only 20 percent unskilled; for female blue-collar workers the proportions were 12 percent and 54 percent respectively. Among male foreign workers the share of skilled persons (22 percent) was clearly well below that for unskilled (35 percent). In a number of countries, but especially in West Germany and France, this has recently intensified the traditional conflict of interest within the manual work force between skilled and unskilled labor, at a time when it faces serious challenges associated with automation, deindustrialization, and unemployment.

Income and Wealth

Global Income Distribution

The distribution of income and property within a society is one of the most central and striking measures of social inequality. It has, therefore, frequently been both the occasion of conflict and the target of attempts to integrate the various social interest groups more closely. From the point of view of the household economy, income largely determines the standard of living. From the point of view of the economy as a whole, it plays an important role in relations of consumption and hence in the entire economy's structure of demand. But despite this central role no entirely adequate statistical measure of income distribution exists; moreover, data that permit comparison with the past or between countries are even rarer. Nonetheless, certain trends can be identified in the available material. A levelling process has clearly been going on, especially since 1950. The rapid increases in national product per capita that have occurred throughout both Western and Eastern Europe imply that the general level of welfare has also risen. Accompanying this was a substantial growth of real wages in Western Europe, which ranged, with due allowance for variations in their calculation, from an increase by a factor of three in Britain to one of six in France (see fig. 2.6). The share of income derived from employment—wages and salaries— in the total national income also expanded during this period.

Aggregated data of this kind can give only a very rough indication of distribution. Statistics on income are more suitable, but these also have their faults. Such statistics are commonly drawn from income tax returns, and the proportion of the employed population paying tax varies from country to country, as do the prospects for evading payment of taxes. Moreover, the difference between pre-tax distribution and

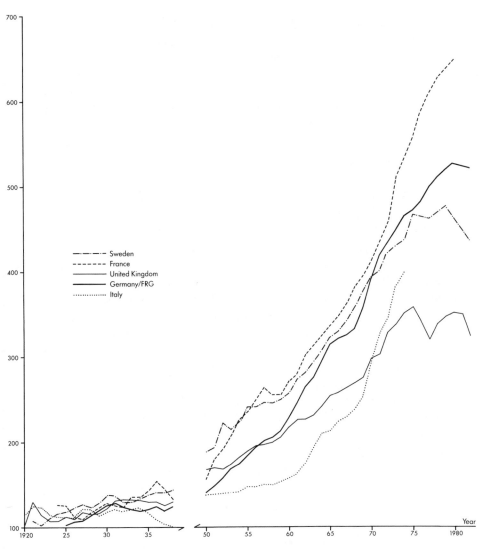

Figure 2.6. Real Wages in Various Countries, 1920–1982 (1913 = 100). *Sources:* E. H. Phelps Brown, "Levels and Movements of Industrial Productivity and Real Wages Internationally Compared, 1860–1970," *Economic Journal,* 83 (1973): 67–68; Sergio Ricossa, "Italy," in *The Fontana Economic History of Europe,* ed. Carlo M. Cipolla, vol. 6 (Glasgow, 1976), pp. 274, 316; ILO, *Yearbook of Labour Statistics 1976* (Geneva, 1976), pp. 617–21, 776–77; *1984* (Geneva, 1984), pp. 600–603, 728–29.

post-tax distribution must be borne in mind. Taking these caveats into account, one can still discern through the course of the twentieth century a slight decline in the inequality of income distribution.

In several countries the share of total personal income accounted for by the wealthiest 10 percent of the population declined from 35–40 percent at the beginning of the century to perhaps 24–31 percent, with the steepest decline occurring in the 1930s and 1940s. The greatest levelling tendency in the developed countries of Western Europe is to be found in Sweden, Denmark, Norway, and Britain; there the proportion of total personal income accounted for by the top 10 percent of the population declined between 1935 and 1948 from 34–36 percent to 27 percent and then dropped by the early 1970s to 21–23 percent. By contrast, in Italy, France, West Germany, and the Netherlands this group's share has remained stable at 29–30 percent. A relatively rapid erosion of income inequality also took place in Eastern Europe after 1945. For example, in Hungary the share of income taken by the richest 20 percent of the population fell from 59 percent in 1930 to 36 percent in 1962; in Czechoslovakia it dropped from 47 percent to 37 percent between 1930 and 1965. Indeed, Czechoslovakia exhibited the most egalitarian income distribution in Europe: since the 1960s the richest 10 percent of the population has accounted for only 14 percent of personal income. This decline in the share of income flowing to the highest groups did not directly benefit the lowest income groups, however. Only in Scandinavia, Poland, Czechoslovakia, and East Germany has the share of income taken by the poorest 20 percent of the population increased noticeably from below 10 percent in the 1930s to the level of 15–20 percent since the 1960s; in the remaining countries, including Britain, it has changed little and has fluctuated between 10 percent and 12 percent since 1950.

Differences in Wages and Salaries
The relations between different groups in terms of income are easier to grasp than these national aggregates. Here also the available data are often incomplete and sometimes misleading, since they are mostly based upon agreed rates of pay rather than actual pay. The most complete time-series treats conditions in Britain; there pay differentials between various categories of employees have diminished considerably between 1913 and 1978 (see fig. 2.7). On the one hand, income differences according to qualification within blue-collar workers and white-collar salaried staff lessened; on the other hand, these two groups

Figure 2.7. Occupational Position and Income of Men in Great Britain, 1913–1978 (100 = average income of unskilled worker). *Source:* Guy Routh, *Occupation and Pay in Great Britain 1906–1979* (London, 1980), p. 127.

as a whole moved closer together. At the beginning of the century skilled workers and craftsmen earned on average respectively 68 percent and 98 percent more than unskilled laborers; in the mid-1950s these figures had shifted down to 43 percent and 80 percent, falling further to 28 percent and 38 percent by the end of the 1970s. This process of equalization was more delayed among salaried employees. Here the highest grades earned three times that of the lowest in 1913–1914 and twice that in 1955–1956. The gap separating lower-intermediary and higher salaried employees and civil servants closed to a figure of around 50 percent only in the 1960s and 1970s. The gap separating lower and intermediate grades, on the other hand, altered far less; in 1913–1914 intermediate grades earned 58 percent more than the lower grades, and in 1978 this figure was still at the level of 46 percent.

Since comparable series for other countries are lacking, it is not possible to assert categorically that the British pattern applies to all Europe for the entire century. Nevertheless, the available data on the period since the 1950s indicate that income differentials between the various occupational groups in other countries have diminished slightly. Differences in wages and salaries not only reflect the varying weight assigned to formal job qualifications but also express traditional status differences. Thus, during the 1970s the divergence between the average incomes of workers and salaried employees in France and Italy was greater than that in Belgium, West Germany, the Netherlands, and Britain. The variance within individual occupational groups was also nationally conditioned, being the greatest in France and Italy and the least in West Germany. The hierarchy of occupations by income has remained relatively stable for all employees and in general is related to the technological condition of the particular branches of economic activity.

In non-communist Europe wage negotiations between employees and employers play the most important role in determining income from employment. In communist Europe, by contrast, central state policy determines wages and salaries. This policy is not aimed at a general equalization of incomes but rather at the management of work incentives and the direction of labor into particular occupations. Skilled workers in Eastern Europe, for example, received incomes during the 1960s and 1970s that were between 30 percent and 40 percent higher than those of unskilled workers. Until the 1970s wages in the agricultural sector were held at a level of 80 percent of the average industrial wage as a means to encourage the transfer of labor from agriculture to industry. The pay differentials between manual and nonmanual work were, however, greatly reduced in Eastern Europe. In all countries except Poland the average income of entry-level salaried employees was below that of blue-collar workers—in Czechoslovakia as much as 20 percent below. Even the income of higher salaried employees—the so-called intelligentsia—was in 1970s only 40–50 percent more than that of the average worker's income, the figure for Czechoslovakia being 20 percent.

Gender is another central factor in the constitution of European income differentials. In both Western and Eastern Europe up to the 1970s female employees earned on average significantly less than males: usually one third less, in Britain even one half less. Lower qualifications, shorter work hours, fewer years of job experience, and other factors played a role here, but this did not alter the simple fact that men were favored as the supposed principal earner and supporter of the family.

Global Distribution of Wealth
Apart from the fact that wealth, or property, is always much more unequally distributed than current income, the relatively unreliable data on the spread of personal wealth enable few specific observations. However, here too, definite signs of a reduction in unequal distribution of wealth are present. The introduction of wealth taxes, inflation, economic crises, the effect of war, and politically motivated expropriation have had an impact in this respect as have the general rise in incomes and the decline of self-employment and the private ownership of means of production. Most notably, the possession of durable consumer goods—cars, televisions, refrigerators, and so on—began to rise in the 1960s as did the ownership of apartments and houses, especially in Western Europe (see fig. 2.9).

A further important element in the accumulation of wealth was the development in the postwar period of social welfare in the form of pensions, health benefits, and so forth. This permitted broad sections of the population to accumulate modest amounts of wealth, and at the same time it markedly diminished the significance of the extremely wealthy. In 1913 the wealthiest 1 percent of the population in Britain owned 70 percent of private economic property, in France 50 percent; by the mid-1970s these figures had declined to 23 percent and 15 percent respectively (see fig. 2.8). If one broadens the definition of the rich to the top 10 percent or 15 percent of the population, then this decline is not so marked; in 1975 this wider group still disposed of 60–70 percent of private wealth.

Estimates for the distribution of wealth in West Germany over this period show a similar pattern. Analysis of the possession of wealth according to socioeconomic position in France and West Germany shows that in the mid-1970s the share of wealth held by blue-collar workers was significantly lower than their proportion in the total population. This relationship was reversed among the self-employed and the higher salariat; these groups possessed a proportion of all wealth greater than that of their relative numbers in the population as a whole. To sum up, the distribution of wealth in Western Europe did broaden in the course of the twentieth century but this broadening did not really overcome distributive inequality.

Living Standards and Life-Styles

How is the composition of society according to occupation, income, and wealth expressed in the life-styles of different social groups? Here

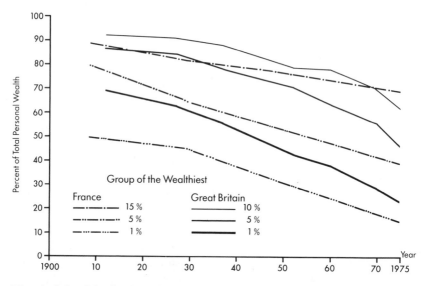

Figure 2.8. Distribution of Wealth in Great Britain and France, 1910–1975 (as percent of total personal wealth). *Sources:* G. P. Marshall, *Social Goals and Economic Perspectives* (Harmondsworth, 1980), p. 95; Adeline Daumard, "L'éclatement de la bourgeoisie française," in *Histoire économique et sociale de la France*, ed. Fernand Braudel and Ernest Labrousse, vol. 3, part 3 (Paris, 1982), p. 100.

again there is a paucity of representative studies on, for instance, consumption and the equipping of households that either cover a long period of time or deal with all strata or countries. Such information about the interwar period is in particularly short supply. But, as in the foregoing, the data available allow one to draw some plausible conclusions.

Until the 1950s considerable differences existed in living standards and life-styles. Especially evident was the extremely low living standard of the bulk of the urban and rural population. Even in "good" years the major part of household expenditure, often more than 75 percent, was devoted to satisfying basic needs—food, clothing, accommodation, and heating. After the deduction of taxes and social insurance premiums, less than one fifth of household income remained for disposition on superior consumer goods, leisure, savings, and so forth. In the households of salaried employees and civil servants, on the other hand, this residual amounted to more than one quarter of larger and more secure incomes. Blue-collar workers were under a permanent threat of loss of earnings from sickness, accident, or unemployment, which worsened an already precarious income situation. Mass unemployment after 1929 was followed by widespread impoverishment throughout Europe, and this left a lasting impression on those affected, an impression that would have major impact on the development of social and economic policy after the Second World War (see fig. 2.14).

Those in regular employment (and this was always the majority of the labor force, even in the crisis years) in the meantime achieved a certain improvement in their living standard, since real wages in most countries rose noticeably, if unsteadily (see fig. 2.6). Food became more plentiful and more varied. Electric lighting and radios increasingly became standard household equipment. By 1938, in France and Britain the automobile was no longer the prerogative of the rich. In Germany, millions dreamed of owning a "people's car" (the Volkswagen) and saved for that day. The bases of a consumer society began to develop in these years in western and northern Europe: brand name goods, consumer credit, cheap retail stores, mail order houses, and advertising all became more widespread.

Almost three decades of constant economic growth in the wake of the Second World War brought about the breakthrough to a society of mass consumption, at least in northern and western Europe. The general increase in prosperity that came with this contributed greatly to the reduction of traditional material inequalities in the life-styles of

European societies. Full employment and constantly increasing real wages improved the levels of consumption enjoyed by the lower strata, and thus living standards in general. The share of household expenditure required for basic needs sank to around one half by 1960, freeing the means to acquire many more consumer goods and services or to accumulate savings. In particular, variations in wage incomes caused by the business cycle or related to stage in life were diminished by the extension of state social benefits.

The data in figure 2.9 illustrate this convergence in consumption patterns for three French social groups whose life-styles had traditionally diverged widely: the higher salariat, peasants, and blue-collar workers. The general trend of these curves also applies to other European countries, although naturally in remote and less-developed regions this process was much slower. This levelling process was especially rapid in northern and western Europe during the 1960s, taking place in eastern Europe only during the 1970s. Moreover, this "democratization" of affluence was quite fragmentary in southern European countries. Aside from Spain and Italy, the possession of the most symbolic consumer good—the automobile—was in 1980 only half as common in southern and eastern Europe as in the remaining parts of Europe (see table 3.15 and fig. 4.2).

The convergence of different levels of consumption naturally does not mean the disappearance of life-style variations deriving from association with a particular social strata. As shown in Chapter 1, variations in demographic behavior—age at marriage, number of children, life expectancy—also contribute to social differentiation. Even in the purchase of higher-level consumer goods such as dishwashers, campers, videorecorders, and personal computers, a differentiating process arising from price-related differences in quality has been evident in Western Europe. In Eastern Europe "class differences" have emerged on the basis of privileged access to those consumer goods frequently in short supply.

At the beginning of the 1980s the duration of free time was more or less the same for the majority of employed persons. However, the manner in which this free time was spent showed marked social inequalities. Demanding working conditions—intense concentration, monotony, shift work—greatly restricted for many workers the possible use of free time. A normal work schedule and physically less demanding occupation allowed for a more creative utilization of work-free time.

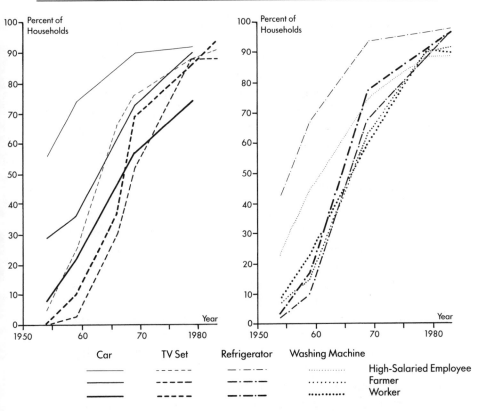

Figure 2.9. Ownership of Consumer Durables in France, 1954–1983 (in percent of households in occupational category). *Sources:* Jean-Pierre Rioux, *La France de la Quatrième République,* vol. 2 (Paris, 1983), p. 243; Jean-Daniel Reynaud and Yves Grafmeyer, eds., *Français, qui êtes-vous?* (Paris, 1981), p. 392; Roger Girod, *Les inégalités sociales* (Paris, 1984), p. 63; Institut National de la Statistique et des Etudes Economiques (INSEE), *Tableaux de l'économie française 1970* (Paris, 1970), p. 302; *1985* (Paris, 1985), p. 77.

A further important factor here was the level of education. Despite the educational explosion beginning in the 1960s, substantial educational differences, especially in respect of general education, still existed between social groups in the 1980s. Different leisure-time pursuits resulted from this, in particular those related to higher-level "cultural consumption": reading, attending concerts and the theater, and so forth. More evident disadvantages exist in the case of holidays. Whereas nearly three quarters of the households of the salariat in western Europe can afford summer vacations, only one half of the workers' households can; peasants are way down the scale, because of the nature of their occupation. Winter vacations, on the other hand, are enjoyed by only a minority of the better-off strata.

In sum, a sociohistorical watershed was crossed in the Europe of the 1960s. Living standards and life-styles are still substantially affected by occupation and income, but these have lost a great deal of their previous weight in determining behavior. From an historical perspective sheer material inequality has been considerably reduced.

Occupational Mobility

Another important dimension of stratification and differentiation is the degree of social mobility or immobility in a society. As ideal types, one can distinguish between the principle of assignation related to inheritance and the principle of achievement through individual effort; the former generates an immobile society, the latter a mobile one. Although the amount of mobility says little about the real degree of inequality inherent in a system of social differentiation, the potential for conflict can be exacerbated or moderated by the degree of openness or closedness of social groups. In addition, the stability of such groups has a major impact on the character of social relations, the constitution of social identity and solidaristic behavior.

Several factors have influenced the development of social mobility in twentieth-century Europe: (1) socially differentiated demographic behavior—fertility, life expectancy, and so on; (2) the changes in occupational and economic structure brought about through industrialization, technological advances, and bureaucratization—the decline of agriculture, the reduction in the number of the self-employed, expansion of the service sector; (3) the increase in domestic and international migration; (4) the increase in appointment to occupational positions according to formal qualifications related to actual achievement; and (5) the growing degree of social and economic intervention on the part of the state.

Theoretically, these factors must have enhanced social mobility. The historical trend can be demonstrated only very vaguely, however, since until recently systematic studies of the composition and change of social groups according to background and aspirations have been lacking. Not until the early 1970s was reliable and exact information collected, for the most part distinguishing occupational groups on the basis of internationally comparable indices, so that relatively certain observations could be made concerning intergenerational mobility in various countries.

From the point of view of the individual, the most important feature of mobility is the change from one position within a social hierarchy to another; shifts of position are felt mostly as social advancement or decline. The available studies show that the pattern of mobility among European men is marked by the "inheritance of position," although one must bear in mind that the findings are heavily influenced by the number and composition of the social categories used (see fig. 2.10). In Britain, Sweden, West Germany, Hungary, Poland, and Czechoslovakia, on average two thirds of workers' sons remained blue-collar workers themselves. The degree of continuity among sons of unskilled and semiskilled workers, at 70 percent, was more marked than among sons of skilled workers, at 60 percent. At the other end of the social pyramid around 60 percent of the sons of the higher salariat, academics, the self-employed, and entrepreneurs "inherited" the social position of their fathers. Here again, if one disaggregates these groups, a clear difference in the degree of intergenerational succession emerges: among academics and the higher salariat the quota of social inheritance was almost 70 percent, among intermediate civil servants and salaried employees only 55 percent. The succession to the parental position among peasants and owners of small businesses was much more rare, at around 25 percent. In both these latter cases this was the result of the shrinkage of the occupational group itself: mobility was in effect forced. The degree of succession was lowest in the case of sons of low-level white-collar employees and civil servants, at around 15 percent. Although this group was not declining in size, it obviously served as a transitional position from which sons in almost equal part ascended or descended in the social hierarchy.

Social ascent or descent took place mostly by stages over short social distances. Half of the sons of peasants and rural workers transferred to the urban working class, one third to unskilled and semiskilled labor. The most frequent shift of unskilled and semiskilled workers' sons was to the category of skilled laborer. Twenty-one percent of the sons of skilled workers by turn then fell to unskilled or semiskilled status, but a relatively large group succeeded in making the leap into the middle salariat. For 23 percent of the sons of small-business owners mobility meant a decline into skilled manual employment. This was also true of 26 percent of the sons of the lower salariat, although in this group almost exactly the same number ascended to the intermediate salariat.

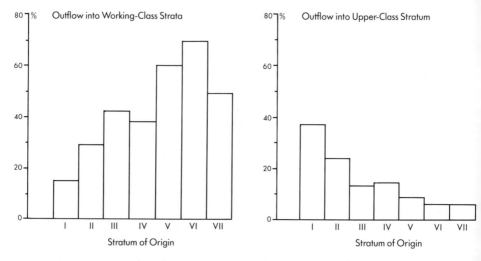

Figure 2.10. Intergenerational Social Mobility in the Early 1970s (in percent). *Sources:* Robert Erikson, John Goldthorpe, and Lucian Portocarero, "Intergenerational Class Mobility in Three Western European Societies," *British Journal of Sociology*, 30 (1979): 432; Karl Ulrich Mayer, "Berufsstruktur und Mobilitätsprozess," in *Soziale Indikatoren im internationalen Vergleich,* ed. Joachim Hoffmann-Nowotny (Frankfurt, 1980), p. 125.

Unweighted averages of the values for four countries: England and Wales, France, Sweden, and the Federal Republic of Germany. Social categories: I = higher-grade professionals, administrators, and officials; managers and proprietors of large industrial establishments; II = lower-grade professionals, administrators, and officials; higher-grade technicians; managers in small business and industrial establishments; supervisors of nonmanual employees; III = routine nonmanual employees in administration and commerce; sales personnel; other rank-and-file service workers; IV = small proprietors; master artisans with and without employees; farmers and smallholders; self-employed fishermen; V = lower-grade technicians; supervisors of manual workers; skilled manual workers; VI = semi- and unskilled manual workers not in agriculture; VII = agricultural workers. Groups V and VI constitute the "working class," group I the "upper class."

Around one quarter of the sons of academics, self-employed, and entrepreneurs, as well as of higher salaried employees and civil servants, shifted into the intermediary strata of white-collar employees, and vice versa.

Another important dimension of mobility is the relative homogeneity of individual strata. Here the question is from which social groups a stratum recruits its members. The degree of self-recruitment is strongly influenced by the expansion or contraction of the stratum concerned. Unsurprisingly, the rapidly increasing group of low-level salaried employees and civil servants recruited only 10 percent of its members from its own social ranks. The expansion in the number of other higher salaried employees likewise weakened the effects of internal succession; self-recruitment in Western Europe accounted for one third, in Eastern Europe less than one fifth. Among blue-collar workers in Western Europe the degree of self-recruitment at 60 percent coincided almost everywhere with the degree of status inheritance. In Eastern Europe, by contrast, the relatively late development of the industrial working class limited the potential for self-recruitment, whose quota amounted to only 50 percent. In both Western and Eastern Europe the degree of self-recruitment was strongest among peasants: around 90 percent of peasants were themselves sons of peasants.

The expansion of the service sector, combined with the stagnating or even declining numbers of industrial workers, rendered that most important of social barriers—between manual and nonmanual labor—more porous, and in both directions. One third of the sons of skilled workers and one quarter of the sons of semiskilled and unskilled workers made the change to nonmanual occupations. More than half of the lower salariat was composed of these social climbers. Even among academics and higher civil servants these groups took up one quarter of the available positions. Although many of the sons of the lower salariat and owners of small businesses descended into the working class—around 30–45 percent—these made up less than one fifth of blue-collar workers. Whether these downward changes in occupational status always entailed a decline in material standards of living is a very complex issue that cannot be considered here.

This pattern of mobility, derived from studies in France, Britain, Sweden, and West Germany, applies to many European countries. There were, of course, national peculiarities arising from the varying developmental stages of occupational structure and from political factors. The initial strength of the agricultural sector and the rapidity of its decline greatly influenced the degree of homogeneity of the industrial working class. Among Western European countries this homogeneity was most marked in Britain, where 80 percent of the working class at the beginning of the 1970s was recruited out of its own ranks, with only 5 percent coming from agriculture. By contrast, just half of the French and Swedish working classes came from workers' families and over a quarter from a rural background. In Eastern Europe the rural upwardly mobile constituted one third of the industrial blue-collar workers in Czechoslovakia and one half in Poland. A second structural feature affecting mobility is the strength of the service sector.

The rapid expansion of this sector in Sweden helped make the transition from manual to nonmanual occupations much more common there than elsewhere in Europe. Nearly two thirds of those in nonmanual occupations in Sweden came from workers' families; in other Western European countries less than half.

The political determinants of mobility relate in particular to the structure of occupational qualifications and the degree of democratization of the educational system. With respect to social mobility they had the greatest effect on the social composition of the highest stratum—self-employed professionals, entrepreneurs, higher-level managers, and civil servants. Formal qualifications, such as the second state examination for lawyers in West Germany or graduation from one of the elite *grandes écoles* in France, had a marked effect in limiting the pool of recruits. At the beginning of the 1970s in both these countries little more than a quarter of the higher strata came from families of manual occupation; in Sweden and Britain by contrast 44 percent did. In this respect Eastern European society constituted the greatest exception. As a result of ideologically determined mechanisms of selection, persons from a manual and rural background occupied two thirds to three quarters of the positions in the upper strata.

In conclusion, one must emphasize that this so-called half-open pattern of mobility still contained much inequality of opportunity. The chance of the son of a blue-collar worker ascending into the middle strata was half that of those who were born into this strata. The relative probability of ascending into the upper strata was even smaller; it was one seventh of that of a son whose father already belonged to an upper occupational group.

Integration and Conflict

Social differences generate a lasting tension between integration and conflict, within society as a whole and within individuals and groups. The very complex nature of the relationships that arise from this cannot be examined here in detail. Taking a lead from the British sociologist T. H. Marshall, the following discussion focuses on one centrally important ideological and institutional element of social integration and conflict, namely, citizenship and its associated rights. Two particularly important aspects of citizenship in the twentieth century will be considered: nationality, and participation in political and economic decision-making.

Nation-States, Nationalities, and National Minorities

The nation has been a central sociopolitical category in European history since the end of the eighteenth century. Whether regarded as a cultural nation united by a single language and popular traditions, or as a nation-state with a common political tradition, the nation has played a crucial role in the integration of state and society. The democratic principle of popular sovereignty elevated the nation to the sole legitimate principle of state formation and subordinated the state to the interests of the nation. From this developed the claim of differing national groups to political self-determination, usually in the form of their own sovereign nation-state, which united territory and people. The notion also arose that a state could have only a single nationality, a "state-people" in whose name the assimilation of other national groups within the state's territory was demanded. The social process of nation-building assumed, therefore, a contradictory stance: on the one hand, emancipatory, democratic, and integrationist; on the other, repressive, authoritarian, and belligerent.

The principle of nationality—that is, the notion that every nation should have its own independent state—only partially prevailed in the state system of nineteenth-century Europe, which was the result of historical dynastic power struggles. Although a united Germany and a united Italy were created, and the independence of Belgium, Greece, Bulgaria, Rumania, and Norway as states was achieved, numerous national groups at the beginning of the twentieth century were still without their own state, or without rights to self-determination. Apart from Italy, all the great European powers before 1914 included more than one national group, and disputes over national interests had prime domestic significance. The political development of Austria-Hungary was especially overshadowed by lasting disagreements on the nationality problem.

The First World War raised hopes and expectations that the nationality principle would at last prevail and thereby secure the free and peaceful development of Europe. The peace treaties enacted between 1919 and 1921, in accordance with the Wilsonian doctrine of "self-determination for all peoples," reorganized the European map into nation-states defined by linguistic criteria. Only the Basques, Catalans, Bretons, and Welsh remained without their own state. The new frontiers were, however, themselves the occasion of much dispute. It was hardly possible to take equal account of the national, economic, and strategic needs of all peoples in the nationally mixed areas of central and eastern Europe. Frontier disputes and conflicts broke out—between the Germans and the Poles, the Poles and the Lithuanians, the Slovaks and the Hungarians, the Hungarians and the Rumanians, the Italians and the Slovenes, and so on—and even democratically conducted plebiscites produced only temporary solutions.

All the newly created states also included several national groups: in Poland and in Rumania the national majority was only two thirds of the total population. In Czechoslovakia and in Yugoslavia, which called itself the Kingdom of Serbs, Croats, and Slovenes until 1929, similar conditions prevailed, with the difference that even the "state-peoples" were nationally mixed. Thus the question of minorities and national integration became one of the most difficult and recalcitrant problems faced by European societies during the interwar years. It was soluble neither by the right of minorities to protection secured in the peace treaties and supervised by the League of Nations, nor through attempts to reach agreement in international congresses of European nationalities. Many governments mistrusted the national minorities and pursued a repressive policy of assimilation. In turn, many of these minorities—especially the Germans in Czechoslovakia and Poland—behaved as if the new states were simply fashionable creations without social and political legitimacy.

Most peoples did not ground their national identity simply on a common language. Social recognition as a full member of the nation frequently presupposed a particular ideological orientation and religious conviction. A good Irishman, Pole, or Spaniard could scarcely be a Protestant; in Britain, Scandinavia, the Netherlands, and Germany, national consciousness and Roman Catholicism were a dubious combination. Jews or persons of Jewish descent, despite having formal equality as citizens, were discriminated against almost universally. The so-called Jewish question dogged the process of nation-building particularly in central and eastern Europe. The national sentiment of socialists and pacifists was also questioned in most countries, and many of them suffered repression or persecution.

The fascist movement, especially German National Socialism, marked the ultimate perversion of the national idea as a principle of social order. It took up the distinction between nations by racial characteristics that had developed towards the end of the nineteenth century, a distinction designed to demonstrate the natural superiority of certain nations, and in this way laid the foundations for a violent policy of nationalistic expansion. All individualism had to bow before a community conceived in racial terms. The Second World War was conducted by the National Socialists as a struggle of the German people for living space, whose necessary corollary was the enslavement, exile, and systematic extermination of the racially "inferior" ethnic groups.

These excesses placed the idea of the nation-state in question. By the end of the 1940s the first supranational institutions had been formed as a result of the pressure of growing East-West tension. The foundation of the EEC in 1956–1957 represented the temporary high point of the movement for Western European unity. Even if it fell short of many hopes, the EEC promoted a large measure of cooperation, equalization, and understanding between member states, in direct contrast to the aggressiveness of interwar nationalism. The relapse into national interest that emerged in the economic crisis of the 1970s did at least seek to preserve the level of integration already achieved and not, as had occurred earlier, to pursue aggressively the individual advantage of one state at the expense of others. In Eastern Europe occasional reference to national peculiarities served to justify the pursuit of policy that deviated from the Soviet model. But only Yugoslavia succeeded in developing its own national version of socialism.

In theory, the problem of minorities was solved during the postwar years in Eastern Europe through a policy of forcible resettlement and eviction. By 1960 only Rumania continued to have a large Hungarian minority, amounting to 15 percent of the country's total population. Allegedly, all communist governments guaranteed their minorities equal rights and cultural autonomy. In Czechoslovakia and Yugoslavia the postwar constitutions recognized two or more official languages. Tensions between ethnic groups persisted in many states, but they were usually disguised as factional disputes within the various communist parties.

Problems with national and linguistic minorities also existed in some Western European countries after 1945, although only in the instances of Northern Ireland and South Tyrol was a second state involved. After many years of difficult negotiation and occasional terrorist outrages, an agreement was signed in 1970 ending the dispute over South Tyrol, which had simmered since 1919. The extremely violent and bloody conflicts in Northern Ireland still show no prospect of settlement in the late 1980s. In other countries minority groups demanded cultural recognition and greater political self-government, without at the same time denying the legitimacy of the existing nation-state—the Catalans and Basques following the dissolution of the Franco regime and the introduction of democracy to Spain; Bretons, Corsicans, and Alsatians in France; the Welsh and the Scots in Britain; and the Slovenes in Austria. All these groups sought greater decentralization on the grounds that an overblown and anonymous central bureaucracy ignored the particular interests of specific sections of the population. Apart from Basque and Corsican extremists, these minorities pursued their goals by peaceful means; none of them sought a real destabilization of their existing societies. The millions of foreign workers and their families who have become resident in the industrial countries of northern and western Europe since the mid-1970s have once more posed the problem of the assimilation and integration of social and national minorities, although this time against a quite different sociocultural and historical background.

Participation in Political and Economic Decision-Making

Political Domain
The principle of popular sovereignty entails the participation of the citizen in the processes of political opinion-formation and decision-making, in particular determining the political composition of the government. The twin pillars of participation in political affairs—parliamentarism and democratic elections—were only incompletely realized in most countries up to the First World War. By then many countries had, of course, introduced universal suffrage for adult men and established parliamentary assemblies. The political responsibilities of these parliaments were, however, often extremely limited, as in Germany, Austria-Hungary, Italy, and Sweden.

The final breakthrough in the parliamentarization and democratization of political systems was achieved in the wake of the First World War, as in the case of the development of nation-states. The war not only discredited the ruling elites, but also undermined the legitimation hitherto enjoyed by the aristocratic-authoritarian system of rule. With the exception of Yugoslavia, the new states of 1918–1919, Germany included, endowed themselves with republican constitutions. All those countries that had not yet introduced universal male suffrage did so; and the right to vote was extended to women in most countries, the exceptions being Belgium, France, Greece, Italy, Switzerland, and Spain. Where parliaments did not exist, they were written into the constitution. Thus the foundation was laid for the democratic participation of a variety of social interests in the process of political decision-making.

As a rule, these interests articulated themselves by means of political parties. In the European pluralistic system, which was first able to develop fully in the years following the First World War, political parties could be distinguished according to the coordinates of four basic dimensions of social conflict: (1) ethnic and linguistic conflicts; (2) confessional conflicts; (3) conflicts between town and country, or between agriculture and industry; and (4) conflicts between worker and employer, or between capital and labor.

Parties that saw themselves exclusively in terms of the interests of particular ethnic groups emerged only in multinational countries such as Spain, Belgium, and the east-central European, Baltic, and Balkan countries. The dispute over the secular state emerged in a number of countries in the form of confessional, usually Catholic, parties, which fought above all to maintain religious education—for example, the Center party in Germany, the Italian People's party, the Christian Social party in Austria, the Belgian and Dutch Catholic parties, or the Dutch Calvinist party. The strength of the peasant parties in northern and eastern Europe, as well as in France, Ireland, Switzerland, and Bavaria, affirmed the persistent conflict between industrial and agrarian interests in those areas and countries. The struggle between labor and capital gave rise to the classical workers' parties, mostly of a Marxist cast. The fields of conflict were naturally not entirely comparable from country to country, so that these parties were not uniformly distributed in each country; in addition, distinguishing sharply between fields of conflict is difficult, and parties were rarely one-dimensional. Thus in Czechoslovakia, for example, Catholic peasants' and workers' parties also split along national lines, with separate organizations for the Czechs, the Slovaks, the Germans, and the Hungarians. The oldest political parties—the liberals and the conservatives—arose out of the conflicts of the eighteenth-century ancien régime and thus cannot be assigned definitively to any one of these four fields.

The party landscape that emerged in the phase of political mobilization following the First World War changed little—with a few important exceptions—until the 1970s. For about half a century European party systems were, in the word of the Norwegian political scientist Stein Rokkan, "frozen." Apart from short-lived fluctuations, often associated with specific crises, even the balance of forces in elections remained surprisingly stable. This was especially apparent in the case of non-communist workers' parties; from the early 1920s to the late 1960s only the Norwegian, Swedish, and British labor parties managed to enlarge significantly their electoral base. The development of conservative and Christian parties was also exceptionally stable; only in Norway and Sweden did the proportion of votes cast for the conservative parties decline in the 1940s. In most countries the consequence of democratization of the electoral system was that liberal parties lost their previous position. A particularly sharp decline occurred in Norway, Sweden, and Britain, where further ground was lost during the 1930s.

The most important exceptions to these continuities were in countries where fascist or communist governments assumed power. In a number of countries after the First World War, the newly established democratic party system was unable to cope with the social, economic, and political crises of the time. These conditions favored the rise of fascist and authoritarian governments. Democracy was abolished in the 1920s in Hungary, Italy, Poland, Portugal, Spain, and Yugoslavia; Germany, Austria, and the remainder of eastern Europe, except Czechoslovakia, followed suit in the 1930s. These anti-democratic governments declared social conflict illegitimate or even non-existent and forced the "integration" of diverse social interest groups into a solidaristic national or folk community. In eastern Europe after the Second World War communist regimes soon replaced the newly reconstituted pluralistic party systems with the monopoly of Communist parties founded upon the principles of Marxism-Leninism. In Bulgaria, East Germany, Czechoslovakia, and Poland a few peasant and bourgeois parties continued to exist, but they were not permitted to exercise a genuine representation of separate interests and had to acknowledge the hegemony of the country's Communist party.

In those states where democracy was re-established—Italy, West Germany, and Austria—the previous parties of the right were in general discredited. Instead, Christian-democratic people's parties were founded to integrate the non-socialist electorate. By contrast, the parties of the left have maintained a strong continuity. An exception to this was the German Communist party (KPD) in West Germany. During the 1950s it was banned; when it was allowed to reconstitute itself in the 1970s, it could not repeat the electoral successes of the Weimar Republic and sank into insignificance. Thus the venerable German Social Democratic party (SPD) undertook by itself to represent the greater part of the country's leftist electorate. In Italy, on the other hand, it was the Communist party that developed into the largest party on the left, clearly overshadowing the social democratic party, which received only half as many votes. In France the question of continuity was even more complex. During the Fourth and Fifth Republics the strongly personalized Gaullist party created a national-conservative coalition that ultimately embraced the bulk of the French right.

Relative continuity in voting behavior and party structure contrasts markedly with the discontinuity in political culture. This was characterized in the interwar years by embittered ideological conflicts, confrontation, and polarization. In simple terms, two political currents confronted one another: conservative forces that ultimately rejected the democratic system and sought to retain or restore an authoritarian form of government and a hierarchical social order, and revolutionary forces that likewise sought to overturn bourgeois democracy and install a socialist society, in part via the dictatorship of the proletariat.

The Russian Revolution, revolutionary uprisings in other countries, and the creation of the Comintern aroused aversion and fear in bourgeois and peasant strata with respect to political movements that quite evidently sought to seize power under the flag of socialism. Such anxieties, in turn, promoted the formation of anti-labor electoral and government coalitions. The workers' parties were themselves divided over whether to follow a revolutionary or reformist path. They had a hard time ridding themselves of the forms of consciousness and behavior built up during decades of anti-capitalist struggle, and also developing the political will for compromise so necessary to the formation of coalitions. The majority of workers' parties, therefore, split irreconcilably into social democratic and communist wings. In France, Finland, Italy, Czechoslovakia, and Germany, in particular, this split not only undermined the solidarity of the workers' movement but also weakened its influence in general. With the exception of Sweden, Denmark, and Norway, where the bourgeois block broke up and the workers' parties were able to steer a clear reformist path, during the interwar period parties associated with the labor movement remained for the most part politically and ideologically isolated. In these circumstances the new party systems of the 1920s contributed to social and political conflict more often than to consensus. Unstable political conditions—short-lived coalitions and minority governments—hindered the solution of the great economic and social problems such as general economic in-stability, inflation, high unemployment, world economic crisis, social inequality, or socioeconomic backwardness.

The irreconcilability of political conflict and the collapse of political culture prior to 1939, together with the experience of general political cooperation in governments in exile and resistance movements during the war, created a new basis for political participation in Western Europe after 1945. The democratic idea was emphatically affirmed by, for instance, the introduction of general female suffrage in France, Italy, and Belgium, as well as by the abolition of the Italian monarchy. A pragmatic tolerance displaced the dogmatic defense of ideological positions in many parties. Non-communist workers' parties no longer stood outside the spectrum of candidates for coalition formation; in-stead, in most countries they participated in governments of the 1940s and 1950s. West Germany was a major exception in this regard. The Second Austrian Republic provides a good example of the new postwar political mood. The two most important political groupings, the Cath-olics and the socialists, who had been locked in internecine struggles in the First Republic, joined forces in a grand coalition government from 1945 to 1966 and again after 1986. A similar fundamental change also occurred in Belgium and in the Netherlands.

Theoretical positions and practical politics were emptied of ideo-logical content in the wake of the Second World War, and a degree of convergence took place. The major parties saw themselves as middle-of-the-road "people's parties." Differences between them were further erased as a consequence of continuing economic growth—the change of occupational structure, increasing prosperity, increased social mo-bility, urbanization, the decline of agriculture, the import of foreign labor, and so on. The differentiation of parties by distinct and ho-mogeneous socioeconomic and sociocultural constituencies was grad-ually dissolved. The general reduction of the voting age to eighteen increased the demographic weight of voters who were politically so-cialized after 1945 and therefore insulated from the extreme party and political categories of the interwar years.

By the end of the 1960s the "frozen" party systems began to thaw. Identification with a particular party became weaker, and the fluctua-tion of voters increased. Thus, in 1971 the Austrian social democrats achieved for the first time in Austrian history an absolute majority of votes; on the other hand, the Norwegian, Danish, and Swedish social democrats had to take great losses and, for the first time in decades, relinquish the reins of government. The Dutch Catholic party, which since 1918 had united virtually all Catholic voters in the country and maintained an electoral share of 30 percent, lost practically half of its votes between 1963 and 1972; in 1976 it joined with the two Dutch Protestant parties and in 1980 it was dissolved.

Parallel to this change in traditional voting behavior, new conflicts arose, deriving from the structural social and political deficiencies of modern industrial capitalism. From the early 1970s protest movements developed in many countries that criticized the materialism of the bureaucratized affluent society and questioned the monopoly of interest articulation and decision-making by the established parties, big business, and state institutions. The new parties that emerged from this movement, based for the most part on a constituency drawn from the highly educated middle strata, pursued non-material goals such as a better quality of life and environment, and greater political participation for the individual citizen through the decentralization of political opinion-formation and decision-making. Until the 1980s these environmental and protest parties achieved successes mostly in regional and local elections; but since then they have won seats in the national parliaments of Denmark, Belgium, West Germany, and Austria.

From the very first, the postwar constitutions of eastern European countries endowed all citizens over the age of eighteen with full rights of political participation. Elections with a high turnout regularly took place, but with few exceptions (in East Germany, Poland, and Hungary) only members of the Communist party were permitted to stand as candidates, and furthermore there was only one candidate for each position, so that these elections cannot be considered democratic in the normal fashion. Under such conditions political participation became for the electors merely a ritual that confirmed the given relations of power and government.

Economic Domain
Participation in the economic sphere, as in the political sphere, depends on the extension of political and social rights. In addition, however, such participation is also heavily influenced by economic factors: the state of the labor market, the level of technology, the particular economic sector, the state of the economy, the size of enterprises, the concentration of ownership, and, not least, the degree of organization among the workers. Participation in economic decision-making is demanded and advanced above all by trade unions.

By the beginning of the twentieth century trade unions had already achieved formidable organizational power. As a rule, these trade unions were defined in terms of a particular social or political tendency, and were closely identified with a political party. Their legal status was ambiguous in most countries, which contributed to their insecure position. Provisions such as the Danish agreement of 1899 between the employers' associations and the trade unions' association, or the British laws of 1906 and 1913 governing liability in the event of strikes or political agitation, remained the exception. In spite of this the readiness to strike in support of political and economic demands remained. A general strike by Belgian unions forced the extension of the right to vote. In 1909 the Swedish Trade Union Congress organized a one-month general strike in support of a rise in wages (without success). In the final years before the outbreak of the First World War labor struggles greatly increased.

During the war trade unions and the state struck a deal in most countries: the unions supported the war effort in return for the state's undertaking to improve their legal and economic status. A genuine law of association replaced a purely formal right of association. The right of a union to negotiate wage agreements and working conditions on behalf of its members was recognized. The actionable nature of such collective contracts was given legal foundation in most countries, with the exception of Britain. Works councils, bodies of elected workers' representatives whose task was both to represent the interests of the workers in the running of the enterprise and to monitor the implementation of the collective agreement, were introduced in Germany, Austria, and Czechoslovakia. The Austrian parliament also instituted a public-law Chamber of Workers and Salaried Employees, which could pronounce on questions relating to the economy and the working world in general and thus promote workers' interests beyond the workplace. The International Labor Office, founded in 1919 and associated with the League of Nations, confirmed that trade unions were the legitimate representatives of employees.

The revolutionary climate of the immediate postwar years was another factor in the steep rise in trade union membership; in some countries unions achieved in these few years the highest levels of membership of the century. A wave of strikes rolled through Europe, variously demanding the nationalization of heavy industry, railways, banks, and mines, higher wages, and better working conditions. The employers, pointing to falling profits and the difficult economic climate, often reacted by raising norms of output, reducing wages, laying off workers, and even in some cases—as in Italy—with violent and intimidatory measures.

The political climate altered as early as 1920. The momentum built up by the unions was suddenly halted, and they experienced a series of heavy reverses. The consequences were far-reaching; membership fell sharply in nearly all countries, sometimes even by as much as half. The position of unions was further weakened by internal disputes as well as by the high level of unemployment. The greatest struggle of the 1920s—the British general strike of 1926—was a failure and led to frustration and disappointment among British workers. In Germany, the autonomy of the different agencies in the labor market was increasingly limited; the process of compulsory arbitration first introduced during the inflationary crisis of 1923 was applied ever more frequently. The majority of French, Belgian, and Dutch employers refused to negotiate collective agreements with the unions. In the eastern European countries (excluding Czechoslovakia) unions had to fight against state repression; this was also true of Spain. From the mid-1920s Mussolini's Italy and Cormona-Salazar's Portugal proclaimed a general ban on trade unions.

During the 1930s the extremely high level of unemployment crippled the power of the unions to resist wage reductions and the deterioration of working conditions. The seizure of power by the National Socialists in Germany in 1933, and the formation of an authoritarian regime in Austria in 1934, resulted in the destruction and proscription of the hitherto strongest union movements in Europe. A similar fate befell the Spanish unions with the victory of Franco. In all three countries corporatist workers' associations with compulsory membership were introduced, just as earlier in Italy and Portugal.

On the other hand, in France in 1936 the reunited communist and non-communist unions succeeded, through a wave of strikes, factory occupations, and the intervention of the newly elected Socialist prime minister Léon Blum, in establishing for the first time the principle of collective agreements with employers' association (the Matignon Accord). Among other things this agreement envisaged the creation of elected workers' representatives *(délégués du personnel)* charged with the supervision of wages and working conditions. At the end of 1936 compulsory arbitration was introduced in France as well. These successes, which immediately led to an expansion of union membership, did not last long. In 1938 Blum's coalition government collapsed. A general strike against the succeeding government of Daladier failed. The policy of national renewal introduced by the 1940 Vichy government led to the dissolution of all unions.

At the beginning of the 1930s labor disputes also flared up in Norway and Sweden. The electoral successes that followed enabled workers' parties in both countries to form governments. The continuing world economic crisis and the new domestic situation led to a moderation of the confrontational policies hitherto pursued in both countries by the employers' associations and the unions. In 1935 and 1939, respectively, the two groups in each country arrived at basic agreements on social partnership that have provided the basis for collective negotiations since that time.

After the end of the war a new era opened in the prospects for participatory influence in the economic domain. New unions were founded everywhere, except in Spain and Portugal, where they remained forbidden until the mid-1970s, and in Britain, Sweden, and Switzerland, where they had never been outlawed. In Austria and West Germany new unions were organized around particular industries and economic subsectors, rather than around political and social tendencies, as had been the case in the prewar years. Attempts at coalition failed in France, Italy, Belgium, and the Netherlands; in these four countries trade unions re-emerged along political and confessional lines. The mood of optimism of the postwar years brought the unions new members and strengthened their confidence. Major strikes occurred in virtually all Western European countries, as unions sought to realize their social and economic aspirations in the process of reconstruction, to protest against the shortages and injustices deriving from the economic conditions of postwar Europe, and to achieve higher wages and other associated improvements.

By contrast with the class struggles of the interwar years, however, labor relations after 1945 were increasingly characterized by the concept of social partnership and the cooperative regulation of conflict, although this was not true of all countries to the same extent. Various factors contributed to this development: at the political-ideological level, the final integration of workers' parties into the political establishment and the adoption of the idea of the social state by all political parties led to a stronger recognition of the right of social participation; at the business managerial level, increasing concentration of businesses depersonalized labor relations and required longer-term planning for production. Taken together, these factors promoted the institutionalization of measures for the regulation of employer-worker conflict and hence a rational and cooperative attitude. Continuing prosperity over almost three decades also equalized the bargaining power of employer and employee. The tight labor market strengthened the position of the unions; rising productivity and favorable economic conditions meant that employers were better able to meet increasing wage costs without curtailing profits. Finally, changes in occupational structure also played a role. The growing numbers of white-collar salaried employees and public officials increased the influence within the labor force of occupational groups that were only weakly unionized and lacked a tradition of class struggle.

The levels of strike activity represented in figure 2.11 embody this break in continuity. One must keep in mind, however, that the data are not controlled for the size of the work force in each country. Because the curves register the absolute number of workdays lost in strike action, they reflect the temporal trend within each country, but they do not allow straightforward comparisons between countries. In order to accommodate the wide numerical range, the vertical axis is logarithmic, which further renders comparison difficult. The two broad groupings that emerge are, in fact, quite widely separated; the average loss of work through strikes in the countries of the lower group amounts to only 5–10 percent of the average loss incurred by those in the higher group.

The level of strike activity generally corresponds to the existing condition and quality of worker participation in each country. In Belgium, the Netherlands, Austria, West Germany, Switzerland, and the Scandinavian countries a relatively comprehensive network of employee representation was created in the immediate postwar years, partly by legislation and partly through agreements reached between unions and employers' associations; this system of representation contributed to the weakening of more traditional means for the furtherance of specific demands. In this process works councils were formed and charged with the supervision of workers' interests within the individual business concern. The Belgian and Scandinavian unions also managed to establish separate union representation within each enterprise. The West German laws on worker codetermination, promulgated in the early 1950s, which provided for the election of employees' delegates to the supervisory directorates of large companies in specific industries, remained virtually unique into the 1970s. Elsewhere similar provisions can be found only occasionally and only with respect to state enterprises.

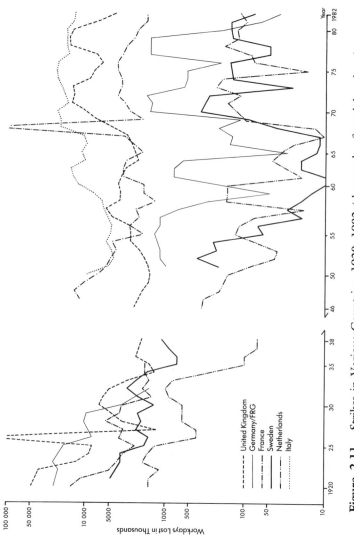

Figure 2.11. Strikes in Various Countries, 1920–1982 (thousands of workdays lost in a three-year moving average). *Sources:* Brian R. Mitchell, *European Historical Statistics 1750–1970* (London, 1975), pp. 173–83; ILO, *Yearbook of Labour Statistics 1979* (Geneva, 1979), pp. 596–98; *1984* (Geneva, 1984), pp. 828–30.

Germany/BRD: Strikes were forbidden during the National Socialist regime. Italy: Strikes were forbidden during the Fascist regime. United Kingdom: General strike in 1926. France: General strike in 1926 and 1968.

Nonetheless, the participatory rights of employees were strengthened generally through the formation of corporatist social and economic advisory councils. The two best-known instances—the Austrian Joint Commission on Wages and Prices, and the Swedish National Council for the Labor Market—developed into general mechanisms for social and economic management. The degree of union organization was very high in these countries. Apart from West Germany, the Netherlands, and Switzerland, by 1950 more than half of wage earners and salaried employees were members of unions; and this figure rose to two thirds by 1980, and in Sweden as high as 90 percent. By contrast, in West Germany, the Netherlands, and Switzerland the level of membership remained around one third of the dependent work force.

The situation was quite different in Italy and France. After a brief initial period of unity, the union movement split. Competition between unions placed a premium on the preparedness to strike as a mark of strength. Since the largest union organizations in these countries were led by communists, the struggle for worker participation involved a supersessionary element absent elsewhere. This, in turn, strengthened the traditionally extreme anti-unionism among paternalistic employers. Collective agreements were the outcome of confrontation rather than peaceful negotiation. Although since the late 1940s legislation provided for the representation of workers, this requirement was often ignored. The May 1968 events in France and the "hot autumn" of 1969 in Italy resulted in a definite extension of employees' rights. An institutional framework for collective negotiations was created; union representation within enterprises was finally achieved; and in Italy elected works councils were established. Despite these achievements strike activity remained at a relatively high level compared with that of other countries. Since working-class interests were still inadequately represented in society in general, workers and trade unions continued to use strikes as a means to assert broad social and economic demands. Under these circumstances labor relations based upon the idea of social partnership could scarcely develop. Even the Socialist party's electoral victories in France in 1981 contributed little to the amelioration of the prevailing conflictual atmosphere.

In Britain another variant of worker participation exists, one that involves conflict more than social partnership. The high frequency of strikes in Britain is usually attributed to the occupational fragmentation of the labor movement and the extreme decentralization of trade union organization. Without a doubt both characteristics hinder the formulation of common demands and their realization in negotiation. In addition, declining industrial sectors, such as textiles, mining, heavy industry, and shipbuilding, played a greater role in the British economy than elsewhere; as a consequence the social tensions arising from restructuring were correspondingly higher.

In the later 1960s and early 1970s, not only France and Italy but practically the whole of Western Europe experienced a wave of strikes. This activity not only provoked discussion concerning the reform of existing participatory structures but produced actual changes. For instance, in West Germany the right of the works council to participate in managerial decision-making was substantially extended. The 1976 Law on Codetermination decreed that one third of the seats on corporate supervisory boards be reserved for employees' representatives. Similar proposals in Belgium, Finland, France, and Britain failed to find the support necessary to translate them into law.

In the state socialist systems of Eastern Europe a comprehensive participation in economic decision-making was deemed automatically achieved through the leading role of the party of the working class— the Communist party—and by the socialization of the means of production. Unions continued to exist, but they had an entirely different position and function than those in the capitalist market economies of the West. They were bound by party directives and were supposed chiefly to support production initiatives such as socialistic competition. All those in employment were enrolled automatically as members, and strikes were forbidden. Close party control of trade unions was not relaxed anywhere in Eastern Europe until the end of the 1960s, when Hungary adopted an economic reform program, the New Economic Mechanism, that permitted unions to express their members' interests openly and critically to management.

In the remaining Eastern European states trade unions continued to have no real participatory role. As far as can be judged from the information available, their activities were rejected by workers virtually unanimously. At the beginning of the 1980s Polish workers established their own trade union, Solidarity, independent of the Polish Communist party. Its initial overwhelming popularity precipitated a crisis in the Polish political system that culminated in late 1981 in the prohibition of the new union and the imposition of martial law throughout the entire country for several years. In spite of the prohibition, Solidarity has continued to function more or less openly as a voice of popular opposition to governmental measures.

The course of economic participation took a different tack under Yugoslavian communism. As early as 1951 the Yugoslavian Communist party developed a model of workers' self-management. Works councils elected by employees selected the workplace managers and were supposed to take part in all important decisions relating to its business guidance. These organs of self-management, however, remained without real influence until the final abandonment of central economic planning in the mid-1960s. In 1971 the councils were reformed; the various occupational groups within an enterprise were organized as autonomous entities, which by mutual negotiation defined the policy to be executed by the elected managers.

In sum, during the course of the twentieth century relatively far-reaching provisions for participation in political and economic decision-making were institutionalized in all European societies. Theoretically, at least, this should have strengthened the legitimacy of the decisions arrived at in these processes, increasing the degree of social integration and control, if not altogether ameliorating social conflict. If the twentieth century is viewed as a whole, this is no doubt the case. The loss of revolutionary potential on the part of the labor movement is just one example of this tendency. Yet broadening the social basis of legitimation for the political system also promoted the growth of the state's influence in economy and society. Institutionalized participation in decision-making also entailed political and economic obligations. Since decision-making was profoundly influenced by big, organized interest groups, however, neo-corporatist tendencies emerged that worked counter to the ideal of pluralistic democracy; the representation of diverse interests was thereby restricted and public political responsibility for decisions arrived at limited. Even the state's room for maneuvre was reduced—and not merely in the social and economic domain. Many interest groups used the influence they derived from a firmly anchored position in the given socioeconomic structures to extract special advantages for themselves. Not infrequently this led to economic inefficiencies and socially unjust policies.

Socialization

Human social behavior is substantially oriented to social and cultural norms and values. Their communication, and their impact upon social roles and relationships arising from them, is known as socialization. The process of socialization takes place as a constant interplay between the individual and the social environment, and includes all spheres and stages of life. Generally a distinction is made between formal and informal agencies of socialization, which are differentiated by the degree of conscious direction of values and association with the process of political decision-making. Formal agencies are schools, political parties, the military, and other sociopolitical organizations such as trade unions. The family, peer groups, and the world of work are considered informal agencies. Churches and the mass media come somewhere in between, depending on the time and the place. The following section restricts itself to those four transmitters of roles and values deemed most important in modern European societies. Family and church are long-established social institutions; by contrast the school and the mass media assumed central importance only in the nineteenth century. These two spheres will here be treated in ideal-typical fashion as contrasting institutions and fields of orientation, although this contrast cannot be maintained so clearly in practice.

Family and Church

Family

Without any doubt, the family is the most important agent of socialization in European societies. It is the basic unit of biological and social reproduction. Through it, generations are bound together economically and emotionally. The transmission of property and status in society is effected primarily through the family. It therefore assumes a key position in the process of social development. Because of the family's centrality, discussion of its nature and role in society is never-ending and often contentious.

In theory at least, the family in traditional society fulfilled several important social functions: biological reproduction, welfare, education and socialization, and economic production. Economic, political, cultural, and demographic changes since the eighteenth century both conditioned and enabled a fundamental shift in the social role of the family. Usually this shift is seen in terms of the loss of family functions. The process of industrialization gradually displaced the family enterprise and led to the separation of places of work and habitation. The growing supply of finished goods and services, together with increasing real wages, rendered the domestic production of food and clothing superfluous. The state assumed a central role in the socialization and education of children and young persons. Changes in sexual and reproductive behavior and the employment of married women outside the home accompanied this general loss of function.

Instead of treating this change as indicative of the decline of the family, as conservative criticism of modern society has tended to do, one should view it as a process of emancipation. The shedding of functions enabled the traditional patriarchal family to reconstitute itself on a more individualistic basis, or one of partnership. The propagation of this pattern was obstructed in most countries until well after the First World War by the legal privileges of the husband. The widespread introduction of female suffrage shortly after the First World War did not at first have any great impact on patriarchal family law. Nonetheless, in the course of the 1920s Norwegian and Swedish wives won equal footing with their husbands in respect to the administration of property and income, child-rearing, the location of domicile, the right to divorce, and other familial matters. During the 1930s Britain abolished the remaining legal inequalities between spouses. However, after 1945 a restorationist family policy, aimed at the "reconstruction of the family" in the wake of difficult wartime conditions, predominated in most countries. Despite constitutional affirmations of the equality of the sexes, it was only in the 1960s and 1970s that substantial revisions were undertaken in family law in several countries (including some in Eastern Europe). Even though they did not completely realize the model of the "partnership family," these new measures did point in that direction: every family member—adults and children alike—was accorded, as least in law, greater independence and individual responsibility. Such provisions corresponded with the general social process of democratization of these years.

Moreover, the shedding of previous functions does not necessarily mean lack of function. The family context is still today decisive in the pattern of social mobility. Many studies in different countries also show that family life influences education and achievement on the part of children and young persons. In addition, the reduction in family size and the dissolution of rigid structures of parental authority enhanced the level of domestic intimacy, and thus the family gained in meaning as a focus of emotional support and context for personal development. This process did not, however, lead to a general social isolation of the nuclear family, as had at one time been feared by those who took up Talcott Parsons's sociological theses. Studies carried out during the 1960s and 1970s in many countries showed that contact between relatives was extremely intensive. In the majority of cases, adults saw, telephoned, or wrote their parents weekly; similar contact occurred between siblings at least monthly.

Church

The realization of the post-patriarchal family required not only the alteration of particular laws, but also a change of sentiment. Particularly important in this respect was the changed place of the church in European societies, for Christian social thinking espoused the dogma of marriage as an indissoluble sacrament whose chief purpose was the raising of children and emphasized the authority of the man and of the father. Although many intellectuals since the Enlightenment had criticized or even rejected the church, this institution still had a leading social, cultural, and political role in all countries at the beginning of the twentieth century. With important exceptions such as France, Italy, and Portugal (after 1910), where the church was alienated from the state by anticlerical governmental policy, it provided moral legitimation to state authority and the ruling social structure. In several countries, a specific religious confession was associated with national consciousness.

Political and socioeconomic changes and the associated questioning of traditional norms and values both during and after the First World War had repercussions for the role of the church in European society. The democratic-republican revolutions in Germany and in the successor states of the Austro-Hungarian monarchy fractured the old connection between throne and altar. The process of democratization increasingly projected the social and economic problems and demands of the mass electorate into the foreground. The church's special status was attacked as an unjust privilege and its values derided as irrelevant and reactionary. Working-class parties particularly adopted a decidedly anticlerical, even atheistic, posture, assailing the church as a bourgeois instrument for the suppression of workers' interests. In the face of such attacks, spokesmen for the church were for the most part helpless and uncomprehending and as a result rejected social progress. Outside Britain and Scandinavia, they regarded the democratic system with great scepticism, if not outright hostility. Almost all of them—especially the Catholic authorities—were closely associated with traditional structures of thought and power, rejected materialism and class struggle, insisted on the importance of church and religion in education, and treated contraception and divorce as sins.

The shift in the social significance of the church in Europe was neither uniform nor simultaneous. Adherents were lost first among the urban population, the lower strata, men, and young people. Among the rural population, the higher strata, women, and the elderly, by contrast, the church continued to find support. In general, three different national paths of secularization can be distinguished: (1) countries in which the Protestant church dominated—Britain and Scandinavia; (2) countries with a Protestant majority and a significant Catholic minority—Germany/FRG, the Netherlands, Switzerland, Northern Ireland; and (3) countries in which the Roman Catholic church dominated—France, Italy, Spain, Belgium, Austria, Portugal, and the Irish Republic. Eastern European countries after 1945 followed yet another path, in part because they contained other religious confessions than Roman Catholicism and Protestantism, in part because their Communist governments officially espoused atheism.

In the first group the Protestant church did not seek to dominate state and society. Secularization took an individualistic path, affecting personal attitude to religious belief; church institutions were not, as a rule, a subject of open public conflicts. In the second group Catholic and Protestant churches were relatively closed and had associated subcultures and social networks. In addition, a nondenominational group developed in the later nineteenth century; in Germany it was primarily made up of social democrats. This situation produced constant dispute on confessional issues, but also a sociopolitical stalemate that effectively stabilized the existing conflict. In the third group an organizational unity existed between the Catholic church and society. Every sally against the institutional position of the church, against the religious value system or the existing social order, provoked massive reaction. The struggle between clericals and anticlericals periodically dominated the history of the French Third Republic. In Spain, Portugal, and Austria this polarization led during the 1930s to uprisings or civil war and the establishment of authoritarian clerical or fascist regimes.

The horror of war, the material and social poverty of the immediate postwar years, as well as the question of guilt or responsibility for mass crimes renewed interest in religion and the church. The works of such theologians as Karl Barth and Pierre Teilhard de Chardin were widely read throughout the 1950s. Churches attempted to become more responsive to the wishes of their congregations, thus showing that they had learned some lessons from the prewar experience. The role of lay organizations in church administration was strengthened. Pastoral activity and doctrine were adapted to contemporary needs; in France hundreds of priests, the so-called worker-priests, labored in factories in an attempt to win workers back to the church. Ecumenical conversations were taken up energetically; Christians and Marxists even undertook dialogues with one another. The most prominent and decisive point in the modernization of the Catholic church was the Second Vatican Council (1962–1965) summoned by Pope John XXIII.

But these signs of renewal were not enough to counteract a secularization driven along ever faster by urbanization and growing affluence. Virtually everywhere church attendance fell dramatically. The trend in West Germany reflected the general picture faithfully: in 1953, 60 percent of Catholics and 18 percent of Protestants regularly attended church services; by 1980 the figures had fallen to 37 percent and 5 percent respectively. Even in Spain and Italy only one third of Catholics attended mass on a regular basis by 1980. Recruitment into the ranks of the clergy was no longer assured after the 1960s. The number of newly ordained Catholic priests fell in France from 1,028 in 1951 to 501 in 1968 and further to 99 in 1977; in the Netherlands it fell from 345 in 1955 to a mere 32 in 1975.

Withdrawal from the church also became more frequent. In the Netherlands—admittedly an extreme example—the proportion of the population without formal confession doubled over the period 1949–1977, from 16 percent to 35 percent. At the same time, decrees and prohibitions issuing from the church increasingly lost influence in political and personal life. This was most evident in the case of birth control among the European Catholic population; although the Curia repeatedly and emphatically prohibited it, the practice spread rapidly, as testified by the falling birth rates throughout Europe. Despite heavy intervention on the part of bishops and even the pope, the Catholic church suffered heavy defeats in the Italian plebiscites on divorce and abortion in 1974 and 1981. Such failures were telling indicators of the diminishing power of the Catholic church even in its historically most faithful countries.

This trend did not mean, of course, that the church, or even religion, had completely lost its social significance. The majority of Europeans— even in Eastern Europe—retained an allegiance to church ritual, especially that of baptism. In matters of welfare and the care of the sick the church still today plays an important role. Confessional education continues to be the rule in a few countries. The uproar during 1983–1984 in France over a planned alteration of status of Catholic schools indicates that confessional issues still retain explosive force. The cases of Poland and Ireland are quite varying instances of the power that the church continues to have in state and society. For both countries religion is, because of historical circumstances, a central component of national identity. In Poland the church also plays a role as spiritual opponent of the ruling state of ideology, to an extent greater than in any other communist state.

School and Public Domain

Schools

From its inception the Protestant church has furthered the role of the school both as a medium for the transmission of elementary knowledge and as an institution for the socialization of a wide stratum of the population; in this guise, however, schooling served mainly religious ends. During the eighteenth century the absolutist state transformed these pedagogical goals into popular schooling of a general and emphatically secular nature. Supervision of the school system was to be the prerogative of the state, not the church, and the curriculum was to be organized according to political interests, such as loyalty of subject to ruler, as well as economic demands such as reading and writing, and the cultivation of such "moral" values as industriousness and a striving for competency. The educational ideas of the Enlightenment and of liberalism lent new impulse to these general goals; schooling was to contribute towards the comprehensive development of the personality and to be a substantial component of the social process of emancipation. The diffusion of democratic principles such as popular sovereignty, the nation-state, and participation in state activity enhanced the significance of the school as an instrument of nation-building, social integration, and political education. Democratic citizenship presupposed at least general elementary education. The growing demands of technological advance in the workplace also contributed to the extension of schooling.

Compulsory schooling, usually from the age of six to the age of twelve or fourteen, was introduced during the nineteenth century in almost all European countries. The installation of state authority within the educational system placed the traditional role of the church in question; in many countries the ensuing conflicts between church and state were settled only after long and bitter struggle. In Prussia, Denmark, Sweden, and Norway—countries with an established Protestant church—compulsory schooling was introduced before the mid-nineteenth century. During the 1860s and 1870s similar legislation was promulgated in Spain, Rumania, Hungary, Austria, Scotland, Switzerland, Italy, and England/Wales, although in some of these countries the practical realization of such measures followed much later. The French Third Republic initiated compulsory schooling in 1882 and created a system of secular state-run elementary schools; but despite this more than one quarter of all pupils continued to attend private Catholic schools. During the 1890s Ireland and Finland also adopted compulsory schooling. Belgium and the Netherlands followed a different course. Here the constitutional guarantee of freedom of education led to separate confessional school systems: a secular and public system, a "free" Catholic system, and, in the Netherlands, also a Calvinist system. Lengthy disputes over finance and equality developed in both countries, and these were not settled until 1914 and 1920 respectively. Because of these disputes, compulsory schooling came relatively late: in 1900 in the Netherlands and in 1914 in Belgium.

The extension of schooling meant that increasingly more people completed an elementary education. By 1910 between 66 percent and 75 percent of children aged 5–14 in northern and western Europe attended elementary school. Adult illiteracy sank below 10 percent; in Germany and the Scandinavian countries it was virtually nonexistent. The picture in southern and eastern Europe, however, was quite different. In Portugal, Spain, Greece, Rumania, and Bulgaria before the First World War almost two thirds of the population could neither read nor write. In the Habsburg Empire the situation was more or less the same, except among the Czechs, Germans, and Hungarians, whose adult populations were largely literate. As with virtually all socioeconomic phenomena in Italy, the ability to read and write was very unevenly distributed among the regions. By 1911 in the provinces of Piedmont, Liguria, and Lombardy only 13 percent of those over the age of six could neither read nor write, but the figure for Apulia was 59 percent and for Calabria as high as 70 percent.

Although compulsory schooling was in principle democratic and egalitarian, in practice this was true only of elementary education at first. After a few years' attendance this single stream divided in all countries. The vast majority of children continued in practical and vocational courses of instruction, leaving school for working life at the age of twelve or fourteen. A much smaller proportion went on to secondary schools, in which they followed a more demanding curriculum emphasizing classical languages. Although such schools were for the most part administered by the state, they were not tuition-free. The pupil in this type of school left at the age of eighteen or nineteen without any specific vocational training. The diplomas gained at this level were nonetheless required for many posts in state administration and the church, as well as for entry into university.

This restrictive and hierarchical structure in state schooling reinforced existing socioeconomic inequalities and deepened the division between social strata. The small proportion of secondary pupils in the 10–19 age-group testified to the exclusivity of secondary education: in 1910 it was more than 3 percent only in Denmark, Sweden, Norway, and Germany. The proportion of university students in the 20–24 age-group was even smaller: in 1910 it was nowhere over 2 percent, and was in most cases around 1 percent. The social background of such pupils and students was correspondingly narrow; children from working-class families were little in evidence. Moreover, recruitment discriminated heavily between the sexes. The share of girls in secondary schools in 1910 was over 40 percent only in Britain and Finland; in Denmark, Norway, Ireland, and Germany it was around 33 percent, and in Belgium, Austria, Italy, and Sweden it was under 10 percent. Women made up less than 10 percent of university students in all countries.

The wave of democratization in political life after 1918 also affected educational opportunity. Many reform groups, particularly workers' parties, demanded the reconstruction of schooling on the basis of equality of opportunity. Implementation of such a principle of equality entailed abolishing the dualistic system: the secondary level would have to be unified and linked institutionally to the primary level. These far-reaching plans soon provoked bitter disputes in nearly all countries, with party-political, ideological, and financial dimensions. By contrast with the contemporary problem of unemployment, however, such educational issues could be postponed relatively easily. In Britain reforming legislation was introduced in 1918, 1926, and 1936, but financial shortages meant that the individual reforms were not fully implemented. The opponents of a restructuring of the school system in France and Germany argued, among other things, that the classical secondary school was a central cultural vehicle whose disappearance would severely weaken the national culture. In the Netherlands and Belgium similar reform proposals stood no chance of realization because of the fragile equilibrium between state and church school systems. By contrast, Norway, Sweden, and Denmark had done away with the dualistic school system even before 1918. During the interwar years the social democratic governments in these three countries reinforced this process of integration; following elementary school came a general middle school for all pupils, and only then a higher secondary school similar to the German *Gymnasium* or the French *lycée*.

In spite of this stagnation in the development of education policy, the proportion of secondary school students doubled in several countries between 1920 and 1940 (see fig. 2.12). Still, the numbers remained very small and on the eve of the Second World War represented more than 8 percent of all 10-to-19-year-olds only in Denmark, the Netherlands, and Britain. On the other hand, more girls attended secondary schools than before; by the mid-1930s girls constituted one third of all secondary school pupils in all western and northern European countries, with the exception of Belgium and Switzerland. Similarly, the number of female university students rose, although it varied greatly from country to country. By the end of the 1930s only in France and Finland did women make up a third of university students. In Britain, Ireland, Austria, and Sweden they made up one quarter, and elsewhere the proportion was less than 15 percent. The low level prevailing in Germany in the 1930s was largely a result of the general discrimination against women practised by the National Socialist regime.

After the Second World War the development of the welfare state contributed to the expansion and democratization of education. Education was to be as much a civil right as social security. All citizens were to be able to fully develop their educational potential. Structural change in the labor market—the increasing technological level of industrial occupations, the decline of agriculture and of self-employment, the constant increase in administrative personnel and in the service sector—stimulated the need for more and better schooling. This demand pertained above all to secondary and university training. Most countries, especially after 1960, undertook steps to meet these enlarged educational needs. Several raised the legal school-leaving age to sixteen. Everywhere, new schools, in particular vocational schools, were built. In almost every country new universities were founded, sometimes through the transformation of existing teachers' colleges. School and college fees were either abolished or reduced through generous state support.

Once again, the question of the democratization of the entire educational system was brought up. After the war the Scandinavian coun-

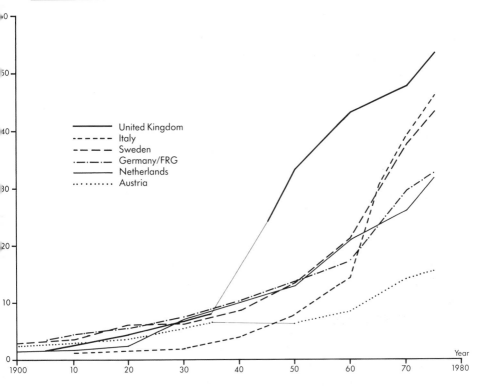

Figure 2.12. Secondary School Attendance in Various Countries, 1900–1975 (number of pupils as percentage of the 10–19 age-group). *Source:* Reinhart Schneider, "Das Bildungswesen in den westeuropäischen Staaten 1870–1975," *Zeitschrift für Soziologie,* 11 (1982): 223.

tries continued their integrationist and egalitarian school policies. In 1962 Sweden combined its separate elementary and middle schools into comprehensive institutions in which all pupils, regardless of social origin or vocational orientation, spent nine years of compulsory schooling. This model was imitated within a few years by Finland, Norway, and Denmark. Other countries in Western Europe did not go so far. In Britain the Educational Act of 1944 at first simply renamed all pupils over the age of eleven as "pupils in secondary education"; a genuine comprehensive school was developed after 1965, but the decentralization of school administration militated against the imposition of a single type of school. The attempt in West Germany to fundamentally reconstruct secondary education into unified comprehensive schools likewise broke down because of the federal structure of education administration; by 1980 such schools had become an officially recognized type only in Bremen, West Berlin, Hamburg, and the state of Hesse. In the early 1960s France and Italy established four-year middle schools, diminishing in this way the obstacles in the transition to college and university.

The communist governments of Eastern Europe had a far clearer view of schooling as an instrument of social and economic mobilization. The first objective after 1945 was the final eradication of illiteracy, especially among the rural population (except in East Germany and Czechoslovakia, where it was unnecessary). Second, the link between educational system and labor market was strengthened by the retreat from the ideal of general education. Only East Germany and Bulgaria completely replaced the traditional structure with a new type of school characterized by a polytechnic curriculum. Still, by the mid-1970s, more than half of Polish, Czech, and Hungarian secondary pupils also attended technically oriented institutions. Successful completion of those studies entitled them to enter university.

The result of such policies was a remarkable educational explosion throughout Europe. The number of school pupils rose sharply from 1950 to 1975; in many lands the number trebled, in some it even quadrupled (see fig. 2.12). Almost everywhere, between a third and a half of the 10–19 age-group attended a secondary school in 1975; the figure was significantly lower, below 15 percent, only for Austria and Switzerland. The number of university students rose even more steeply. In 1950 less than 4 percent of the 20–24 age-group in Western Europe was registered at an institution of higher education; in 1960 the figure was 7 percent, by 1970 over 14 percent, and in 1978 as high as 24 percent. Only in Switzerland, Portugal, and Greece was the figure in 1978 still below 20 percent. Sweden registered the highest proportion: 36 percent. The number of students also increased greatly in Eastern Europe during these years, although the policy of state management of college entry and recruitment to the labor market moderated the overall rise. In 1978 the proportion of 20 to-24-year-olds studying at university varied between 10 percent (for East Germany) and 18 percent (for Bulgaria and Poland).

Education opportunities for women increased especially—a sign of changing perceptions of women's social role that were also expressed in the increase in paid employment of women outside the home. The average proportion of female students in all colleges and universities doubled in Western Europe from 22 percent in 1950 to 39 percent in 1975. Even in those countries with the lowest female participation rates—the Netherlands, West Germany, and Switzerland—women made up over 30 percent of all students by 1975. Eastern European countries had since 1945 deliberately used higher education policy to promote equality of opportunity for men and women. In 1950 female students already made up on average 34 percent of the total student population; in 1975 they constituted nearly 48 percent.

Such expansion of the education system was naturally costly. Expressed as a proportion of national product, spending on education over the two and half decades following 1950 rose almost everywhere from 2 percent to over 5 percent. The school became one of the most important agencies of socialization, in which socioeconomic, political, and cultural norms were transmitted. It became the source of professional qualification for an increasing number of occupations. The promotion of fundamental scientific research remained an important function of universities and colleges. Coping with these diverse responsibilities was difficult in itself; the sheer volume of pupils and students created further problems. Major demographic changes such as the declining birthrate and a high level of internal migration added to the difficulties of educational planning. Overflowing classes, lack of equipment, and technical backwardness of vocational training prompted criticism in practically all countries. Such difficulties fed the already existing controversies over method and content of teaching. The hope that social barriers might be removed through educational policy was also shown to be somewhat misplaced. Children from the lower strata continued to be underrepresented in the colleges and universities of all European states, including those of the East. The aim of enhancing social mobility through the democratization of the education system was therefore only partially achieved. Moreover, from the second half of the 1970s graduates of higher education faced growing difficulties in finding occupations commensurate with their qualifications. In consequence, the leading premise behind the expansion of educational facilities, namely, that the labor market needed a large numbers of recruits with academic qualifications, was increasingly called into question.

Mass Media
The educational expansion of the twentieth century contributed to the formation of a more egalitarian, democratic society, in which many more people were able to participate more fully in their country's cultural life. The extension of mass media also aided this development.

In France they even became known as parallel schools *(école parallele)*. Because of the media's central role in forming social and political opinion, struggles over who would influence and control them have occurred from the very beginning. The role of the state is a crucial factor in this issue. In some countries the state merely supervises the media; in others it controls them more or less directly. Unsurprisingly, the question of access, in terms of freedom of the press, has always occupied a central position in debates on a more democratic society.

In the course of the twentieth century means of communication were greatly extended. This was indicative in part of the commercialization of everyday life, but also of the broader social impact of intellectual mobilization. After the First World War the censorship of the press practiced in several countries was abandoned; as a consequence the press flourished. Alongside a more specialized press aimed at specific political, social, or religious groupings, which in part attained literary quality, a new mass press emerged, seeking a high level of sales through sensationalist reports and illustrations. During the interwar years this trend was most marked in France and Britain. At the beginning of the 1930s Britain had five daily papers with sales over one million, and France had three; two of the British tabloids, the *Daily Mail* and *Daily Express,* claimed circulations over two million. The circulation of the biggest German newspaper, the *Berliner Morgenpost,* was by comparison much lower at 600,000. The decline of democratic parliamentarism in several countries interrupted this positive development of the press. Fascist and authoritarian regimes dissolved many newspapers and introduced press censorship.

With exceptions such as Spain and Portugal, freedom of the press was reintroduced after 1945, and newspaper sales climbed almost everywhere until the early 1960s. The mass circulation newspapers enjoyed the greatest growth: two British tabloids had daily sales of over four million copies each, and the similar *Bild-Zeitung* in West Germany had sales of 2.5 million. But not all newspapers were able to compete, for costs increased and the competition from other media—radio and television—became steadily more intense. The ensuing reorganization to achieve economies of scale encouraged the tendency to concentration. The number of newspapers fell, and a few leading publishers such as Beaverbrook, Rothermere, Hersant, and Springer gained dominating positions. This transformation of the market came primarily at the cost of the specialist press; the relative "depolarization" in domestic political debate eroded support for the party press, and venerable institutions such as *Vorwärts* (Berlin), *Arbeiterzeitung* (Vienna), or *L'Humanité* (Paris) had to fight for survival. As a consequence of these difficulties, by the mid-1960s the newspaper market in many Western countries entered a period of stagnation; circulation figures noticeably declined in Britain, France, Belgium, and Italy. At the same time, however, the Eastern European countries experienced an expansion of the press. This was partly a result of the achievement of universal literacy, but also a consequence of the different function of the press as an instrument of propaganda. In addition, the survival of newspapers in the East did not depend upon success or failure in the marketplace.

The much-discussed "communications revolution," however, pertained not to the propagation of the press, but rather to that of the new media such as film, radio, and television. It began with film. The first cinema was opened before the First World War, and during the 1930s giant film palaces were constructed in many cities. The motion-picture theater assumed an important role in social contact and communication. Annual cinema attendance in Britain from 1934 to 1940 was around one billion; in 1933 in Germany it was a quarter of a billion, in 1942 one billion.

The intensive effects of film, radio, and television on their audiences are evident, if hard to specify exactly. The direct visual form of representation in film (with sound added after 1927), is a supreme medium for information, but also for manipulation. Film's ability to influence opinion and behavior was recognized very early not only by commercial producers, but also by politicians. The weekly newsreels, documentaries, and feature films produced by the National Socialist Ministry for Propaganda and Popular Enlightenment constitute undoubtedly the most infamous example of employing film to insinuate and reinforce ideology. Elsewhere, too, film was used both during and immediately after the war for decidedly ideological purposes. Nonetheless, after the war the real box office hits were the non-political and uncritical thrillers, musicals, or westerns that had been so successful in prewar years. Films that seriously addressed themselves to political and social questions generally found a better reception among film reviewers than among the broader public. The high point of the cinema was reached towards the end of the 1950s, after which the industry entered a period of lasting crisis. The numbers of cinemagoers fell continuously, and many movie theaters closed. In 1980, for example, West Germany had only half as many cinemas as in 1959, the year in which the greatest number were in operation. Attendance peaked in 1956 at 818 million; in 1980 it amounted to only 144 million.

Whereas the press and the cinema were primarily private commercial undertakings, radio and television were from the very first heavily influenced, if not directly controlled, by the state. Regular radio broadcasts began in the mid-1920s. Within a decade the radio became a mass medium, which in the case of many countries reached two thirds of all households. Here again it was the German National Socialists who best used radio as an ideological instrument for the manipulation of the population. During the 1930s live transmission of major political, sporting, and cultural events was in many countries a major contributor to national integration. In the course of the Second World War the airwaves were employed for psychological warfare, a practice continuing after 1945 between communist and capitalist Europe.

Television, which combines immediacy and visual concreteness, is certainly the most direct of all the mass media. It spread very rapidly after its introduction in the late 1940s (see fig. 2.13). By 1970 the majority of households in all European countries apart from Yugoslavia, Rumania, Portugal, and Greece possessed a television set. Television had a profound impact on individual and social life. Being switched on for two hours on average every day, it altered the division of time with respect to habits of socializing, eating, and sleeping. Critics soon surfaced to bemoan television's harm to family life and sociability; they also warned of risks—overtiredness, overstimulation, imitative criminality, and so on—especially to children. The poor general quality of television programming was attacked as well: the cultural level of the offerings was undemanding, uncritical, and predominantly oriented to maximizing viewer quotas; commercial advertising promoted a psychosis of affluence and spread a pervasive consumerism among the population; the coverage of politics, which was too short, superficial, and lacking analytical content, contributed little to the enlightenment of the citizenry. The critics furthermore contended that the behavior of political leaders was becoming increasingly geared to the demands of television, with politics degenerating as a result into a media spectacle.

Although these criticisms contain a kernel of truth, both radio and television have nonetheless enriched sociocultural and political life. The transmission of cultural performances enabled them to escape the confines of theater or concert hall and provided access to a broader spectrum of the population. School broadcasting on radio and television

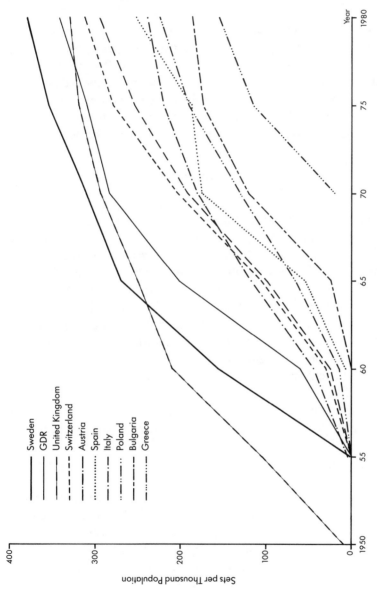

Figure 2.13. Ownership of Television Sets in Various Countries, 1950–1980 (number of sets per thousand population). *Sources:* A. S. Deaton, "The Structure of Demand 1920–1970," in *The Fontana Economic History of Europe*, ed. Carlo M. Cipolla, vol. 5 (Glasgow, 1976), p. 125; World Bank, *World Tables*, 3rd. ed., vol. 2: *Social Data* (Baltimore, 1983).

likewise enhanced the educational offerings of schools themselves, while being also available to the regular domestic audience. The belief that mass media could contribute to the democratization of education led to the foundation in Britain in 1960 of a university of the air— the Open University; a few other countries, including West Germany, followed this example in the 1970s. The live coverage of political events and politicians did not have only negative aspects. It supplied a large part of the population with an increased amount of up-to-date information and better enabled them to form their own opinions. In this and other ways the electronic mass media contributed decisively to the sociocultural and political integration of European societies.

Welfare

Every society must face the vital problem of securing the existence of its members in exceptional circumstances. Until well into the nineteenth century, non-state institutions such as the church, local communities, or kinship groups fulfilled this important protective function. The state limited its responsibility primarily to promulgating poor law legislation, which laid down the legal and organizational framework of the semi-private system. Despite this legislation, welfare provision was everywhere typified by administrative arbitrariness, inadequate support and social stigmatization; in all countries the receipt of welfare entailed a loss of civil rights. From the mid-nineteenth century the industrial and democratic revolutions undermined the social, economic, and political foundations of this traditional system. As a result the state increasingly assumed responsibility for the welfare of its citizens, who thus gained a legally secured claim to their security of existence.

Social Insurance

Traditionally, the origin of modern social policy is traced to the German legislation of the 1880s. Between 1882 and 1889 Germany created the first system of state insurance against the risks of sickness, accident, old age and infirmity. Several states rapidly followed this example (see table 2.2). By the end of the century Italy, Denmark, Belgium, and Austria-Hungary had introduced legislation covering at least two of the three areas; by the First World War all European countries apart from Bulgaria, Finland, Greece, and Spain had followed suit. The sequence in which the three forms of insurance were introduced had no uniform pattern, although generally speaking accident insurance came first, followed by coverage for sickness and old age and infirmity. The central objective was protection against loss of income in the case of inability to work. Different systems for each area of insurance emerged, distinguished by the cause of inability to work and following very different principles of administration and support.

The rapid diffusion of state social legislation in nearly all European countries reflected the general necessity to undertake more effective measures against mass poverty. A generalized European debate on these matters developed, sustained by study trips, specialist international periodicals, and, from 1889, meetings of the International Congress for Social Insurance. These discussions covered detailed administrative or fiscal questions as well as the central principles of this new insurance system—whether participation was to be voluntary or compulsory, whether coverage would be restricted to industrial workers or extended to other social groups, whether the state would participate in its costs. Two contrasting models of social policy emerged: universal social welfare assistance versus group-based social insurance. The choice had more than technical importance, for the question was one not simply of ameliorating poverty, but also of defining the position of the worker in society and the relation of the state to its citizens.

Underlying the first model is the idea that a community bears a collective social responsibility to care for those of its members in difficulties; each has a claim to support, and thus insured protection should be a general social right of citizenship. The second model emphasizes instead the concept of individual responsibility and the principle of self-help. Since the risk of poverty varies widely, insurance funds should be separated according to occupation, and financial support in the case of a claim should be limited to the amount of contributions paid. The first model found limited acceptance initially because of the relatively egalitarian nature of its assumptions and also because of the considerable costs and administrative difficulties of a social insurance system constructed on these lines. Before 1945 it was therefore applied only to pensions and relief assistance, and even then only in Denmark (1891), Britain (1908), and Norway (1923).

The subsequent elaboration and realization of social protection depended on a variety of factors: the party-political composition of the government, the degree of administrative centralization, the extent of local autonomy, the strength of the labor movement, and the attitude of non-governmental institutions such as the church. Liberals as a rule

Social Structures

Table 2.2. Initial Legislation on Social Security by Country

		Sickness	
	Accident	Voluntary	Compulsory
Northern Europe			
Sweden	1901	1891	1953
Denmark	1898	1892	1933
Finland	1917		1963
Norway	1894		1909
Western Europe			
Germany/FRG	1884		1883
United Kingdom	1897		1911
France	1898	1898	1930
Netherlands	1901		1913
Belgium	1903	1894	1944
Austria	1887		1888
Switzerland	1911	1911	
Ireland	1897		1911
Eastern Europe			
Poland	1921		1920
Yugoslavia	1922		1922
Rumania	1912		1912
Germany/GDR	1884		1883
Czechoslovakia	1919		1924
Hungary	1907		1907
Bulgaria	1924		1924
Southern Europe			
Italy	1898	1886	1928
Spain	1922	1929	
Portugal	1913		1919
Greece	1914		1926

Sources: Peter Flora, Jens Alber, and Jürgen Kohl, "Zur Entwicklung der westeuropäischen Wohlfahrtsstaaten," *Politische Vierteljahrsschrift*, 18 (1977): 767; ILO, *Studies and Reports*, Series M (Social Insurance), no. 13, *International Survey of Social Services 1933*

preferred an insurance system based on the voluntary participation of those involved. The financial contribution of the state here only underwrote the private fund. In this way liberal principles such as freedom of contract, individual responsibility, cooperative self-help, and the liability of employers in cases of accident were maintained, but at the

Table 2.2. (Continued)

Old Age		Unemployment		Family Allowance
Voluntary	Compulsory	Voluntary	Compulsory	
	1913	1934		1947
	1891	1907		1952
	1937	1917		1943
	1936	1906	1938	1946
	1889		1927	1954
	1908		1911	1945
1900	1910	1905	1967	1932
	1913	1916	1949	1939
1900	1924	1920	1944	1930
	1927		1920	1948
	1946	1924	1976	1952
	1908		1911	1944
	1927		1924	1947
	1922		1927	1949
	1912			1944
	1889			1945
	1924	1921		1945
	1925		1957	1938
	1924		1925	1942
1898	1919		1919	1936
	1919	1931	1954	1938
	1919			1942
	1922		1945	1958

(Geneva, 1936); ILO, *Studies and Reports,* New Series, no. 42; *Unemployment Schemes* (Geneva, 1955); Guy Perrin, "Reflections on Fifty Years of Social Security," *International Labour Review,* 99 (1969): 249–292.

same time the element of state contribution gradually brought into existence the idea of a social balance between higher and lower earners. Compulsory insurance, whereby state legislation required that specific socioeconomic groups (at first only industrial workers) had to enroll in the program and in which the state (and in some cases the employer) shared financial and administrative responsibility with the insured, corresponded to conservative and paternalistic traditions. Moreover, this form of insurance provided the opportunity of using social welfare as an instrument of domination against the political claims of an oppositional labor movement, or as bait for gaining workers' loyalty to the state.

Before the First World War the principle of compulsory membership was applied to all main types of social insurance—sickness, accident, old age and disability—only in Germany, Austria-Hungary, Luxembourg, Norway, and the Netherlands. Other countries favored the provision of subsidy to voluntary systems, although both principles frequently coexisted. Participation in the insurance programs was usually limited to industrial workers. Salaried employees were brought into compulsory insurance only in Austria (1906) and Germany (1911); in both instances this involved establishing separate organizations and principles of support. The scope of these early programs was very limited. Only in four countries did the percentage of insured within the total work force exceed 15 percent—Germany with 45 percent, Denmark with 26 percent, and Britain and Belgium with 18 percent each. Benefits were limited to the insured person; except in Germany, the claim to a pension died with the original claimant. In addition, the level of benefit was set at the lowest possible level. Total expenditure on social insurance did not exceed 2 percent of the national product in any European state before 1914. Obviously, the redistributive effect of these early social policies was minimal.

Before 1914 only five countries introduced measures aimed at the fourth cause of loss of earnings, namely, unemployment. Several reasons accounted for this delay: in the first place, persons of both laissez-faire and paternalistic persuasions considered unemployment the result of sloth or malingering and not of impersonal economic forces; hence publicly aided relief to unemployed individuals was unwarranted. Second, financial arguments were brought against unemployment insurance; the wide fluctuations of unemployment brought about by cyclical variations and crises rendered a serious attempt to cover this risk extremely complicated. It was not clear how the contributions could be held to an affordable level for the individual worker and yet provide the resources necessary for massive amounts of support in the event of a crisis.

The first unemployment insurance funds were organized in the second half of the nineteenth century by the emergent trade union movement. From 1890 on they were increasingly supplemented by communal assistance programs. The best-known such program was initiated in 1901 by the Belgian city of Ghent. This "Ghent model," quickly copied by many European cities, consisted of publicly funded contributions to the unemployment benefits paid out by the trade unions; the "Cologne system," which was widely practiced in Germany, was similarly structured. Another relief action, the public labor exchange or employment office, emerged around 1900 in France, Germany, Britain, Austria, and Belgium. State subsidy of established union unemployment insurance funds was first introduced at a national level in France in 1905, shortly followed by Norway, Denmark, Belgium, and the Netherlands. In France and Norway, however, the trade union movement saw this intervention of the state as an infringement of its independence and declined to cooperate.

In 1911 the German Congress of Municipalities demanded the creation of uniform, nationwide unemployment insurance, but this effort broke down over differences between political parties. In the same year the English Liberals, under the social reformist leadership of David Lloyd George and Winston Churchill, did a complete about-face on social policy and introduced the first national law establishing compulsory unemployment insurance. The cost was to be shared equally by the insured, the employer, and the state; every insured person paid a uniform premium. As with other workers' insurance programs of the time, the level of benefits did not exceed a bare subsistence minimum and qualification for payment involved various controls such as a minimum period of employment, a minimum number of contributions, a waiting period before the start of payment, and so forth. Moreover, only those workers belonging to seven occupational groups held to be especially vulnerable to unemployment—covering around 10 percent of the economically active population—were insured. Nevertheless, this measure decisively enlarged the role of the state in British society and economy.

Social Security

After the First World War the general political and economic conditions of state protection underwent a fundamental transformation. The labor movement, even before 1914, had played a major role in state social policy, although mostly as the object of measures taken by the state. In the course of the war, to maintain the loyalty of their citizens and to justify the demanded sacrifices, many governments promised to introduce extensive social protection programs once peace had returned. The democratization and parliamentarization of the political system after 1918 endowed workers' parties in many countries with great political influence, and they were thus in a position to realize at least parts of their social programs. The inclusion in the Weimar Constitution of paragraphs promising a "comprehensive system of social insurance," and especially unemployment assistance, signified the new way of thinking. At a different level, the newly established International Labor Office urged its member states to extend social security protection.

The scale of the problem had meanwhile risen enormously. Millions of war victims—invalids, widows, and orphans—needed and demanded assistance. Millions of solders were demobilized and sought work; many failed to find it, or succeeded only after a long search. The influenza epidemic of 1918–1919, which carried away hundreds of thousands, underscored the necessity for the extension of health insurance. The inflation of the following years undermined the bourgeois belief that responsible private saving could cope with the financial crises of life. It also showed up the financial inadequacy of voluntary social insurance and thereby lent support to the contention that only compulsory insurance programs with state financial participation could mobilize sufficient resources to guarantee support in all instances.

The years immediately after the war saw much legislative activity in the area of social policy, particularly in the new states of eastern and southern Europe. Poland, Yugoslavia, and Bulgaria introduced compulsory insurance for industrial workers against the three standard risks—accident, sickness, and old age. Czechoslovakia extended the accident and health insurance system it inherited from the Habsburg monarchy and in 1924 added a workers' pension plan to whose cost employers also contributed. Italy transformed its voluntary pension system into a compulsory one covering all workers and salaried employees up to a certain income level. Portugal and Greece had begun to develop accident insurance shortly before the war; between 1919 and 1926 they added compulsory health and old age insurance. Spain also created a statewide workers' insurance network in this period. In many countries the number of persons covered and the amount of benefits provided were small, but the simple fact that such protection existed at all implied a new relationship between society and state.

Those northern and western European countries that were especially progressive in social policy gradually transformed their systems of workers' insurance into programs of generalized social insurance. By 1930 these countries had extended accident insurance to rural workers, and benefits were paid no longer only for factory accidents, but also for occupational diseases. The number of compulsory subscribers to health insurance was enlarged, and many countries—Norway, Germany, France, Italy, and the Netherlands—included medical treatment of the family members of insured persons as a standard benefit. The number of Europeans covered by the three branches of insurance rose significantly from 1910 to 1930: as a percentage of the economically active population, those covered by accident insurance increased from 31 percent to 51 percent, by health insurance from 15 percent to 47 percent, and for old age pensions from 8 percent to 44 percent. Nonetheless, the share of social insurance expenditure in the national product remained modest. It was higher than 2 percent in only four states: Austria (4.4 percent), Denmark (2.6 percent), Germany (7.8 percent), and Britain (4.6 percent). On the other hand, the new measures implied a subsequent rise in expenditure.

State social policy after 1918 did not limit itself to the creation and consolidation of traditional measures of social insurance but also entered new areas. One of these was the construction of housing. The problem of poor housing and housing shortages had been a subject of concern and study in a number of countries before 1914. The halt to construction brought about by the war aggravated the condition of the housing market even more. The urgency of the housing problem at the end of the war was demonstrated by its explicit mention in the Weimar Constitution and in Lloyd George's 1919 election slogan— "Homes fit for heroes." Many countries sought to ameliorate, if not to solve, this problem by a combination of tenants' rights and state subsidization of housing construction costs. The construction of almost half of the new residential buildings in Germany from 1924 to 1931 was assisted with payments from the Housing Rent Tax introduced in 1924. In Britain municipal councils, aided by central government funds, built one third of all housing constructed during the 1920s and 1930s. France and Sweden also pursued large-scale housing construction projects. The public housing policy undertaken until 1934 by the Social Democratic city council of Vienna gained international recognition.

Another innovation during the interwar years was the family or child allowance. It was first introduced in Belgium in 1930 as a compulsory state measure, following a number of private arrangements in several branches of industry. France passed a similar law in 1932. In both countries the payment of family allowances was associated with other measures aimed at promoting population growth. Since the entire burden of its cost fell on the employer, implementation of the program was linked to pay policy. This connection was especially evident in the case of the similarly financed Italian Family Allowance Law; it was promulgated in 1936 shortly after a general reduction in industrial wages.

The most intractable and most contentious social problem remained without doubt unemployment. The persistently high levels of unemployment were a sombre theme of the interwar years. As the data in figure 2.14 indicate, in the wake of the postwar boom unemployment levels in many European countries rose as high as 10 percent of the work force and remained at that level for the rest of the 1920s. The official figures, moreover, underestimated the actual extent of unemployment since, depending on the country, they included either only unemployed trade union members or only persons registered as unemployed at an official labor exchange. The collapse of the world economy after 1930 dramatically worsened the condition of the labor market.

At the high point of the crisis in 1932–1933, one quarter of economically active persons in Sweden and Britain were without work; in the Netherlands, Germany, and Norway the figure was as high as 30 percent; in Poland 40 percent of industrial workers were unemployed. Apart from Germany, where the rearmament program of the National Socialist government quickly restored full employment, unemployment generally fell very slowly over the 1930s; by 1940 it had receded to the level prevailing during the 1920s—which was itself distressingly high. In some countries, such as the Netherlands and Norway, the level of unemployment remained throughout the 1930s double that of the 1920s.

The enormous number of unemployed was an unprecedented phenomenon; so, too, was the duration of unemployment. A large proportion of the unemployed were concentrated in a few industrial sectors—mining, textiles, shipbuilding, iron and steel—where a restructuring process was under way, caused by the combined effects of mechanization, rationalization, and altered conditions in world markets. In addition, such industries were strongly concentrated in particular regions, where they provided a great proportion of the available

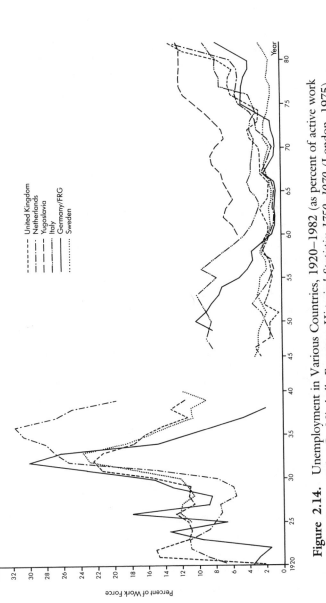

Figure 2.14. Unemployment in Various Countries, 1920–1982 (as percent of active work force). *Sources:* Brian R. Mitchell, *European Historical Statistics 1750–1970* (London, 1975), pp. 166–72; ILO, *Yearbook of Labour Statistics 1979* (Geneva, 1979), pp. 240–42; *1984* (Geneva, 1984), pp. 455–59.

Germany/FRG: 1920–1928 unemployed among trade union members, from 1929 registered unemployed. United Kingdom: 1920–1922 unemployed among trade union members, 1923–1939 registered unemployed among insured workers. Italy: 1925–1932 unemployed among insured workers; 1933–1954 registered unemployed; 1954– unemployed according to monthly sample surveys. Yugoslavia: registered unemployed. Netherlands: registered unemployed. Sweden: 1925–1955 unemployed among members of trade union benefit funds, from 1956 unemployed among members of insurance funds.

jogs. Consequently, very few alternative sources of earnings for the unemployed were available.

As noted above, prior to 1914 very few systems of national insurance against unemployment existed, and only the British one had any real effect. In 1920 it extended the number of persons covered to include the majority of workers and low-level salaried employees. Despite the urging of the International Labor Office, only Italy, Austria, Poland, Bulgaria, Yugoslavia, and finally Germany (in 1927) adopted the compulsory model of unemployment insurance. The financial participation of the employer was disputed everywhere, since such contributions not only increased production costs, but also implied the admission of the employer's joint responsibility for the existence of unemployment. However, the politically "cheaper" solution of directing financial aid towards trade union relief funds instead was adopted only in Czechoslovakia, Switzerland, Spain, and Sweden.

Ultimately, the extreme levels of unemployment during the interwar years overstrained the relief systems of all European countries. The low levels of benefits—from 25 percent to 35 percent of gross pay—and their short duration—from fifteen to twenty-six weeks—could not ameliorate effectively the poverty associated with long-term unemployment. By 1922 so many British unemployed had exhausted their contributions that the government was compelled to introduce special measures of welfare compensation. The program's initial actuarial calculations also went awry. By the end of the 1920s, two thirds of the payments were met from general taxation, which prompted the introduction of a means test for recipients. In Germany, where national unemployment insurance had started only in 1927, the rapid rise of claims during the economic crisis overwhelmed the new system's financing. Since the Brüning government's policy of retrenchment precluded state aid to the fund, benefits had to be cut drastically. By mid-1932 only a quarter of the German unemployed received insurance benefits; the remainder had to rely on the extremely low sums available as emergency relief assistance, or on benefits from communal unemployment schemes. The trauma of unemployment did not remain without political consequence. For one thing, it contributed to the radicalization of the political climate; at the same time it forced a reorientation of the state function of protection, from which the modern welfare state emerged.

The Welfare State

Capitalist Western Europe

The far-reaching social consequences of the Second World War drove the process of reassessment of state responsibility for citizens' welfare further. Universal comprehensive social security was advocated in the 1941 Atlantic Charter of Allied war aims, and then in the 1948 Declaration of Human Rights of the United Nations, as well as in several national constitutions. The underlying idea was that the concept of citizenship involved not merely a right to participate in political decision-making, but also a right to share in the general welfare of society. Social policy should not remain limited to a system of social insurance aimed at replacing income lost through no fault of the insured person; it should not just offer a reactive protection. The task now was to transform the traditional system of insured relief when want occurred into one aimed at prevention of want itself, improving thereby the general welfare of the citizen.

Britain was the first country to realize this idea. The Labor government elected at the end of the war introduced a series of measures between 1946 and 1948 aimed at implementing the recommendations of the enthusiastically received 1942 Beveridge Report, which had called for a comprehensive revamping of the coverage for health, pensions, poverty, accident, and unemployment. In addition, it instituted a new form of family allowance, which varied according to the number of children in a family. The leading principles of this new social security program were universality of participation (basically all citizens), comprehensiveness of coverage, and equality of contributions and benefits. It was the linchpin of a wide-ranging social reform package, which included a democratic educational policy, progressive fiscal policy, measures to promote housing construction, and, above all, an interventionist economic policy, primarily directed at achieving and maintaining full employment.

Only the state socialist countries of eastern Europe created a similarly comprehensive system of state welfare—"from the cradle to the grave"—and there it embodied quite different ideological objectives. Otherwise, the Scandinavian countries came closest to the British example. Here universal public insurance against old age and infirmity had been introduced before the Second World War. All four countries established family allowances directly after the war and also initiated a conscious policy of income redistribution. In addition, Norway and

Sweden founded credit associations, which very soon came to finance the majority of new housing. In 1953 Sweden introduced the principle of national insurance into the health care system, followed by Norway (1956), Finland (1963), and Denmark (1971). The financing of these measures was underwritten by highly progressive income taxes, which were also structured in such a way as to further promote socioeconomic equality. The most important difference in these otherwise uniform state welfare systems was in the provision of unemployment insurance. Here the Scandinavians retained the voluntary principle, supplemented by state subsidy, a situation made possible by the strength of the trade union movement. Norway alone departed from this northern European practice; it had adopted compulsory state unemployment insurance in 1938.

Although Switzerland and the Netherlands were the only countries besides Britain to follow the state welfare model in introducing national old-age pensions (in 1946 and 1956 respectively), all countries in Western Europe ultimately adopted the principle of a citizenship based upon social rights as their guiding ideal in social policy. No longer was social policy a means for the legitimation of power or simply a manner of securing the existence of the industrial worker: it had become the expression of an expanded social welfare concept that sought to achieve a broader social balance. The comprehensive extension of social security in France in 1946 derived, for instance, from an all-party agreement in the National Resistance Council and was intended to promote the solidarity and renewal of French society. The Basic Law of West Germany declared that the new state was a "social state"; the first West German government claimed to pursue the creation of a "social market economy." Unlike in Britain and Scandinavia, however, the new benefits and extended coverage in West Germany were incorporated into existing and revived socioadministrative structures. In many instances, despite the extension of coverage to the self-employed and non-employed, social insurance remained markedly fragmented along occupational lines. The survival of status differentiation between different social strata and occupational groups was evident in the continued autonomy of separate insurance funds for blue-collar workers and white-collar salaried employees.

The welfare state was greatly augmented during the 1950s and 1960s in Western Europe. In 1950 the average proportion of the economically active population covered by accident, health, old-age, and unemployment insurance was greater than 70 percent only in Denmark, Britain, Norway, and Sweden. In 1975 it was below 70 percent only in Greece,

Portugal, and Spain. The process of convergence indicated here did not, however, proceed uniformly. Most widespread in 1975 was pension insurance, which covered 89 percent to 100 percent of the working population; only Greece, Portugal, and Spain had lower proportions. Almost as many people were covered by health insurance; in 1978 even Italy adopted the Anglo-Scandinavian model of universalized health care, establishing a national health service financed in part by state funds. Least common and most widely varying in 1975 was unemployment insurance. In nine countries—among them France after the 1967 law establishing compulsory insurance—it covered two thirds of the working population. In Denmark and Switzerland, on the other hand, it covered less than 40 percent.

Continuous and strong economic growth during these years favored the extension of social benefits. Pensions became linked everywhere to the cost of living—first in West Germany in 1957, finally in Britain in 1975. Many countries supplemented original schemes of income-based pensions with minimum state pensions—France and Austria in 1956, Italy in 1965, West Germany in 1972. By contrast, Sweden, Denmark, Norway, and Britain, whose state pensions originally had a single flat rate, introduced differentials based on income in the mid-1960s, thereby adopting elements of status maintenance. Compensation for family costs was dealt with through the increase of family allowances and child deductions built into income tax as well as through new supplementary benefits such as pregnancy allowance, maternity allowance, maternity leave, child care supplements for single mothers, and subsidies for the costs of day-nursery care and housing.

In many countries the state took over direct administration of all social assistance, although the share it bore of the costs was not uniform. The apportionment of the financial burden of all social insurance in Western Europe in 1950 was on average 30 percent to the insured person, 37 percent to the employer, and 29 percent to the state; in 1974 the shares were still roughly the same at 29 percent, 40 percent, and 27 percent respectively. With respect to individual types of insurance and individual countries, however, the cost-sharing pattern and its trend of development differed significantly. In France and Italy, for example, the employers bore more than half of social welfare expenses in 1950 and 1974, in part because they financed the entire cost of family allowances. In Norway the share contributed by the employer rose to 50 percent by 1974, enabling the share paid by the insured to fall from 48 percent to 31 percent. In the Netherlands the reapportionment went in the opposite direction: whereas the employer's contribution declined from 46 percent to 29 percent and the state's from 34 percent to 10 percent, the share paid by the insured person rose from 20 percent to 51 percent. In other countries the share paid by the state increased, although it amounted to more than a third in only three countries—Sweden, Ireland, and Denmark; in Denmark the state's share of welfare expenses topped 88 percent in 1974.

Communist Eastern Europe

Although the development of the welfare state in state socialist Eastern Europe after 1945 was also based on the idea of cementing society together and the principle of a single comprehensive insurance, the political and ideological objectives differed fundamentally from those in capitalist Western Europe. The purpose was not to secure the welfare of the individual citizen, but rather to satisfy human needs and interests "according to the standard of the general social interest." Social policy therefore belonged within the overall planning framework for socioeconomic development and was not permitted to develop its own dynamic. Even the very terms "social policy" and "welfare state" were initially dismissed as bourgeois capitalist concepts. Apart from federally organized Yugoslavia, social insurance was centrally managed as a part of the state budget, even though in East Germany and in Czechoslovakia the trade unions participated in its administration. As a rule, the state and the enterprises bore the entire cost. Only in East Germany and in Hungary did the insured individual pay premiums, but their amount did not influence the level of benefits received. Since unemployment had no official existence in socialist states, insured protection against it was abolished everywhere except in Yugoslavia, Hungary, and Bulgaria, although East Germany did not make such a move until 1978.

Only those who actively participated in the socialist construction of society had a definite claim to social benefits. Czechoslovakia, alone of the Eastern European states, created in 1948 a national insurance system unrelated to work activity, but this system was abandoned in 1957 because of financial difficulties. The connection of social insurance to participation in the construction of socialism meant that the self-employed and peasants were for several years, except in East Germany and Czechoslovakia, left out of social insurance coverage altogether. This was not changed in Hungary until the beginning of the 1960s; Polish peasants had to wait until 1972 for access to the national health system and until 1978 for admission to the state pension plan.

This relatively strong coupling of the social security system to the productive sphere also expressed itself in the casual way the authorities treated areas not immediately relevant to production, such as old age pensions. Czechoslovakia and Hungary did set the age of retirement quite low—at sixty for men and fifty-five for women—but the level of claimable pension was a bare subsistence minimum, as in other socialist countries. Up to the 1960s old age pensions averaged little more than one fourth of the normal gross wage. Subsequently, pensions were raised considerably. As of 1968 both white-collar and blue-collar workers in East Germany could supplement their statutory pension through additional voluntary payments, and many made use of this provision. There was, however, nowhere a complete indexing of pensions to the cost of living as in the West. The closest any state socialist country came to the dynamically indexed model was an annual 2 percent increase in pension levels decreed by Hungary in 1972. In addition, from that date on Hungarian pensions were set at 75 percent of preretirement income; however, this new level was not applied retroactively, and the formula was not adopted by any other Eastern European country. The generally low level of old age assistance in Eastern European states meant that many persons continued to work well past the official retirement age.

From the end of the 1960s the socialist states greatly extended their family-oriented welfare programs, in part as a reaction to the serious decline in the birthrate, but also because of the increasing shortage of labor. Child allowances doubled in a few countries. Maternity and infant benefits were introduced. More generous terms than existed in capitalist Western Europe could be found above all in the case of maternity leave for working women: it ranged from sixteen weeks in Poland to twenty-six weeks in Bulgaria, East Germany, and Czechoslovakia.

Crisis of the Welfare State

The rise in the number of persons entitled to assistance and the improvement of benefit levels greatly increased social welfare expenditures. The average for Western Europe rose from 9.4 percent of the national product in 1950 to 13.4 percent in 1965, and 22.4 percent in 1977. In figure 2.15 one can see how the various rates of growth are closely related to the starting point. In the later 1950s the share of social expenditure in the national prduct passed the 10 percent mark in Belgium, West Germany (which with 14.5 percent started with the highest share), France, Britain, and Austria. Until the mid-1960s, however, little increase occurred; but from then on social expenditure everywhere rose steadily to the late 1970s, by which time it had almost doubled (in France and Belgium more than doubled). A similar rate of growth took place in Ireland and Switzerland; in the rest of Western Europe the proportion of social expenditure with respect to the national product rose by 1977 to a level three times that of 1950, in the Netherlands four times. By 1977 Sweden was far out in front with almost one third of its national product taken up by social expenditures.

Another cause of the rise in expenditure was the changing age structure of the European population; an ever greater part of the population was of retirement age and thus drawing pensions. This demographic shift also increased demands for medical care, the costs of which skyrocketed because of the greater reliance on expensive medication and technology. The share of national product represented by health expenditures virtually doubled in almost all European countries in the decade from the mid-1960s to the mid-1970s. In some countries— among them Italy, the Netherlands, Ireland, and Denmark—spending on health care exceeded that on pensions after 1970.

The welfare state entered a state of crisis in the mid-1970s. The enormous rise in costs collided with the abrupt end of the long years of strong economic growth. Increasingly, the discussion of social policy turned on issues such as measures for the reduction of costs, alternative financing techniques, and the stabilization or reduction of benefits. Renewed mass unemployment in many states—consequent partly upon the entry of those born during the baby boom into the labor market, partly upon cyclical or structural problems—placed additional burdens on social security systems.

This situation led to a fundamental and systematic critique of the welfare state. Conservatives claimed that it had become too expensive and inefficient, and they proposed it be dismantled: benefits should be limited and social services privatized. They attacked state welfare systems for being dominated by legalistic bureaucracies as well as for limiting the scope for individual initiative and hence weakening personal motivation. Criticism also came from the radical side, although with a quite different purpose: here the opponents of the welfare state contended that the exclusive focus on consumption and the excessive emphasis on material welfare typical of the 1950s and 1960s had completely neglected non-material human needs and promoted an extreme individualism without sense of community.

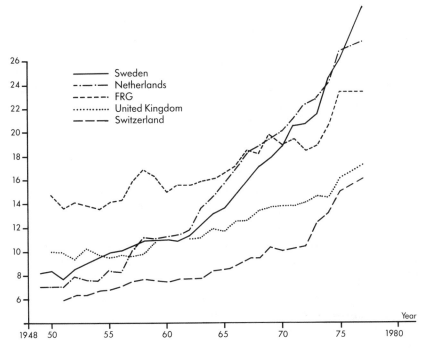

Figure 2.15. Social Expenditure in Various Countries, 1949–1977 (as percent of gross domestic product). *Sources:* Peter Flora, ed., *State, Economy, and Society in Western Europe 1815–1975: A Data Handbook,* vol. 1 (Frankfurt, 1983), pp. 453–551; Jens Alber, "Wohlfahrtsstaat," in *Pipers Wörterbuch zur Politik,* gen. ed. Dieter Nohlen, vol. 2: *Westliche Industriegesellschaften,* ed. Manfred G. Schmidt (Munich, 1983), p. 535.

Computed according to the ILO definition of social expenditure as comprising social security benefits, public health benefits and services, family allowances, social welfare benefits, social benefits for civil servants, and pensions for war victims.

Summary

In the course of the twentieth century social structures and the spheres of social activity changed fundamentally in all European countries. The sectoral displacement of the occupational structure, that is, the migration of labor from agriculture via industry to services, constituted the initial major transformation. This "tertiarization" had far-reaching direct and indirect consequences for European societies. Among the most important was the de facto disappearance of a small independent peasantry and hence of a central social group of traditional society whose lifestyle and mentality differed substantially from that of urban-industrial civilization. The process of tertiarization also lay behind the growing size and improved position of the female labor force, a development that reflected the changing role of women in twentieth-century European society. Further, it contributed to changes in the quality and quantity of work, which in turn affected life-styles and the social role of such important agents of socialization as the family, the church, and the mass media. Since all these changes altered the composition and strength of the major socioeconomic groups, tertiarization thus also influenced the development of political parties and interest groups.

A second central transformation was the socialization of the state, or rather the development of the social welfare state. In the course of the twentieth century the state assumed a central place in social change. This was especially true of Eastern Europe after the Second World War, where the state—the instrument of the Communist party—controlled and guided virtually all areas of social and economic life with the objective of realizing a socialist society. In non-communist Western Europe the objectives remained more diffuse, but here too the state was meant to contribute to the creation of a more social and just society. This altered function of the state was embodied in the dense network of social security protections against the consequences of sickness, unemployment, infirmity, old age, and so on. The egalitarian, redistributive impulses that lay behind this were reinforced by corresponding developments in the system of taxation and transfer payments. The meaning and purpose of the state education system were also increasingly seen as the increase of social mobility and the creation of social equality. Furthermore, the state assumed responsibility for the promotion and management of the job market, indirectly through appropriate economic and fiscal policies and directly through the high number of persons employed in public enterprises, for public means of production played an ever greater role in the capitalist states of Western Europe as well.

Although both processes of transformation had their origins in the nineteenth century, they only really began to develop fully after the Second World War. European society has thereby achieved a level of welfare, integration, and equality unique in its history. Despite this positive outcome, however, the last decade has shown that social progress is neither automatic nor achievable without cost, neither finished nor irreversible.

CHAPTER 3

Continuity and Change in Economic Structures: Development and Creation of National Product

The systematic organization of the next two chapters follows the structure of national income accounting, a form of accounting that measures the money value of all economic transactions—goods and services—within an economy over time. As a rule, the account is divided according to the origin, utilization, distribution, and financing of the national income or national product. The first of these explains the creation of national product according to economic sector or branch. The second form of account concerns who dispenses the total consumption and investment in the national economy: private individuals or the state. The third form of account deals with the personal distribution of the national product by household and individual and with the functional distribution according to size of income and wealth. The financial account shows the means employed by private households, enterprises, and the state to finance their respective purchases. The complete national account is usually also supplemented by an exact representation of the interconnectedness of productive activities between the individual branches of the economy in the form of input-output tables and also by a representation of international economic links in the form of a balance of payments.

Development of National Product

Development of Production

Growth of National Incomes
The description of the long-term development of national economies is extremely difficult. Economic relations are too complex for a passably

accurate picture to be constructed out of one or more statistical indicators of the growth process. Data relating to prices, unemployment, industrial production, accumulation of capital, and so on certainly deal with important areas of the economy, but they can provide only snapshots of specific, limited sections. In view of this difficulty, general economic development is usually now presented in terms of the growth of national product. The historical estimation of national product, which comprises the sum of the money values of all produced goods and services in an economy during a specific period, is fraught with numerous problems that limit reliability and meaningfulness of the projections. Nevertheless, at the moment there is no superior alternative approach. The following outline of the national product in the various European economies must therefore remain provisional.

The curve in figure 3.1 traces a hundred years of the collective national product of all countries in Western Europe—that is, in the regions of northern, southern, and western Europe. The absolute value for the years 1899–1901 is set at 100 and all other values are expressed in terms of this index number. The following characteristic phases are apparent: (1) modest but relatively steady rate of growth up to the First World War; (2) uneven development during the interwar period, in which the break in trend caused by the First World War and the sharp decline brought about by the Great Depression of the early 1930s are strikingly clear; (3) the enormous growth during the 1950s and 1960s after yet another abrupt break in trend caused by the Second World War; (4) the slowdown in growth since the mid-1970s. No data exist for the years of the two world wars nor for those immediately following them. The inclusion of the eastern European national product would not substantially alter the picture.

The same data are used in figure 3.2, but they are presented in logarithmic form so that the fitted straight line indicates the relative changes in national product. Equal intervals on the vertical axis signify equal percentage changes and not absolute changes: the flatter the line, the slower the growth of the economy; the steeper the line, the faster the growth. The dotted line extrapolates the long-term trend. In this figure also the four phases of growth are discernible. Up to 1914 the Western European national product followed the trend line closely and then fell behind between the wars; in the two decades after 1945 its rate of growth clearly exceeded the long-term trend, but in the 1970s it moved closer to the trend line once again.

The development of the European national product is shown in yet

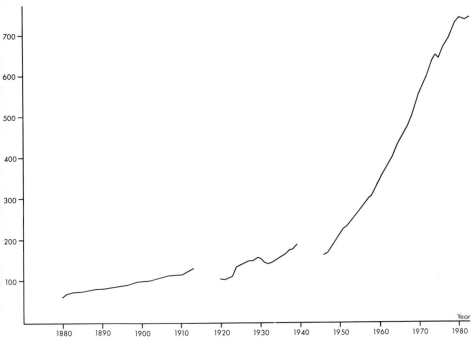

Figure 3.1. Western European National Product, 1880–1982 (1899/1901 = 100, arithmetic scale). *Sources:* Paul Bairoch, "Europe's Gross National Product 1800–1975," *Journal of European Economic History,* 5 (1976): 314; OECD, *National Accounts: Main Aggregates,* vol. 1: *1953–1982* (Paris, 1984), p. 82; OECD, *Economic Outlook,* 32 (December 1982): 154; UN (ECE), *Economic Survey for Europe in 1969,* part 1: *Structural Trends and Prospects in the European Economy* (New York, 1970), pp. 3–12, 46–54; *1982* (New York, 1983), p. 104.

another perspective in figure 3.3, namely in annual percentage changes. Here again the various phases of growth are evident. Most striking are the uneven development of the interwar years and the high but gradually falling growth following the Second World War.

When in the following account exact figures—sometimes to two decimal places—are given for the development of the national product in Europe as a whole and in individual countries, one must remember that they express an only apparent exactitude. The data have been taken from the few available studies; despite their exactness, they remain extrapolations and estimates. According to such calculations, the European national product declined absolutely a few times in this century. The drop during the First World War was perhaps 30 percent, that during the Second World War somewhat less. The period of recon-

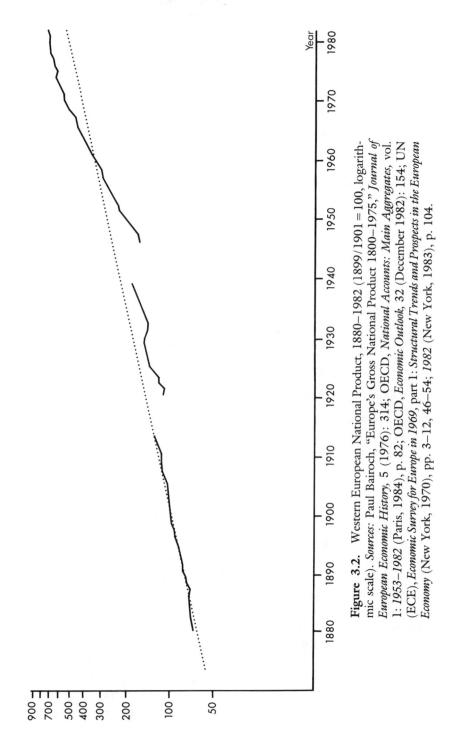

Figure 3.2. Western European National Product, 1880–1982 (1899/1901 = 100, logarithmic scale). *Sources:* Paul Bairoch, "Europe's Gross National Product 1800–1975," *Journal of European Economic History,* 5 (1976): 314; OECD, *National Accounts: Main Aggregates,* vol. 1: *1953–1982* (Paris, 1984), p. 82; OECD, *Economic Outlook,* 32 (December 1982): 154; UN (ECE), *Economic Survey for Europe in 1969,* part 1: *Structural Trends and Prospects in the European Economy* (New York, 1970), pp. 3–12, 46–54; *1982* (New York, 1983), p. 104.

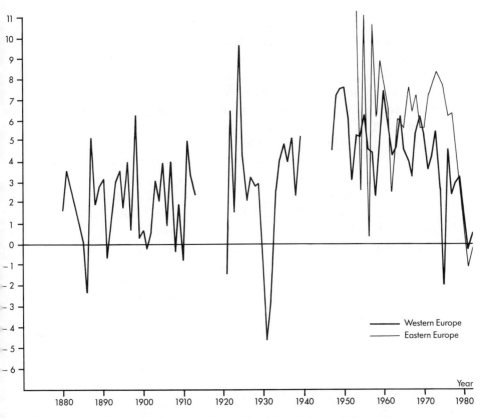

Figure 3.3. Rates of Change in National Products of Western and Eastern Europe, 1880–1982 (in percent). *Sources:* Paul Bairoch, "Europe's Gross National Product 1800–1975," *Journal of European Economic History,* 5 (1976): 314; OECD, *National Accounts: Main Aggregates,* vol. 1: *1953–1982* (Paris, 1984), p. 82; OECD, *Economic Outlook,* 32 (December 1982): 154; UN (ECE), *Economic Survey for Europe in 1969,* part 1: *Structural Trends and Prospects in the European Economy* (New York, 1970), pp. 3–12, 46–54; *1982* (New York, 1983), p. 104.

struction was also shorter after the Second World War: to regain prewar levels of national product after 1918 took five or six years, after 1945 only four. Apart from the war years, European national income fell absolutely in 1901, 1908, 1910, 1920–1921, 1930–1932, 1974, and 1981.

The source of the high degree of instability and the low level of economic growth in the interwar period lay in the world economic crisis of 1929–1933. Although the annual rate of growth averaged 3.9 percent for the years 1920–1929 and 1.1 percent for 1929–1938, the beginning of the second decennium marked the only peacetime period in the twentieth century when the European national product declined three years in succession: 0.54 percent in 1930; 3.34 percent in 1931; and 0.63 percent in 1932. Compared with the wartime drops, the decline during the Great Depression appears relatively small because the crisis hit individual countries with varying intensity at different times and because the data in figures 3.1–3.3 are simple statistical averages. If an average rate of change is calculated taking into account only the sharpest falls of the individual countries in the years between 1929 and 1934, the drop in the European national product (excluding the Soviet Union) during the Great Depression amounts to 12.3 percent, for the industrialized countries of western Europe (including Italy) 14.5 percent, and for this group but excluding Britain 18.2 percent. It took until 1935 (i.e., six years) to regain the level of 1929. Fundamentally, then, the low average rate of economic growth between 1913 and 1946—a mere 0.6 percent—can only be explained by the effects of the two world wars and the world economic crisis. During the 1920s and the second half of the 1930s the rate of growth averaged over 4 percent. This was not so high as in the 1950s, but it was nevertheless superior to the average of the nineteenth century and that of the first two decades of the twentieth. Between 1950 and 1973 the European national product grew by around 4.9 percent per annum, something that had never happened over such a long period since the beginning of industrialization. This unprecedented growth did not slow until the middle of the 1970s. In the decade 1975–1985 the growth rates fell markedly, but they still were above those of the interwar period.

Figure 3.3 also includes for the period after 1950 the rates of change in the national products of Eastern European centrally planned economies (minus the Soviet Union and Yugoslavia). Economic development in Eastern Europe in the 1950s was less continuous than in Western Europe, although the rates of growth were actually higher. Throughout the entire postwar period, however, the trend line of Eastern European economic growth paralleled that of Western Europe. This held true for the period of slowed growth beginning in the mid-1970s. However, data on national income in capitalist Western Europe and state socialist Eastern Europe cannot be compared without qualification; important differences exist in the mode of calculation. In Eastern Europe the system of national income accounting distinguishes between "material production" (or "productive activities") and "non-material production" (or "non-productive activities"), and this distinction influences the meaning of all macroeconomic aggregates. National product in Eastern European countries corresponds to the "sum of net product values" only in the sphere of material production: industry including mining and artisanal crafts, construction, forestry and agriculture, trade, the restaurant and hotel industry, and transportation and communications; appropriately, it is then called officially "net material product" (NMP). A great part of the "non-productive" service sector is thus not included: for example, banking and insurance, health services, state administration, scientific agencies, education, and the arts. Comparison is also made difficult by state control of prices, which are set according to political rather than economic criteria and whose overall structure is frequently revised. Despite these difficulties studies commissioned by the United Nations have concluded that economic growth in state socialist Eastern Europe has generally exceeded that in capitalist Western Europe.

Although the growth of national product in the individual European states showed a degree of synchronization, it followed a distinctive course in each country. The trend line of overall European developments shown in figures 3.1–3.2 is naturally heavily influenced by the larger countries such as France, Germany, Britain, and Italy and so should be used only as an initial orientation. Figure 3.4 presents the growth trends for six specific countries, which fall into three groups. The criterion for selection was the level of development achieved at the beginning of the century as defined by the degree of industrialization, gross national product per capita, and the proportion of agricultural labor in the total work force. Britain and Belgium, as the classic industrialized countries, had attained together with the German Empire the highest level of development in Europe by the beginning of the century; this was undoubtedly a major reason why the national product of these countries subsequently grew rather slowly. Within this group Germany was an exceptional case, in that during the 1930s its growth rate was above average. After the Second World War the two German states—West Germany and East Germany—have also experienced more rapid economic growth than Britain or Belgium.

The second group is made up of states that were relatively highly developed at the beginning of the century although at a distinctly lower level than those in the first group. Exemplary in this category are France and Czechoslovakia, whose economic growth curves are shown in figure 3.4. The Netherlands, Denmark, Austria, Italy, Hungary, Norway, and Sweden also belong to this group, which occupies a middle position in the pattern of European growth. A third group comprises those countries that were underdeveloped agrarian economies at the beginning of the century. Along with Finland and Portugal, whose growth curves are traced in figure 3.4, Greece, Bulgaria, Rumania, and Yugoslavia fit this category. Spain, with some reservations, could also be included. In theory, Ireland belongs here as well, although its subsequent growth curve, one of the weakest in all Europe, did not conform to that of the other countries in this group.

Not all countries can be unambiguously assigned within this schema,

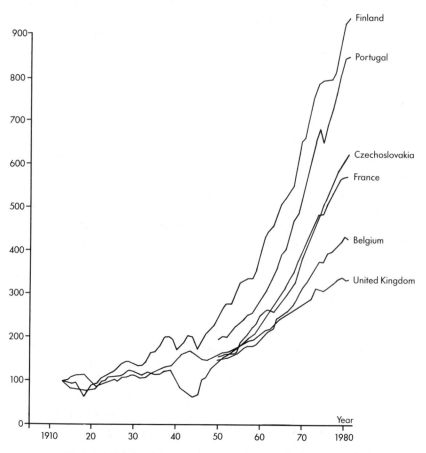

Figure 3.4. National Product in Various Countries, 1913–1982 (1913 = 100). *Sources:* Angus Maddison, "Economic Policy and Performance in Europe 1913–1970," in *The Fontana Economic History of Europe,* ed. Carlo M. Cipolla, vol. 5 (Glasgow, 1976), pp. 497–506; OECD, *Economic Outlook,* 35 (July 1984): 152–53.

and a degree of arbitrariness is unavoidable. For one thing the number of indicators used is very small; moreover, these indicators themselves have limited empirical significance. The data on decennial growth rates given in table 3.1 show the full variety of growth experiences. One must also bear in mind that within most national economies in Europe strong regional variations in development have continued to exist throughout the twentieth century.

National Product per Capita

The comparison of absolute levels of national product country by country showed that in the course of the century a catching-up process took place in which the less-developed countries achieved a higher than average rate of growth. Whether this led to a convergence in standards of living, levels of consumption, or social welfare (to name just a few relevant measures) is another question. Some indication is provided at the macroeconomic level by the figures for national product per capita population or per capita national income. But this is only a very crude indicator. It disregards the distribution of income and wealth, and hence the distribution of purchasing power, as well as the social security system, the state of training and education, and the infrastructure.

Between 1800 and 1913 European per capita national income rose at an annual rate of 1.2 percent; over the period 1913–1950 the rise was 0.9 percent, and from 1950 to 1975 around 4.5 percent. Over the period 1800–1948 altogether it increased 225 percent; by contrast, between 1948 and 1975 alone the European per capita national income grew by 250 percent. Thus more economic growth occurred in the quarter century following the Second World War than in the previous century and a half. Although a growth process that reinforced economic disparities between individual European countries prevailed throughout the nineteenth century and up to the mid-twentieth, it weakened noticeably after the First World War. After the Second World War this growth process finally reversed itself, and a relative levelling of national per capita incomes occurred.

Table 3.2 presents the per capita income of selected countries representing the four different regions of Europe in relation to the per capita income of Britain. Once again it must be noted that a whole series of statistical problems limit the significance of such figures. The data in the left half of the table are based on per capita national income expressed in U.S. dollar equivalents; the figures in the last two columns on the right are based on numerous physical indicators assembled by

Table 3.1. Average Annual Rates of Growth of Real National Product by Country, 1913–1981 (in percent)

	1913–29	1920–29	1929–38	1950–60	1962–73[a]	1974–81[a]
Northern Europe						
Sweden	2.3	2.6	2.6	3.4	4.0	1.6
Denmark	1.9	3.9	2.0	3.3	4.2	1.5
Finland	2.2	5.3	3.8	5.0	4.7	2.7
Norway	2.8	2.7	2.9	3.2	4.1	3.6
Western Europe						
Germany	1.1	4.5	3.9	—	—	—
FRG	—	—	—	7.8	4.4	2.1
United Kingdom	0.7	1.9	1.9	2.7	3.1	0.6
France	1.4	4.9	−0.5	4.6	5.6	2.5
Netherlands	3.4	4.2	0.3	4.7	5.2	1.8
Belgium	1.5	3.5	0.0	2.9	5.0	2.0
Austria	0.3	5.2	−0.5	5.8	4.9	2.6
Switzerland	2.8	3.7	0.6	4.4	4.1	0.3
Ireland	—	—	—	1.7	4.0	3.4
Eastern Europe						
Poland	—	—	—	4.6	4.9	−1.0
Yugoslavia	2.1	4.5	1.3	5.7	4.7	3.2
Rumania	—	—	—	5.8	6.3	6.5
GDR	—	—	—	5.7	2.9	3.0
Czechoslovakia	2.7	6.0	−0.2	4.9	3.2	3.0
Hungary	1.2	5.2	1.1	4.6	4.6	3.0
Bulgaria	—	—	—	6.7	6.9	5.9
Southern Europe						
Italy	1.7	3.0	1.4	5.8	5.1	2.5
Spain	2.2	1.6	−3.0	5.2	6.9	2.0
Portugal	—	—	—	3.9	7.0	3.1
Greece	—	—	—	5.9	7.4	3.0
Western Europe	1.9	3.6	1.2	4.4	4.6	2.2
Eastern Europe	1.7	6.3	2.1	5.6	4.9	3.5
Soviet Union	0.9	3.9	6.1	6.6	5.3	4.1
Total Europe (excl. Soviet Union)	1.9	3.9	1.1	4.7	4.9	2.6

Sources: Angus Maddison, "Economic Policy and Performance in Europe 1913–1970," in *The Fontana Economic History of Europe,* ed. Carlo M. Cipolla, vol. 5 (Glasgow, 1976), pp. 451, 478; UN (ECE), *Economic Survey of Europe in 1982* (New York, 1983), p. 104.

Note: Because of the different definition of national product in the state socialist economies, the growth rates of Eastern European countries after 1950 are not truly comparable either with those of Western European countries after 1950 or with any rates before 1950.

[a] Countries in Eastern Europe: 1960–1968/69 and 1976–1981.

the economics staff of the United Nations and thus give a much more realistic impression of the different standards of living. Since the important issue is the similar trend indicated by both sets of data, their differing empirical basis is not of major concern.

Prior to the First World War, Britain, Switzerland, and Belgim were in the lead. Portugal, at the beginning of the nineteenth century still one of the richest countries in Europe, had by 1900 become one of the poorest. Whereas Switzerland managed to maintain its leading position throughout the twentieth century, Britain and Belgium fell behind; they were caught up with and even overtaken by Germany, France, Sweden, Norway, Finland, the Netherlands, and Austria. Ireland, Portugal, Spain, and Greece were able to reduce the gap between themselves and the leaders, but they are today still very much behind, with per capita incomes well below the European average.

Over the entire twentieth century, per capita national income grew fastest in the countries of northern Europe, although the rate of growth in southern Europe was almost as high. Western Europe followed at a considerable distance. Scandinavia's leading position is due to the rise of per capita income there during the interwar years. By contrast, in the southern European countries per capita income scarcely increased at all during that period, but after the Second World War climbed at by far the highest rate in all Europe. The high rates of growth in southern Europe were not only due to an expansion of domestic product. They are also attributable to the transfers of foreign exchange

Table 3.2. Per Capita National Product in Various Countries, 1900–1973 (in percent, UK = 100, current frontiers)

	1900	1925	1950	1950	1973
United Kingdom	100	100	100	100	100
France	69	92	84	70	91
Germany/FRG	73	73	69	72	103
Sweden	52	79	126	106	120
Finland	48	59	76	63	98
Italy	38	49	44	48	72
Portugal	33	33	28	34	48
Poland	—	25	41	42	61
Rumania	31	33	24	25	48

Sources: Paul Bairoch, "Europe's Gross National Product, 1800–1975," *Journal of European Economic History*, 5 (1976): 286, 297; UN (ECE), *Economic Bulletin for Europe*, 31:2 (1979): 28–31.

earned by nationals working in other countries, principally western European.

Comparisons on per capita income between East and West are problematic. Data for the period before 1939 are extremely limited, and for the postwar period the differences in systems of national income accounting present the usual problems. The Swiss economic historian Paul Bairoch, who has computed one of the few existing East-West comparisons on this issue, concludes that per capita income actually increased rather more quickly in postwar Eastern Europe than even in southern Europe. The UN figures presented in table 3.3 confirm Bairoch's contention that these increases were bringing about at the same time an equalization of per capita income throughout Eastern Europe.

Once again the often strong regional economic variations within the individual national economies must be considered. This variation was (and is) significant not only with respect to the contrast between the industrialized regions of north Italy and the underdeveloped areas of the Italian south. The same phenomenon existed in the juxtaposition of the heavily industrialized Rhine-Ruhr area in Germany's west and the agrarian areas of Germany's east before 1945. Likewise in West Germany the contrast between East Friesland, a rural backwater, and booming urban agglomerations such as Stuttgart and Munich is stark. Great differences existed already at the beginning of the century between the Basque country and Andalusia in Spain, and they continue to exist today. Even prosperous Switzerland still has "rich" and "poor" areas. Many further examples could be mentioned. Even taking these contrasts into account, though, the trend of twentieth-century devel-

Table 3.3. Per Capita National Product in Eastern European Countries in 1950 and 1973 (in U.S. dollars, percentage figures in parentheses)

	1950	1973
Poland	339(68)	2482(79)
Yugoslavia	199(40)	1801(57)
Rumania	209(42)	2082(60)
German Democratic Republic	530(106)	3301(104)
Czechoslovakia	515(103)	2507(99)
Hungary	324(65)	2433(77)
Bulgaria	216(43)	2507(79)

Source: UN (ECE), *Economic Bulletin for Europe,* 31:2 (1979): 28–31.

opment is plain: regional disparities waned almost everywhere. In some countries this process proceeded more quickly, in others more slowly, but generally, and the exceptions prove the rule, an equalization of per capita income has taken place. This was the outcome not only of a more equitable distribution of economic activities but also of a growing spatial concentration of population.

Figure 3.5 presents a rough overview of the regional distribution of per capita income that shows plainly the falling off towards the European periphery. It also underscores the fact that a country's average value only conditionally indicates the internal regional distribution. Differences between countries would become even more pronounced if a more sensitive regional classification of per capita income were used.

Europe in the World

To conclude this initial overview, some points should be made concerning Europe's place in the world economy. At the beginning of the century Europe's share of the world's national product probably exceeded 50 percent. The effects of two world wars and the Great Depression reduced this proportion by 1950 to 37 percent, but the enormous economic growth of the 1950s and 1960s propelled it back to a level of just over 50 percent by the end of the 1970s. In this regard one must remember that in 1980 Europe contained a mere 11 percent of the world's population. Europe's share of world industrial output also declined. In 1913 Europe (excluding Russia/Soviet Union) accounted for 50 percent; this fell in the interwar period to about 42 percent and by the 1960s to around 33 percent. In 1980 European industry still produced 28 percent of the world's total industrial output; if the Soviet Union's industrial production is included, the European share comes to about 43 percent. Logically, Europe's position in world trade has been equally prominent. In 1913 its exports accounted for 60 percent and its imports for 65 percent of the respective world trade totals. Following each world war both shares declined, and by the early 1980s they amounted to 46 percent and 48 percent respectively. In general, then, in the course of the twentieth century Europe has lost its domination of the world economy, but it still remains, alongside the United States, the single most important economic area of the world. This contention is substantiated graphically in figure 3.6, a world map in which the size of individual countries is determined by their share of the world national product.

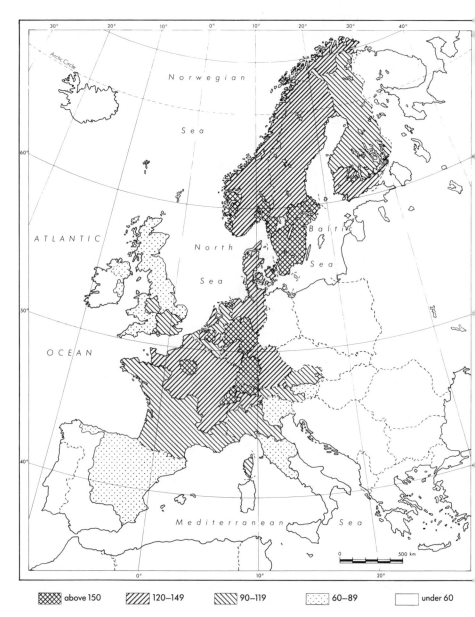

| above 150 | 120–149 | 90–119 | 60–89 | under 60 |

Figure 3.5. Geographic Distribution of Gross Domestic Product in Western Europe in 197
(overall average = 100). *Source:* William Nicol and Douglas Yuill, "Regional Problems an
Policy," in *The European Economy: Growth and Crisis,* ed. Andrea Boltho (Oxford, 1982),
410.

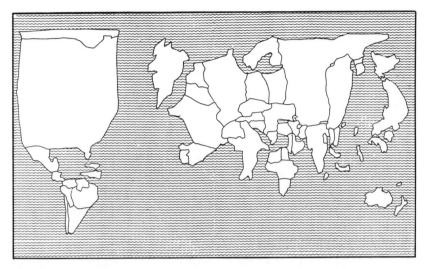

Figure 3.6. The World in 1984 Scaled According to National Product. *Source: The Globe and Mail* (Toronto), 9 September 1985.

Development of the Factors of Production

The development of national product depends on the development of the factors of production, in classical terms land, labor, and capital. However, since the growth of national product originates not only through the increased use of these factors but also through their more efficient organization and combination, another element—technical or organizational progress—is now recognized as a fourth independent factor of production. In modern industrial economies land no longer plays the decisive role it did in pre-industrial economies; its importance has declined even in agriculture. If, on the other hand, one enlarges the meaning of "land" to include such concepts as regional development planning, environmental protection, geographic location, or natural resources, then land continues to have the major influence on economic development that it had in the past. Nonetheless, this survey is restricted to the latter three factors of production: labor, capital, and technical progress. Specific aspects of land as a factor of production will be covered in the treatment of agriculture later in this chapter.

Labor
The most important determinants of the volume of labor have already been dealt with in Chapters 1 and 2: natural population growth and

migration, along with other demographic features such as age structure, sex ratio, participation rates, working hours, and unemployment. In this section, therefore, only the two most important components of volume of labor—the number of persons in actual employment and the hours worked—will be discussed anew. Figure 3.7 shows the development paths of these elements in ideal-typical form; the important issue is the indicated trend. Evidently, the number of employed persons in Europe has grown continually throughout the century. The rise, however, was not always at the same pace; it was interrupted briefly by the two world wars and has flattened out perceptibly since the 1970s. In some countries the number of employed persons has actually stagnated. Work time experienced a similar but inverse development. Hours of work fell continually: more slowly in the interwar years and then at an accelerated pace from the 1960s on. The volume of labor, the arithmetical product of the number of workers and the number of hours worked, has scarcely altered throughout the course of the century. From the end of the nineteenth century to the First World War a slight increase occurred and since the 1960s there has been a slight decrease. Individual countries deviated from this general pattern, but by and large it is valid for the great majority of Western European countries. The development of the national product in Western Europe is shown in figure 3.7 in order to emphasize how much the national product has grown despite an unchanging or even falling volume of labor. This means that one unit of labor has produced ever more national income; in other words, the productivity of labor must have risen substantially in the course of the century.

Labor productivity is the ratio of output to labor input, the latter often expressed as the number of workers or the number of man-hours. National income accounting usually measures labor productivity as gross domestic product per man-hour. The productivity of labor is of central economic importance. Leaving land to one side, labor is a factor of production that cannot be increased arbitrarily, as is the case with capital. Production can therefore be increased only by raising the efficiency of the workers. This can be done in various ways. At the level of the enterprise, labor productivity is a function of the training of the work force, the use of the factors of production, the efficiency of workplace organization, and above all the technological level of the machinery employed. The same factors play a role at the level of the national economy, although on a different scale. In the long run labor productivity is determined by the volume of labor and the quality of

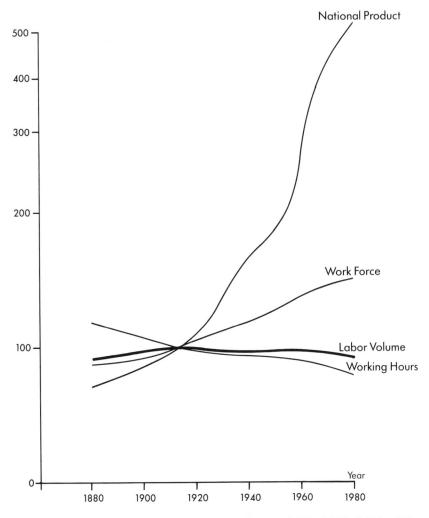

Figure 3.7. Volume of Labor in Western Europe, 1880–1980 (1913 = 100, logarithmic scale). *Sources:* UN (ECE), *Economic Survey of Europe in 1977,* Part II: *Labour Supply and Migration in Europe* (New York, 1979), pp. 18–20; ILO, *Yearbook of Labour Statistics 1984* (Geneva, 1984), pp. 33–43; Paul Bairoch, "Europe's Gross National Product 1800–1975," *Journal of European Economic History,* 5 (1976): 314; OECD, *National Accounts: Main Aggregates,* vol. 1: *1953–1982* (Paris, 1984), p. 82; OECD, *Economic Outlook,* 32 (December 1982): 154; UN (ECE), *Economic Survey for Europe in 1969,* part 1: *Structural Trends and Prospects in the European Economy* (New York, 1970), pp. 3–12, 46–54; *1982* (New York, 1983), p. 104; ILO, *Hours of Work in Industrialized Countries,* by Archibald A. Evans (Geneva, 1975), pp. 141–42; ILO, *Yearbook of Labour Statistics 1938* (Geneva, 1938), pp. 85–87; *1956* (Geneva, 1956); pp. 164–65; *1964* (Geneva, 1964), pp. 287–88; *1974* (Geneva, 1974), pp. 442–43; *1984* (Geneva, 1984), pp. 542–44.

labor and capital; in the short run it is determined by the degree of utilization of existing productive capacity. In general, the level of labor productivity is one of the most important indices of an economy's stage of development.

Compared with the levels prevailing before the First World War, labor productivity in the interwar period scarcely increased. This altered after the Second World War; in the subsequent twenty-five years labor productivity rose almost three times more than it had in the previous eighty years, before the rapid expansion flagged in the 1970s. Throughout the century the levels of productivity in the various European countries tended to converge. Particularly following the Second World War the eastern and southern European countries as a whole managed to reduce the collective lead of the northern and western European states, and within each major European region the productivity levels in the individual countries also drew closer to one another. Substantial differences still persist, of course, not only between countries but also between regional areas inside individual national economies. The trend towards convergence of productivity levels is also evident in comparison of the Western European and the American economies. Whereas immediately after 1945 the level of productivity in the United States was double that in Western Europe, by the early 1980s it was only about one third higher.

During the 1970s an exceptional situation arose with respect to employment policy. Rising labor productivity means, after all, that the same amount of production can be achieved with a smaller volume of labor (fewer workers and/or shorter hours of work). If the volume of labor does not change and labor productivity increases, then output must also grow in order to employ all the workers, and in fact it must grow at least as fast as the rise in productivity. Throughout the course of the century this had always happened. Not until the 1970s were laborsaving advances in productivity no longer covered by higher rates of growth in the national product; even in the interwar period of weak growth, national product had expanded faster than productivity. As a consequence the link between economic growth and employment was broken. The effects on the labor market were all the more severe since technical progress was by this time more than ever oriented to laborsaving rationalization and because altered sociodemographic structures—reduced mortality, more married women in the work force, entry of baby-boom children into the work force—as well as the sociopolitical strength of the workers' movement hindered an appropriate compensatory shrinkage in the size of the labor force.

A survey of the sectoral development of employment has already been given in Chapter 2. This discussion focuses on the sectoral development of labor productivity. If one compares the sectoral distribution of the work force with the sectoral distribution of value-added product, then one can draw conclusions about the relative productivity of the various sectors. Historically, productivity has varied greatly from sector to sector in economies having a low level of development. This is typical of heterogeneous economic structures, in which each sector's market for factors of production and for products are only weakly interconnected, and the productive technologies employed combine capital and labor in quite differing intensities. Especially striking is that in underdeveloped economies agriculture has the lowest productivity and industry the highest. The sectoral productivities converge in the course of development as agriculture, and later services, achieve particularly large advances in labor productivity. This development pattern fits all European economies. After the Second World War increases in productivity accelerated in all sectors. But in contrast with the situation in the first half of the century, growth of productivity in agriculture now clearly exceeded that in industry and services. Increases in productivity in the service sector were previously always below those in agriculture and industry, but after 1945 they pulled even with advances in the industrial sector.

On average the service sector still has the lowest productivity today, although the large variations between individual branches of this sector—banking and insurance, state bureaucracy, household services, and so on—must be kept in mind. Moreover, measuring the productivity of services is very difficult; often the value of output can be determined only indirectly because many services have no true market value, or are even offered free of charge.

In the relation between sectoral productivities and sectoral proportions of the total work force a common pattern emerged after 1945 first in northern and western Europe and then spread in lagged phases to southern and finally to eastern Europe. Because of a rapid rise in sectoral productivity, agriculture's share of the work force declined more quickly than its share in national product. As a result of the also above-average increase in productivity in industry, the relative size of the industrial labor force grew more slowly than the sector's output.

By contrast, because of below-average productivity, employment in services expanded faster than the sectoral output; but of course the number of service jobs is more closely related to demand than to productivity. The differential rates of sectoral productivity played an essential role in the shifting relations of sectoral employment noted earlier. Only because agriculture achieved such substantial advances in productivity were so many workers able to leave the agricultural sector after the Second World War. The service sector absorbed so much labor because its productivity rose relatively slowly. Generally speaking, sectoral differences in productivity still exist today, despite a clear levelling out.

Capital

Alongside labor, capital has a decisive impact on economic development. Capital can create additional jobs, but it can also destroy existing ones. Capital replacement (substituting new capital for old) or capital widening (adding fresh capital to the existing capital stock) are the usual means for introducing new technologies into the production process. As a rule, these technological inputs then increase overall output as well as enhance the productivity of both labor and capital. Unlike labor, capital can be expanded at short notice and temporarily. Capital accumulation and investment thus determine not only the process of long-term economic growth but also short-term economic fluctuations.

As in the discussion of labor, the first topic to be examined is the development of the volume of capital in the European economy. This is not a straightforward exercise since most countries have little reliable data concerning the long-term growth of national capital stock. However, some estimates do exist for the larger economies of Western Europe. These indicate that the stock of capital grew relatively slowly in the interwar period, then very rapidly—even more rapidly than in years before the First World War—in the first postwar decades; since the mid-1970s expansion of capital slowed noticeably, but it remained stronger than in the first half of the century. The growth of capital investment thus corresponded to that of national product, which comes as no great surprise given the importance of capital accumulation for overall economic development. The pattern of capital accumulation traced here is also confirmed by the levels of ongoing investment.

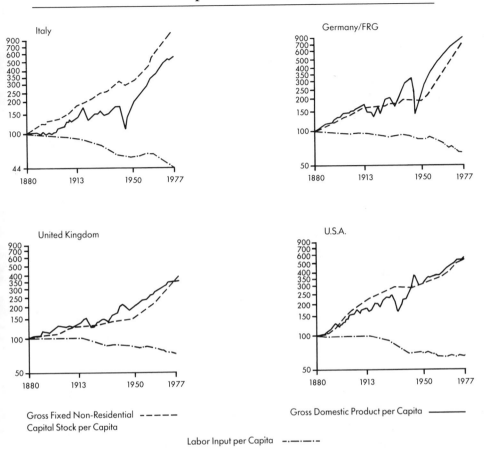

Figure 3.8. Growth of per Capita Capital Stock (Capital Intensity), per Capita National Product (Labor Productivity), and per Capita Labor Supply in Various Countries, 1880–1977 (1880 = 100). *Source:* Angus Maddison, *Phases of Capitalist Development* (Oxford, 1984), p. 55.

A further central economic indicator is capital intensity. This is the ratio of capital to labor, expressed in terms of amount of capital stock per capita of the work force or per capita of the total population. In general, capital intensity rises with the level of economic development, for human beings have historically always sought to alleviate their labor, or increase its capacity, by using machines. Figure 3.8 shows for selected countries the long-term evolution of capital intensity (gross capital stock per capita) and, for comparative purposes, labor productivity (output per capita) and the volume of labor (labor input per capita). The following relationships are important to note:

1. Capital intensity and labor productivity (in other words, capital and output) moved relatively uniformly within the individual countries, especially compared with labor input, which took an almost diametrically opposite course; the slope of the curves, however, differed considerably from one country to the next.
2. Capital stock, or capital intensity, developed much more evenly than national product and labor productivity, whose courses were affected by business cycles, the Great Depression, and two world wars.
3. Capital intensity and labor productivity reacted differently to economic depressions, wars, and their aftermaths. Obviously some amount of capital capacity remained temporarily unused, and these reserves then enabled the rapid growth of national product in the phases of reconstruction.
4. A rough international pattern of development is shown in all four countries, as the growth of capital intensity and labor productivity slowed during the interwar period and then accelerated again after the Second World War.
5. Labor productivity and economic growth were closely related; a rapid rise in capital stock was evidently a necessary, but not sufficient, condition for rapid economic growth.

The increasing intensity of capital also accelerated after 1945 in the remaining European states. Although actual data covering the first half of the century exist for few countries, one can assume from the prevailing lower levels of industrialization that the difference in growth rates of capital intensity before and after the Second World War was even greater than in the more developed economies of western Europe.

The close relationship between labor productivity and capital productivity has already been noted. Just as the former is measured in output per unit of labor, so capital productivity is expressed as output per unit of capital. A unit of capital can be a single machine, for example, but since machines vary considerably and no common denominator such as "number employed" or "hours worked" exists, capital productivity is measured in purely nominal terms: for example, output per thousand dollars' gross capital investment. As a rule, capital productivity increases by means of the technical progress embodied in ever more efficient machinery. This happens not only when new machinery widens the existing capital stock but also when it replaces older machines. The stream of new technology therefore flows into production through gross investment in the capital stock. In the long run the decisive factor for the improvement of capital productivity is undoubtedly technical progress. In the short run, though, capital productivity can rise or fall depending simply on whether the existing productive capacity is being fully utilized. Capital productivity thus is also a function of the business cycle.

Since data on long-term trends in national capital stock exist for few countries, statements on the development of capital productivity must be derived indirectly by relating the amount of current investment to the incremental growth of national product instead of by the direct comparison of total capital stock with total national product. This so-called marginal productivity of capital remained during the interwar years at a level below that of the pre–First World War period, although in some countries it deviated substantially from the European average. Moreover, throughout the 1920s and in the second half of the 1930s it declined gradually overall. After the Second World War marginal capital productivity recovered noticeably, but its expansion slowed in the 1960s and then fell sharply during the 1970s. As with other central macroeconomic indicators, a process of equalization between countries is also evident; although differences still exist, marginal capital productivity in the eastern and southern European states has generally caught up with the levels prevailing in northern and western Europe.

The long-term movements in capital productivity have been largely caused by reduced economic growth and idle productive capacity, which negatively affected capital productivity above all in the interwar period and since the mid-1970s. The positive relationship between overall economic growth and advances in capital productivity, as with labor productivity, is once again unsurprising since such advances occur primarily through investment embodying the most advanced technology, which takes place during periods of economic expansion. This is true for the economy as a whole as well as for its different sectors and branches. During the immediate postwar years capacity effects were very favorable; small amounts of capital investment sufficed to set entire manufacturing plants in operation again. Once this phase passed, however, increasing amounts of investment went into the replacement of spent capital equipment and an ever smaller amount into the widening and deepening of existing capital stock; in consequence capital productivity tended to decline. Nonetheless, the productivity of capital still typically rose faster than the productivity of labor. National variations in the development of capital productivity can be explained by, among other things, different innovation processes resulting from varying capabilities of line management or different economic systems and policies.

Despite the lack of data on the sectoral structure of national capital stocks, one can assume from the pattern of general economic development that in the course of the first half of the century this structure shifted clearly in favor of industry—at least in the more advanced economies of northern and western Europe. An increasing proportion of capital widening investment flowed into industry, whereas the portion destined for agriculture declined. The situation altered after 1945: the proportion of agricultural investment continued to fall, but industrial investment also began to decline relatively. By contrast, capital investment in the service sector increased.

For the countries of southern Europe no reliable data exist, but the strong growth of industrial output in the immediate postwar years in these countries implies that industry's share of the national stock of capital increased. In Spain and Portugal this trend did not level off until the 1970s. In Greece, on the other hand, the share of capital investment in services rose strongly, particularly in shipping and tourism.

The Eastern European states have also followed their own path in this area. Here, too, agriculture's share in the national capital stock declined but so did that of the service sector. In conformity with state socialist development strategy, capital investment flowed above all into industry. In the 1970s Eastern Europe fell into line with the Western European development path: the share of industrial investment fell back and that of investment in services increased. Ultimately, then, in all four European regions the sectoral structure of investment and of capital stock reflects the sectoral structure of output and employment.

Technical Progress

The third autonomous factor of production to be dealt with here is technical progress. Given the natural limits of the potential supply of labor and the diminishing marginal productivity of capital, the prospect of additional inputs that would extend the frontiers of growth is of vital significance to economic development. The construct "technical progress" embodies the variety of possible determinants that, alongside the traditional factors of labor and capital, influence the growth of national product. The question of what this very vague term really means was often debated in the years following the Second World War, when technical progress had assumed more significance than ever as the most important and ultimately decisive growth factor in an otherwise fully employed economy.

Technical progress can first be used simply as a synonym for the concept of a global increase in productivity, as a way of saying that total output rises faster than the purely quantitative inputs of factors of production. Of course the question of where this increase in productivity comes from arises immediately. A whole series of causes could be put forward that were already mentioned in the discussion of the productivity of capital and labor and that have only an indirect connection to technical progress. Such is the case when the efficiency of the entire supply of factors within an enterprise is enhanced by, for example, better organization and management, or when the efficiency of some of the factors is augmented through, for instance, the introduction of new machinery. The necessary inventions and the transformation of the inventions into actual means of production—the dual process of invention and innovation—depend on a wide variety of very different ingredients: the society's general level of economic development and hence educational level and quality of educational system; the existing facilities for scientific research and the amount of experience in research and development; the extent of technological transfer between countries; the degree to which a society is prepared to live with technological change and its consequences; and so forth. The development of technical progress in the twentieth century is, in general, characterized by division of labor, specialization, and diffusion.

The vague definition of technical progress and the multitude of its components hinder both a simple, let alone quantitative, description of its evolution and an unambiguous analysis of its causes and effects. Some general observations can be offered, nonetheless. On the input side, in the course of the twentieth century in most European countries both the proportion of the national work force employed in research and development as well as the share of the national income allocated to research and development have increased. Not only did private industrial research expand, but also the state increasingly promoted science and education. This research input varied greatly from country to country to be sure, but in general the relative size of national expenditures devoted to research in the individual states has converged since 1945, and especially since the 1960s.

The output of invention and innovation is usually measured in one of three ways: as the results of basic research appearing in scientific publications, the registration of patents (especially abroad), and the export of licenses for products or technologies; as the share in total production of a product or production process embodying a leading technology; or as the commodity structure of exports and the competitiveness of individual export goods. Long-term studies of the innovative strength of individual countries based on these indicators do not exist. Very generally, then, only the following can be asserted with confidence: the number of patents registered has grown throughout the century, and the scientific level of applied industrial technology has risen. At the end of the nineteenth century fundamental technological innovations were made above all in metalworking and the production of metals, in the generation of electricity, and in the chemical industry, whereas in the interwar period they were concentrated in petrochemical production; since the Second World War research and innovation have been especially intensive in the aerospace, electronics, pharmaceuticals, and chemical industries as well as in certain areas of toolmaking.

The profit mechanism of capitalist market economies forced Western European entrepreneurs to be more sensitive to new techniques than their counterparts in the state socialist economies and hence to apply innovations to the production process as soon as possible. Labor, an expensive factor of production, had to be exchanged as quickly as possible for the cheaper factor, capital. This substitution process often led to the dismantling of plant that was in itself still productive though no longer profitable; it also placed high demands on the performance of individual workers with corresponding personal and social consequences. The slower rate of innovation in state socialist systems was a sign of economic inefficiency, but it also expressed a different attitude towards technical progress and its effects. In the West the process of "creative destruction" (Joseph Schumpeter), which remains substantially market-driven despite the concentration of ownership and state interventionism, impelled the capitalist system into a condition of permanent structural change; in the East this process was slowed by the recognition of the political and social consequences entailed by changes that were originally purely technical or managerial-operational. Not that belief in technological progress was less widespread in the state socialist countries than in the capitalist countries. In both systems a practically unbroken optimistic faith in the blessings of technical progress has held sway up to the present. Technology has without doubt ameliorated human labor, freed humankind from various constraints, and increased the social welfare, but it has also imposed new constraints and destroyed jobs as well as the natural environment. Above all in Western Europe, the potentially negative consequences of technical progress have recently once again moved into the forefront of public consciousness.

Theories of Economic Development

Up to now the development of the European economies has been only described, not explained. Any general explanatory approach attempting to deal with European development as a whole must necessarily be at a very high level of abstraction if it is to comprehend the different paths followed by specific regions and countries. Such an attempt naturally runs the risk of oversimplifying and of forcing disputable facts into a unitary interpretive model. A few of these explanatory approaches will be presented here, nonetheless, in order that one does not lose sight of the general process of economic development amidst a welter of detail.

Although the economic, social, and political history of Europe in the twentieth century did not exactly unfold continuously and uniformly, economists particularly have a propensity to search it for regularities and "laws." Many initially concluded that industrial development since the nineteenth century had followed a basically stable and linear long-term path of growth (see fig. 3.2). According to this "linear trend hypothesis," fluctuations related to the business cycle occurred continually around the trendline, but serious deviations happened only as a result of the exogenous disturbances of two world wars, after which the national economies attempted to rejoin the trend through a phase of reconstruction with especially rapid economic growth. A number of intransigent circumstances prevented this recovery from happening after the First World War, but the period of dynamic growth following the Second World War does represent a successful "reconstruction" of the long-term trend.

In the 1960s the German economist Franz Janossy developed a comprehensive theory of trend and reconstruction. He postulates first that the growth trend characteristic of "normal," that is, crisis-free economic development was primarily determined by the size and qualification of the labor force. The affinity with neoclassical growth theory, which presupposes that the increase of national product is in long-term equilibrium with the economically active population and labor productivity, is obvious. Janossy's second postulate dealing with the actual period of reconstruction draws on post-Keynesian growth theory, which analyzes economic fluctuations around a long-term growth path in terms of population growth and technical progress. According to the theory, these two factors constrain economic growth in the long run but not in the short run. Janossy believes that at the beginning of a reconstruction period, even after such major interruptions as wars, the labor force potential remains unchanged and embodies in the structure of qualifications of its members the technical progress vital to further economic growth. Only capital is lacking. In such an instance the productivity of capital is relatively high; even modest investment suffices to achieve above-average rates of growth. Capital productivity then continuously diminishes in the course of the reconstruction period until finally the disequilibrium between labor force, qualifications, and technical progress on the one side and capital on the other has been corrected and the economy has resumed its long-term growth trend.

This hypothetical model of historical trend and reconstruction assumes that the long-term potential of economic development is linear. The assumption is confirmed by the relatively steady growth rate of population (and hence labor potential) as well as of technical progress despite two world wars and severe economic depressions. That the very different economic systems of Western and Eastern Europe would experience equally strong economic growth after 1945 also fits this interpretive model. It is further supported by the fact that the economic development of those states less heavily affected by the wars did proceed more evenly and as a rule without any phase of above-average dynamic growth. And finally, the model holds true for the "normalization" of economic development after the extraordinary reconstruction period: since the 1970s the Western and Eastern economies have been growing at a pace roughly similar to that which prevailed before the First World War.

On the other hand, one must then ask why the European economies reacted so differently to similar disturbances. Why did they sink into stagnation after the First World War, and yet after the Second produce unprecedented economic boom, if in each case they were after all only trying to reconstruct normality? Methodological problems make it impossible to check the supposed return to economic normality by an empirical reconstruction of an allegedly existing natural rate of growth. Furthermore, the trendline is decisively influenced by the decades of economic growth before the First World War, for which no reliable data exist. The calculation of the historical trend seems therefore rather arbitrary.

Ever since the emergence of a visible slowing in the rate of growth of European economies in the 1970s, the "long-wave hypothesis" that figured so prominently in the 1920s and 1930s has returned once more into fashion. This explanatory approach contends that since the beginning of industrialization national economies have developed in long growth cycles of fifty to sixty years' duration: an upswing of twenty to thirty years followed by a downswing of another twenty to thirty years. Opinions differ on the exact dating, duration, and character of these cycles, but most writers accept the periodization of 1780–1840, 1840–1890, 1890–1940, 1940–? The dating of cycles in the twentieth century has been especially disputed, and an unequivocal choice is not possible.

Quite diverse causes have been cited for this long-wave variation. The best-known explanation comes from the Austro-American economist Joseph A. Schumpeter, who identified basic technological inventions and the associated innovative activity as the key factor in stimulating the long economic upswings. The fundamental innovations promote output and demand, stimulate innovatory improvements through increased profitability, and hence lead to expansive development. Over time this process, however, loses its dynamism. New inventions pointing to future trends do not emerge. Innovatory improvements and innovation that simply widens the capital stock eventually saturate the market and exhaust innovatory power; technical progress is reduced to mere rationalization. Labor is set free, demand falls, the downswing sets in. The process bottoms out and reverses only when new basic innovations overcome the "technological stalemate."

Following Schumpeter's interpretation, the first growth cycle—the real beginning of industrialization—was based upon textile machinery and the steam engine; the second, beginning in the mid-nineteenth century, on iron and steel and especially the railway; the third, starting at the end of the nineteenth century, on the chemical and electrical industries; and the fourth, after the 1940s, on motor vehicles and aircraft, petrochemicals, and computer technology. Prognoses of the length of the downswing that began in the 1960s and 1970s depend greatly on their authors' subjective judgment of the development prospects in the highly industrialized countries. Optimists see the basic innovations for a fifth upswing in microelectronics, bioengineering, alternative energy exploitation, and other ecologically oriented technologies. Other versions of this interpretive hypothesis, which like Schumpeter's date from the interwar period, propose alternative components for the formation of the long waves. All of them assume a close relationship between long-term economic growth and investment activity but differ in their specification of the various determinants of investment levels: basic innovations, rates of interest and capital market conditions, demand anticipation, profit expectation, wage levels, policy framework, and so on.

The arguments of each of these versions would have to be considered in detail for a thorough, critical appreciation of their potential validity. However, just as with the hypothesis of the linear historical trend, statistical considerations compel scepticism that the existence of long cycles could ever be proven empirically. Yet the entire hypothesis stands or falls on this issue. The Schumpeterian variant, especially, raises numerous obvious questions that have so far been unanswerable: Why do the apparently decisive innovations come in bunches? What constitutes a basic innovation, and how does it differ from emulative innovation? Why does innovatory power ever diminish? How are technical inventions translated into innovatory processes and hence into economic growth? Finally, as already pointed out, technical progress itself is so vaguely defined that it cannot be measured exactly.

The interpretive approaches dealt with so far have been very economistic and, to a degree, unhistorical. The "hypothesis of structural discontinuity" seeks to pay greater attention to the actual historical process and thereby also to historical discontinuities. The representatives of this interpretation presuppose the existence of a number of phases, stages, periods, or epochs, each of which possesses its own structure and thus requires its own specific set of explanations. In general, a socioeconomic structure can be understood as the internal network of social, political, and economic interrelationships; hence these latter elements gain more recognition than was the case in the previous interpretations. Unsurprisingly, many authors see the two world wars as breakpoints of structural discontinuity: the interwar period is separated from the pre-1914 period as well as from the post-1945 period. Plainly, both world wars effected major changes in the demographic situation, the system of nation-states, the organization of society and social relations, and the organization of the economy and politicoeconomic policy. These changes are interpreted as indicating that an existing socioeconomic structure collapsed in the course of each war and that a new structure, requiring a new set of explanations, emerged thereafter. In addition to the two world wars, the world economic crisis of the early 1930s is also treated as a structural break because, owing to the shift in politicoeconomic paradigm, national economies subsequently supposedly developed along new lines.

The economic crisis since the mid-1970s has posed particular difficulties for this explanatory approach. Is it only an especially severe crisis within the framework of the post-1945 world and European socioeconomic structures, or does it represent a fundamental structural break? Many authors are not yet able to decide and talk of structural displacements, of additional new structures, or of partial structural transformation. In all this a weakness of this approach becomes manifest. Since all economies undergo structural change constantly, the ascertainment of a structural discontinuity is difficult and, to some extent, arbitrary. It is no accident that the structural breaks in economic history are usually attributed to exogenous factors such as wars. But one strong point this structural discontinuity does have is that it offers considerable interpretive latitude. It also permits very specialized, rather than generalized, explanations of the process of economic development.

This third approach, therefore, conforms particularly closely to the historical reality of the twentieth century. For an age when economic, social, and political relations were so closely intertwined and in which societal changes affected economic structures and processes so strongly, explanatory models confined to the economic sphere alone can have only limited validity. Moreover, this last approach has the advantage of at least partially subsuming the first two approaches.

Creation of National Product

Macroeconomic Structures

National product, or national income, has thus far been treated as an indicator of economic development. The following sections examine the relative contributions of the primary, secondary, and tertiary sectors to its creation.

In those countries already highly industrialized at the beginning of the century, namely Britain, Belgium, and Germany, the agricultural sector contributed only 15 to 20 percent of the overall national income. In the course of the century this share dropped further, until in the early 1980s it amounted to only 2 percent. The industrial share rose to about 50 percent by midcentury; between then and the 1980s it fell to below 40 percent. West Germany was an exception, for its industrial share continued to rise into the 1960s to well over 50 percent and in the early 1980s was still at 50 percent. The service sector's contribution to the national income expanded in all three countries; already 45 to 50 percent at midcentury, it rose by the early 1980s to around 60 percent (but only to 50 percent in West Germany).

Scandinavia, the Netherlands, France, Austria, and, until 1948, Czechoslovakia belong to a second group of countries in which industrialization began later and developed less vigorously. Here the share of agriculture in the national income was rather higher—close to one third—at the beginning of the century, and in the 1980s it was still around 5 percent, or double that in the first group. The contribution of the industrial sector also rose strongly, but it peaked at only 40 percent in the years following the Second World War. As in the case of the first group of countries, the service sector expanded more or less continuously and accounts today for around 60 percent of the national product.

In those countries still emphatically agrarian in 1900, the development of other sectors' contribution to national income took place much later. At the turn of the nineteenth century probably 80–90 percent of the Greek, Irish, Spanish, and Portuguese, as well as Rumanian, Bulgarian, and Yugoslavian national income originated in agriculture. The level prevailing today in the southern European economies— around 15 percent in the early 1980s—is comparable with that prevailing in Britain a century ago. In these countries the contribution of the industrial sector is still growing or has recently stabilized at a level of 35–40 percent. As in the more advanced economies, the proportion of the national income derived from services has increased and now hovers around 40–50 percent; Greece is an exception in this regard with a share of 60 percent.

The deliberate strategy of industrialization adopted in the Eastern European communist states after 1945 pushed industry's share of national income strongly upwards. On average the industrial contribution rose from one third in the early 1950s to more than one half in the early 1980s. In consequence, economic structures that were originally very different became increasingly similar. In the early 1950s the proportion of national income derived from industry ranged from a good

40 percent in the industrialized national economies of East Germany and Czechoslovakia to about 20 percent in the Bulgarian and Rumanian economies, which at that time still gained more than one half of the national income from the agricultural sector. At the beginning of the 1980s, the industrial share of national income was between 60 percent and 75 percent in all Eastern European economies; the agricultural share varied from 7 percent to 16 percent and the share of services from 16 percent to 24 percent. During the 1970s as a result of the gradual move away from the strategy of forced industrialization the industrial share receded somewhat, and the service, or tertiary, sector, whose relative position remained constant or even slightly declined during the 1950s and 1960s, increased everywhere. The only exception to this last trend was East Germany, which, together with Rumania, had the lowest share of services; yet, according to its general level of economic development and the Fourastié-Clark-Fischer three-sector hypothesis, it should have had the relatively strongest service sector in Eastern Europe. The discrepancy can be explained only by the different objectives of the economic policies pursued in East Germany. More so than elsewhere in Eastern Europe, East Germany has deliberately limited the service sector and its value-added capacity, through pricing policy among other measures. This example shows, incidentally, that although the evolution towards a service economy is a general phenomenon, it can be obviously be influenced by economic policy.

The data in table 3.4 summarize the sectoral shifts that have occurred in the formation of national product since the Second World War. As mentioned earlier, differing definitions of national product mean that the data for state socialist Eastern Europe and capitalist Western Europe are not directly comparable.

Agriculture

Human beings can only exist if agriculture provides them with the necessary foodstuffs. This fundamental truth also applies to Europe. One tends to give little recognition to the agricultural sector in highly industrialized regions, yet a few figures suffice to demonstrate the continuing importance of agriculture in twentieth-century Europe. Although in 1900 agriculture was no longer, as in 1800, the basis of existence for three quarters of the European population, it still em-

Table 3.4. Formation of National Product by Region, 1950–1981 (in percent of total product)

| | Sectoral Distribution | | | | | | | | | | | |
| | 1950–52 | | | 1958–60 | | | 1967–69 | | | 1979–81 | | |
	A	I	S	A	I	S	A	I	S	A	I	S
Western/northern Europe (incl. Italy)	11	34	56	9	37	54	7	39	54	5	37	58
Southern Europe (excl. Italy, incl. Yugoslavia)	38	25	37	30	32	38	24	37	39	15	38	47
Eastern Europe (excl. Yugoslavia, incl. Soviet Union	41	39	20	36	45	19	18	64	18	13	67	20

| | Average Annual Rates of Change | | | | | | | |
| | 1950–69 | | | | 1973–81 | | | |
	A	I	S	Total	A	I	S	Total
Western/northern Europe (incl. Italy)	2.3	5.4	4.4	4.6	1.5	1.5	2.9	2.2
Southern Europe (excl. Italy, incl. Yugoslavia)	3.2	8.6	5.8	6.0	1.9	2.8	3.6	3.4
Eastern Europe (excl. Yugoslavia, incl. Soviet Union)	3.1	9.6	6.4	7.0	0.7	6.9	7.1	5.2

Sources: UN (ECE), *Economic Survey of Europe in 1971,* part 1: *The European Economy from the 1950s to the 1970s* (New York, 1972), pp. 8–10; *1982* (New York, 1983), p. 105; OECD, *Historical Statistics 1960–1981* (Paris, 1983), pp. 45–46.
Note: A = Agriculture; I = Industry; S = Services.

ployed roughly 40 percent of the work force (somewhat less in western Europe and considerably more in southern and eastern Europe). When the proportion declined to around 10 percent in the early 1980s, in absolute numbers this still amounted to almost thirty million people. Persons employed in agriculture, then, were and remain of central importance—both as producers and as consumers—for the development of European national economies.

Development of Agricultural Production

Figure 3.9 presents data on the growth of European grain production (wheat, rye, barley, oats, and corn) over the century. Grain production has been chosen because it has always been one of the most important branches of agriculture and because its pattern of growth is generally representative of other commodities.

At first glance the curve follows the same trajectory as that of European national product. With the First World War came a sharp fall, which was only made up in the course of the 1920s; the Great Depression brought about a renewed drop in grain production in the early 1930s, and the Second World War resulted in an even deeper collapse than had the First. The interwar years were generally characterized by a worldwide agricultural crisis, which hit European agriculture especially hard. Increased overseas competition, overproduction, and collapsing prices were the results, and for many producers they meant high indebtedness, substantial losses of income, or bankruptcy. In consequence of the combined effects of wars and depression, overall grain production hardly expanded during the first half of the twentieth century. Following the Second World War, however, it rose enormously. Beginning in 1950 data on total agricultural output are available, assembled by the Food and Agricultural Organization (FAO) of the United Nations. Indices for Eastern and Western European total agricultural output are also presented in figure 3.9, whereby the average total production in 1952–1956 (representing the return to pre–Second World War levels) constitutes the base number. As with all data pertaining to economic development in East and West after 1945, these figures are not strictly comparable even though they represent physical quantities. Nonetheless, clearly agriculture underwent strong and relatively steady growth in both parts of Europe with Eastern European growth beginning somewhat later but expanding more rapidly. As in the case of national product, the 1970s brought a slowdown in the growth of agricultural output. The causes of this generally dynamic growth process lie in the very favorable general economic conditions and the associated transformation of agricultural technology. Modern forms of mechanization, fertilization, pest and disease control, animal husbandry, and so on were much more intensely practised not only in the more-developed countries of western and northern Europe but also in southern and eastern European states, where traditional production methods dominated in agriculture until after the Second World War.

Figure 3.9. Grain Production in Europe, 1899–1981 (in million tons, excl. Russia/USSR), and Total Agricultural Production in Western Europe and Eastern Europe (incl. USSR), 1950–1982 (1952/56 = 100). *Sources:* International Institute of Agriculture, *International Yearbook of Statistics* (later *Yearbook of Food and Agricultural Statistics*) *1909–1938/39* (Rome, 1910–1940); Food and Agricultural Organization, *Production Yearbook 1955, 1958, 1961, 1965, 1969, 1971, 1974, 1977, 1980, 1983* (Rome, 1956–1984).

Factors of Production

Land as a factor of production, that is, the agriculturally cultivated area, generally decreased in Europe during the twentieth century. Only in two periods—the interwar years and the years immediately following the Second World War—did it increase briefly and temporarily. For a closer comparative examination only arable land should be used since it is subject to fewer national differences in definition. In western Europe the amount of arable land has declined steadily. In northern Europe as a whole tilled land continued to expand slowly until the 1950s, after which its area shrank rather rapidly. The major contributor to this drop was Sweden; in Denmark and Norway the extent of arable land changed little, and in Finland it continued to expand into the 1960s. The southern European countries have also increased their tilled area right up to the present; it had fallen by almost 10 percent in the interwar period. The greatest fluctuations in the amount of land under tillage occurred in eastern Europe. During the interwar years it was expanded; especially in the Balkans there was much fallow to bring under cultivation. The Second World War caused a substantial contraction, but in the 1950s and 1960s tilled acreage increased once more and began to recede sightly only in the 1970s. Table 3.5 provides some basic data on areas under cultivation in the different regions of Europe. In order to show the long-term trend, the German acreage for 1913, 1921, and 1939 has been divided according to the post-1945 political boundaries and assigned appropriately to either the western or the eastern European region. No figures for Europe as a whole are given on account of territorial shifts associated with the redrawing of borders with the Soviet Union; this problem also naturally reduces the accuracy of the data on eastern Europe.

Of almost greater importance for agricultural production than the absolute extent of the cultivated area is the division of that area into individual economic units. Great landed estates and subsistence-farmed small holdings operated unproductively in the past compared with medium-sized holdings run by an independent peasantry. Before the First World War latifundia and small holdings determined the agricultural property structure in eastern and southern Europe. By contrast, small and medium farms dominated in western and northern European countries. The political upheavals in the wake of the First World War did, to be sure, bring about changes; agrarian reforms were introduced in twelve eastern European countries and millions of hectares were redistributed. Except in the Baltic states, however, the re-

Table 3.5. Cultivated Area by Region, 1913–1981 (in million hectares)

	1913	1921	1939	1951	1965	1981
Western Europe	44.64	43.02	41.98	41.41	40.45	37.89
Northern Europe	8.89	9.53	9.58	9.74	9.34	8.82
Southern Europe	33.66	32.63	30.88	42.94	43.90	40.39
Eastern Europe	52.74	55.55	59.84	52.43	54.79	52.90

Sources: International Institute of Agriculture, *International Yearbook of Statistics* (later *Yearbook of Food and Agricultural Statistics*) *1909–1938/39* (Rome, 1910–1940); FAO, *Production Yearbook 1955, 1958, 1961, 1965, 1969, 1971, 1974, 1977, 1980, 1983* (Rome, 1956–1984).

Note: Unweighted averages of country data. Data for individual countries do not always correspond exactly to the year indicated.

forms did not create more efficient farming units. Either the juxtaposition of large estates and parcellized holdings continued, or the number of very small, marginal plots increased even further. Whatever the case, these uneconomical operational structures were a major reason why the modernizing potential of the agricultural sector was realized less in these two regions than in western and northern Europe.

The years following the Second World War brought radical changes. In all eastern European countries giant cooperatively organized agricultural collectives and state farms were created through compulsory collectivization and nationalization. In southern Europe, on the other hand, the centuries-old latifundia remained in existence long after 1945. Not until the mid-1970s did Portugal and Spain carry out agrarian reforms that weakened somewhat the predominance of latifundia and small holdings. The reduction in the total number of farms in both countries resulted from the abandonment of many extremely small units, which had for the most part been operated merely to supplement income from other sources. This phenomenon also occurred in western European countries, where the number of agricultural enterprises fell by more than a third after 1945. After 1958 the agricultural policy of the EEC consciously strove to create viable and profitable medium-size farms.

In consequence of all these changes, a relatively major reorganization of the European land under cultivation took place over the course of the twentieth century. After the First World War the number of productive units increased, and the average size of holding decreased. After the Second World War the pattern was exactly reversed: the number of enterprises dropped and their average size rose.

Labor as a factor of production in agriculture underwent much greater changes than the production factor of land. Before 1914, 67.5 million persons were employed in European agriculture (see table 3.6). During the First World War this number did not change, but it rose distinctly in the interwar period and exceeded seventy million on the eve of the Second World War. The eastern European countries accounted for almost all of this increase. In the western and northern European states the number employed in agriculture fell slightly during this period. Thereby began the decline in the absolute number of agricultural workers in the developed industrial states; the relative size of the agricultural work force had already started to shrink some decades earlier in most of the countries in these two regions. During the 1940s European agricultural employment fell as a result of the war, and by 1950 it numbered barely sixty-two million, well below the interwar level. In the following three decades it was radically cut back and by 1980 amounted to just thirty million.

The countries of eastern and southern Europe, above all, suffered from rural overpopulation until after the Second World War; the large number of persons seeking to make their living from agriculture could barely support themselves. Even today the agricultural sector in these countries is overmanned by comparison with western and northern Europe, although this overall condition does not exclude the possibility of regional and seasonal labor shortages. The rapid drop in agricultural employment after the Second World War coupled with only minor decreases in total cultivated area raised the ratio of land to labor input: one person tilled an ever larger piece of land. Such development was made possible only by the investment of increasing amounts of capital.

Table 3.6.   Agricultural Employment by Region, 1913–1980 (in millions, percentage figures in parentheses)

	1913	1930	1950	1980
Western Europe	19.25(28.5)	19.15(27.5)	14.93(24.1)	5.12(16.8)
Northern Europe	3.12(4.6)	3.12(4.5)	2.50(4.0)	0.85(2.8)
Eastern Europe	29.41(43.5)	31.58(45.3)	29.13(47.0)	17.20(56.7)
Southern Europe	15.76(23.3)	15.89(22.8)	15.39(24.8)	7.15(23.6)
Total	67.54(100.0)	69.74(100.0)	61.95(100.0)	30.32(100.0)

Sources: Angus Maddison, "Economic Policy and Performance in Europe 1913–1970," in *The Fontana Economic History of Europe*, ed. Carlo M. Cipolla, vol. 5 (Glasgow, 1976), p. 496; UN, *Statistical Yearbook 1982* (New York, 1984), pp. 86–93.

Capital and technical progress as factors of production in the agricultural sector refer to mechanization, use of chemicals, introduction of new breeds of animals and new strains of crops, methods of cultivation, and animal husbandry. Use of the steam plow, the steam thresher, and the drilling machine spread in the second half of the nineteenth century, but the overall degree of mechanization still remained low in the first half of the twentieth century; the tractor gained importance only in western and northern Europe. After 1945 conditions changed radically in a short time. In 1939 about 270,000 tractors were operated in the whole of Europe; by the early 1980s there were over eight million. Moreover, the tractor developed from a simple pulling machine into an integrated work vehicle capable of being used in multiple tasks and of replacing much human and animal labor.

Tractors, seeders, harvesters, threshers, and a whole series of other agricultural machinery that decisively transformed both crop farming and animal husbandry were finally adopted on a widespread basis throughout Europe shortly before and after the Second World War. The latest state of mechanization has been the application of microprocessors to automate the execution of specific tasks. The precondition for this step, of course, has been the comprehensive electrification of agricultural areas. Although mechanization has reached almost all areas of Europe in one form or another, great differences persist. It is especially far advanced in the states of western and northern Europe, whereas in the eastern and southern European countries mechanization had still not reached western European levels by the mid-1980s.

The increasingly intensive methods of cultivation meant that the soil had to be enriched or replenished by fertilization. The use of mineral fertilizer to supplement the organic fertilizing process began in the nineteenth century. As with mechanization, the spread of this technique accelerated throughout the more developed states of western and northern Europe, above all in the smaller countries such as the Netherlands, Belgium, and Denmark where agricultural practices were especially intensive. The larger, extensively farmed agrarian economies of southern and eastern Europe followed at a considerable distance. Only in the postwar period, and really only since the 1960s, have mineral fertilizers (nitrates, phosphates, and potash) become widely used in these two regions; their consumption has grown particularly strongly in eastern Europe, while in southern Europe the rise has been more moderate. The gap between the major regions, however, continues to be large. In some countries—Belgium, the Netherlands, West Germany, and even East Germany—the process of soil enrichment seems to have reached a point of saturation. Overfertilization can be increasingly discerned, giving rise to an ever more threatening chemical contamination of foodstuffs. The continued rise of applications per unit of agricultural land in these countries results from the increased use of mineral fertilizers on pastures and meadows rather than on tilled soil.

A sustained increase in agricultural output is possible only if pests and diseases can be effectively controlled. The utilization of chemical pesticides (insecticide, fungicide, herbicide, rodenticide) has evolved similarly to the use of artificial fertilizers. Significant use began again first in western European agriculture and spread to other European regions only after the Second World War. Pesticides have enabled the almost complete extermination of specific pests such as the Colorado potato beetle as well as the control of specific epidemics such as hoof-and-mouth disease. Just as with fertilization, the extensive use of pesticides in certain European regions entails the threat of growing contamination of agricultural products.

Mechanization and the application of chemicals certainly express most clearly the enormous increase of capital investment in the agricultural sector. But research into new methods of husbandry and cultivation also requires capital, which is usually provided by the state. The so-called second agricultural revolution after 1945 refers to the fundamental transformation of agricultural production techniques brought about by the factors just discussed. A rising volume of capital investment combined with a declining labor force meant that capital intensity in agriculture rose rapidly after the Second World War, even exceeding that prevailing in many branches of industrial and craft-based production. At the same time, though, capital costs increased in relation to produced value; in other words, farmers were faced with ever-higher costs of production.

Table 3.7 contains data on the development of the major inputs in agricultural production in the postwar period. Comparisons between conditions in Hungary and Poland, on the one hand, and the other European regions, on the other, must remain tentative, for the differing methods of calculating prices mean that the data do not have an equivalent basis. Nevertheless, at the beginning of the 1980s capital costs were clearly lowest in southern Europe and highest in northern and western Europe. In eastern Europe they were likewise high in the more developed Czechoslovakian and East German economies, whereas their level was noticeably lower in the less developed Polish and Rumanian economies. The proportion of capital costs in gross value of production doubled in postwar northern and western Europe; it tripled in southern Europe, as it probably also did in eastern Europe. One must note, however, that the data in table 3.7 cover only a portion of the total costs of production and that even capital costs are not fully listed. Almost everywhere all capital costs and write-offs together amount to 60 percent or more of agricultural production value.

The rising capital intensity promoted specialization of production, since sophisticated machinery incurred supplementary costs that could be recouped only by concentrating on the production of particular crops and livestock. In grain production uniform patterns of crop rotation emerged that enabled a highly efficient full mechanization of planting, tending, and harvesting and thus achieved high labor productivity. Production of root crops was also adjusted to incorporate new planting sequences that raised the intensity of land use and ensured a higher level of productivity. The growing pressure of production costs and rationalization affected animal husbandry as well; in this area, too, mechanization was increasingly the rule.

Factor Productivity

Why did agricultural productivity rise so strongly over the last hundred years despite the period of interwar stagnation? It cannot have resulted from the purely quantitative increase in the employment of factors of production. On the contrary, acreage declined somewhat and labor inputs fell greatly. Capital investment did play an ever greater role, but the large increases in agricultural output cannot be attributed merely to the enlargement of the volume of capital. To achieve them, a substantial enhancement of factor productivity was necessary: land and labor, with the assistance of capital, had to produce more per factor unit employed.

In addition to the continual refinements in the quality of seed stocks and animal breeds, improvements in yields per hectare or per head of livestock in the second half of the nineteenth century were due principally to more intensive use of artificial fertilizers and protein-rich feed. The intensification of land use and the change of cultivating techniques—above all the extension of root crops—also played a role. In Germany, the Netherlands, Sweden, Belgium, and Denmark, for example, land productivity rose annually at an average rate of 1 percent to 2 percent between 1880 and 1913. French agriculture, on the other hand, made hardly any advances in productivity. No reliable data are

Table 3.7. Expenditures in Gross Agricultural Product by Region, 1950–1982 (in percent)

	1950–52	1960–62	1970–72	1980–82
Northern/western Europe				
Fodder, seed, livestock	9.4	15.8	19.9	21.5
Fertilizers	4.9	5.6	6.5	7.9
Pesticides	0.6	0.6	1.2	2.1
Fuel, lubricants, electicity	2.4	3.1	3.3	4.3
Maintenance, repairs	5.9	5.9	6.4	6.9
Total	23.2	3.1	37.3	42.6
Southern Europe				
Fodder, seed, livestock	3.4	7.1	13.3	15.3
Fertilizers	2.5	2.7	3.3	3.7
Pesticides	0.7	0.7	1.0	1.2
Fuel, lubricants, electricity	0.7	1.1	2.3	4.1
Maintenance, repairs	1.2	1.3	2.0	3.1
Total	8.5	12.9	21.9	27.4
Hungary				
Fodder, seed, livestock		4.4	27.1	24.9
Fertilizers		2.5	5.0	5.5
Pesticides		1.7	0.9	1.9
Fuel, lubricants, electricity		2.8	2.2	3.1
Maintenance, repairs		4.5	3.2	4.1
Total		15.9	38.4	39.5
Poland				
Fodder, seed, livestock		1.9	12.5	18.3
Fertilizers		3.6	5.9	5.4
Pesticides		0.3	0.5	1.0
Fuel, lubricants, electricity		2.1	2.4	3.9
Maintenance, repairs		3.4	4.3	4.7
Total		11.3	25.6	33.3

Sources: UN (ECE), *Economic Survey of Europe in 1971,* part 1 (New York, 1972), p. 609; *1982* (New York, 1983), pp. 136–44; *1983* (New York, 1984), p. 134.

available for the majority of eastern and southern European countries, but given the inefficient structure of operational units in these regions the productivity of land presumably rose very slowly. Thus, before the First World War yields per hectare in European agriculture varied widely. In the developed countries of northern and western Europe they were twice as high as in the backward lands of eastern and southern Europe.

These differences also persisted throughout the interwar period, during which yields per hectare generally increased only slowly or even stagnated; the agricultural crisis of the late 1920s and 1930s halted the process of agricultural innovation in every respect. This stagnation was all the more remarkable in that outside Europe at this time agricultural producers achieved great advances in productivity.

After the Second World War the second agricultural revolution brought about an enormous increase in the productivity of land, possibly a doubling between 1950 and 1980. The combined effects of more and better factor inputs were the primary cause of this increase; the importance of traditional and natural factor inputs generally declined. This substitution process is quite evident in the following estimates of the percentage contribution made by various production components to increases in grain yield in Czechoslovakia between 1948 and 1978 (derived from the UN data listed in table 3.7):

	1948	1978
Natural soil fertility	40	10
Climatic conditions	20	15
Ground preparation	20	10
Seed quality/planting methods	5	20
Pesticides	5	15
Fertilization	10	30
	100	100

Since 1945 agricultural productivity has developed along quite similar lines in the various major European regions; only in southern Europe has it risen more slowly (with the exception of Italy). The eastern European states have caught up to some extent but have not yet matched the high levels of productivity achieved in western and northern Europe.

Figure 3.10 presents data on wheat yields in four countries representing different levels of economic development. The lack of growth during the first half of the century is plain, as is the strong increase in crop productivity following the Second World War. The converging tendency of yields per hectare during the phase of rapid growth and the persisting lag between East and West are also evident.

Other crops and animal products experienced a similar pattern of development. So far a modest slowing of growth has occurred only among particularly highly bred species of plants and animals and in very intensively farmed areas, whose yields in any case lie far above the average. Considering European agricultural production on the whole, the "law of diminishing returns" has not yet come into force.

An ever greater agricultural output produced by ever fewer workers necessarily means that labor productivity has greatly increased. To cite

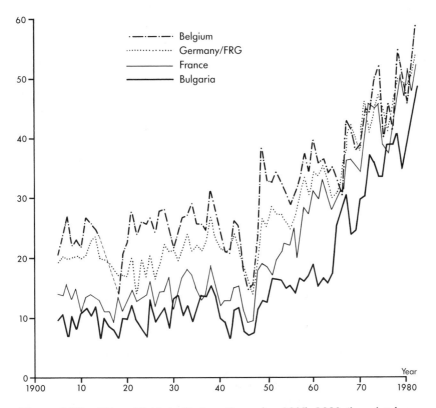

Figure 3.10. Wheat Yields in Various Countries, 1905–1982 (in quintals per hectare). *Sources:* International Institute of Agriculture, *International Yearbook of Statistics* (later *Yearbook of Food and Agricultural Statistics*) *1909–1938/39* (Rome, 1910–1940); Food and Agricultural Organization, *Production Yearbook 1955, 1958, 1961, 1965, 1969, 1971, 1974, 1977, 1980, 1983* (Rome, 1956–1984).

just two examples: in Germany at the beginning of the century one unit of labor could produce sufficient food for five persons, in mid-century for six, and in 1980 for thirty-five; moreover, the per capita consumption of food also rose during this time. In Britain, the various tasks associated with the production of wheat required 120 work hours per hectare in 1900, 80 in midcentury, and only 15 in 1980, even though the amount of wheat yielded per hectare meanwhile increased substantially. As with the productivity of land, labor productivity also depended on larger and higher quality inputs of capital. The elimination of underemployment (explicit or implicit unemployment) also played a role. Both ingredients generally determined the huge leaps in labor productivity—five- to sixfold increases in nearly all countries—following the Second World War as well as the lagged response in the different regions; particularly rapid advances occurred in northern and western Europe during the 1950s, in eastern Europe during the 1960s, and in southern Europe during the 1970s.

Altogether this added up to a transformation of the character of European agriculture, particularly apparent after 1945. Mechanization, employment of chemicals, biological innovation, structural and organizational changes, and an ever closer interlinking with other economic sectors meant that in certain branches the boundaries between agricultural and non-agricultural methods of production disappeared. Despite this basic trend, however, one should not overlook that in northern and western Europe, and especially in eastern and southern Europe, farming is in part still conducted along very traditional lines.

Regional Variations in Agricultural Production

The twentiety-century transition from an extensive production of raw commodities to an intensive production of refined foodstuffs emerged first in northern and western Europe. Denmark and the Netherlands were the pacesetters. They used the agricultural crisis of the late nineteenth century to introduce far-reaching structural changes based on the importation of agricultural raw commodities and the exportation of processed animal and vegetable products. The two countries thereby achieved by the beginning of the century the highest levels of productivity in European agriculture. The other countries reacted to the initial agricultural crisis by imposing protectionist measures, which were then intensified during the subsequent agricultural crisis in the interwar period. The existing framework of production was thereby preserved and the necessary structural changes delayed.

The modernizing drive that all European countries experienced after the Second World War affected above all the methods of production. The composition of production, that is, the crops and animals used, altered considerably more slowly. In the final analysis, the other European countries caught up with the intensive methods of crop raising and livestock rearing long used in Denmark and the Netherlands. Eastern and southern European rural economies had a particularly large gap to bridge. In eastern Europe crop farming, especially of grain and corn, traditionally determined the structure of productivity, although extensively organized livestock rearing played a certain role. Up to 1939 little changed; only after 1945 was grain acreage reduced and intensive crops such as fruits and vegetables planted more widely. Only since the 1960s has livestock rearing increased through the buildup of large factory farms with stall-fed herds.

The modernization of agriculture has made great progress in eastern Europe, but the sought-after "agrarian-industrial complex" was still a long way off in the mid-1980s. The difficulty of changing methods of production in agriculture is demonstrated by the continuing gap in the level of intensity of the farming methods practiced in the individual countries throughout the century. As before, three groups can still be distinguished: the least industrialized Balkan countries with the lowest intensity, highly industrialized Czechoslovakia and East Germany with the highest level, and Poland and Hungary in the middle.

Even further behind western and northern Europe were the southern European countries. Right up to the present, nearly one half of the entire area under cultivation in the south has been devoted to grain. In addition, typical Mediterranean products have been of great importance. Common climatic, topographical, and historical conditions (in Italy primarily in the *mezzogiorno* region) meant that the product composition of agriculture changed extremely slowly and the methods of production remained considerably more backward than elsewhere in Europe.

A characteristic feature of the transition to an agricultural processing industry is the increasing share taken by animal products in the total value-added output of agriculture. In western European countries after 1945 this share fluctuated between 65 percent and 70 percent. It was lowest in France at 50 percent and highest in the Irish Republic at over 80 percent. Since Ireland certainly does not possess an especially progressive agricultural sector, the high Irish share demonstrates that particular structures of production can also determine the relative position of animal and vegetable products. In eastern Europe until into the 1960s the proportion of animal products in total agricultural output remained unchanged or climbed only slightly; in the mid-1980s it averaged around 40 percent, reaching 60 percent in East Germany and Czechoslovakia. In the southern European countries the share is even smaller.

Although the conditions of agricultural production—land quality, climate, operational structures, and so on—in principle provide great scope for product specialization, the emergence of such rationalized, complementary systems of agricultural production has been very slow. Up to the Second World War, in fact, most countries organized their respective agricultures on a national basis. Only in the course of postwar politicoeconomic integration in West and East has a process of specialization gradually set in.

Europe in the World

No reliable data on world agricultural production exist for the years before the Second World War. According to an estimate of the International Institute of Agriculture in Rome, Europe accounted for 30 percent of world agricultural production in 1934–1938; after the war, Europe's share fell to 20 percent. Such global figures are of limited use, of course, since the production of the various agricultural commodities is geographically quite unevenly distributed. For instance, Europe accounts for only a small portion of the world's annual rice crop, yet it grows a considerable proportion of the world's potato output. It is therefore worthwhile recounting relative figures for some specific crops. Before 1914 one third of the world's output of wheat came from Europe (excluding Russia); in 1980, one fifth. Over the same period Europe's share of the world rye crop fell from 56 percent to 46 percent and that of oats from 80 percent to 40 percent. The European contribution to world output in other animal and vegetable products declined as well, so that Europe's overall significance has fallen in the course of the twentieth century. On the other hand, Europe still remains one of the leaders in terms of the intensity of agricultural production. Nowhere else, apart from North America and a few other smaller regions, are such high yields obtained by so little labor; moreover, the productivity of the land itself is exceptionally high, especially in the smaller countries of western and northern Europe.

Industry and Crafts

Industrial and artisanal methods of production differ according to the degree of mechanization, the quantity produced, and the place of the worker in the enterprise. In some instances, goods that were produced in small-scale handicraft workshops at the beginning of the century are today produced in large-scale industrial factories. In other instances, goods produced in one country by individual skilled craftsmen are at the same time produced in another country by mechanized industrial techniques. The boundaries between industrial and artisanal production are thus fluid, and consequently the overview presented here cannot distinguish precisely between industry and crafts. Just as the primary sector is for brevity's sake referred to only as "agriculture," so the secondary sector is frequently described in the single term "industry." The following account adheres to this customary usage, but one must remember that secondary sector comprises not only the manufacturing and processing industries (raw materials, producer goods, capital goods, consumer goods, and foodstuffs) but also mining, construction, and the production of gas, water, and electricity.

General European Development

Industrial production. In Europe since at least the beginning of the Industrial Revolution the course of industrial production has decisively determined overall economic development. Those countries with the highest levels of industrialization have set the tone of the European economy, and those in which agriculture remained the dominant economic activity until well into the twentieth century have played only a secondary role. Unsurprisingly, then, the growth curve of European industrial output paralleled that of national product, although the fluctuations were more pronounced. During the first half of the nineteenth century European industrial output doubled. From the mid-nineteenth century to the First World War it rose four- to fivefold as industrialization spread to more countries and more areas of economic activity. In the forty years from 1913 to 1953 European industrial output doubled despite the effects of two world wars and the Great Depression; and in the following three decades to the mid-1980s, it more than trebled. Looking over the past hundred years, three major phases of growth in industrial output can be discerned, as was the case with national product (see figs. 3.12 and 3.1). In the period before the First

World War industrial output expanded relatively constantly. In the years between the wars the pattern of industrial growth was extremely uneven. The period after the Second World War was marked by a dynamic process of growth that definitely began to slow down only in the second half of the 1970s.

To what extent did the paths of individual national economies deviate from the European norm? A partial answer is provided by the data on the growth of industrial output in several countries presented in figure 3.11. Plainly, all four countries experienced a strong spurt of industrial growth after the Second World War, although in varying intensities. As was the case with national product, the European countries can be separated into several groups depending on the strength of postwar industrial expansion.

Belgium and Britain once again form a distinct grouping; both countries, already highly industrialized at the beginning of the century, have since then experienced a relatively moderate growth of industrial output. A second group, initially not so industrialized, comprises Austria, France, the Netherlands, Norway, Sweden, and Switzerland; in these six countries industrial output after 1945 expanded much faster than in Belgium and Britain, perhaps twice as fast. Industrial product rose even more dynamically in a third heterogeneous group composed of Czechoslovakia, West Germany, Finland, East Germany, Hungary, and Italy. At the beginning of the twentieth century the territories now included in the FRG, the GDR, and the CSSR were among the most industrialized areas of Europe; Italy, Finland, and Hungary, however, were still largely underdeveloped agrarian states. The most dynamic spurt of industrialization occurred in the fourth group of countries, which, apart from a few local or regional concentrations, had practically no industry at the end of the nineteenth century: Greece, Portugal, Spain, and Yugoslavia. As seen in figure 3.11 the trendline of Greece's postwar industrial growth rises far above that of the countries representing the first three groups. A fifth group comprises the remaining eastern European countries whose figures on industrial output are, like those for Czechoslovakia, East Germany, and Hungary, not strictly comparable with Western data due to differing methods of calculation; according to their official statistics, these countries—Bulgaria, Poland, Rumania, and the Soviet Union—experienced exorbitant rates of increase.

It must be emphasized that the curves of industrial production in figure 3.11 were computed for each country individually. Using the

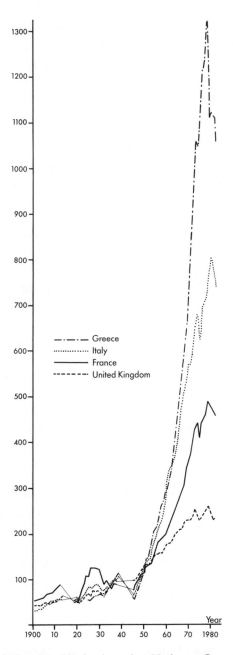

Figure 3.11. Industrial Production in Various Countries, 1901–1982 (1957 = 100). *Sources:* OEEC, *Statistical Bulletins: Industrial Statistics 1900–1959* (Paris, 1960), p. 9; UN, *Statistical Yearbook 1960* (New York, 1961), pp. 82–87; *1967* (New York, 1968), pp. 160–64; *1976* (New York, 1977), pp. 155–59; *1982* (New York, 1984), pp. 585–89.

same index year of 1957 naturally does not mean that the absolute industrial production in that year was the same in all four countries; the levels were in fact extremely unequal. Despite a moderate rate of growth in the twentieth century, British industrial output in the early 1980s was still in absolute terms four times higher than Greek output, whose curve of growth was many times steeper than the British curve.

In some instances, the assignment of countries to one of the groups is problematic. This, however, does not affect the overall trend towards a general convergence of levels of industrialization. Those countries that were more industrialized at the beginning of the century experienced a relatively slow rate of growth throughout the twentieth century, whereas those countries that were less developed in 1900 followed a much more dynamic growth path, especially after 1945. In consequence, the regional disparities prevailing between northern/western and southern/eastern Europe were reduced, as were differences between individual countries. In addition, the geographic distribution of overall industrial output shifted in favor of countries on the European periphery.

To round out the picture and to avoid leaving a false impression, comparative data on the absolute levels of industrial production in all European countries are presented in table 3.8. It shows indexed values calculated using the British industrial output in 1900 as the base value. Despite the slow growth of its industrial sector throughout the twentieth century, Britain was still in 1980 the strongest industrial power in Europe (excluding the Soviet Union) after West Germany. Rumania's industrial product, on the other hand, in spite of enormous growth since 1945, had by 1980 barely exceeded the British output of 1900. Industrial output in Bulgaria, Greece, and Portugal in 1980 roughly equalled the British level of the mid-nineteenth century. Yet these data still show a trend towards reduction of disparities. In 1913 British industrial production was 127 times higher than Greece's, but in 1980 only 17 times higher. The degree of convergence would be even greater if the industrial output were computed on a per capita basis. As with other aggregate data on national product, one must treat the accuracy of these figures with considerable scepticism. Whether, for example, the absolute industrial output of Bulgaria in 1913 amounted to 1 percent of the British level in 1900 or only 0.1 percent cannot really be clarified.

Structure of industrial production. The evolution of the structure of industrial production will be examined first in terms of western Eu-

Table 3.8. Levels of Industrialization by Country, 1913–1980 (in percent; U.K. output for 1900 = 100)

	1913	1928	1938	1953	1963	1973	1980
Northern Europe							
Sweden	9	12	21	28	48	80	83
Denmark	2	5	7	16	24	42	44
Finland	2	4	5	5	17	34	43
Norway	2	3	5	11	15	24	24
Western Europe							
Germany	138	158	214	—	—	—	—
FRG	—	—	—	180	330	550	590
United Kingdom	127	135	181	258	330	462	441
France	57	82	74	98	194	328	362
Belgium	16	22	18	25	41	69	76
Netherlands	4	11	13	24	42	75	84
Austria	—	9	10	15	26	49	59
Switzerland	8	9	9	20	37	57	54
Ireland	—	2	3	4	5	9	12
Eastern Europe							
Poland	—	16	19	31	66	129	169
Yugoslavia	1	5	7	11	32	70	103
Rumania	2	4	5	15	37	85	118
GDR	—	—	—	44	86	125	157
Czechoslovakia	—	22	23	36	65	103	129
Hungary	—	6	9	21	42	69	86
Bulgaria	1	2	3	6	11	21	28
Southern Europe							
Italy	23	37	46	71	150	258	319
Spain	11	16	14	22	43	122	156
Portugal	2	3	4	5	10	23	31
Greece	1	3	4	3	7	20	26
Soviet Union	—	72	152	328	760	1345	1630

Source: Paul Bairoch, "International Industrialisation Levels from 1750 to 1980," *Journal of European Economic History,* 11 (1982): 299, 331.

ropean industry as a whole. Figure 3.12 shows the twentieth-century growth curves not only of overall industrial output but also of the most important branches, or subsectors, of manufacturing industry: chemicals, metal products or metalworking, primary metals, food and beverages, and textiles.

The rapid rise of the chemical and metal products industries is es-

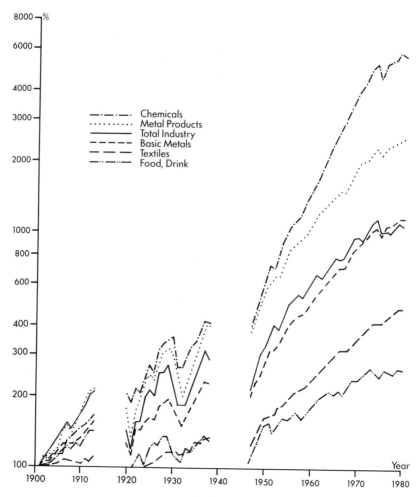

Figure 3.12. Structure of Industrial Production in Western Europe, 1901–1980 (1901 = 100, logarithmic scale). *Sources:* OEEC, *Statistical Bulletins: Industrial Statistics 1900–1959* (Paris, 1960), p. 8; UN, *Statistical Yearbook 1960* (New York, 1961), pp. 82–87; *1967* (New York, 1968), pp. 160–64; *1976* (New York, 1977), pp. 155–59; *1982* (New York, 1984), pp. 585–89.

pecially striking; since 1920 they have persistently increased at a considerably higher rate than that of industry overall. The designation "chemical industry" includes not only the production of basic industrial chemicals such as sulfuric acid but also the manufacturing of synthetics such as rubber and plastics. The subsector "metal products, machinery, and equipment" is composed of a conglomeration of products and branches: machine construction, vehicle construction, electronics, electrical machinery, shipbuilding, aerospace, precision engineering, optics, office equipment, and data processing, among others. Compared with the levels at the beginning of the century, production in each of these subsectors had risen fourfold by 1939. Between 1939 and 1980 output in the chemical industry rose another fourteenfold, making the total increase of output since 1900 almost sixtyfold. Output in the metalworking industry over this eighty-year period expanded almost as much with a fifty-fivefold increase. By contrast, overall industrial output in western Europe grew only tenfold between 1900 and 1980. Whereas the rates of growth for metalworking, primary metals, and overall industry roughly paralleled one another, food and beverages and textiles grew considerably more slowly; in consequence the total growth over the century was only fivefold and threefold respectively. The growth curves for mining and energy (oil, gas, and electricity) have not been included in figure 3.12. Mining output followed the pace of the textile industry. The energy subsector's rate of growth, however, exceeded even that of the chemical industry, its total output between 1900 and 1980 increased eighty-fivefold.

This diversity in rates of growth shifted the composition of overall industrial output. The changes that occurred in the manufacturing sector are indicated by the data in table 3.9. At the beginning of the century food and beverages and textiles taken together still accounted for almost 50 percent of western European industrial production; by 1975 their share had been more than halved to 17 percent. The relative position of chemical and metal products changed almost inversely to that of food and textiles; it amounted to 21 percent of total industrial output in 1901 and rose to 53 percent in 1975. The share of primary metals remained more or less constant, ranging between 7 percent and 10 percent.

From a long-term perspective these changes indicated a fundamental transformation of western European industrialization. Those branches that were the focal point of nineteenth-century industrialization and carried the process forward—mining, textiles, and food processing—

Table 3.9.   Sectoral Development of Industry in Western Europe, 1901–1975
(in percent of value of production)

	1901	1913	1929	1937	1953	1961	1975
Food, drink	27	19	16	15	14	13	12
Textiles	20	18	14	12	9	7	5
Metals production	7	10	10	10	8	8	8
Metalworking	16	24	27	28	33	35	38
Chemicals	5	6	10	10	10	13	15
Other	25	24	23	25	26	25	22

Sources: V. Paretti and G. Bloch, "Industrial Production in Western Europe and the United States, 1901–1955," *Banca Nazionale del Lavoro Quarterly Review,* 9 (1956): 205; UN (ECE), *Structure and Change in European Industry* (New York, 1977), pp. 103–104; UN, *The Growth of World Industry* (later *Yearbook of Industrial Statistics) 1962* (New York, 1964); *1976* (New York, 1978).

lost ground during the twentieth century. Their central roles were gradually taken over by the chemical and metalworking industries, whose importance was only beginning to become evident at the end of the nineteeth century but that today form the core of a modern industrial structure. In this historical development structural change and growth in output were interconnected: the faster the rise in total industrial output, the more rapid the transformation of industrial structure. Structural change was slowest in the troubled interwar economy and accelerated during the postwar boom, slacking off only after the mid-1970s.

Bringing the state socialist countries of Eastern Europe into the discussion would not substantially alter the general pattern of industrial development just outlined. This is not to say that no differences exist between the industrial structure of Western and Eastern Europe.

Europe in the world. Europe is the cradle of the Industrial Revolution, which began in the eighteenth century in northwestern Europe, chiefly England, and spread southeastwards. For a long time the rest of the world was not able to industrialize, with the exception of areas settled by Europeans, chiefly North America. The European share of world industrial output rose to almost 60 percent by 1914 (see table 3.10). Five countries alone accounted for 75 percent: France, 6.1 percent; Germany, 14.8; Britain, 13.6 percent; Russia, 8.2 percent; and the United States, 32 percent. As a consequence of the First World War the distribution shifted further in favor of the United States. The

European share fell to under 50 percent, but it recovered somewhat during the interwar period despite the Great Depression.

The effects of the Second World War on Europe's position in world industry paralled those of the First. During the immediate postwar years, when Europe's economy lay devastated, easily half of the world's industrial production occurred in North America. In spite of rapid reconstruction Europe's share of world industry was no more than 42 percent in 1953. The "economic miracle" of the 1950s and 1960s enabled Europe to regain the relative level it had held at the end of the 1920s, namely 47 percent, but by 1980 the European contribution to world industrial output had slipped back to 44 percent. During these years the United States lost even more ground than Europe, its share falling from 45 percent in 1953 to 32 percent in 1980. Thus, world industrial output has become geographically somewhat less concentrated. In the early 1950s—the high point of geographic concentration—9 percent of the world's population (Canada, Britain, Sweden, Switzerland, and the United States) produced 57 percent of worldwide total industrial product; in 1980 these countries produced only 36 percent. Nonetheless, the predominance of Europe and North America

Table 3.10. Shares of European Countries in World Industrial Production, 1913–1980 (in percent)

	1913	1928	1938	1953	1963	1980
Belgium	1.8	1.7	1.1	0.8	0.8	0.7
FRG	—	—	—	5.9	6.4	5.3
Germany	14.8	11.6	12.7	—	—	—
France	6.1	6.0	4.4	3.2	3.8	3.3
United Kingdom	13.6	9.9	10.7	8.4	6.4	4.0
Italy	2.4	2.7	2.8	2.3	2.9	2.9
Sweden	1.0	0.9	1.2	0.9	0.9	0.8
Spain	1.2	1.1	0.8	0.7	0.8	1.4
Switzerland	0.9	0.7	0.5	0.7	0.7	0.5
Eastern Europe (excl. USSR)	7.6	7.2	7.3	5.3	6.7	6.3
Russia/USSR	8.2	5.3	9.0	10.7	14.2	14.8
Total Europe	57.6	47.1	53.6	42.1	47.4	44.0
United States	32.0	39.3	31.4	44.7	35.1	31.5
Japan	2.7	3.3	5.2	2.9	5.1	9.1
Rest of world	7.5	7.2	7.2	6.5	8.5	12.0

Source: Paul Bairoch, "International Industrialisation Levels from 1750 to 1980," *Journal of European Economic History,* 11 (1982): 304.

in world industry has not fundamentally changed throughout the twentieth century.

Regional and National Development before 1945

Western Europe. In the countries of western Europe the industrial sector was already of primary economic importance at the beginning of the twentieth century. In Britain it employed under 50 percent of the labor force, in Belgium and Switzerland about 45 percent, and in Germany 40 percent. Industrial employment was noticeably lower in France, the Netherlands, and Austria, but in these countries its share of the national work force still amounted to approximately one third. Only in Ireland, whose economic structure resembled that of the agrarian states of southern Europe, was industry very weak, employing only 15 percent of the country's labor force. In striking contrast to developments in the other European regions, the relative strength of the industrial work force in western Europe changed little up to the Second World War. In addition, during the interwar period industrial output rose more slowly in western Europe than elsewhere; only Dutch industry approached the growth rates occurring in most countries of northern, southern, and eastern Europe. Of course, one must remember that the absolute level of industrial output before 1939 was much higher in the western European economies than in the other major regions, and that it is easier to obtain high growth rates in a developing economy than in an advanced one.

The process of industrial growth before the First World War was broadly similar in all countries. After the war, Britain, Germany, and Austria had the most difficult time. But Germany and Austria, along with Belgium and France, were able to accelerate industrialization in the second half of the 1920s. The British industrial economy stagnated largely because of its obsolescent structure. A large part of domestic capital and four fifths of the industrial work force were concentrated in coal mining, shipbuilding, and textiles—that is, in areas whose importance would decline as the structural transformation of modern industry evolved and, even more important in the short run, which were heavily export-oriented and encountered serious difficulties in the increasingly protectionist world market of the 1920s and 1930s. For the British economy the interwar period was a time of transition from the old nineteenth-century industrial structure to a modern one, but the pace at which this proceeded was slower than elsewhere.

The course of industrialization was quite different in France, where up to the First World War advances had been made in only a few branches of the economy. The war, the reacquisition of Alsace-Lorraine, and the rapid rise of industrial output during the 1920s brought about such substantial structural change that people even spoke of a "second industrial revolution." The share of output contributed by producer and capital goods industries as well as by metalworking and chemicals expanded while that contributed by consumer and luxury goods, including food and beverages and textiles, declined. The application of the latest technologies led to considerable increases in productivity. During the Great Depression not only did this surge in industrial output collapse but also the process of industrial structural change first slowed, then stopped, and in some instances were even reversed. This did not happen in Germany, where structural change continued throughout the 1930s. The National Socialist rearmament policy directed a large part of available investment capital into the producer and capital goods industries. Machine construction, electronics, chemicals, toolmaking, and other modern branches of industry benefited from this deliberate management of capital and labor. Together with the Netherlands, in the first half of the century, Germany underwent the most pronounced change in industrial structure of all national economies in western Europe.

Northern Europe. Throughout northern Europe the secondary sector's role was more or less the same in the individual national economies. At the beginning of the century between 25 percent and 32 percent of the Danish, Norwegian, and Swedish labor force was engaged in industrial or artisanal occupations; these proportions rose insignificantly up to the Second World War. Finland, until 1918 part of the Russian empire, constituted an exception; the share of its work force in industry was only 10 percent before the First World War and rose to 20 percent by 1939.

Both agricultural and industrial output attained an initial highpoint in northern Europe during the First World War. The recovery from the collapse of the war boom was very slow, but from the mid-1920s until 1940 industry in all four northern European countries expanded at a rate above the average for western Europe. The Scandinavian economies were relatively less damaged by the world economic crisis of the 1930s than other European economies. Sweden and, above all, Finland underwent a particularly favorable industrial development in the interwar years: between 1913 and 1939 manufacturing output more than doubled and trebled respectively. During the same period in Denmark it barely doubled; in Norway, the hardest hit by the Great Depression, manufacturing output rose by only 70 percent.

Productivity fluctuated in the decade after 1910 and in the 1930s, both rising and falling; by contrast, it increased in all countries in the 1920s. An important initial stimulant for the expansion of productivity was the introduction of the eight-hour day, in place of the ten-hour-day in 1918–1919 just as wages increased, industrial prices declined, and foreign competition intensified; in logical consequence, costs of production rose, and profits fell. To counter this situation, entrepreneurs adopted strong rationalizing measures that resulted in increased industrial output at lower cost. The industrial expansion of the 1920s concentrated on the export market, that of the 1930s more on domestic consumption. By the 1930s all four countries had adopted national economic policies featuring protectionist measures such as foreign exchange controls and import restrictions, and these, in turn, stimulated the spread of an autocentric, import-substituting industrialization.

Structural transformation, the central development trend in modern industry, was also evident in northern Europe. The relative size of output in food and beverages and textiles fell, that of metalworking and chemicals rose. But, of course, the individual economies did have different starting configurations. In Sweden these two contrasting major industrial groupings were in 1913 roughly on an equal footing, each accounting for 30 percent of the total value-added product of manufacturing industry. Up to the Second World War, metalworking, especially machine construction, expanded its output; in some fields Swedish products gained worldwide recognition for embodying the latest competitive technology. One of the leading economic branches in Sweden, as in all Scandinavian countries, was the forest products industry, which during the first half of the twentieth century completed the shift from simple production of lumber to the manufacturing of paper and cellulose. Thus, within individual industries themselves there was a move towards products that entailed a higher degree of processing and refining. By 1939 Sweden not only was the most industrialized country in northern Europe, but it also had the most diversified industrial structure and the highest degree of business concentration.

In Norway at the beginning of the century foods and textiles contributed 40 percent of the country's industrial output, a level twice as high as that of metalworking and chemicals. But the abundant water power available for the generation of electricity created favorable conditions for certain areas of industry: electrochemicals, electrometallurgy, and electrotechnology. In consequence, during the interwar period the production of both ferrous and non-ferrous metals (especially aluminum) increased greatly as did the output of both lumber and finished forestry products. By the Second World War the relative positions of the two major industrial groupings had reversed, with metalworking and chemicals becoming twice as important as foods and textiles.

In Denmark the food and beverage industry accounted for over half of all industrial output in 1900. In the latter half of the nineteenth century the modernization of agriculture and the shift to the processing and refining of food products got industrialization underway and promoted the growth of consumer goods industries. During the decade after the First World War capital goods' share of total industrial production expanded to exceed that of consumer goods. This process of industrial structural change slowed by the 1930s. Nonetheless, the share of metalworking and chemicals in the Danish industrial output rose from 10 percent in 1900 to 30 percent in 1939.

In Finland only the barest outline of an industrial base was evident at the beginning of the century: sawmills and factories for cellulose, rubber, veneers, and cement. Although up to 1939 Finnish industry had the strongest growth in all Scandinavia, its structure changed very little. The consumer goods industry, based on small-scale, labor-intensive enterprises, was dedicated almost entirely to the domestic market. The shift from simple lumber production to semi-finished and finished forestry products was virtually the only structural transformation in Finnish industry during the interwar period.

Southern Europe. In general, at the beginning of the twentieth century the secondary sector was relatively weaker in economies of southern Europe than in those of northern and western Europe. The industrial work force represented 27 percent of all employment in Italy, 22 percent in Portugal, 16 percent in Greece, and 14 percent in Spain. By the early 1930s Spanish industry had expanded to employ 26 percent and Italian industry to employ 31 percent of their respective national work forces: in Portugal and Greece no significant change occurred. The figures on employment cannot, however, be translated directly into growth of industrial output. Italian industrial production climbed rapidly in the 1920s but fell sharply in the Great Depression, and at the end of the 1930s was barely higher than at the end of the 1920s. Spain's industry grew more slowly than Italy's and was not so hard hit by the world economic crisis, but the civil war that started in 1936 brought about a catastrophic drop in industrial output to about half the level of 1913. Greek industry expanded rather rapidly throughout the interwar period despite its unchanging share of the country's labor force. Industrial output in Portugal, about which little data exist, seems to have risen moderately.

At the beginning of the century the southern European secondary sector was overwhelmingly based on small workshops and artisanal methods of production; there was little industrial plant in the sense of large-scale mechanized factories. The production of food and beverages and textiles was of supreme importance and remained so up to the Second World War. In Italy and Spain the share of these low technology branches in total industrial output declined from 60 percent before 1914 to 40 percent in the late 1930s, but in Portugal and Greece the proportion remained unchanged at two thirds throughout the interwar years.

Structural and geographic heterogeneity were a further characteristic of southern European industry. The Italian and Spanish economies began to industrialize seriously in the first half of the century, but only on a local or regional basis. Industry was strongly concentrated in northern Italy (Lombardy, Piedmont, Liguria, and Veneto) and in Catalonia and the Basque country; for example, in 1911 Lombardy alone contained over one fifth of all industrial workers in Italy. The First World War sparked the beginnings of structural change in Italian industry. The fastest growing branches in the secondary sector was machine construction, vehicle construction, and shipbuilding. The chemical industry grew as well, and the output of sulfuric acid, phosphate, and synthetic fibers achieved a level impressive even by world standards. Yet despite this expansion in the producer and capital goods industries, textiles remained the largest single industrial branch, and up to the Second World War the food and beverages branch contributed a higher proportion of the total value-added output of industry than the production of iron and steel.

During the first third of the century the mining industry in Spain stagnated, but the output of manufacturing industries expanded moderately. This implies that export-oriented industries tended to decline, and that industries oriented to domestic demand began to grow. The most important capital goods industries in Spain were locomotive construction, bridge and shipbuilding, and construction of agricultural machinery and machine tools. The most important products of the consumer goods industries were food and beverages, leather, paper, and soap. The Spanish chemical industry primarily produced soda and ammonia salts, aniline, and other products used in the textile industry.

Industrialization in Greece and Portugal in the first half of the century remained rudimentary by comparison. The large food and beverage industry in these two countries made little progress in the adoption of higher stages of processing and refining; it stuck with the production of olive oil, wine and other alcoholic beverages, flour, and confections. The next most important branch of the countries' secondary sector was textile production. It operated in both countries with obsolete, inefficient machines and was not internationally competitive; in Greece it served the domestic market exclusively, whereas in Portugal it enjoyed a monopoly of supply in the country's overseas colonies as well. A few other branches of industrial production had a certain importance: chemicals (soap, turpentine, and rosin), leather, footwear, paper and printing, milling, and, in Portugal, cork. Before the Second World War neither country had a producer and capital goods industry to speak of.

Eastern Europe. Eastern Europe's industry was also extremely underdeveloped at the beginning of the century. In Rumania, Bulgaria, Yugoslavia, and Poland a mere 8–10 percent of the labor force were employed in industry and crafts; in Hungary, about 20 percent. Czechoslovakia, the most industrialized country of the region, had about one third of its work force in the secondary sector. Up to the Second World War these proportions rose somewhat overall, but the short-term fluctuations in industrial growth were considerable. The First World War brought not only physical destruction but also political, social, and economic upheavals associated with the breakup of the Austro-Hungarian and Russian empires and the emergence of new states. The economic benefits after the war were illusory because of inflation and devaluation, and most of the eastern European countries (Bulgaria and Czechoslovakia being the exceptions) did not regain 1913 levels of industrial output until the second half of the 1920s. The Great Depression affected industry in eastern Europe diversely. In Rumania industrial output declined somewhat, but in Bulgaria it rose slightly, primarily because petroleum production increased. Yugoslavia was affected more heavily; Czechoslovakia, as the most industrialized country with considerable foreign trade in industrial goods, was hardest hit. The effects on Polish and Hungarian industry were rather less. Overall, eastern Europe industrial output in the 1930s increased more strongly than western Europe's. The fact that industrialization was just beginning in most of the eastern European countries qualifies the significance of this faster growth, however. In Bulgaria, for example, the entire value-added industrial product at the end of the 1920s still amounted to only one fifth of the value of the grain harvest or one tenth of the total agricultural output.

Despite the differences between the individual national economies, certain common characteristics did exist in the industrial structure of all eastern European countries. As in southern Europe the absolutely dominant branches of the economy were food and beverages and textiles. At late as 1938–1939 their share of total industrial product far exceeded 50 percent in most countries. The food and beverage industry were especially significant in the agrarian states of Yugoslavia, Rumania, and Bulgaria, where flour, sugar, tobacco, and distilled spirits were the most important products. With reservations this applied to Hungary as well, whereas in Poland and Czechoslovakia the textile industry occupied first place. Third place in all countries was taken by the production of industrial raw materials. Especial progress was achieved in the output of coal and mineral oil, iron and steel, and cement. Output of wood and wood products was also not unimportant, especially in Yugoslavia, Rumania, and Poland. The remaining branches of industry were of far lesser importance. The lack of production of highly refined industrial goods was an important hindrance to autocentric industrialization; this applied particularly to the underdeveloped state of the metalworking and chemical branches. There were exceptions, of course. In Hungary, where machine construction and the electrical industry began to play a limited role, the production of agricultural machinery was far advanced, as was textile machinery in Poland. With the partial exception of Czechoslovakia, the structure of industry in the countries of eastern Europe was generally one-dimensional and uneven. Low-quality, unsophisticated consumer goods dominated industrial production; higher quality capital goods were just beginning to appear.

The production structure of eastern European industry were imbalanced in yet another respect. As in southern Europe, a multitude of small-scale craft enterprises were juxtaposed with a few large industrial factories. This dualistic structure, a pronounced feature of eastern European economies since the late nineteenth century, hardly changed at all during the interwar period. Despite their low levels of productivity, the small enterpises remained viable because of the sufficient supply of cheap labor. The structure of domestic demand for industrial products also favored the small workshops and prevented the larger enterprises from benefiting from theoretically greater productivity; methods of modern mass production were hardly developed, and the majority of large firms served the very limited domestic market with a large variety of goods produced in small numbers.

In this respect Czechoslovakia once again does not really fit the model of the "typical" eastern European economy, and Poland and Hungary do only with reservations. Large areas of western Czechoslovakia were highly industrialized; machine construction and the electrical industry were quite advanced, and agricultural machinery, locomotives, and armaments were produced in large quantity. Czechoslovakia was additionally a major producer of consumer goods. All things considered, interwar Czechoslovakia should be treated as half-belonging to western Europe.

Regional and National Development after 1945
The following discussion of post-1945 industrial growth compares western and northern Europe as a unit with southern Europe and eastern Europe. It is largely based on UN studies and, very importantly, in contrast with previous usage in this book counts Italy as part of industrialized northern/western Europe instead of southern Europe.

Industrial production. Industrial output developed in all three European regions along roughly parallel lines. Over the period as a whole, from 1945 to roughly 1985, eastern Europe expanded its industrial output most rapidly and northern/western Europe most slowly. Except for southern Europe (Greece, Portugal, and Spain), the highest rates of growth were achieved in the 1950s, after which the pace of expansion slowed. In the countries of southern Europe, however, industrial output grew even faster in the 1960s than in the decade before. The decline in growth rates was not constant. A definite break in the trend occurred in 1974–1975; this is downplayed in table 3.11 because it shows the average of widely deviating annual rates over the time period 1971–1975. The growth of industrial employment also slackened. In southern and eastern Europe the absolute size of the industrial work force continued to increase into the 1980s, but in northern/western Europe it had begun to fall in the early 1970s.

The expansion of industrial output in capitalist Western Europe as a whole (northern/western and southern) was more closely tied to advances in productivity than was the case in state socialist Eastern Europe, even though productivity in these latter national economies

Table 3.11. Industrial Production and Industrial Employment by Region, 1949–1982 (mean of average annual rates of change in percent)

| | 1950–60[a] | | 1961–70 | | 1971–75 | | 1976–82[b] | |
	Prod.	Empl	Prod.	Empl	Prod.	Empl	Prod.	Empl
Western/northern Europe	5.6	1.6	5.5	0.7	2.7	−0.5	1.3	−1.4
Eastern Europe	11.5	4.6	8.5	2.9	8.5	2	4.4	0.7
Southern Europe	6.5	2	9.4	2	6.2	1.6	2.8	0.3

Sources: OECD, *Historical Statistics 1960–1981* (Paris, 1983), pp. 28, 45; UN (ECE), *Economic Survey of Europe in 1961,* part 2 (New York, 1962), chap. 3, p. 6; *1983* (New York, 1984), pp. 142–47; UN (ECE), *Structure and Change in European Industry* (New York, 1977), pp. 250–53.

[a] Western/northern Europe and southern Europe 1949–1959.
[b] Western/northern Europe and southern Europe 1975–1981.

climbed especially rapidly during the 1950s. Fundamentally, industrialization in the 1950s and 1960s took place in all countries through the application of labor-intensive as well as capital-intensive methods of production. Wider use of capital-intensive inputs began in the 1960s, but not until the introduction of revolutionary production technologies in the 1970s did a broadly based deepening of industrial capital occur so that proportionally more capital than labor was used to produce national output. Since then, European industry has been in the throes of a far-reaching structural change that has been determined more than ever by technical progress.

Industrial structure. Shifts in industrial structure followed a broadly similar pattern in all countries: the share of output taken by basic materials and producer and capital goods—especially metalworking and chemicals—continued to grow; that of the consumer goods industries—especially food and beverage, textiles, and clothing—declined (see table 3.12). Structural change occurred most rapidly where output itself rose the fastest, namely in the less developed economies. In consequence, industrial structures became increasingly alike throughout Europe.

Despite this process of convergence, differences persist between individual countries and between the major socioeconomic regions. In industrialized northern/western Europe, for a long time only the production of chemicals increased noticeably faster than total industrial output. Increases in metalworking production as a whole were not above average, although there were large differences of performance

Table 3.12. Production and Employment in Industrial Sectors by Region, 1950–1978 (in percent, total industry = 100)

| | 1950–52 | | | | | | 1958–60 | | | | | |
| | Production | | | Employment | | | Production | | | Employment | | |
	EE	IWE	SE	EE	IWE	SE	EE	IWE	SE	EE	IEW	SE
Metalworking	18	34	16	32	32	17	25	36	23	34	35	24
Chemicals	5	10	11	5	5	5	6	10	12	5	7	7
Textiles and light industry	34	26	41	38	36	51	29	24	35	35	32	41
Food, drink	30	14	19	12	12	17	26	13	16	11	11	17
Metals production	10	8	5	7	6	4	10	8	6	7	7	4
Other	3	9	7	6	9	7	4	9	8	8	9	9

| | 1967–69 | | | | | | 1976–78 | | | | | |
| | Production | | | Employment | | | Production | | | Employment | | |
	EE	IWE	SE	EE	IWE	SE	EE	IWE	SE	EE	IEW	SE
Metalworking	33	36	28	40	38	28	40	42	32	43	41	35
Chemicals	8	14	14	6	8	7	11	14	15	7	10	8
Textiles and light industry	23	22	28	30	28	38	19	19	23	25	26	33
Food, Drink	21	12	13	11	10	14	14	11	13	10	10	12
Metals production	10	7	6	7	6	4	8	7	8	4	7	5
Other	4	10	11	7	9	9	8	7	9	10	6	8

Sources: UN (ECE), *Economic Survey of Europe in 1971*, part 1: *The European Economy from the 1950s to the 1970s* (New York, 1972), pp. 43–45; UN, *The Growth of World Industry* (later *Yearbook of Industrial Statistics*) *1962* (New York, 1964); *1972* (New York, 1974); *1982* (New York, 1984); UN (ECE), *Economic Survey of Europe in 1980* (New York, 1981), pp. 227–29.

Note: EE = eastern Europe; WNE = industrialized western/northern Europe, including Italy; SE = southern Europe.

within this very heterogeneous grouping. For example, the output of machines, vehicles, and electrical and electronic appliances increased faster than the overall industrial norm. By contrast, in eastern as well as in southern Europe, both chemicals and metalworking grew faster than average industrial production. Production of primary metals, especially of iron and steel, also developed at differing rates. The deliberate creation of an independent heavy industry in the eastern European states, a policy also followed by southern European states to a lesser extent, resulted in an output curve of metals matching that of total industrial product. In northern/western Europe, on the other hand, metals production rose more slowly than industrial output as a whole. In all three regions the output of textiles, light industrial goods, and food and beverages expanded at below-average rates. The growth patterns of employment in each of these three branches roughly mirrored those of its output, although the differing levels of labor productivity in the branches diminished the degree of variation.

The process of structural convergence, however, is not a universal phenomenon applicable at all times to all types of industrial structure. Moreover, the identification of convergence is influenced by the definition of branches and subsectors within the industrial structure; differences often emerge when large groupings are broken down into their various components. Thus, although the so-called OECD profile of industrial structure has established itself in all industrialized countries in northern/western Europe to such an extent that using its relatively specific definitions of economic branches brings out few differences between individual countries, nonetheless during the 1960s the relative str— gths of chemicals, machines, and textiles in the overall industrial structure did vary. Also, despite the increasing structural similarity between northern/western and southern Europe, a smaller proportion of output in metalworking and a larger proportion in textile and light industrial goods continued to characterize industrial structure in southern Europe. Ironically, in the 1980s the relatively most competitive branches of industrial production, next to specific areas of chemicals and metalworking, are precisely those branches that are designated "sensitive areas" in the EEC and subjected to appropriate crisis regulation: iron and steel, shipbuilding, textiles, and clothing.

Likewise, the process of convergence in the countries of eastern Europe has not led to completely identical industrial structures. Relative levels of production in the more advanced branches of the chemicals and metalworking industries, electrotechnology, and electronics still reflect national differences in overall economic development; unsurprisingly, they are highest in Czechoslovakia, East Germany, and Hungary. Moreover, a clear change in development strategy occurred in the 1970s in most eastern European countries: the production of consumer goods, long neglected, was given a higher priority and grew rapidly in consequence, thereby shifting the relationship between rates of growth in producer and consumer goods in favor of the latter.

The growing similarity of national industrial structures has diminished the degree of industrial specialization in individual economies.

Nonetheless, some countries continue to have branches of industry whose proportion of total industrial output or of the total industrial work force is either under or over the European average. Specialization of this kind, though, says nothing about the absolute weight of the particular branch within the context of the European economy as a whole nor anything about the specialization in individual goods. For example, the share of chemicals in the total industrial output of West Germany corresponds to the European average, yet the West German chemicals industry is one of Europe's preeminent producers in the branch. In Finland machine construction is relatively underrepresented on a European scale, yet it is an international leader in the technology of ships' turbines. Many additional examples could be cited. In the Eastern European economies the level of industrial specialization with respect to separate branches also declined, but in the 1970s a policy of product specialization was initiated. As a result, Comecon countries purchase the majority of their buses from Hungary, their diesel motors from Rumania, and their gas and steam turbines from Czechoslovakia.

The economies of eastern Europe, particularly southeastern Europe, and of southern Europe still suffer from the heterogeneity of their industrial structures. Large numbers of small and medium-sized concerns in need of modernization face a few modern big businesses. Although the share of traditional, labor-intensive enterprises has fallen steadily throughout the postwar years, they still predominate in some industrial branches and geographic regions. In this respect they lag substantially behind countries in northern/western Europe.

General development. By dividing the various branches of industry into four major groupings a general development pattern of structural changes in twentieth-century European industry can be discerned. The first grouping comprises all those branches that experienced a continual fall in their relative position in the total industrial output and total industrial work force throughout the course of the century: food, beverages, and tobacco; textiles; leather goods; ceramics; quarrying; and glass products. These branches played a central role in the early phase of industrialization. At low levels of economic development the income elasticity of demand for these goods was relatively high. Income elasticity relates changes in demand for a particular product to changes in income; a highly income elastic demand for food items would mean that with rising incomes a higher proportion of income will be spent on food. Individual goods or groups of goods, however, do not perpetually retain the same income elasticity; a person's demand for food, for example, ultimately reaches a saturation point beyond which increased income will not increase demand. In the case of the products in this first group, their initially high income elasticity receded as economic development expanded. Consequently, the overall economic importance of these branches declined first relatively, then absolutely.

The second grouping contains branches whose share of output and employment dropped over the long term but whose decline has recently levelled out or even reversed itself. These include certain sections of the food industry; the footwear, clothing, furniture, and paper industries; and a miscellaneous group manufacturing toys and games, sports equipment, and musical instruments, among other products. In general, this grouping produces primarily higher quality consumer goods. The income elasticity of demand for goods made by these relatively labor-intensive branches rose once again after a high per capita income was reached.

Included in the third grouping are those branches of industry whose relative position increased over decades and only recently stagnated or even slipped back slightly: rubber products, oil refining, and the processing of mineral-oil and coal products. However, the development of these branches cannot be assessed straightforwardly, for it varied considerably from country to country.

The fourth grouping brings together the branches whose output and work force have risen continually both relatively and absolutely, namely, chemicals and metalworking (especially the construction of machinery and tools). The income elasticity of these branches' products has remained constantly high.

The usual criterion for measuring a country's level of economic development and hence assigning it a certain type of industrial structure is per capita income. Of course, not all countries with effectively equal per capita incomes have the same industrial structures (contrast Kuwait with Switzerland); there are other determining factors as well. One is the level of industrialization as measured by the relative size of the industrial work force. Increases in the importance of chemicals, iron and steel, or electrotechnological products were more closely related to the expansion of overall industrialization than to rises in per capita income. Plainly, production linkages in the industrial sector favored the growth of demand for the products of these branches. The relative importance of the output of food and beverages and timber and woodworking products, on the other hand, fell as the degree of industrialization rose.

Population size is another determining variable. It was positively correlated with the development of a number of industrial branches, notably oil refining, machine construction, automobile production, and precision instruments, chemicals, and optics. Evidently, the scale of the domestic market played an important role here. In general, countries with large populations have a more diversified industrial production than countries with small populations. Export trade has also been an important factor, as has the presence of natural resources in some countries. The key role of the wood, pulp, and paper industry in the Scandinavian countries is clearly due to their large expanses of high-quality forests. Specific artisanal traditions, consumer preferences, and other national peculiarities must also be considered in order to explain the actual development of each particular country's industrial structure.

The development pattern just outlined applies to the highly industrialized states of northern and western Europe. Despite the variety of explanatory factors, it does seem that the less developed economies of eastern and southern Europe are also following this path of structural change. In every country, food, drink, and tobacco, leather goods, and textiles are among those branches that first industrialized their methods of production. Those branches that typically follow in a second round of industrialization are non-metallic mineral products, rubber goods, and wood, chemical, oil, and coal products. The areas of clothing, paper and printing, and primary metals and metal products usually are latecomers to industrialization. Figure 3.13 presents an ideal-typical overview of the development of this central process of structural change in western Europe over the last century.

Services

The tertiary sector produces not material goods but rather customer services. In the course of the twentieth century its significance has steadily increased such that today the majority of employed persons in almost every European country work in this sector. It covers very diverse branches of economic activity including trade, transportation, money and banking, insurance, public administration, education, scientific research, health services, law, communications, and numerous other public and private services. The selection of activities to be discussed here is somewhat arbitrary. Trade, transport, and money and banking are more or less traditional branches of the service sector; on the other hand, communication has assumed great economic impor-

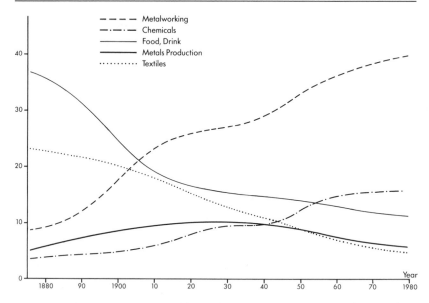

Figure 3.13. Structural Change in Western European Industry, 1880–1980 (in percent). *Sources:* UN, *The Growth of World Industry* (later *Yearbook of Industrial Statistics*) *1962* (New York, 1964); *1972* (New York, 1974); *1982* (New York, 1984); V. Paretti and G. Bloch, "Industrial Production in Western Europe and the United States 1901 to 1955," *Banca Nazionale del Lavorno Quarterly Review,* 9 (1956): 186–88.

tance only since the Second World War. The topics chosen are also the ones about which historical information is the fullest. However, the decisive element is that the branches examined below are directly connected with economic growth and are therefore accessible to economic argumentation, a property not shared by all forms of service.

Trade

The following discussion focuses entirely on foreign trade, primarily on the export and import of commodities. Trade in commodities and services constitutes only one part of external economic relations; yet despite the close integration of the world major financial markets, it remains the most important single indicator of economic relations between states. This is particularly true of Europe, for the limited scale of its separate national economies makes the continent's economic development especially dependent upon the intensive exchange of goods.

Volume of trade. Figure 3.14 presents data on the value of exports

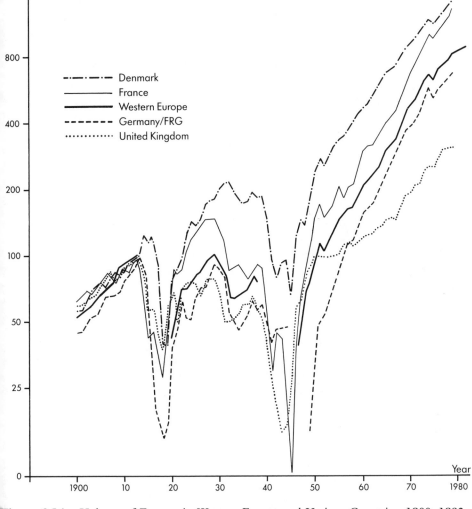

Figure 3.14. Volume of Exports in Western Europe and Various Countries, 1900–1982 (1913 = 100, logarithmic scale). *Sources:* Angus Maddison, *Phases of Capitalist Development* (Oxford, 1984), pp. 248–53; UN, *Yearbook of International Trade Statistics 1982* (New York, 1984).

in western Europe as a whole and in various European countries over the course of the century; the curves are indexed using 1913 as the base year and are presented on a logarithmic scale so that the slopes of the curves represent growth rates. From the mid-nineteenth century until 1913 the volume of trade in western Europe grew strongly and steadily except for a slacking from the mid-1870s to the mid-1890s. The First World War then caused such a drastic disruption of European trade that 1913 trade volumes were not regained generally until 1928. The sharp downturn that soon followed, caused by the Great Depression, was still not overcome in most countries by 1939. Thus, European trade throughout the entire interwar period equalled its pre-World War I volume only during a few years at the end of the 1920s. During the Second World War trade between European countries collapsed once again for the third time within a generation. From the end of the 1940s trade volumes rose as steadily as they had fallen; moreover, apart from a few minor reverses, the rise has continued steadily into the 1980s, although the pace has weakened slightly since the mid-1970s. Individual countries followed different paths, of course, but, as the data in figure 3.13 demonstrate, the overall pattern of growth was quite similar in many cases.

Integration and disengagement. The enormous rise in the absolute volume of trade throughout the century is not necessarily associated with an increasing integration or internationalization of the European economies. If foreign trade rises or falls at the same rate as does national product, then the share of exported or imported goods and services in the country's total output remains constant. The degree of integration, defined as the proportion of exports and imports in total product, would thus be unchanged. To trace the evolution of the integration of the western European economies, an index of export volume in relation to national product was created using 1913 as base year; the value of 100 indicates that the degree of integration was unchanged; values above 100 signify a higher level of integration and internationalization, and values below 100 a lower level (see fig. 3.15).

The curve in figure 3.15 indicates plainly the enormous drop-off of economic integration in the interwar period; even with the aid of the GATT, Marshall Plan, EEC, and EFTA, the western European economies regained the 1913 level of integration and internationalization only in the mid-1970s, and then surpassed it. What is true for western Europe is in principle valid for the rest of the European countries, although with certain exceptions. Measuring integration in terms of quotas of foreign trade—that is, total export and import trade in relation to national product—results in fundamentally the same conclusion. If total national output of commodities alone is used as denominator, then the degree of integration in the 1970s was actually substantially higher than shown here, for in the course of the century

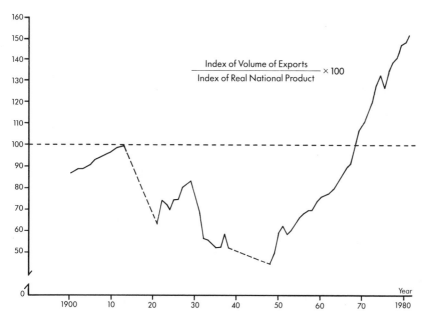

Figure 3.15. Internationalization of the Western European Economy, 1900–1982 (1913 = 100). *Sources:* UN (ECE), *Growth and Stagnation in the European Economy,* by Ingvar Svennilson (Geneva, 1954), p. 292; UN, *Yearbook of International Trade Statistics 1964–1982* (New York, 1965–1984); Paul Bairoch, "Europe's Gross National Product 1800–1975," *Journal of European Economic History,* 5 (1976): 314; OECD, *Economic Outlook,* 31 (July 1983): 124–25; OECD, *National Accounts: Main Aggregates,* vol. 1: *1953–1982* (Paris, 1984), p. 82.

services have contributed a growing proportion of the national product and they can be exported or imported only to a limited degree.

Integration or disintegration in external trade must not be equated with integration or disintegration of the economies themselves. An economy is not simply a quantifiable set of exchanges of goods and services but is also a comprehensive socioeconomic societal process managed in East and West according to distinct principles since the Second World War.

Geographic distribution. From which countries and regions do European imports originate? As the data in table 3.13 indicate, the geographic distribution of European imports has not fundamentally altered throughout the century. The proportion supplied by western Europe declined somewhat and those of the other major regions rose, but this was not a far-reaching structural change. Nor did the distribution by individual country change substantially. Britain and Italy constitute the only exceptions: the British share of total European exports halved between 1913 and 1981, whereas the Italian share virtually doubled. The decrease in the western European share and the increase in the southern European share are almost entirely accounted for by these two countries. All of the countries not included in table 3.13 had shares under 2 percent. For countries such as Bulgaria or Portugal, it did of course make a difference whether they had a 0.2 percent share of European exports, as in 1913, or a 1 percent share, as in 1981. But from a pan-European perspective such tiny shares are of secondary importance.

Approximately one half of all external trade in Europe was conducted among the ten most industrialized countries of Europe itself (roughly northern and western Europe, including Italy). Within these ten France, Germany/FRG, and Britain were preeminent, although this leading position was ceded bit by bit as the role of the other countries enlarged. The second greatest portion—some 40 percent of total intra-European trade—was exchanged between the group of ten and the

Table 3.13. Distribution of Total European Exports by Region and Country in 1913, 1938, and 1981 (in percent)

	1913	1938	1981
Northern Europe	5.4	11.4	8.5
Sweden	2.1	4.4	3.2
Western Europe	70.4	66.9	61.1
Germany/FRG	22.8	20.6	19.9
United Kingdom	24.2	21.7	11.3
France	12.6	8.4	11.1
Netherlands	4.6	5.4	7.6
Belgium	6.5	6.9	6.1
Switzerland	2.5	2.9	3.0
Southern Europe	7.1	7.6	11.5
Italy	4.6	5.3	8.3
Eastern Europe	17.1	14.1	18.9
Soviet Union	7.4	2.4	8.7

Sources: Carlo Zacchia, "International Trade and Capital Movements 1920–1970," in *The Fontana Economic History of Europe,* ed. Carlo M. Cipolla, vol. 5 (Glasgow, 1976), p. 596; UN, *Yearbook of International Trade Statistics 1981* (New York, 1982).

less-developed countries in eastern and southern Europe. During the interwar period this second set of trading relations actually expanded its share somewhat at the expense of the first set, but after the Second World War the trade between the industrialized states of northern and western Europe reasserted its dominant importance.

Before 1939 trade between the less-developed countries of southern and eastern Europe amounted to only about 6 percent of the European total. After 1945 this proportion trebled because the Eastern European states chiefly traded amongst themselves after the establishment of their state socialist systems. In the mid-1980s approximately 14 percent of European trade is conducted within Eastern Europe and 75 percent within Western Europe; East-West trade amounts to 10 percent of the total, having much greater significance for the Eastern European economies than for the Western European ones. Although the East-West split after 1945 certainly rechanneled trade to some degree, one must not overlook that trading relations between regions and countries had developed over the long term and were primarily conditioned by economic and geographical conditions and only secondarily by deliberate external trade policy.

As in intra-European trade, no far-reaching structural change has occurred in extra-European trade. Throughout the twentieth century Europe has primarily traded within its own borders, secondarily with North America, Australia and New Zealand, and Japan, and to a far lesser extent with Asia, Latin America, and Africa. Before the First World War roughly 70 percent of all European exports were exchanged within Europe itself; during the interwar period the percentage rose slightly and then dropped during the Second World War; since 1945 it has climbed once again and amounts to about 75 percent in the mid-1980s. The intra-European share of all imports evolved similarly; its constantly somewhat lower percentage reflects the greater dependence of European economies on extra-European suppliers of agricultural products and raw materials. Generally, then, the intra-European share in the external trade of European countries rose slightly over the course of the twentieth century. Those countries having colonial empires experienced an especially marked rise after the Second World War as decolonization spread. By the mid-1980s of these countries only Britain, Portugal, and Spain continued to diverge from the European average. At that time these three states still sent 40 to 50 percent of their exports to extra-European countries and likewise drew between 40 and 50 percent of their imports from outside Europe.

Table 3.14. Composition of Exports in Manufactured Goods by Region, 1913–1980 (in percent)

	Intra-West			
	1913	1938	1965	1980
Food, drink	11.8	8.2	10.9	9.3
Processed raw materials	17.9	16.9	10.8	4.1
Basic metals	11.7	14.8	9.1	6.5
Machinery	9.8	20.3	32.7	41.6
Chemicals	5.0	7.5	9.1	15.2
Textiles	25.0	14.6	5.9	3.6
Other	16.4	16.2	21.5	19.7

Sources: UN (ECE), *Growth and Stagnation in the European Economy,* by Ingvar Svennilson (Geneva, 1954), pp. 187, 293; UN (ECE), *Economic Survey of Europe in 1967* (New York, 1968), chap. 2, pp. 71–75; UN, *Yearbook of International Trade Statistics 1965* (New York, 1966); *1982* (New York, 1984).

Distribution of goods. The composition of foreign trade according to commodity groups—foodstuffs, raw materials, intermediate and finished goods—relates closely to a country's level of economic development. Generally speaking, in the first half of the century the principal exports of the less-developed agrarian states were foodstuffs and raw materials. In those countries where industrialization was more advanced the composition shifted in favor of semimanufactured and manufactured goods. Those countries that were already highly industrialized in 1900 exported primarily finished products. The relation between level of economic development and structure of exports resulted in a similar evolution in all countries: everywhere the share of foodstuffs and raw materials declined and that of intermediate and finished goods increased. The relatively backward countries of southern and southeastern Europe underwent this structural change mostly after the Second World War. By the 1980s manufactured products constituted the bulk of exports in all European countries.

A close examination of the composition of exported finished products reveals characteristic features associated with the structural change examined earlier in the manufacturing industry as a whole (see tables 3.14 and 3.12). The shares of the commodity group of food, beverages, and tobacco, the processing of raw materials, and the production of primary metals and textiles all declined, whereas the proportions of machinery, transport equipment, and chemicals rose. In other words, goods embodying a low level of processing and semimanufactured

Table 3.14. (continued)

Intra-East		West-East		East-West		Intra-South	
1965	1980	1965	1980	1965	1980	1965	1980
8.3	5.6	8.4	16.9	16.5	11.8	34.8	26.8
16.5	26.0	7.2	9.4	34.5	29.6	4.1	6.8
11.4	7.2	13.4	10.9	12.0	11.5	4.3	6.4
38.4	35.6	37.3	28.2	9.9	13.9	6.5	13.2
4.1	6.1	12.3	16.7	5.6	8.5	4.3	5.6
3.1	1.9	4.7	4.1	2.1	3.1	31.2	24.4
18.5	17.6	16.7	13.8	19.4	21.6	14.8	16.6

Note: Western Europe in 1913 and 1938 refers to United Kingdom, Germany, France, Italy, Belgium, Switzerland, and Sweden; in 1965 and 1980 it also includes Finland, the Netherlands, and Norway; eastern Europe excludes the Soviet Union.

goods taken together lost their earlier significance and were displaced by goods with higher manufactured content. The shift in the structure of exports went further in the industrialized economies of western Europe, followed with some delay by those of northern Europe. The traditional export structures persisted much longer in several eastern and southern European states. In the latter, only in the 1980s did machinery, transportation equipment, and chemicals reach that proportion of total exports typical of the most industrialized European countries before the First World War. Nonetheless, as in the case of overall industrial structures, export structures of the individual countries have also slowly converged, so that the export profile of the lesser developed countries has approached that of the more developed ones.

The structure of imports developed in a similar way to that of exports. In the course of the century the share of primary goods—agricultural products and raw materials—in total imports fell, and that of processed and finished goods rose. The long-term trend also suffered the by now familiar slump during the interwar period.

Relating the geographic distribution of trade to the composition by commodity reveals a trend in international trade that remained characteristic from the late nineteenth century until the 1940s: exchanges shifted away from mutual trade between the highly developed economies towards a complementary trade between the industrialized countries and those supplying foodstuffs and raw materials. The industrialized countries exported proportionately more and more industrial goods and imported increasing amounts of raw materials and agricultural products. The proportion of their total volume of trade conducted with one another also declined. Trade flows were thus diverted from the industrial core economies to the developing and agrarian economies on the periphery. The level of self-sufficiency in industrial goods increased, which partly resulted from the diminishing differentiation of industrial structures in the large European economies of Germany, France, and Britain. The trade of the smaller European economies, by contrast, gained in significance because these countries were less able to supply themselves with a full range of industrial goods through domestic production. The continued exchange of commodities between industrial economies was based on a growing degree of product specialization. The dual process of diminishing differentiation of industrial structures and increasing product specialization was reflected in the declining intraindustrial and rising interindustrial and complementary trade shares; the former involves exchanges between identical branches of industry, the latter exchanges between differing branches.

The collapse of world trade during the Great Depression of 1929–1932 emphatically strengthened the tendency to industrial self-sufficiency by reducing still further the division of labor between industrial economies. What foreign trade remained was concentrated even more around the exchange of industrial goods for agricultural products and raw materials.

This long-standing trend reversed after the Second World War. The interindustrial specialization of trade declined, and the proportion of intraindustrial trade rose. Among other sources this was the outcome of the enormous postwar economic boom, the steady reduction of the share of primary goods in international trade in general, and the spreading product differentiation and diversification of supply that partly supplanted price and quality as the bases of competition. Simultaneously, the commodity structures of foreign trade—measured in terms of the crude groupings in official trade statistics—became more homogeneous. The geographic distribution of trade also shifted, with exchange relations between the traditional industrial countries moving once more into the center of European trade. The postwar internationalization of the European economies was thus more strongly based on substitutive trade—the exchange of similar products differing chiefly in price—than had been the case before the Great Depression, and expressed the comparatively weaker division of labor between the leading industrial economies. This is not to deny, of course, that a substantial portion of intraindustrial trade was grounded in comparative technological advantage and product specialization, nor that interindustrial, complementary exchanges continued to play a major role in European trade.

Europe in the world. The regional distribution of world trade reflects the structure of the world economy. The dominating role of Europe— in particular, of course, western and northern Europe—around the turn of the century appears clearly in the trade statistics: Europe accounted for 60 percent of world exports and 66 percent of world imports; more than 80 percent of world exports were finished manufactured goods, and almost 80 percent of world imports were primary goods. Characteristic of the world economy at the time was the concentration of trade within the European and North American industrialized core and between this core and the developing Pacific economies of Japan, Australia, and New Zealand; trading relations between the European industrial core and its agrarian periphery in eastern and southern Europe were much less intense. As a result of the First World War, the Great Depression, and the restrictive trade and tariff policies of the 1930s the European share of world trade sank markedly. It fell even further during the Second World War, but in the course of the 1950s it rose again to over 50 percent. In the 1970s Europe, like North America, gave up some of its share of world trade, above all to Asia. This diminution was caused generally by the international spread of industrialization, but it was also linked specifically to the emergence of Japan as a world economic power and to the rising prices of raw materials such as oil.

Nonetheless, Europe's predominance in world trade persisted. At the beginning of the 1980s it still accounted for virtually one half of all the world's imports and exports. Throughout the entire twentieth century Europe, the overseas areas of European settlement, and Japan together have constituted the basic network of world trade; other countries or world regions could contribute specific goods and services to that network, but they could not alter the general pattern, and their shares of overall world trade were ultimately insignificant.

Trade and economic development. The growth of world trade faster than world output before 1914 was interpreted by liberal economists of the time as a natural developmental tendency of the world economy and hence as a fundamental condition for future economic progress. The decline of world trade in the wake of the First World War prompted contrary arguments: technical progress, industrialization, rising real income, and other factors would inevitably reduce international exchange of goods and services. According to this thesis, advancing technology would enable both the substitution of natural raw materials by synthetic ones fabricated in the industrial countries and a generally more efficient use of raw material. The spread of industrialization would diminish advantages in comparative costs and would also make it possible for developing countries to produce industrial goods themselves. The increasing convergence of industrial structures and the tapping of new domestic markets in the industrial countries would lead likewise to a growing self-sufficiency. An ever smaller proportion of rising personal incomes would be spent on imported foodstuffs and a greater percentage expended on services produced mainly in the domestic economy. On the basis of these assumptions many economists in the interwar period were again tempted to see something like a natural law in the diminution of trading volumes. Their convictions were reinforced at the time by the generally strong assertion of nationalistic and autarkic policies, the expansion of national monopolies in domestic markets, and the obstruction of international trade through international cartels. Exchange relations between national economies were genuinely declining.

Although elements of this argument continued to be propagated after the Second World War, the renewed growth of economic internationalization demonstrated that world trade had become once more an important impulse of world and European economic expansion. The enormous product differentiation and the high mobility of factors of production and products were scarcely predictable according to previous experience. The share taken by transportation costs in the total value of internationally traded commodities fell substantially. Relatively small differences in products, prices, and profits sufficed to sustain international exchanges and even strengthen them. International monopoly competition reached a greater intensity than had prevailed in the first half of the century.

The simple theory of factor proportions, reducing international trade to complementary or interindustrial exchanges, could account only in part for the rise in foreign trade after the Second World War. Once again, a variety of arguments was posited in an attempt to explain the growing interdependence of national economies. One of the most prominent and plausible is the model of the product cycle. This theory presumes that new products and new methods of production originate in the highly developed countries. Once these products and methods have matured there, they will be taken over by less developed countries with cheaper labor and then reimported by the more developed countries: the closer the interlocking of economies, the faster the transfer of innovations, which in turn promotes further integration. This model could explain not only the expansion of foreign trade after the war but also the secular shift of the shares taken by individual European countries or groups of countries in the total volume of trade. The theory also implies that a developed country will decline in importance if it can no longer maintain its technological advantage through a process of continuing invention and innovation.

Transport and Communications
Since the mid-nineteenth century Europe has undergone a revolution in transport and communications. The use of the term "revolution" is, of course, justified only if one views the history of humanity in the very long term. Persons, goods, and information have achieved a hitherto unknown degree of mobility. During the twentieth century not only have traditional means of transport—including ships and roads—continued to improve, but also additional means have emerged: the automobile initiated a new era in road traffic at the turn of the century, and shortly thereafter the invention of the airplane created a completely new form of transport. In spite of the dynamism with which the older transport systems were modernized and new systems developed, transport and communications nonetheless evolved quite differently from country to country.

Railroads. The railroad first established itself as a central means of transportation during the second third of the nineteenth century and enjoyed its most dynamic phase of expansion between then and the end of the century (see fig. 3.16). The rate of expansion slackened as the amount of trackage approached a saturation point, which was reached in the course of the First World War or shortly thereafter, depending on the country. In the interwar years the rail network grew more slowly and mainly in countries outside western Europe; in several western European countries increasing competition from road traffic even forced a slight contraction of track mileage, a trend that gathered strength rapidly after 1945 and also spread to most other countries of Europe.

In Britain, for example, the rail network of the mid-1980s had roughly the same extent as that of the 1860s. The situation was similar in Germany/FRG-GDR, France, Belgium, and the Netherlands. Those

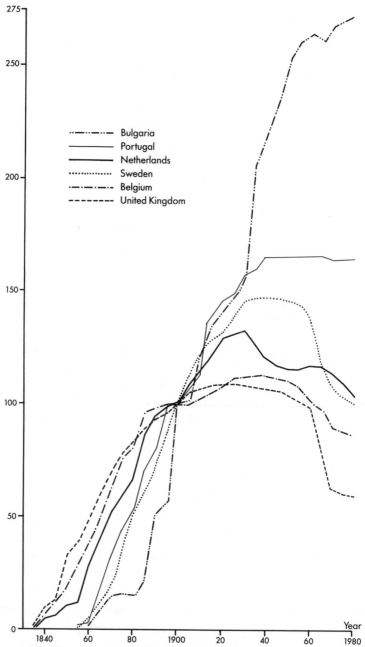

Figure 3.16. Length of Rail Network in Various Countries, 1840–1980
(1900 = 100). *Sources:* Brian R. Mitchell, *European Historical Statistics 1750–1970*
(London, 1975), pp. 581–88; UN (ECE), *Annual Bulletin of Transport Statistics
for Europe 1970–1981* (New York, 1971–1982).

countries that industrialized somewhat later—Denmark, Norway, Sweden, Italy, Austria, Czechoslovakia, and Hungary—followed the same pattern of expansion and contraction but with a time-lag. Even though the rail systems in these countries also started in the 1830s and 1840s, their really dynamic phase of expansion came a few decades after expansion in the first group of countries. The saturation point also came later, in the 1930s, and the phase of contraction did not begin until the 1960s. In a third group of countries—Spain, Portugal, Greece, Finland, Bulgaria, Rumania, and Yugoslavia—the rail network did not expand greatly until the beginning of the twentieth century. Its contraction has begun only very recently in these countries; in Bulgaria the rail network was still being extended moderately in the early 1980s.

Track mileage alone, of course, does not indicate the degree to which a country is opened up to rail traffic. In terms of the amount of trackage per square mile of territory, interwar Belgium had the densest rail network ever constructed. Following Belgium are Britain, Germany/FRG-GDR, the Netherlands, Denmark, Hungary, and Czechoslovakia; in other words, the densest rail networks have always been in western and central European states. The rail system in northern, southern, and southeastern European states has always been much less densely built up. The length of trackage per square mile in 1980 in Finland, Norway, and Greece, for example, was less than had existed in Belgium and Britain in the mid-nineteenth century; moreover, the three countries were beginning to reduce their rail mileage. Variations exist not only between national averages but also between local regions within a country. Even in such densely networked countries as Britain and Germany some areas had a density of rail mileage akin to that in Finland. Conversely, in the urbanized region of southernmost Finland rail coverage compared favorably with that in western Europe; indeed, in the interwar period Finland's rail mileage per capita population exceeded the levels of most other European countries. Generally speaking, if one relates track mileage to the country's population rather than to its physical area, the ranking of countries according to the density of their rail network undergoes considerable modification.

This schematic arrangement of countries into groups must not mislead us into relating the extent of the rail network exclusively to a country's level of socioeconomic development. Geographical conditions, the availability of other means of transportation, and political conditions can also affect the size of a country's rail system. These additional factors especially influenced the geographic layout of rail networks. Some networks, such as the French one, were created around a single node, usually the capital city, with more or less direct radial lines connecting the principal cities; in other networks, such as the German, main lines joined at many junctions from which secondary lines branched off. The eastern European countries had especial difficulties arising from the territorial and political changes after each world war; networks that were originally laid out according to differing principles had to be amalgamated, and some existing networks were torn apart.

The direct relationship between general economic development and the amount of traffic carried by rail is plainly indicated by the curves in figure 3.17. The sharp drop in freight traffic around 1930 mirrors the Great Depression, and the steep rise results from not only the postwar economic boom in individual countries but also the increasing internationalization and integration of European trading patterns. The much slower growth of passenger traffic after the mid-1950s is obviously the consequence of the growing use of cars and buses for the movement of people.

Road traffic. Road traffic now almost always means motorized vehicles. Yet animal-drawn, mostly horse-drawn, wagons continued to have an important place in transport in the first half of the twentieth century. In the agricultural areas of the core industrialized countries they were quite common up to the Second World War. Even in such highly industrialized countries as West Germany or Belgium, horses and oxen finally disappeared as draft animals only in the 1950s. In a few eastern European states, and especially in the lands of southern and southeastern Europe, horses and donkeys were still relatively widely used as a means of transport in the mid-1980s. Nonetheless, the radical reduction in the total number of horses kept throughout Europe underlines the very limited role animals now play in European transport as a whole. Consequently, the following discussion will focus exclusively on the diffusion of motorized vehicles.

The motorization of road traffic began in the 1890s, three quarters of a century after the beginning of the railway. At the turn of the century automobiles were still an exceptional luxury, and their use spread slowly up to the First World War. Until then, even in the more developed countries trucks were used primarily by companies located some distance from the nearest railway station; or they were mostly deployed within city limits or for short stretches into the countryside

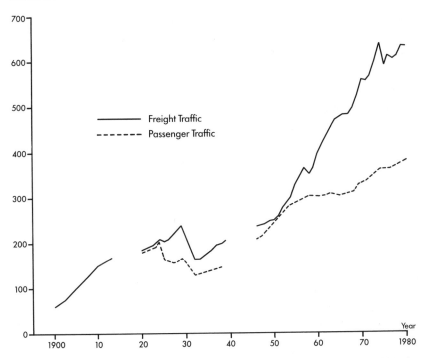

Figure 3.17. Freight and Passengers on European Railroads, 1900–1980 (in billion ton/kilometers and passenger/kilometers). *Sources:* Brian R. Mitchell, *European Historical Statistics 1750–1970* (London, 1975), pp. 589–612; UN, *Statistical Yearbook 1977* (New York, 1978), pp. 528–29; *1981* (New York, 1982), pp. 1002–1003.

to supplement the railway. The First World War fundamentally promoted the motorization of road traffic, although the increase in ownership of private cars slowed somewhat. In the course of the 1920s, however, the number of vehicles rose rapidly. During the Great Depression the diffusion of trucks continued to benefit from the increasing competition between road and rail for the transport of goods, whereas that of private automobiles stagnated. In a few countries especially hard hit by the crisis, the number of licensed cars in the 1930s levelled off or even declined. Once the immediate phase of reconstruction following the Second World War was over and the economic boom had begun, car ownership expanded enormously throughout Europe: the era of mass motoring had arrived. Not until the end of the 1960s did the rate of growth slacken in most countries. Figure 3.18 presents

selected national growth curves indexed to the base year 1913; because
the postwar expansion has been so dynamic, the y-axis uses a logarithmic scale.

As in the case of the railway, national patterns of growth fall into
three rough groupings. In the first grouping, comprising Britain,
France, Belgium, Switzerland, Germany/FRG-GDR, Sweden, Nor-

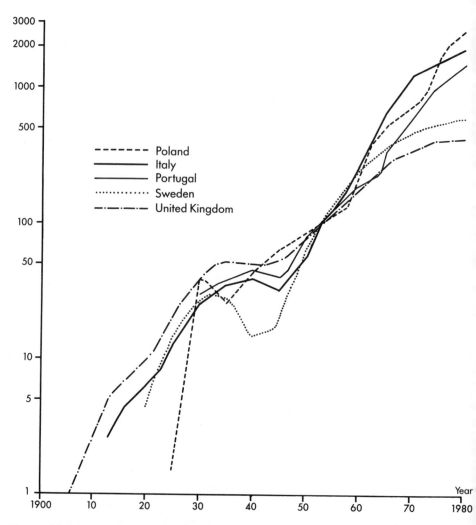

Figure 3.18. Registered Motor Vehicles of All Types in Various Countries, 1906–1980
(1913 = 100, logarithmic scale). *Sources:* Brian R. Mitchell, *European Historical Statistics 1750–
1970* (London, 1975), pp. 639–45; UN, *Statistical Yearbook 1977* (New York, 1978), pp.
542–43; *1981* (New York, 1983), pp. 1009–10.

way, and Denmark, the number of private cars rose quite rapidly in the first third of the century, even though real mass motoring, in which the car as a personal form of transport is taken for granted, did not become established until the 1950s. By the late 1960s the annual number of new registrations slowed as the market approached evident saturation. Italy, Finland, the Netherlands, Austria, and, with some qualification, Spain and Czechoslovakia constitute a second grouping. Here motorization began later and by the end of the interwar period had not yet equalled the level attained by the countries in the first grouping. The postwar growth curve was then even steeper and the expansion did not begin to level off slowly until the early 1970s. In the final grouping of less-developed economies—Greece, Portugal, Bulgaria, Rumania, Poland, Hungary, and Yugoslavia—motorization of road traffic did not really set in until after the Second World War. The spread of motor vehicles was then very rapid especially from the 1960s on, and no signs of market saturation had yet appeared by the mid-1980s.

To appreciate more accurately the impact of motorization on the lifestyle of individual Europeans, one must consider not only the absolute number of cars but also their density: the number of cars per capita population. In 1938, for example, the number of cars per capita in Britain was almost double that in Sweden; during the 1950s the spread of car ownership in Sweden was so much more rapid than in Britain that the relative positions were reversed by 1960, with the number of cars per capita in Sweden being roughly a third higher than in Britain (see table 3.15). By contrast, the number of cars in Portugal and in Poland also rose more quickly than in Britain during the 1960s and 1970s, yet the Portuguese level of automobile density in 1980 was still twenty years behind the British and the Polish level was thirty years behind. In Rumania and Bulgaria the number of cars relative to population has scarcely grown since the interwar period and the per capita figure more or less equals the British level at the beginning of the century.

Inland navigation. Inland shipping began to decline in the mid-nineteenth century. The load capacity and speed of river and canal barges were too low to compete with railways, and barge traffic succumbed everywhere that the railway encountered a poorly built up and inefficient system of inland waterways. This was especially true in areas having many very small canals with correspondingly low-capacity barges and boats. Where large canals or large natural waterways existed,

Table 3.15. Ownership of Passenger Cars by Country, 1922–1980 (automobiles per thousand inhabitants)

	1922	1930	1938	1950	1960	1970	1980
Northern Europe							
Sweden	4	17	25	36	160	285	347
Denmark	5	22	29	28	89	218	273
Finland	—	6[a]	8	7	41	152	255
Norway	—	8[a]	19	20	63	193	300
Western Europe							
Germany	1	8	21	—	—	—	—
FRG	—	—	—	13	81	277	376
United Kingdom	7	25	42	46	105	209	276
France	5	26	42	37[b]	121	252	343
Netherlands	3	9	48	14	45	193	323
Belgium	4	13	11	32	82	213	319
Austria	—	—	17	7	57	162	300
Switzerland	—	12[a]	5[c]	31	95	221	351
Ireland	—	18[a]	18	31	62	134	217
Eastern Europe							
Poland	0.1	1	1	2[d]	4	15	67
Yugoslavia	0.2	1	1	1[d]	3	35	109
Rumania	0.3	2	1	—	1	2	3
GDR	—	—	—	—	18	73	160
Czechoslovakia	1	4	5	—	20	57	149
Hungary	0.4	2	2	—	4[e]	24	95
Southern Europe							
Italy	1	5	8	7	40	192	310
Spain	—	—	—	3	9	70	202
Portugal	2	4	5	7	18	60	128
Greece	—	—	1	1	5	26	90

Sources: A. S. Deaton, "The Structure of Demand 1920–1970," in *The Fontana Economic History of Europe,* ed. Carlo M. Cipolla, vol. 5 (Glasgow, 1976), p. 124; World Bank, *World Tables,* 3rd ed., vol. 2: *Social Data* (Baltimore, 1983); UN, *Statistical Yearbook 1981* (New York 1983), pp. 1009–10; *1983/84* (New York, 1986), pp. 1015–16.

[a] 1928.
[b] 1948.
[c] 1937.
[d] 1955.
[e] 1962.

the situation was different. The technological development of steam power led to bigger and faster boats that enabled inland navigation to remain competitive with the railway in the transport of various bulk commodities such as coal or gravel. Ultimately, inland water traffic could be expanded only if the size of boats could be enlarged and unit freight costs reduced. Where there was an effective artery, such as the Rhine in central Europe or the Danube in southeastern Europe, inland navigation even enjoyed a boom at the end of the nineteenth century.

Traffic slumped during the interwar period but revived again after the Second World War. The total length of navigable waterways continued to shrink, but some stretches were modernized and enlarged to carry large boats and barges. In the 1980s the Netherlands, followed by Belgium, still had the densest networks of inland waterways in all Europe; the gap between these two countries and the rest of Europe is large. In spite of the declining frequency of traffic on the waterways, the amount of freight transported has risen since the Second World War. Overall, inland navigation has steadily lost importance throughout the twentieth century, though rather less than commonly supposed.

Air traffic. In 1903 the Wright brothers made the first successful powered flight. The experience gained in the military use of aircraft during the First World War lent a strong technological and economic impulse to this new form of transport in the interwar period. By 1919 two companies had begun regular flights between London and Paris. In the following years civilian aviation companies were established in a number of European countries such that by the mid-1920s the major cities of Europe were connected by regular air services. Airlines in France, Britain, and the Netherlands initiated overseas flights even though air traffic at the time was still chiefly oriented toward shorter stretches. During the 1930s the routes were continually expanded. Passenger traffic dominated, but the airplane was still far from being mass transportation. Only small, costly, and perishable goods were transported by air freight. In terms of the total volume of European traffic, air transport was still completely insignificant in 1939.

War once again prompted decisive advances in air travel. The range and loading capacity of aircraft were substantially improved in the course of the Second World War. After the war the intercontinental and intra-European network of air routes became quickly denser; flying times became shorter, and fares cheaper. Nonetheless, even in the early 1980s the airplane remained relatively unimportant for everyday transportation in Europe, in contrast to North America, because of the shorter distances between intra-European destinations; but since the 1960s it has become a means of mass transportation for international tourism.

Restructuring of traffic volume. The relative positions of the major types of carriers have shifted noticeably in the course of the century. In the more developed countries the railroads' share of total traffic has declined more or less steadily since the First World War in spite of increases in absolute volume of goods moved. In the less developed countries its relative position continued to rise until the Second World War, after which decline also set in. By contrast the share of motor transport rose continually everywhere. In the carriage of passengers airplanes became increasingly important, and long-distance pipelines assumed an even larger role in the transport of commodities such as oil and natural gas. Tables 3.16 and 3.17 disregard seaborne traffic, despite its importance to domestic transport in countries such as Greece

Table 3.16. Principal Carriers of Inland Passenger Transport for Various Countries, 1952–1983 (in percent total passenger/kilometers)

	Year	Rail	Road[a]	Air
Norway	1952[b]	43	43	0.2
	1965[b]	28	61	6
	1983[b]	25	51	18
FRG	1955	51	49	0.1
	1963	46	51	3
	1983	32	59	9
Netherlands	1970	43	57	0.1
	1983	46	54	0.3
Bulgaria	1965	42	58	0.1
	1983	20	79	1
Italy	1970	48	50	2
	1982	32	66	2

Sources: UN (ECE), *Annual Bulletin of Transport Statistics for Europe 1983* (New York, 1984), p. 15; *Norges Historisk Statistikk 1978* (Oslo, 1978), p. 206; *Norges Statistisk Årbok 1984* (Oslo, 1984), p. 310; *Statistisches Jahrbuch für die Bundesrepublik Deutschland 1965* (Wiesbaden, 1965), pp. 355–56; *1985* (Wiesbaden, 1985), p. 283; CMEA, *Statistical Yearbook 1976* (London, n.d.), pp. 282–83.

[a] Includes street tramways; excludes private passenger cars.

[b] Ferries and boats accounted for 10 percent of passenger traffic in 1952, 8 percent in 1965, and 6 percent in 1983.

Table 3.17. Principal Carriers of Inland Freight Transport for Various
Countries, 1954–1983 (in percent total ton/kilometers)

	Year	Rail	Road	Inland Waterway	Pipeline
Norway	1954	74	26	—	—
	1963[a]	46	54	—	—
	1983[a]	19	44	—	37
FRG	1954[b]	52	18	30	—
	1963[b]	47	20	29	4
	1983	28	43	25	4
France	1954[b]	66	21	13	—
	1963[b]	61	25	10	4
	1982	34	46	6	14
Netherlands	1963	13	23	61	3
	1982	5	38	50	7
Italy	1954	30	69	1	—
	1982	11	82	0.1	7
Czechoslovakia	1954	90	9	1	—
	1963	82	11	4	3
	1982	68	20	3	9
Poland	1963	95	4	1	—
	1982	68	21	1	10
Rumania	1963	87	6	4	3
	1982	80	13	3	4

Sources: UN (ECE), *Annual Bulletin of Transport Statistics for Europe 1959* (New York, 1960), p. 19; *1969* (New York, 1970), pp. 4–5; *1983* (New York, 1984), pp. 16–17.
[a] Including Ofoten Railway.
[b] Excluding short-distance road transport.

and Norway. As the data show plainly, the dominant feature of the restructuring of traffic volumes since 1950 has been the transfer of traffic from rail to road. In the more industrialized countries of western and northern Europe this development went hand in hand with increasing densities of motor vehicles and extension of highway networks.

Substantial differences between individual national patterns of traffic persist, of course. In those countries where cars and trucks were less numerous and roads fewer and of inferior quality, the railroad has remained very important, and even dominant for freight transport. This is particularly true of the eastern Europe countries. In 1980–1981 the rail's share of total goods traffic in Britain and West Germany was 14 percent and 26 percent respectively; in Rumania it was 80 percent, in Poland 67 percent. Yet conclusions about the level of economic development or the modernity of systems of transport and traffic cannot be drawn from these figures without qualification. In Germany/FRG the rail's share in total passenger transportation fell from over 50 percent in the interwar years to just 6 percent in 1980; in the Netherlands it still accounted for 50 percent in 1980. Since per capita car ownership and the technological state of the rail system were roughly equivalent in both countries at the latter date, other reasons must be sought for the Dutch railway's continuing ability to attract passengers. Differences between Bulgaria and West Germany, on the other hand, are clearly a function of the wide gap in levels of economic development. That the rail's share of total passenger traffic in Bulgaria in 1980–1981 was much higher than that in West Germany is attributable, above all, to the far more restricted diffusion of automobiles and the poor state of the road network. In recent years in the most industrialized western European countries the railroad has managed to stabilize its share in the total volume of both passenger and freight traffic. After decades of neglect, rail systems are being extensively modernized to increase capacity and competitiveness; the long-distance, high-speed intercity trains such as the French TGV are but a part of this upgrading program. Behind these modernizing drives is also the recognition that the railroad is for the moment the means of transport most accommodating to growing demands for better environmental protection.

Transport, communications, and economic development. The importance of transport and communications for the development of economy and society cannot be overestimated. Geographic mobility has both social significance and economic significance. National and international division of labor and integration could develop only to the extent to which communications and transport capacities were improved and their costs reduced. The ever more effective exploitation of existing resources, the ever more intensive use of factors of production, and the continuing advancement of factor productivities were directly related to the improved performance of the transport and communications system. Economic development was especially rapid in those geographic areas that already possessed a dense and high-grade transportation network at the turn of the century, whereas it was hindered in areas having dispersed and inefficient systems. In this respect western and central Europe had competitive advantages over the peripheral areas on the European rim. Despite continual improvement the economic development of these areas—particularly those in the far north, the southeast, and the far south—has remained handicapped by inadequate systems of transportation and communications.

Money and Banking

Although the activities subsumed under the rubic of money and banking clearly belong to the tertiary or service sector, they are less autonomous than the previously considered branches of the economy, and an examination of their historical evolution fits somewhat uncomfortably into the organizational scheme followed by this chapter. National and international monetary systems are determined largely by state regulation; in other words, they constitute important means of influencing national product and could be appropriately discussed in the later section on policies of economic management. The evolution of prices and international capital movements could also have been examined under the earlier section on general economic development.

National monetary and banking systems. During the second half of the nineteenth century practically all European countries accepted the gold standard as the foundation of their monetary system and defined their national currencies in terms of a legally set measure of fine gold. In addition to pure gold coins, base metal and silver coinage and paper bank notes also circulated. Originally the bank note was only a money surrogate—a promissory note for gold coin—but it increasingly became accepted as real cash and by the First World War was declared legal tender in all countries. The number of bank notes in circulation was linked to gold through regulations that required note-issuing banks to hold a proportion of their issues in gold reserves; the banks were also obliged on demand to redeem their notes in gold according to the prevailing parity. This mixed gold-currency standard promoted industrialization in the second half of the nineteenth century by creating an elastic money supply, which compensated for the deflationary tendencies that would have otherwise been generated by strong economic growth if gold had been the only circulating currency. Parallel systems of cashless payments based on transfer between current accounts also emerged, thereby enhancing the money-creating capabilities of credit banks. Without bank notes and bank money industrializing economies would have entered a deflationary crisis.

The mixed gold-currency standard broke down during and after the First World War. The obligation to redeem bank notes in gold was abolished; gold coinage was withdrawn from circulation, and backing for currency consisted mostly of foreign-exchange holdings with only a small part in gold. Under the revised system, designated the gold bullion standard, the function of gold backing began to change fundamentally. Throughout the nineteenth century gold cover had been regarded primarily as a means of securing the domestic circulation of money; in the twentieth century it served principally as an international liquidity reserve. This change was possible only because bank notes and base coinage were finally universally accepted as legal tender. Since then, money has not been backed in reality; it is no longer a commodity, and its value is purely a function of its purchasing power. Hence we now speak of purchasing power or paper currency.

In the course of the nineteenth century, the realization spread that the integration of large territories into an economic union with a common monetary system could be achieved only if the state-run coinage were supplemented by a monopolistic concentration of the issuing of bank notes. Throughout Europe the system was centralized. The issuing of bank notes was restricted to one or a few banks; in many countries several banks retained this so-called right of issue until well into the twentieth century. Although these central note-issuing authorities had the legal form of private joint-stock companies, they evolved gradually into public institutions. In return for being endowed with special privileges, they also had special obligations and were subject to special controls.

The independence of banks of issue varied widely from country to country. Following the inflationary period immediately after the First World War banks of issue generally gained a greater freedom to determine their issuing policies autonomously. This move was intended to prevent the misuse of the printing of money by the government, as had happened in several countries both during and after the war. Today note-issuing banks still occupy greatly different positions within the structure of the state. Some are merely subordinate authorities of the government, some are subject only to the government's right of collaboration and codetermination, and still others have virtually a free hand.

Under the gold currency standard, banks of issue restricted their attention to assuring that the issued notes could be redeemed on demand in gold. The abolition of this required convertibility after the First World War and the consequent endowment of note-issuing banks with unlimited liquidity moved the stability of money value into the center of concern. Only after the Second World War did the diffusion of Keynesianism add economic policy objectives. As a result of the extension of their objectives, the central note-issuing banks deployed ever more sophisticated and effective instruments for the management of money and credit supplies.

The modern private banking system also emerged in the nineteenth century. Despite organizational differences between individual countries, almost everywhere large full-service banks were established to deal with all forms of business in money and credit, along with specialized banks that served specific needs or socioeconomic interests. The banking systems in the northern and western European states were fully developed by the First World War, but those in the eastern and southern European economies remained incomplete and inadequate throughout the interwar period.

From the late nineteenth century concentration joined diversification as an important structural element of banking systems. In practically all countries a few big banks with widespread networks of branches emerged and captured a high proportion of the total volume of credit. This process of concentration has continued throughout the twentieth century; after the Second World War it was supplemented by intensified internationalization, either through cooperation between banks or through the foundation of foreign branches and subsidiaries. The increasing influence of the state in the credit sector has also been characteristic in this century. Banking legislation became more voluminous and fine-tuned; bank supervision became an instrument of state economic management; state influence was increased directly through the expansion of public credit, either by forming state or publicly owned credit institutions or by acquiring private ones. A final structural element of twentieth-century European banking systems is the changing definition of specialized banks. Such banks have increasingly assumed new functional tasks and services, and their clienteles have become less and less distinguishable by specific socioeconomic interests.

The international monetary system. The First World War brought the collapse of the international gold standard. After the war the unstable economic conditions and particularly the instability of currencies prompted calls for a rapid return to the gold standard; its advocates believed that before 1914 the gold standard had secured both international free trade and stable foreign exchange rates. Despite this pressure the gold standard was not restored more or less until the late 1920s; by 1931 it had collapsed again for a variety of reasons.

First, the pre-1914 gold standard had operated under very special and favorable circumstances—a stable world economic order and economic growth—that no longer existed after the war. Second, the full gold standard was not restored internationally in the 1920s. Rather, in a partial version known as the gold exchange standard, a few major currencies—the United States dollar, the British pound, the French franc, and to a lesser extent the German Reichsmark—were exchanged on the basis of fixed gold parities and served themselves as the basis of exchange rates for all other currencies. Consequently, a degree of instability remained in the international monetary system. Third, new exchange rates were not established according to the requirements of an orderly monetary system but rather were dictated by vagaries of domestic politics, national aspirations to prestige, or speculative motives. Many countries had the ambition to reintroduce their pre-1914 exchange rates regardless of new economic conditions (figure 3.19 shows three examples of restoration). Such foreign exchange policies resulted frequently in over- or undervalued currencies; for the parity chosen was purely coincidental rather than actually corresponding to the country's existing economic conditions.

Fourth, the new gold exchange standard did not restore the close connection between national and international monetary systems that had existed under the full gold standard when currency was convertible into gold both nationally and internationally. Before the war the creation of money by commercial banks depended on their being supplied with bank notes by the note-issuing banks, whose issues depended, in turn, on the level of gold reserves; this interdependence between money supply and gold linked the national and international money markets so strongly that they formed for all intents and purposes a single entity. After the war, correction of inappropriate rates of exchange would have required in most cases domestic economic adjustments that would have upset the relative stability just achieved. However, the readiness to burden the domestic economy with such adaptive policies, commonly accepted before the war, no longer existed. The functional mechanism of the nineteenth-century gold standard was paralyzed by the attempts of national central banks to neutralize gold movements by the purchase and sale of foreign exchange.

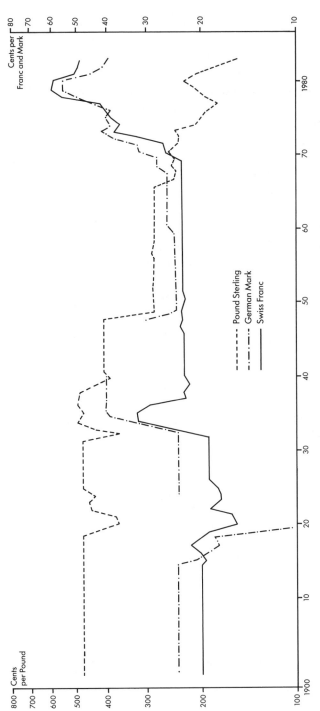

Figure 3.19. Exchange Rates for the Pound Sterling, German Mark, and Swiss Franc against the U.S. Dollar, 1900–1983 (in cents, logarithmic scale). *Sources:* UN, Department of Economic Affairs, *Public Debt 1914–1946* (Lake Success, N.Y.), pp. 67, 137, 147; Fred Hirsch and Peter Oppenheimer, "The Trial of Managed Money: Currency, Credit and Prices 1920–1970," in *The Fontana Economic History of Europe,* ed. Carlo M. Cipolla, vol. 5 (Glasgow, 1976), p. 641; International Monetary Fund, *International Financial Statistics Yearbook 1984* (Washington, D.C., 1984), pp. 286–87, 554–55, 588–89.

Fifth, decisions on currency policy were more than ever before regarded as general economic, and ultimately political, decisions, which indubitably made it more difficult to adjust currency policy to existing economic circumstances. Even though the gold exchange standard did not place national monetary policy under the same externally determined constraints as the earlier gold currency standard, the newly (and mostly falsely) fixed foreign exchange parities could not be sustained for long. The financial crisis of 1931 brought collapse. In September of that year Britain abandoned gold: obligatory convertibility was abolished and the pound devalued. Numerous countries followed suit shortly thereafter.

After the collapse of the gold exchange standard, various monetary unions sprang up, whereby several countries joined forces to maintain their similarly based currency systems. In 1931 the sterling bloc was established, uniting Ireland, Portugal, the Scandinavian states, Estonia, and Latvia alongside the countries of the British Commonwealth. The sterling bloc survived the Second World War, but the gold bloc formed in 1933 by France, Belgium, Italy, Switzerland, Poland, and the Netherlands lasted only a few years. The attempt to maintain gold parities in the face of the beggar-thy-neighbor policies that predominated in the 1930s was bound to fail. No European state belonged to the dollar bloc. An informal Reichsmark bloc also emerged, encompassing those central and southeast European countries that came under German economic domination as a consequence of National Socialist expansionist policies after 1933. Such currency blocs expressed the prevailing disorder of the 1930s: limited convertibility, arbitrary manipulation of floating exchange rates, control of foreign exchange, and so on. A generally recognized international monetary system no longer existed.

In the 1930s Britain, France, and the United States started negotiations on the foundation of a new international monetary system. During the Second World War these were taken up again and led to the Bretton Woods Agreement of 1944: currencies were once more to be expressed in terms of gold; fixed exchange rates were created and free convertibility guaranteed (see fig. 3.19). As had occurred after the First World War, certain "hard" currencies—primarily the United States dollar—were designated reserve currencies alongside gold reserves. The International Monetary Fund (IMF) was set up as a multilateral institution to promote cooperation and stability in the international money market and charged with tiding members over temporary balance-of-payments deficits by supplying them with foreign exchange. Member countries were permitted to alter their exchange rates only in conditions of "fundamental disequilibrium"—when maintenance of the original rate would entail unacceptably high costs, such as high unemployment—and even then only after consultation with the IMF. Otherwise the individual central banks were obliged to insure through the purchase and sale of foreign exchange that the going exchange rate of their national currencies did not fluctuate more than 1 percent of the originally fixed parity. The new system thus represented a compromise between the rigidities of the full gold standard and the unstable monetary condition of the 1930s. It accepted the pursuit of individualized domestic economic goals but ruled out the arbitrary manipulation of exchange rates as a means of achieving them.

The economic difficulty of the immediate postwar years prevented the full terms of the Bretton Woods Agreement from immediately coming into force. Although foundation of the European Payments Union (EPU) in 1950 created a clearing system for multilateral money transfers between the countries of Western Europe, the fixed-exchange-rate system supervised by the IMF did not function fully until the return of the major Western European currencies to full convertibility at the end of the 1950s. None of the Eastern European states participated in the reformed international monetary system, maintaining instead draconian controls over foreign exchange. Like the interwar arrangements, the Bretton Woods system also had a relatively short life span; in 1971 its central policy of fixed exchange rates was abandoned in favor of floating rates. The most important reason for this breakdown was that world economic forces had gradually shifted to the disadvantage of the United States economy, which undermined the dollar's strength. United States gold reserves declined to the point that the gold dollar standard became a "paper dollar standard." In 1968 the United States restricted the convertibility of dollars at the official rate of $35 per ounce of fine gold to transactions between central banks, and in 1971 it suspended convertibility altogether. The system of floating currencies thus began; an initial attempt to restrict floating to more widely set margins around previous par values collapsed by 1973, after which Western European currencies floated freely against the U.S. dollar and most other currencies (see fig. 3.19).

Since then the international monetary system has no longer been a "system" as such; its basic constitutive structural elements are either ambiguous or completely missing. Binding rules on the procedures to be followed for changing rates do not exist any more. Instead of an exclusive international reserve asset there are now several: the major currencies (U.S. dollar, British pound, West German mark, Swiss franc, Japanese yen), gold, or Special Drawing Rights (SDR) with the IMF. Official convertibility is no longer a substantive obligation. Moreover, there are no stringent rules of adjustment for the maintenance or attainment of balance-of-payments equilibrium.

Beginning in 1973 many Western European countries agreed to restrict the fluctuation of the exchange value of their currencies within a specific range in order to avoid the uncertainties of free-floating rates. The so-called European Monetary Union, comprising the major EEC countries (except Britain and Italy) as well as Sweden and Norway, set a range for the floating of its constituent currencies as a bloc against the U.S. dollar, a policy that came to be known as the "snake-in-the-tunnel" principle. The formation of the European Monetary System (EMS) with its own official currency, the European Currency Unit or ECU, in 1979 was also intended to promote currency stability. However, the new system has had only limited success in furthering complete monetary union in Western Europe; it was far more an expression of a new regionalization of Europe than the construction of a new international monetary system.

International capital movement. The First World War transformed the international relations of money and capital. Until then both had possessed a relatively high degree of stability; after the war they both became unstable and speculative. Numerous weaknesses emerged in the international network of short- and long-term capital movements that generally burdened both the European and the world economy. The most contentious among them were the high reparations and war debts, which were never effectively settled but which put great strain on the debtor countries without ever really benefiting the creditor countries. Ultimately, they were only expressions of the fundamental reversal of international capital flows. Before the First World War, Europe, particularly Britain, France, and the German Empire, was the greatest net creditor in the world; the United States by contrast was a net debtor. After the war the positions were reversed. The United States was now the net creditor; Britain did not regain its prewar level of foreign assets until 1930; France's external assets had fallen to one half of their prewar level; and Germany as the most indebted country in the world had become a net importer of capital.

Large-scale speculative flows of capital, which as a result of the increased wartime and postwar liquidity moved back and forth between the great financial centers of London, New York, Paris, and Berlin, also promoted monetary destabilization. In general, the proportion of short-term capital in the overall capital movement was relatively high, and since short-term investments reacted extremely sensitively to economic and political crises, this further contributed to instability. The volatility of short-term capital presented particular problems in the debtor countries—primarily the eastern European states in addition to Germany and Austria—because the banks there turned short-term foreign credits into long-term domestic loans; a sudden withdrawal of the credits would inevitably provoke a liquidity crisis. In the later 1920s many debtor states received smaller amounts of long-term credits than they paid out in interest, dividends, and repayments to foreign creditors. To maintain solvency, these states thus had to increase short-term indebtedness, which heightened the overall economic instability even further.

The problem of instability was not confined to short- and long-term capital markets but also existed in the commodity sphere. On the one hand, debtor countries were accused of placing the foreign capital in low-yielding investments instead of channeling it into more productive areas in order to create the conditions of its repayment; after all, the creditors claimed, the repayment of debts could be obtained only through careful economic management. On the other hand, the creditor states, primarily the United States, put substantial obstacles in the way of such conditions by imposing restrictions on imported goods.

In the summer of 1931, at the height of the Great Depression, the international money and payment transactions broke down. Capital exports from the creditor countries dried up, which hit the economies of the debtor states very hard: investment ceased; already limited stocks of gold and foreign exchange shrank dramatically; banks collapsed and dragged other enterprises with them into bankruptcy. The collapse of the international money and capital market was simultaneously a consequence of the world economic crisis and a cause of its deepening. For almost a quarter of a century thereafter this market was seriously disrupted. What capital still crossed national frontiers did so primarily within existing or developing currency and economic zones. London capital flowed into Commonwealth countries, Swedish capital into the other Scandinavian states; Belgian, Dutch, and Swiss capital was exported to France, whose own external investments preferred the other member states of the gold bloc. In general, capital was no longer invested in the debtor states but rather in other creditor countries, less in Europe and more in the United States, and investment funds were channelled more according to political considerations than potential profitability.

Although the starting position after the Second World War was considerably more favorable than after the First—no reparations or war debt payments, an inward capital flow thanks to the Marshall Plan—the European money and capital markets recovered full operation only at the end of the 1950s when convertibility was restored for all major currencies. Over the years Western European capital exports rose rapidly from an initial low level, but they never quite regained the importance they had possessed before the First World War. Their structure changed as well. The proportion of direct investment, as opposed to portfolio investment, in long-term capital exports rose from 10 percent before 1914, to over 25 percent in the interwar period, to 50 percent in the 1970s. From a macroeconomic perspective these direct investments played only a secondary role, but they gain in importance if the foreign output thereby produced is compared with the total national product. The foreign output of Western European conglomerates in 1975 amounted to one quarter of the total European national product. The geographic distribution of capital exports promoted the economic interdependence of the highly industrialized countries. Capital no longer flowed, as before the Second World War, between industrial and agrarian economies nor between economies with a capital surplus and those with a capital shortage; instead its movement was confined largely to the relatively homogeneous group of advanced economies. In the case of direct investments at least, the driving impulses behind the capital flows were akin to those furthering intraindustrial trade competition between highly developed industries. A final structural change has been the growing influence and participation of the state in international capital transfers since 1945. Associated with this trend are Marshall Plan funds, overseas development aid, state sureties, European Development Fund assistance, and jointly sponsored projects.

Fundamentally, the international and European money and capital markets in the last several decades have been characterized by greater stability than in the interwar period. But they have not been placid by any means. One element of instability emerged through the so-called Eurodollar or Eurocurrency market, where large quantities of money and short-term capital were shifted between European banks in order to take advantage of spreads in international interest rates and to speculate on devaluation or revaluation of specific currencies. A further element of instability arose in the early 1980s when many developing countries—but also Poland, Rumania, and Yugoslavia—were no longer able to pay interest charges or redeem the principal of loans contracted with Western banks. Only a combination of moratoria on payment, debt refinancing, and state sureties has prevented the financial collapse of many debtor countries, a collapse that would also affect European banks.

Price movements. Price movement over the last one hundred years can be divided roughly into three periods (see fig. 3.20) For decades before 1914 prices remained quite stable. During the interwar period they fluctuated irregularly and tended to decline. Since 1945 general price levels have increased continually; the rise accelerated from the early 1970s to the early 1980s and has only recently slowed.

These three periods were bounded by the two world wars and their respective immediate postwar years during which prices rose sharply in almost all countries. In some of them the wartime upsurge in prices could be dampened after the war; in others it became an uncontrollable hyperinflation such that only a drastic currency reform could restore order to the country's monetary system. Austria, Hungary, Poland, and Germany experienced such hyperinflation after the First World War and Greece, Hungary, and Rumania during and after the Second World War. In the first years after 1945 many Western European states kept the price increases under control and avoided rampant inflation only by introducing currency reforms or similar price-damping measures; among these were Austria, Belgium, Denmark, West Germany, France, the Netherlands, and Norway. The communist-run Eastern European states also undertook monetary reforms and expanded the system of price controls into an important instrument of the centrally planned economy.

When the past century is divided into these three phases, the relation between the curves of prices and general economic growth corresponds to the traditional cyclical model that predicts price increases during an upswing and price decreases during a downswing. If these periods are examined more carefully, however, greater deviations from this overall pattern appear. For example, prices began to fall slowly in the second half of the 1920s even though the economy was expanding. This "structural deflation" had several causes: the generally weak economic recovery overall, persistent high unemployment, overproduction of foodstuffs, overcapacity in particular branches of industry, restrictive

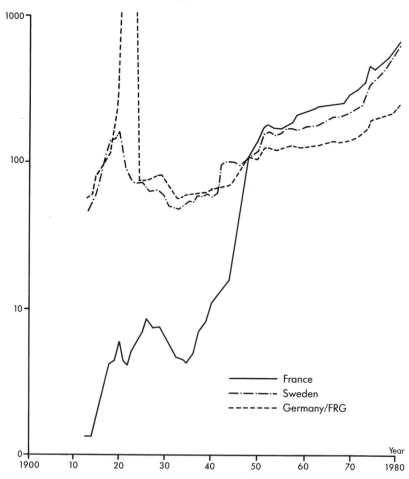

Figure 3.20. Wholesale Price Indices for Various Countries, 1913–1980 (1950 = 100, logarithmic scale). *Sources:* Brian R. Mitchell, "Statistical Appendix," in *The Fontana Economic History of Europe,* ed. Carlo M. Cipolla, vol. 6 (Glasgow, 1976), pp. 721–26; Federal Republic of Germany, Bundesregierung, *Jahresgutachten 1983/84 des Sachverständigenrates zur Begutachtung des gesamtwirtschaftlichen Entwicklung* (Wiesbaden, 1983), p. 288.

conditions in money and capital markets. After the Second World War prices began to rise permanently and independently of economic fluctuations. Moreover, just as the European economy entered a crisis in the 1970s, the upsurge in prices accelerated. Many reasons were advanced for this new phenomenon of "stagflation" in which stagnation and inflation coincided: psychological and rational behavioral changes or "inflation mentality"; expansion of national and international liquidity; rapid growth of the money supply; public sector deficits; sudden and large hikes in oil prices; continuing demands for high wage increases despite growing unemployment; price-fixing by oligopolistic conglomerates; and insulation of incomes from the effects of the business cycle by the social security system. In the early 1980s rates of inflation began to recede again, but the conjunction of deflation and recession that had persisted historically in the 1930s did not reappear.

CHAPTER 4

Continuity and Change in Economic Structures: Utilization and Management of National Product

Utilization of National Product

Macroeconomic Structure of Expenditures

Having described where and how European national income is created, it is now time to consider how that national income is consumed. Three fundamental problems arise:

1. The relation between domestic and foreign consumption in overall national expenditures. If exports exceed imports, the domestic economy consumes and invests less than it actually produces; should imports exceed exports, the situation is reversed. If such imbalances persist for a long time, the country's economy can encounter serious difficulties. Generally, therefore, national economies strive to maintain external economic equilibrium.

2. The structural components of domestic demand. What share of national income is devoted to domestic consumption of goods and services (private or state) and what share to domestic capital investment (private or state)? This question is of considerable importance for employment and economic growth policies. The proper relation between consumption and investment as well as which of their macroeconomic aggregates should be promoted are both hotly debated issues.

3. The agencies of demand. What share of consumption and investment is controlled by the private sphere and what share by the public sphere? This question, too, is the focus of intensive debate because, like the previous one, it bears decisively on economic and political affairs. At stake, in the final analysis, is the multiple relationship between two sets of macroeconomic aggregates: consumption versus investment vis-à-vis private versus public expenditure.

Table 4.1 provides data on the distribution of national expenditure in several countries over the course of the twentieth century. The universal coincidence of a declining share of private consumption with a rising share of state consumption and capital investment is striking. Between 1901–1910 and 1971–1980 the state's share of national expenditure trebled, and the share taken by investment doubled. By contrast, the share of private consumption fell by about a third, from 75–80 percent to 50–60 percent. This structural change was not continuous; it quickened after the Second World War and then slowed somewhat in the 1970s. One must remember, however, that these data are nominal magnitudes. Since the prices involved in state consumption (for example, civil service salaries) rose faster than those related to private consumption, the more rapid relative growth in state expenditure resulted at least in part from differential price movements. In real terms the distribution of national expenditure has changed little since 1945. Moreover, a not inconsiderable portion of private consumption has simply been shifted over to the state sector in the course of the century. Thus, the costs of education and health care, which were mostly privately financed in 1900, constituted by the 1980s a large part of state expenditure. These provisos nonetheless do not alter the fact that in twentieth-century Europe the state has consumed an ever greater portion of the national product and that the relative amount of capital investment has practically doubled.

Comparing developments in Eastern and Western Europe after the Second World War is difficult because of the differing methods of calculating national income and consequently the different interpretations of the relevant macroeconomic aggregates; ultimately, though, the process just described occurred also in the state socialist countries. The share of so-called personal consumption declined, and the proportions of social consumption and accumulation increased.

Private Consumption

Despite its relative decline, private consumption still represents the most important single component of domestic demand. Its structure, that is, its composition in terms of goods and services, is at once a driving force and a consequence of economic development; it also reflects the general living standard of a society. In conjunction with the enormous growth of national product and real wages in the course of the century, this structure has shifted fundamentally. The share of

Table 4.1. Utilization of National Product in Various Countries, 1901–1980 (in percent)

	1901–10	1911–20	1921–30
Denmark			
PCE	79	81	80
GCE	7	7	9
GNCF	14	12	11
United Kingdom[a]			
PCE	85	—	82
GCE	7	—	9
GNCF	8	—	9
Italy[b]			
PCE	75	—	79
GCE	10	—	6
GNCF	15	—	16
Norway			
PCE	78	71	72
GCE	6	6	8
GNCF	17	23	20
Austria[c]			
PCE	—	—	79
GCE	—	—	10
GNCF	—	—	14
Sweden			
PCE	82	80	79
GCE	6	6	8
GNCF	12	14	13
Portugal			
PCE	—	—	—
GCE	—	—	—
GNCF	—	—	—
Greece			
PCE	—	—	—
GCE	—	—	—
GNCF	—	—	—

Sources: Ole Krantz, *Die skandinavischen Länder: Schweden, Norwegen, Dänemark und Finnland von 1914 bis 1970* (Stuttgart, 1980), p. 42; A. S. Deaton, "The Structure of Demand 1920–1970," in *The Fontana Economic History of Europe,* ed. Carlo M. Cipolla, vol. 5 (Glasgow, 1976), pp. 93–94; OECD, *Historical Statistics 1960–1980* (Paris, 1982), pp. 58–65; Angus Maddison, *Economic Growth in the West: Comparative Experience in Europe and North America* (New York, 1967), pp. 76, 103, 239–42.

Table 4.1. (continued)

1931–40	1941–50	1951–60	1961–70	1971–80
79	72	68	62	56
9	11	13	16	24
12	17	19	22	22
80	—	67	64	61
11	—	17	19	20
9	—	16	17	19
74	—	68	64	64
9	—	12	13	15
17	—	20	23	22
70	57	52	52	53
8	9	11	13	18
22	33	37	35	32
82	—	63	59	55
13	—	13	14	17
5	—	24	28	29
74	69	65	60	53
9	11	12	15	26
17	20	23	25	21
—	—	77	73	71
—	—	11	14	15
—	—	12	13	14
—	—	77	71	67
—	—	12	12	15
—	—	11	17	18

Note: PCE = Private Consumption Expenditure; GCE = Government Current
Expenditure; GNCF = Gross National Capital Formation.
[a] United Kingdom: 1901–13; 1921–29; 1930–39; 1950–58.
[b] Italy: 1901–13; 1950–59.
[c] Austria: 1924–30; 1931–37.

basic necessities—food and tobacco, clothing and footwear—in overall private consumption has declined sharply, by contrast, the share of secondary needs in utility goods—services and durable consumer items—grew considerably. This development implies an unexampled increase in the material standard of living; it also heightened the sensitivity of consumer behavior to the vagaries of the business cycle with corresponding effects on general economic growth. Another general economic result of the changing structure of private consumption has been the emergence and expansion of an entirely new branch of economic activity, namely advertising, that is supposed to stimulate and channel private consumer demand.

Behind this aggregate shift, of course, lies a more variegated pattern of change. As already pointed out in Chapter 2, the material life-styles of the various social strata have always differed both quantitatively and qualitatively. Unsurprisingly, national differences in timing and extent of the shift of private consumption away from basic necessities towards higher quality goods and services also existed (see fig. 4.1). During the interwar period the structure of private consumption remained essentially unchanged, reflecting the slow upward movement of real wages (see fig. 2.6). But between 1950 and 1980 the share taken by food, drink, and tobacco in private consumption declined almost continuously by more than one third. At the same time, a large gap between northern/western Europe and southern/eastern Europe has persisted throughout the century. In the 1920s and 1930s expenditure on food, drink and tobacco represented only one half of total private consumption in most countries of western Europe; in the Scandinavian countries and the Netherlands it was less than 40 percent. By 1980 the proportion had fallen to around 25 percent in all states of these two major regions. In southern and eastern Europe, by contrast, these primary necessities still accounted for nearly 60 percent of private consumption in the 1950s, and only in Spain and Italy did their share fall below 40 percent by 1980. According to obtainable data on the consumption of foodstuffs in eastern Europe—continuous and comparable data are unavailable—corresponding quotas for the consumption of food and drink in Hungary, Poland, Czechoslovakia, and East Germany were between 42 and 46 percent in the mid-1970s.

The declining relative cost of food and drink not only reduced the overall share of these items in private consumer's budgets but also enabled an increase in the variety and quality of food consumption. The extent of this diversification differed according to the traditional

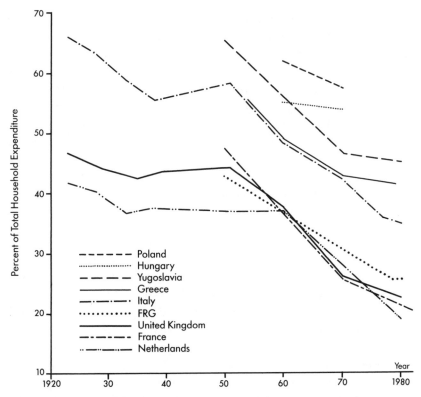

Figure 4.1. Expenditure on Food, Drink, and Tobacco in Various Countries, 1922–1982 (in percent of total household expenditure). *Sources:* A. S. Deaton, "The Structure of Demand 1920–1970," in *The Fontana Economic History of Europe,* ed. Carlo M. Cipolla, vol. 5 (Glasgow, 1976), p. 104; UN, *Yearbook of National Accounts Statistics 1957* (New York, 1959); *1961* (New York, 1963); *1971* (New York, 1973); *1981* (New York, 1983); François Caron, *An Economic History of Modern France* (New York, 1979), p. 214; V. Cao Minna and S. S. Shatalin, *Consumption Patterns in Eastern and Western Europe* (Oxford, 1979), pp. 50–52.

eating habits of each country and nationality, but the tendency was universal: reduction in the consumption of bread, grains, milk, and dairy products in favor of meat, vegetables, and fruit. A number of factors besides relative prices contributed to this shift: altered production structures in agriculture, improved marketing arrangements for perishable goods (packaging, transport, and storage), as well as a broadening of supply and of personal tastes as a result of the spread of foreign restaurants and foreign tourism.

Since Europeans after the Second World War had to spend relatively less on food, they were able to increase the amounts dispensed on other needs and new products. After food, housing is the most basic requirement of private consumption. In nearly all states outside eastern Europe, the shortage of housing resulting from the war and a rapidly growing population brought about a rise in the proportionate expenditure on rents, from around 10 percent of household expenditures in 1950 to over 15 percent, in some countries even 30 percent, in 1980. (In eastern Europe strict state control of rents and the housing market kept the proportion down to around 4–5 percent.) Yet one must not forget that the quality of housing was also comprehensively improved. In the 1950s apartments supplied with inside running hot and cold water, separate toilet facilities, electricity, and central heat were still in the minority in many areas. From about 1960 in western Europe and from about 1970 in eastern and southern Europe, this level of facilities had become the standard rule. Individual home ownership also increased in many countries: in 1963, 41 percent of households in Britain were owner-occupied, and by 1980, 54 percent.

But the clearest sign of the rise of modern consumer society was increasingly widespread ownership of consumer durables such as radios, televisions, washing machines, refrigerators, and, of course, automobiles. Above all, the costs of purchasing and operating means of transportation and communication (including the telephone) represented a relatively new category of expenditure, whose share in total private consumption in many countries trebled between 1950 and 1980 from about 5 percent to roughly 15 percent. The growth of ownership of four key durable goods is indicated by the curve in figure 4.2; France represents the western and northern European pattern (including Italy), and East Germany represents the eastern and southern European pattern. In the case of the state socialist countries of Eastern Europe, the curves also reflect a transformation in economic development policy: the "discovery" of the consumer at the beginning of the 1960s and the gradual retreat from the Stalinist mode of accumulation.

State Consumption

Next to private consumption, state or public consumption is the second largest aggregate in total national expenditure. Since public services are supplied mostly free of charge, their total value must be determined according to the costs of those services rather than according to their market prices. State consumption is thus constituted above all by the

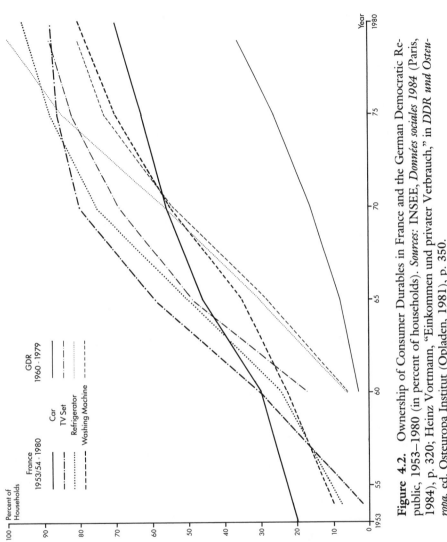

Figure 4.2. Ownership of Consumer Durables in France and the German Democratic Republic, 1953–1980 (in percent of households). *Sources:* INSEE, *Données sociales 1984* (Paris, 1984), p. 320; Heinz Vortmann, "Einkommen und privater Verbrauch," in *DDR und Osteuropa,* ed. Osteuropa Institut (Opladen, 1981), p. 350.

salaries and wages of civil servants as well as by the purchase of goods, manufacturing taxes paid by the state, and write-offs and prepayments on state property.

An unambiguous determination of current state expenditure is not easy; for earlier times it is even more problematical. To distinguish among state consumption, public investment, and transfer payments, which together constitute total state expenditure, is especially difficult. Transfer payments rose faster than other types of state expenditure until by the 1980s they amounted on average to more than half of total state expenditure in many Western European countries. After taking public investments into account, actual state consumption—the operational outlay for general administration, armed forces, economy, communications and transport, education, and so on—made up about 40 percent of total state expenditure. This figure was much higher at the beginning of the century, since capital investments and transfer payments assumed significance only with the rise of the interventionist social welfare state. In view of the difficulty of separating state consumption from investments and transfer payments, the following discussion deals with the development of state expenditures as a whole, but the trends undoubtedly apply as well to state consumption in the narrower sense.

The increase of state expenditures during the century was naturally accompanied by structural change in those expenditures. The changing composition of state expenditures and the changing function of state activity were closely interconnected: if state expenditures can generally be considered the financial expression of state activity, then changes in the structure of expenditures ultimately reflect changes in the social and political system. Given the data available one can posit the following conclusions about structural change in public expenditure in northern and western European countries (including Italy). In the nineteenth century expenditures on the classic state functions such as justice, finance, and defense plainly occupied the center stage (see fig. 4.3). Larger amounts of money were spent on them than on economic and social affairs; not uncommonly they consumed more than three quarters of state spending. Even in the Scandinavian countries, which were relatively untouched by war, military expenditures exceeded those for general administrative activities. During the final decades of the nineteenth century, however, a gradual change set in. The proportion of spending for military and adminstrative tasks receded, and that for economic purposes, including social purposes, rose; the foremost component of social expenditure was public education. In a few progressive countries, for example, Britain and the German Empire, the outlay for social and economic purposes had become the largest items in state expenditure even before the First World War.

This important structural change in public spending was clearly accelerated in many countries by the political transformation brought about by the war. An internal realignment within social expenditures also appeared; in the interwar period many states began to spend more on social security, health care, and housing than on education. The path to the modern welfare state was first trodden by Germany, Britain, and the Scandinavian countries; in the course of the 1950s the Netherlands, Belgium, Italy, and France followed suit, and most recently the remaining southern European countries. At the beginning of the 1980s no state in Western Europe spent less than half of its total outlay on social and educational affairs. The more or less continuous growth of this component is certainly the most significant structural shift in the composition of total public expenditure in the last hundred years. The decline of military expenditure during the same period—discounting the wars—to below 10 percent of total public expenditure is likewise striking.

Capital Investment

As mentioned earlier, capital investment has become one of the key components of the modern industrial economy. To follow its course historically and comparatively, it is commonly presented in relation to national product, which results in a measure variously designated the investment ratio or the rate of capital formation. Unsurprisingly, historical data on capital formation exist for only a few countries, but the movement of the investment ratios in the major economies of Western Europe should provide a reasonably valid guide to overall European development. In examining the record over the last hundred years the familiar tripartite periodization emerges. During the interwar period investment ratios were barely higher than those prevailing before the First World War and plainly lower than those after the Second World War. The economic boom of the 1950s and 1960s entailed extraordinarily high rates of capital formation. Between the mid-1970s and the mid-1980s investment ratios declined slightly, but they were on average still twice as high as the interwar figures and were also higher than the rate of the early 1950s. From this historical perspective, at

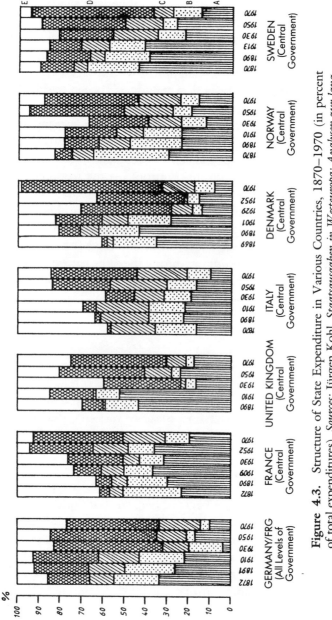

Figure 4.3. Structure of State Expenditure in Various Countries, 1870–1970 (in percent of total expenditures). *Sources:* Jürgen Kohl, *Staatsausgaben in Westeuropa: Analysen zur langfristigen Entwicklung der öffentlichen Finanzen* (Frankfurt, 1984), p. 230. A = military. B = administration, justice, police. C = industry, commerce. D = social security, health, education. E = other expenditures.

least, the economic crisis of the 1970s and 1980s looks mild. Indeed, the long-term trend is one of rising rates of capital formation, which also applies to the economies of eastern Europe. Applying Western categories of national income accounting, despite the attendant difficulties, to Eastern economies reveals that the investment ratios in state socialist and capitalist Europe after the Second World War were rather similar, in the East they were initially somewhat lower, but they rose more quickly than in the West.

The investment ratios indicate only the proportion of the national product used for capital formation, not the actual volumes involved. This is also true of the data in figure 4.4, where the long-term trend values of the investment volumes have been set at zero, to bring out the volume fluctuations around the rising trend more clearly. The volume of investment was above the trend in the decade before the First World War, fell below it during the Great Depression, and moved above it from the 1950s to the mid-1970s, at which time investment volume fell below the trend once again.

With respect to annual growth rates of the volume of capital investment after 1945, state socialist Eastern Europe clearly lay ahead of capitalist Western Europe (see table 4.2). The very rapid growth in investment in the centrally planned economies of Eastern Europe in the 1950s and 1960s can be partly attributed to the relatively low initial levels of capital formation. The Stalinist development strategy of forced accumulation is undoubtedly another reason. The data in table 4.2 also indicate that the rates of investment growth have diminished in both capitalist and state socialist Europe; the slowdown was most marked in the 1970s in the West, in the 1980s in the East.

Management of National Product

Structure of Macroeconomic Management

Up to now the economic system has been treated as a relatively isolated subsystem. Connections with other parts of the social system—especially with the political subsystem—have been disregarded for the most part. Such an approach is legitimated only by heuristic and analytical considerations. In reality, economics and politics are closely interconnected. The state, the largest and most important formal organization in the political subsystem, is tied into the economy in numerous ways. Fundamentally, two central areas of state responsibility

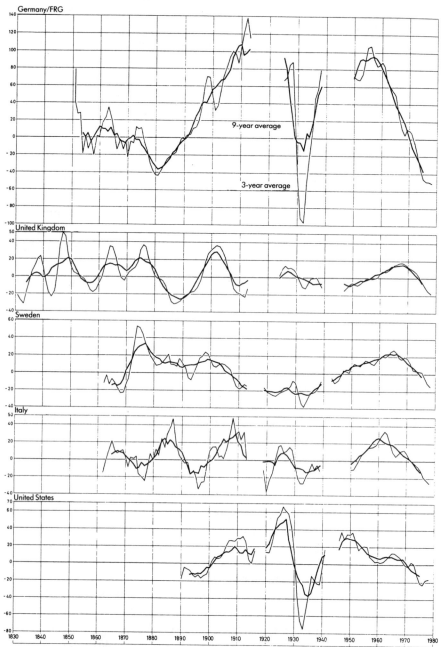

Figure 4.4. Long Waves in Investment Activity in Various Countries, 1830–1979 (deviations from a moving three-year and nine-year average expressed in percent of trend value). *Source:* H. H. Glismann et al., *Lange Wellen wirtschaftlichen Wachstums: Replik und Weiterführung* (Kiel, 1980), p. 24.

Table 4.2.   Gross Capital Investment in Western and Eastern Europe, 1950–
1982 (average annual rate of change in percent)

	1950–59	1960–73	1973–80	1979	1980	1981	1982
Western Europe	6.5	5.6	0.3	3.7	2.2	−3.6	−2.2
Eastern Europe[a]	12.0	7.9	4.0	−1.0	−2.2	−7.2	−4.5

Sources: UN (ECE), *Economic Survey of Europe in 1971* (New York, 1972), p. 8; *1982* (New York, 1983), pp. 20, 115, 168, 216; *1983* (New York, 1984), pp. 17, 109.
  [a] Eastern Europe (excl. Soviet Union): 1950–60; 1960–78; 1971–80.

in socioeconomic affairs can be distinguished: the influencing of economic processes by means of economic and social policy; and the provisioning and distribution of public goods. The first area comprises the multitude of laws, decrees, economic planning measures, and ad hoc interventions. These not only provide the general framework in which a socioeconomic order is created but also directly influence the formation, development, and distribution of national product. Included in the second area of economic public goods are all those material goods and services provided by the public purse. Here the state participates as producer in the formation, development, and distribution of national product.

The Interventionist State

From the various attempts to identify and legitimate state responsibilities in historical development only the hypotheses advanced by the American political economist Walt W. Rostow will be presented here. Explicitly organizing his stage theory along economic and social-historical lines, Rostow posits three universal issues for which the state must assume responsibility:

1. Security: the state must guarantee the territorial integrity of society and preserve national interests.
2. Welfare and growth: the state must look after the general welfare of society.
3. Constitutional order: the state must regulate the filling of positions of authority and the exercise of power.

In the course of historical development these three spheres have had varying degrees of relevance; highest priority at any given time was assigned to the sphere with the most pressing problems. The following account is devoted primarily to the sphere of welfare and growth.

According to Rostow economic development passes through six stages, in each of which the three spheres of issues form different constellations and have differing internal composition: the traditional society; the preconditions for take-off; the take-off, when self-sustaining economic growth begins; the drive to maturity; and maturity or high mass consumption. Individual countries pass through these stages at different times, but all countries undergo these development stages in the same order, which determines state policy and makes it comparable in principle.

In the phase preceding take-off the political, social and institutional framework that will make industrialization possible is created. The state must build up the infrastructure necessary for the capitalist mode of production: a bureaucratically organized state administration, especially a financial administration; a rational system of law with a corresponding administrative substructure; and participation in the creation of a system of banking and credit as well as of a physical infrastructure such as roads, railroads, and so forth. In the actual take-off phase—the final breakthrough to industrialization—these tasks are extended. In the drive to technical maturity and to ever more complex industrial systems the new conditions of production require a qualified work force that can be supplied only by a public educational system. Also necessary is the inauguration of a state social policy. Rostow does not reduce this necessity to mere economic contingency—the securing of biological reproduction or the reduction of the reproduction costs of labor—but instead emphasizes the social structural changes and shifts of social power that accompany industrialization. The subsequent stage of mass consumption brings relatively few qualitatively new tasks, according to Rostow. The social security system, the public infrastructure, and the system of economic management must be expanded. The biggest change in state activity arises from the growing demand that the state secure the employment and purchasing power of the masses and promote general economic growth. Rostow interprets the most recent past—the 1960s and 1970s—as a stage dominated by the search for "quality of life." The negative consequences of extensive industrial growth became apparent and mobilized forces opposing the further destruction of the social and natural environment. From this emerged new tasks for the state that go beyond the traditional forms of social and infrastructural security.

This means primarily that the state increasingly influences the market-based distribution of resources. It has increasingly become a formative, regulatory, managing, and controlling institution. This is also shown by its rising importance in setting the legal norms of the politico-economic order. In its laws the state codifies not only the basic conditions of social exchange but also the conditions of production, labor, and so on. Civil, criminal, public, commercial, labor, and social law represent legal norms with which the state establishes the fundamental structures of society and economy. This normative function of the state has increased since the nineteenth century. Whereas the chief concern during the period of classical liberalism was the creation of a rough legal framework within which the economy could operate more or less freely, in the course of the twentieth century the state has had to fill out this framework with growing complexity, interconnecting law with all spheres of life. A multitude of laws and decrees regulate economic and social processes today. If one understands by the term "social and economic order" the entirety of organizational principles, norms, mechanisms for management and decision-making, institutions, and forms of behavior that, taken together, constitute the basis on which economic activity in a society is conducted, then the legislative intervention of the state determines an ever greater portion of this order.

Rostow's developmental model can, of course, provide only a basic orientation. It must never be applied mechanically to the development path of specific countries. Even if individual countries are supposed to pass through the various stages, they do so in historically varying contexts. Whether the political systems, or rather the state, react similarly to such challenges is likewise left open. Rostow himself has emphasized that societies at similar stages of economic and technological development are confronted with varying political options. To move from mere description to analysis of the evolution of state tasks, a multitude of non-economic factors would have to be taken into account.

The State as a Source of Expenditures
Every newly acquired or augmented state task is associated with outlay and results in rising state expenditures. Since the nineteenth century, therefore, the state in all European countries has called upon an ever greater share of national product to fulfill its purposes. The importance of the state is usually measured nowadays by setting public spending in relation to national product. The reliability of the conclusions drawn from this so-called state-quota is limited by a number of statistical and methodological problems, but it does help in gaining an initial impres-

sion of the growing importance of the state in the twentieth century.

Figure 4.5 shows the evolution of the state-quota in various European countries. During the nineteenth century, which is not shown in the figure, the share of total public spending in the national product varied between 6 percent and 16 percent. The proportions in many continental European countries—Italy, France, Germany, and Switzerland—were much higher than those in Britain and the Scandinavian countries. Before the First World War a rising tendency in the state's share of national expenditure was evident only in Germany and Norway; in some countries the quota was even falling. After the war and especially in those countries directly affected by the war and its social and political consequences—Germany, Austria, France, Italy, Belgium, Britain—normal state spending resumed at a far higher level than had

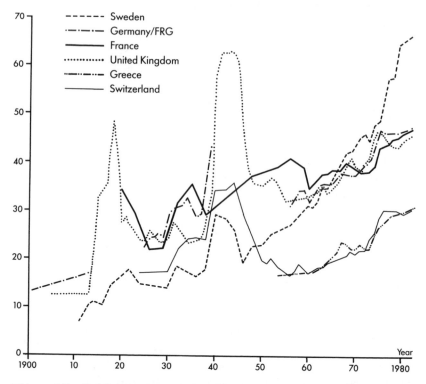

Figure 4.5. Public Expenditure as a Proportion of National Product ("State-Quota") for Various Countries, 1900–1982 (in percent). *Sources:* Peter Flora, *State, Economy, and Society in Western Europe 1815–1975: A Data Handbook,* vol. 1 (Frankfurt, 1983), pp. 345–449; OECD, *Economic Outlook,* 31 (July 1982): 148–49.

prevailed before the war. Only in Scandinavia and Switzerland, which had remained neutral during the conflict, did state expenditures stay initially at a relatively low level, although even in these countries the share of national product represented by state outlay rose.

With respect to the interwar period one must bear in mind that because of the large drop in national income during the Great Depression the proportion of the state's outlay in the national product still rose when the actual amount of expenditure remained stable or even declined, though at a slower rate than the national product. Compared with the great fluctuations of the interwar years, the postwar period after 1945 was characterized by a relatively steady expansion of public sector spending. The increase was most marked in Scandinavia, the Netherlands, and Belgium, where the state's share of the national product almost doubled. In most other countries it rose by almost one half.

The trend of rising state-quotas was thus typical of all European countries, although to a varying degree. If only the beginning and end points of the past hundred years are compared, the rise in the other European countries (excluding Finland) is particularly pronounced. There the share of national product taken by state spending amounted to over 60 percent in the mid-1980s. The western European states represented the European average, both in terms of the rate of growth and the absolute level: in the early 1980s the quota was about 50 percent. One exception to the western European pattern is Switzerland, which together with Greece, Portugal, Spain, and the eastern European countries before the Second World War had a very low quota; in 1980 public expenditure in Switzerland still amounted to only about 30 percent of national product.

The rising relative level of public outlay did not occur at a constant pace but rather in intermittent bursts. One might logically suppose that these bursts of public spending were stimulated by the two world wars, introducing either an abrupt upward shift of the level or an acceleration in the expansion of public spending. This pattern certainly fits some countries, especially those involved in the wars, but it is not open to generalization without qualification.

The Fiscal State

Naturally, the states had to finance their growing outlay by increasing their revenue. Disregarding the eastern European countries after 1945 for the moment, European states have never possessed sufficient productive sources of their own to finance their activities; consequently,

they have had to draw off revenue from privately organized and produced value-added output. The concept of the "fiscal state" indicates
that the bulk of public expenditure is financed by taxation. The broadening of the tax base and the taxation rate have been the means by
which the state sought to increase its income. As the data in figure 4.6
indicate, tax revenue has increased in all European states not only
absolutely but also in relation to the national product.

The data in figure 4.6 refer only to taxes assessed by the central
government, which at the end of the nineteenth century covered between 50 percent and 60 percent of all taxes paid and in the 1970s
accounted for over 75 percent of the total tax intake. The share of total
taxation in the national product was thus in fact rather high and rose
somewhat more moderately than indicated by the curves in figure 4.6.
The pattern of evolution in most European countries was broadly
similar from the mid-nineteenth century on. Up to the First World
War the share of tax income was very low and hardly changed from
one decade to the next. The war then brought about a definite increase,
which was only partly reversed after the war. In a few countries the
share did fall sharply in the immediate postwar years, but then rose
during the remainder of the interwar period. A similar pattern occurred
both during and after the Second World War. There were, of course,
exceptions to this evolution. But the important point remains that the
European states, as fiscal institutions, had to finance their growing
expenditure out of private net output and that they therefore skimmed
off a growing proportion of the national product in the form of tax.

If other forms of state revenue such as social security contributions
were combined with formal taxes, the figures just mentioned would
have to be revised upwards. In the mid-1980s the share of this more
broadly defined tax revenue in the national product amounted to
around 55 percent in the northern European economies, 45 percent
in the western European, and 35 percent in the southern European.

The State as Producer

The state not only collected through taxation an even greater share of
the national product, which it then expended, but also contributed
substantially to that national product on its own account through the
production of public goods. The comprehensive activities of the state—
the public sector—can be separated roughly into three areas. The first
area pertains to narrowly defined economic productive activities. State-
owned enterprises provide large portions of the economic infrastruc-

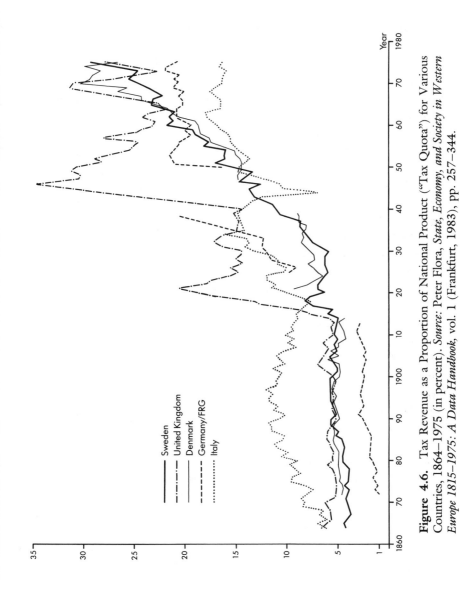

Figure 4.6. Tax Revenue as a Proportion of National Product ("Tax Quota") for Various Countries, 1864–1975 (in percent). *Source:* Peter Flora, *State, Economy, and Society in Western Europe 1815–1975: A Data Handbook,* vol. 1 (Frankfurt, 1983), pp. 257–344.

ture. This is true both for the supply of water and energy and for the supply of services such as transportation, post, and telecommunications. The state owns banks and insurance companies, research institutes, housing construction firms, trading companies, and industrial, agricultural, and forestry enterprises. All these activities are subsumed under the term "public economy," whose significance varies considerably from country to country. The public economy is not very large in the Scandinavian countries, for instance, but in Italy its dimensions are huge: half of all the country's industrial enterprises belong to the state. A second important area of the public sector includes the variety of state institutions concerned with health, education, and welfare: nurseries, schools and universities, hospitals, and so on. The third and most important area of the public sector comprises the general administration, justice and police, and the military. The methodological and statistical difficulties in measuring the value of the goods and services produced by the public sector are so considerable that the contribution of the state to the formation of national product cannot be determined with exactitude and its historical evolution scarcely at all. Clearly, though, the form and extent of publicly created goods and services have grown constantly in the course of this century.

An important indicator of the state's significance as a producer in the national economy is the number of public employees expressed as a proportion of the total work force. Figure 4.7 shows the evolution of this share in a number of Western European countries over the past century. Unfortunately, the data include only a minority of public employees, namely, those within general administration, postal services, railways, and education. Workers and salaried employees in the public economy as well as in social welfare and health are not represented. Yet even this restricted group clearly demonstrates the trend of public sector employment. One must bear in mind, of course, that the data are available only over a few years; movement (especially in the war years) quite possibly did not follow such a straightforward course. But that would not alter the overall trend: the share of publicly employed persons in the total labor force has risen since the late nineteenth century in all European countries. The proportion has been remarkably uniform from country to country: in 1870 it was around 2 percent and by the 1970s over 10 percent, representing a fivefold increase. Since over this same period the total labor force was also growing, the absolute number of public employees actually rose by a factor of from seven to ten.

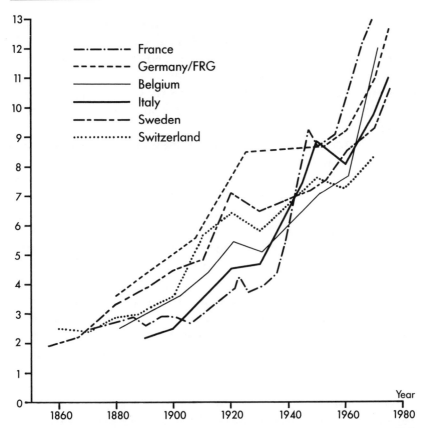

Figure 4.7. Employment in the Public Sector in Various Countries, 1850–1975 (in percent of total work force). *Source:* Peter Flora, *State, Economy, and Society in Western Europe 1815–1975: A Data Handbook,* vol. 1 (Frankfurt, 1983), pp. 193–243.

Although the number of public employees cannot be quantified precisely, it can be roughly estimated. The omission of data on public economy, social welfare and health means leaving out precisely those areas in which the publicly employed work force expanded most rapidly in the twentieth century. The growth of total public employment thus not only occurred from a much higher level, but also increased much more rapidly. In the 1980s a substantial proportion of the total work force was occupied in the public economy alone in many countries: 12 percent in West Germany, 15 percent in Britain, 25 percent in Italy, and 30 percent in Austria. If those employed in general administration, public hospitals, welfare agencies, and social insurance administration were included, then state employees would constitute about one third of the labor force in West Germany, Britain, and France and possibly over one half of the labor force in Italy and Austria. Even in those countries in which the public economy does not play such an important role—the Netherlands, the Scandinavian countries, Spain, and Portugal—the share of public employment is substantially greater than indicated by the curves in figure 4.7.

Public employment in the Eastern European countries took a leap forward after the Second World War. If socialized and collective enterprises are counted as state-owned enterprises—officially they are accounted for as social property—then over 90 percent of the work force is in public employment. More important here is the trend: in all European countries, Eastern and Western, the number of workers and employees in the public sector rose during the twentieth century and today constitutes a large part of the total work force.

Thus, the significance of the state in economic life has generally increased since the nineteenth century. The state has also increasingly attempted to direct economic processes, as can be seen in the course of economic policy throughout the twentieth century. Instead of examining thematic areas separately over time, the following discussion considers economic policy as a whole within specific time periods. This approach provides an overview of the different phases of European economic history and makes it easier to understand chronological developments. Of course, the variety of state activities affecting the economy cannot be presented in any detail—they are far too complex. Our account concentrates on the identification of different economic orders or systems and deals with at least some of the basic instruments through which the state sought to influence the course of economic development.

Politicoeconomic Reconstruction after the First World War

The desire to restore prewar relations determined the economic policy of the 1920s. This reflected the beliefs and interests of the ruling circles in politics and the economy, for whom the decades before the war represented an epoch of stable economic growth and social certainty. By contrast, directly after the war, Europe experienced a wave of revolutionary and quasi-revolutionary change that shook the social orders of many countries to their foundations. The organization of the world economy was also out of joint: the domination of the European industrial and imperialist heartlands was called into question. The nostalgic view of the past, partly realistic, partly idealized, overlooked the structural changes underway before 1914 that the war had only accelerated. It also ignored that relations had changed beyond recall.

International Policy

An inability to assess the new situation realistically characterized the peace negotiations. No state was sufficiently interested in a cooperative approach to problems. The United States, politically and economically the most powerful country, simply wished to withdraw as quickly as possible from the confusion of European affairs and was not prepared to assume leadership in the reconstruction of the world economy. France and Britain pursued their old rivalries between themselves and in common against Germany; Russia, the fourth European great power, entirely withdrew from international affairs. Even though the political usefulness of attributing moral guilt for the war was cast in as much doubt as the economic purpose of war debt and reparation payments, these were the issues that exercised international conferences. Those who had begun the war should be punished; those who had built up debts in the course of the war should repay them. Few realized that the grave condition of the European and world economy raised more important problems requiring international solutions.

Aside from the direct negotiations on peace, debts, and reparations, examples of the failure of international cooperation were numerous. Large-scale reconstruction programs could be neither organized nor financed. Helpful as the emergency support measures were in combatting want and hunger, they could not replace more comprehensive projects. No comprehensive plan for the restoration of the war-damaged areas of Europe emerged, and even partial plans got little further than the barest outlines. Instead of being expanded, the wartime interallied organizations, such as those created to solve the problem of raw materials, were dismantled immediately after the war.

International cooperation also made little progress throughout the 1920s. In 1922 at an international conference on foreign exchange the return to the gold standard—the prewar currency system—was decided, but no agreement was reached on a binding international plan. There was even less willingness to coordinate activities in the area of trade and tariffs. The spread of protectionism, which hindered the recovery of world trade in the 1920s, could not be significantly checked even by the world economic conference convoked in 1927 specifically to deal with the problem. Numerous other conferences, held under the auspices of the League of Nations, sought solutions to particular problems in international trade and finance, and innumerable reforms were proposed. No concrete action resulted, however. On the contrary, the disintegration of the European and world economy continued on its way; the complex network of international economic relations, torn apart in 1914, could not be reconstituted.

The idea that the return to the gold standard would by itself secure a well-functioning liberal world economic order was certainly one reason for the lack of readiness to genuinely reorder the world economy. Another was the belief that national protectionism and self-interest could moderate the effects of the international crisis on the individual national economies. This attitude ignored the fact that not only the structure of the world economy had altered, but also the social and political forces influencing domestic economics. National economies could no longer be integrated so easily into a world economic system that left little scope to domestic economic policy, as was the case under the gold standard. On the contrary, economic policies directed to national interests had become the priority. This circumstance should have made international cooperation all the more necessary, for this new economic nationalism reinforced the prevailing tendencies towards disintegration.

National Policy

Alterations in economic policy. Middle-class public opinion in most European countries still clung to the politicoeconomic model of laissez-faire liberalism, according to which state intervention in the economy should be as limited as possible. Yet the war, and the shift in political balance of the immediate postwar years, had sharpened awareness of state intervention and promoted a readiness to use it. This did not, however, alter the basic structure of capitalism in the European states, as was evident from the actual policy measures adopted in the wake of the war.

The state systems for planning and management that had guided the economy during the war were dismantled with the arrival of peace. Specific forms of control remained in place during the period of transition, so that the transformation of a wartime economy into a peacetime one could be supervised; but by the early 1920s the state had once more generally removed itself from the economy.

Laws on property and title rights altered as little as did the organization of production. State ownership of means of production increased nevertheless, since some governments had participated directly in war production as entrepreneurs; in addition, railroads and particular areas of raw material supply had been nationalized. In a few southeastern European countries extensive nationalization programs were at first hinted at and then pursued vigorously. Undoubtedly more important, though, were the agrarian reforms carried out in twelve countries—all eastern European states, including Estonia, Latvia, Lithuania, Greece, and Finland. In total, twenty-four million hectares—11 percent of the entire area of these countries—were redistributed.

The various attempts to democratize economic decision-making brought no direct alterations of property rights, but they did change the structure of coordination and communication to some extent. At the level of the individual enterprise, works councils, introduced in Germany, Austria, Czechoslovakia, Britain, and Norway, were conceded the right to a say in social issues. At the national economic level, the beginnings of corporatist elements—the joint elaboration of socioeconomic policy by government, workers' organizations, and employers' associations—appeared in the system of liberal competitive capitalism. Such change, however, did not mean that the economy and economic policy were subjected to real democratization.

Economic motivation was changed not only through the extension or introduction of social welfare legislation, but also through a fundamental reform of the system of taxation and finance that in many countries substantially altered the financial position of the public domain and the nature of the redistributive system. This was also true of tax relief and subsidies, which were extended to increase their effect on investment. The measures ranged from traditional policies of subsidization to the first steps in a broadly conceived state strategy of industrialization in southern and eastern Europe. However, even in the western European economies the share of investment originating from the public sector was considerably greater than before the war.

All of these changes remained within the existing economic framework. Systematic change occurred only in Russia following the October Revolution of 1917. Nonetheless, the role and function of the state altered significantly both during and after the First World War; and these changes were compatible with the model of the liberal laissez-faire state only to a limited extent.

Monetary and financial policy. In no other sphere of policy were such economic wonders expected from the mere return to earlier conditions as in monetary policy, which was assigned priority above all other areas of the economy. This is hardly surprising given the chaotic state of monetary relations after the First World War. Extreme fluctuations of exchange rates and inordinate inflation, especially in the central European states, aroused widespread uncertainty. Yet the inflationary pressures were not coincidental. The war economy had concentrated on producing goods intended for destruction, thereby creating a nominal demand and purchasing power but no real supply of goods. The methods of financing the war also played an important role. Domestic considerations led many governments to avoid fully financing military expenditures by taxation, even though tax revenues were noticeably increased. Instead they resorted to domestic borrowing or to the central bank's printing press. With the arrival of peace, the budget deficits and debts still remained because of the continuing high levels of military spending, the social costs of the war, the repayment of war debts, or the payment of reparations. Monetary and financial policies were thus closely connected: monetary stabilization could succeed only if public finances were placed on a new footing, and vice versa.

The manner in which stabilization was affected varied, both with respect to the setting of a new parity with gold (the relation of the national currency to gold) and to the measures adopted for the domestic stabilization of money value. The group of countries actually returning to prewar parities included Britain, Switzerland, the Netherlands, Denmark, Sweden, and Norway. A second group, the largest, had to devalue by varying amounts; in relation to the prewar exchange rate against the gold-standard U.S. dollar, Estonia devalued its currency by 1.1 percent, Rumania 3.7 percent, Bulgaria, 3.7 percent, Portugal 4.6 percent, Greece, 6.7 percent, Yugoslavia 9.1 percent, Finland 12.5 percent, Belgium 14.3 percent, Czechoslovakia 14.3 percent, France 20 percent, and Italy 25 percent. A third group—Austria, Hungary, Poland, the USSR, and Germany—failed to control inflation by conventional means; after a period of uncontrolled hyperinflation, these countries had to introduce entirely new currencies.

What measures were actually used to stabilize currencies? Though some countries returned to prewar parities, this did not mean that their currencies had lost no value during and after the war; in fact, all currencies fell in real terms between 10 percent and 20 percent against the U.S. dollar. The return to prewar parities thus necessitated extensive deflationary measures to reduce prices. By increasing taxation and cutting expenditures, governments attempted to reduce public budget deficits or to achieve budget surpluses. Public borrowing was limited. Monetary policy was tightened to limit the freedom of banks to create credit. Wage scales were frozen, or even reduced. These measures contributed to a weakening of economic recovery or a strengthening of recessive tendencies. Sweden was the first to succeed in reducing the level of prices and wages and in revaluing its currency; it returned to the gold standard in 1924. In Britain deflationary policy and the attendant recessionary effects lasted until 1925. In Norway and Denmark the deflationary crisis took place between 1925 and 1928; its effects in Norway were perhaps more serious then those of the Great Depression of the early 1930s.

Despite quite drastic economic measures in some cases, success in matching costs to prices was limited. The return to prewar parities thus overvalued currencies with respect to gold and the dollar. This then burdened the various national economies, since the ability to export was thereby reduced: the overvaluation of the currency meant that domestically produced goods were relatively expensive on the world market, whereas imported goods were cheaper. Almost all countries suffered from this reduced competitiveness, although to varying degrees. The only real exception was Sweden; not only did its domestic price level fall by an amount necessary to maintain international competitiveness, but its economy proved flexible enough to react to altered conditions in the world market.

Increase of revenue and reduction of spending, restrictive money and credit policies, and the consolidation of public debt were other measures by which those countries that returned to the gold standard in devaluing their currencies attempted to restore internal and external stability. Latvia (which as a newly founded independent state had to introduce a new currency) and Czechoslovakia were the forerunners in this regard. Both countries successfully choked off incipient inflation shortly after the war through rigorous fiscal and monetary measures. Other countries, such as France, Belgium, and Italy, managed this in the course of the 1920s. The revaluation in some countries, such as France and Belgium, led to undervaluation against the dollar and the other European currencies; in some countries, Italy for instance, an overvaluation with respect to the prewar parity persisted despite the revaluation.

This practice also had advantages. The timid attempts at stabilization did not bring about real deflation. On the contrary, inflation continued at what was for the time a moderate level, and this had positive results.

Investment, consumption, and the business cycle were thereby stimulated, which eased the burden of deficit financing on the part of the public sector. Taxes were increased in many countries, but not to such an extent that the already low levels of consumption were further reduced. Inflationary processes set in train a redistributive process—whose existence few recognized—in favor of entrepreneurs, owners of capital, and debtors (among whom was the state) and to the disadvantage of rentiers, savers, and also, in part, wage earners. In the economic sphere inflation generally eased postwar reconstruction; at any rate, those countries with inflationary processes overcame the 1921 crisis better than those without inflation. Moreover, inflationary tendencies relaxed heightened domestic social and political tensions. After the return to the gold standard, the undervalued currencies also enhanced the international competitiveness of their national economies.

The eastern European countries found themselves in a particularly difficult situation. Given the poor state of the economies involved, deflationary policies could only intensify recessive tendencies. But, on the other hand, they were required to reassure foreign investors and hence to secure further capital imports. An exchange rate set too high worsened the prospects for exports, but it also made the future repayment of debt that much easier. For these reasons, among others, the Balkan countries, including Greece, initially held fast to their ultimately unrealistic and overvalued official exchange rates in the Great Depression of the 1930s.

The advantages of inflation were also in the minds of the governments of those countries that subsequently experienced hyperinflation. This attitude was actually appropriate so long as the rate of price increases did not diverge from that in other countries. However, as the inflation spiral grew ever more rapid and then went totally out of control, these advantages quickly became disadvantages. Financial chaos and economic collapse were the consequence. The conventional instruments of monetary and financial policy were after a certain point ineffective in keeping price increases in check; instead, stabilization became the precondition of an orderly financial and fiscal policy. Currency reforms had to be introduced, and these were accompanied by serious crises. Austria and Hungary sought the support of the League of Nations, which underwrote the fresh start in monetary policy through financial restructuring plans and international loans—for Austria in 1922 and Hungary in 1924. Advisors from the League supervised the finances of both countries up to 1926. Once trust in the new currency had been secured, fiscal policies began also to be effective, making a balanced budget possible after a short while. Germany introduced a new currency in 1923–1924, and Poland in 1927. Thereafter, orderly financial management was once more possible in these countries as well.

Trade and tariff policy. That the liberal era of the gold standard was gone once and for all with the First World War became strikingly clear in the development of trade and tariff policy. Protectionism became global. The absence of European competition during the war years had allowed new industries to develop in Japan, India, Australia, and a few South American countries, and after the war these industries needed protection. But no liberalization occurred in North America or Europe either. Indeed quite the opposite: many countries in the 1920s introduced an effective tariff barrier for the first time, or increased already existing tariffs. Restrictions on trade ranged from the licensing of exports and imports through application of quotas and prohibitions of foreign exchange controls. In this way protectionist thinking crept in during the 1920s to a degree inconceivable before 1914. All countries were affected: those with a protectionist tradition as well as those with a liberal, laissez-faire tradition; those with primarily industrial exports as well as those who principally exported agricultural products. To cite just a few examples: in Britain the turn from free trade began with the McKenna Act of 1915, which to increase revenues and to save shipping space imposed a 33 percent duty on cars, motorcycles, and other manufactured goods. Characteristically, the terms of this act not only remained in force at the end of hostilities, but were extended to a longer list of goods; in addition, the Safeguarding of Industries Act and the Dyestuffs Importation Act assured further British products of protective duties.

Whereas the British duties were on the whole very low, in Spain protectionism had such a revival that it led in the second half of the 1920s under Primo de Rivera to the highest customs barriers in Europe. In Italy the Fascists first abandoned high tariffs in 1922, but in 1925 raised the rates once more and introduced import quotas. In eastern Europe the new industries developed during or after the war were given tariff protection. Most of the countries in this region had higher duties after the war than before it. In 1926 Czechoslovakian duties were on average 36.4 percent of the total value of imports, double the rates that had prevailed in Austria-Hungary. The new Hungarian duty was on average 31.1 percent, whereas the earlier duty had averaged 18.9 percent. These rates were higher than those in the other countries of the region.

Perhaps even more complex than the inter-European duties were those of the United States, which were introduced with the Fordney-McCumber Tariff of 1922. This tariff—the highest ever in American history—was scarcely reconcilable with America's new role as the most important world creditor. It made it more difficult for European debtor nations to earn dollars by exporting goods to the United States, precisely when they needed these dollars to pay interest and repay loans.

Summary

The single most important politicoeconomic consequence of the First World War was the altered position of the state in the economy. State interventionism gained in importance, although conceptions of a liberal laissez-fair state were not yet abandoned. The question of whether the modern interventionist state really had its origins in the First World War will be left open here. This development was associated with a shift in priorities: integration into a liberal world economy, which necessitated the subordination of domestic objectives to the goal of external economic stability, no longer had pride of place; instead, measures to stabilize individual national economies were emphasized. International cooperation was not yet dismissed altogether, but the large number of problems that could only be solved internationally remained undealt with.

International cooperation also suffered because the return to the gold standard was expected to bring with it an automatic solution to many open questions. Exchange rates and monetary policy moved into the center of economic policy, and the regaining of prewar parity and the stability of money value became elevated into dogma. The fundamental contradictions that arose as a result went unrecognized: the gold standard could function—if at all—only in a liberal world economy with the appropriate adaptive mechanisms. The gold standard did not permit the existence of domestic monetary policy and ultimately of domestic economic policy. The absolute priority given to monetary goals over all other problems in economic policy ran the risk of undermining the intended social and economic stability. The social and economic costs of such a policy were ignored, and measures were adopted to protect the national economy from foreign competition even though these very measures—high tariffs and import restrictions—themselves undermined the preconditions for the functioning of the gold standard.

From Liberalism to State Interventionism in the 1930s

The Great Depression of the 1930s is more often considered a decisive turning point in the relation of state and economy than the First World War. According to this view, the Depression separates the epoch of the classic liberal state from that of the modern interventionist state. Even if one holds the conviction that the historical process is more or less a continuum with few genuine caesuras, one must admit that a decisive change in economic policy occurred during and after the crisis. The transformation in economic thinking and policy-making can be regarded as the first new paradigm of political economy in this century. Above all, this change affected the domestic economy. In the international sphere the disintegration of the European and world economy continued on its way.

International Policy
International cooperation hit an all-time low in the 1930s. The few attempts made to revive such cooperation were short-lived. At a time when exchange controls, high duties, and quotas obstructed the flow of trade, bilateral agreements emerged in compensation. Bilateral treaties not only aimed at a revival of trade, they sought to do so without resort to internationally convertible currencies. The simplest form of such agreements was barter, the exchange of commodity against commodity without the use of money. Examples of such compensatory deals was the exchange of German coal for Brazilian coffee, or of German artificial fertilizer for Egyptian cotton. A considerable portion of the Greek and Bulgarian tobacco crop found takers in central Europe in this way, who for their part sought export possibilities for manufactured goods. Mostly these bilateral deals, whether conducted by states or by private concerns, were organized under clearing or settlement agreements that minimized the amount of foreign exchange necessary. Germany was the first country to use such settlement agreements extensively. By 1937 it had secured such agreements with every European country except Britain and Albania, although this did not mean that all traffic in goods and services was settled in this fashion. Eastern European countries, which had very close trading links with Germany,

likewise conducted the greater part of their external trade through clearing agreements.

The distintegration of international economic relations led not only to the bilateralization of external trade and external trade policy; at least on the regional level, attempts were made to form multilateral agreements. Southeastern European states sought to stop the fall in their export profits through closer cooperation. Avowals of solidarity made at a series of conferences of eastern European agrarian producers did not suffice to bring about the cartel-like agreements necessary to prevent ruinous mutual competition. These countries nevertheless moved closer together and presented a more united front to the major consumers of their agrarian products. A limited degree of economic cooperation also emerged between Italy, Austria, and Hungary in the Rome Protocol of 1934. The connection of the so-called Oslo Group of 1930, which included alongside the Scandinavian countries the Netherlands, Belgium, and Luxembourg, also represented an attempt to make limited regional cooperation work. Partners to the convention agreed neither to increase existing duties nor to introduce new ones without prior notice to other signatories. No practical consequences followed from this convention, however. This was also true of the Ouchy Treaty of 1932, which envisaged closer cooperation between the Netherlands, Belgium, and Luxembourg. The most important agreement of this period was without doubt that reached in Ottawa in 1932 between the Commonwealth states. It created the Imperial Preference System with preferential duties, internal import reliefs, and intensified external restrictions. Countries of other one-time colonial empires also came together on the issue of trade. The currency blocs formed in these years likewise expressed the regionalization of international economic relations.

These trading agreements—whether bilateral or multilateral—were naturally no substitute for a liberal world economic order. They were solely an emergency solution aimed at preventing the worst consequences of the collapsing European and world economy. No trade was thereby created; rather its decline was moderated and redirected. Long-established trading relations and traditional forms of the international division of labor were abandoned and only partially replaced by new forms. Trade policy was used to a greater extent than in the preceding decade as a means of moderating the effects of the international economic crisis on the domestic economy and of shifting the costs onto other countries.

National Policy

During the 1920s endeavors to return to prewar relations derived not only from self-interested policies or confused memories of the "good old days," but also from the conviction—at least at the level of economic theory and policy—that the premises of the classical model were still valid and that the model accurately identified the functional context of the capitalist economy. This classical model postulated that under competitive conditions the price mechanism assured the existence, in both the short and the long term, of an equilibrium between supply and demand in all markets (whether for goods, capital, or labor) and hence assured general economic equilibrium. In this model prices coordinate the multitude of individual economic intentions through the operation of the "invisible hand" (Adam Smith); interference on the part of the state will only upset this mechanism. The postwar crisis did shake belief in the self-healing powers of the economy, but only the complete collapse of national economies in the world economic crisis prompted a rethinking. This crisis was interpreted not as another cyclical downturn, but rather as an unprecedented depression that questioned fundamentally the functional capacity of the liberal capitalist system. From this point on the view that the state had to assume greater responsibility became more and more widespread. The state should no longer confine itself to the assumption of the social costs of the capitalist economy but should itself influence the course of economic development.

Theoretical alternatives to the classical model had been put forward already in the 1920s, but it was left to the British economist John Maynard Keynes in the mid-1930s to formulate a comprehensive countermodel. According to the Keynesian model, the market economy not only tended to progress through fluctuations, it also had a tendency to operate at a permanent level of underemployment. Supply and demand need not coincide; the price mechanism guarantees neither the sale of all goods on the market, nor the investment of all available capital, nor full employment. The task of economic policy was therefore the matching of supply and demand through the introduction of global measures. Keynes proposed that the proper approach to the crisis of the 1930s, characterized by underemployed productive capacity, was to stimulate aggregate demand by public spending. This would stimulate producers to increase their output, creating in turn new incomes and hence new demand, which then would lead via increasing sales, more intensive utilization of capacity, and higher profits to an increased rate of investment. In this way a circular flow of money would be set in motion through which the economy—if it could be got going in the first place—could pull itself out of the crisis by its own resources. The following sections examine how various European governments sought to find a way out of the crisis, whether by traditional classical liberal means or modern interventionist Keynesian strategies.

Germany. Perhaps the most radical break with previous economic policies occurred in Germany: not only economic policy but the entire politicoeconomic system changed. This break came with the seizure of power by the National Socialists in early 1933. Though there had been signs of cautious countercyclical economic management under the Papen and Schleicher governments, the general approach to the crisis up to 1933 stayed within the classical deflationary framework. Since the German central bank, the Reichsbank, held firm to the gold standard, it was compelled to counter the prevailing economic conditions with a restrictive monetary policy and high rate of interest in order to prevent an outward flow of gold and foreign exchange. The fiscal and social welfare measures of the government also intensified the cyclical downturn: increase of public revenues, reduction in welfare payments and wages, and so on. Only the traditional ruling circles in industry, in the banks, and in agriculture were spared. Quite apart from how individual deflationary policy measures might be assessed with respect to the prevailing conditions, taken together they worsened the crisis.

To distinguish clearly between measures of economic policy and those aimed at changing the economic system is impossible; but an attempt will be made here to sketch out some of the changes to the politicoeconomic order that were introduced under National Socialist rule. This included those measures intended to realize an organic economy along corporatist lines. At the level of the enterprise, employees were stripped of their rights; the entrepreneur was assigned wider powers in his new role as "enterprise leader" (*Betriebsführer*). At the level of associations, existing trade unions were dissolved and one single union, the German Work Front, lacking any rights, was formed. In agriculture, craft production, industry, and trade a new form of organization emerged that retained the autonomy of the individual enterprise in principle, but at the same time strengthened the power of monopolies or monopolistic groups within sectoral associations, whose authority was in turn reinforced. Since the associations and the state worked together closely, the influence of the state over the economy thereby also increased.

A very particular form of economic organization developed, comparable to the corporatism of Italian Fascism, or, even more appropriately, to Spanish syndicalism. But the economic order—the transformation of ideology into practice—was not as important as the task it was to fulfill. The purpose was to maintain the private capitalist system and yet to increase state influence to secure an adequate measure of planning and management for the rapid and decisive advancement of preparations for war.

The National Socialist regime introduced substantive economic measures immediately after the seizure of power in early 1933. First came a wage freeze and the regulation of prices, then an employment program, which in the final analysis continued the countercyclical measures of the two previous governments. Since direct state investment was concentrated almost exclusively on the building of canals, railroad lines, public buildings, and highways, the indirect effects of the job creation program primarily benefited the private construction industry. The introduction of compulsory military service, the introduction of compulsion into the hitherto voluntary paramilitary Labor Service for young men, the intensive propaganda against women's engagement in paid labor, and, above all, an ever more intensive program of rearmament brought about more or less full employment by 1936, with overemployment even emerging in some sectors.

Not until 1936 was a more comprehensive approach to economic planning and management introduced, at a time when shortages of raw materials and foreign exchange threatened the rearmament program. From this point on the most important raw materials were subjected to quotas; the labor market was given more direction and investment was surpervised. Foreign trade was for the most part subordinated to a quota system and exchange controls. The ultimate goal was economic autarky. Nonetheless, an effective planning and administrative apparatus was not created, nor was any such attempt seriously undertaken; the targets could be met more efficiently by using unrestricted state spending in the existing monopolistic private capitalist system than through a cumbersome state planning bureaucracy. The system was financed less by rigorous fiscal controls with respect to income and property than by extensive public borrowing associated with an extraordinary expansion of the money supply. The control of wages and prices accounted for the absence of open inflation; inflationary tendencies were simply dammed up.

The economic success of these policies cannot be denied. Whether they were decisive in overcoming the crisis or merely added to the eventual general recovery is a very complex question that cannot be answered here. The strong recovery of the German economy in the second half of the 1930s was certainly related to rearmament. And this in turn makes it quite clear that National Socialist policy was in fact not a deliberate countercyclical and job creation policy that took into account the basic functional relationships in a private market economy. Instead, it was a policy of rearmament with side effects for employment. When necessary, it went far beyond the normal rules of the previous economic system, in part with dictatorial methods.

Italy. Although by the peak of the Depression, Fascism had already held power for ten years in Italy, it had not until then applied an economic policy aimed at transforming the system. Only in 1934 did the putative corporative system begin to be realized with the foundation of actual corporations embracing all sectors of the economy and their subsectors. The corporations were composed equally of employers, employees, representatives from the party, and representatives of the relevant ministries; their task was to regulate labor relations and to intervene directly in production and sales through the determination of quotas and fixing of prices. Later they were endowed with supervisory powers over the compulsory cartels envisaged, and they also gained the right of approval for industrial investment. Corporatism remained a piecemeal affair, since the corporations' spheres of activity and decision-making competence were never unambiguously defined. Instead, as in Germany, ministerial bureaucrats and employers' associations worked closely together and were the ultimate arbiters of wages, prices, and output.

The deflationary policy pursued up to this point with respect to currency, money, and finance was now finally abandoned. Exchange controls were tightened and the use of import quotas extended. The policy of import substitution was expanded and, as in Germany, endowed with an elevated status by use of the term "autarky." The de facto abolition of backing in gold for the lira in 1935 was followed in 1936 by the de jure departure from the gold standard. The rate of interest was lowered and credit made easier. After 1936 the occupation of Ethiopia and the beginning of rearmament led to an expansionist domestic budget, which, as in Germany, was financed by borrowing. But in contrast to Germany, the emergent inflationary pressure of money and purchasing power was only partially restrained by inadequate price controls.

The close relationship of financial and industrial capital—the two largest commercial banks, together with the Bank of Rome, controlled a good third of the capital of large- and medium-size Italian enterprises—meant that, by supporting banks threatened by collapse, the state assumed control of their industrial assets. These were brought together in the Institute for Industrial Reconstruction (IRI), founded in 1933, which owned over 20 percent of the capital of all Italian joint stock companies and through shareholdings in fact controlled 42 percent—large sections of the iron and steel industry, shipbuilding, transport, and communications, plus smaller parts of machine construction, chemicals, and other industries. In addition, the IRI controlled the entire capital of the three largest commercial banks. At this same time in Germany, by contrast, the stockholdings in the major banks that the previous middle-class government had acquired in the course of its shoring-up actions were reprivatized by the National Socialists.

In general, even the Fascists in Italy were unable to realize the model corporative economy and society. As in Germany, the basic structure of the capitalist system was untouched, despite massive state ownership of enterprises; but state dirigisme was strengthened in such a way that the Fascist regime was more or less able to achieve its objectives through a mixture of cooperation, compromise and force.

Eastern Europe. The eastern European countries (excluding Czechoslovakia) can be dealt with here as a group despite numerous national particularities by restricting the discussion to a few key issues. All of these countries, apart from Poland, reacted to the crisis by imposing an extremely restrictive tariff and trade policy and comprehensive exchange controls. Another common characteristic was the deflationary cast of the policies adopted, which ran along well-known lines: restriction of money and credit, reduction of price and wage levels, reduction of the size of the budget, and balancing of the budget. Such policies were not, of course, always followed to the letter. Despite the massive intervention of foreign suppliers of credit, the public budget was sometimes in serious imbalance. Simultaneously, the state adopted an ever more interventionist stance. Trade in agricultural products was placed under state control. The state regulated the production of crops with industrial uses, and gave bonuses for the expansion of livestock rearing and premiums for taking certain kinds of land out of production. With subsidies, tax breaks, deliberate promotion of some sectors, and other measures the government sought to bolster industrialization through import substitution. The state began to control directly the process of production via a whole range of laws, decrees, and special authorities constituted to oversee enterprises and their output.

As elsewhere, the crisis forced the state into rescuing actions for various enterprises, with the result that these enterprises passed either partly or wholly into state hands. A number of factors reinforced this nationalization policy in the 1930s. The policy of "naturalization," driven by nationalist sentiments, led to the takeover by the state of many of those enterprises ruled by foreign capital. Its openly stated purpose was to reduce foreign influence in domestic industry and to transfer key enterprises to state ownership.

Although the policy of industrialization continued in the 1930s, it had a number of critical weaknesses. In part, rather unproductive investments were made. Within the industrial sector, capital flowed primarily into textiles, foodstuffs, and light industry—that is, into precisely those branches lacking the capacity to provide a basis for broader industrial growth. Public finance was limited and was unable to substitute for the slump in foreign capital imports. The naturalization policy had conflicting effects: foreign investors were discouraged from making further investments, and yet domestic capital could hardly be mobilized because of the restrictive money and capital markets. The attempt on the part of semi-fascist southeastern European states to pursue an import-substituting industrialization thus created conflicts that were scarcely soluble. Both domestic and external economic policies should have pursued a more aggressive line, based on actual productive potential.

But this was not possible. On the domestic political front, the established power structures were not dissolved: a landed aristocracy, a financial oligarchy, and a traditional state bureaucracy opposed the dynamization of industrial development and thus blocked modernization. Externally, the high level of foreign indebtedness and the related pressure of foreign investors, upon whom these states were still dependent, necessitated restrictive policies. In addition, the strong influence of National Socialist Germany prevented an autonomous industrializing process. These developmental dictatorships, founded on a mixture of corporatism and nationalism, represented a particular response to the crisis, but they were unable to break away from the peripheral capitalist situation.

Scandinavia. Sweden, and with some reservations Norway and Denmark, were the countries that found, within the framework of a liberal-democratic system, the most modern response to the crisis. After 1932 the policies of the Swedish Social Democrats were heavily influenced by the so-called Stockholm school of economics, which like Keynes had developed a countercyclical, demand-oriented model that endowed the state with a degree of responsibility for the recovery of economic stability. At least some of the actual economic measures introduced sought to translate theory into practice: in the area of money and credit, interest rates were lowered, bank liquidity was extended, and the kroner was devalued. State spending was increased and deficit financing introduced on a limited scale—from 1932 state borrowing rose slightly. Public programs aimed at the creation of jobs were started and various economic sectors supported with subsidies. Private demand was strengthened through improvement in social legislation. From 1935, after the crisis had bottomed out, some of these measures were cancelled, public indebtedness was reduced, and the budget deficit was eliminated.

Care must be taken in assessing the extent to which this first example of countercyclical policy actually contributed to the recovery. Sweden had after all undergone extremely dynamic growth in the 1920s; it was hit later and less hard by the world economic crisis than other countries. The devaluation of the kroner, which exceeded that of the pound, led to a rise in exports. The expansion of the British economy certainly had positive effects on Sweden, especially for the armaments industry. Additionally, domestic forces independent of state economic programs—housing construction, the consumer goods industry, and specific capital goods industries—contributed to recovery. Hence Swedish economic policy probably supported the economic recovery, rather than bringing it about. Nevertheless, the Swedish policies differed positively from those pursued in other countries—which intensified the crisis rather than ameliorating it—and thus represented an early version of the modern crisis management later practiced in the majority of non-communist European countries.

Britain. By contrast, economic policy in Britain followed a self-contradictory path. Financial policy remained conducted along orthodox lines. Neither countercyclical deficit financing nor special expansive measures were adopted. The monetary policy pursued, on the other hand, did facilitate recovery. The gold standard was abandoned in 1932 and with it the overvalued pound; interest rates were lowered, the availability of credit to foreigners limited, and the money supply and bank liquidity increased. In addition, the de facto flexible exchange rate was stabilized with the assistance of a special currency equalization fund. Through a series of individual programs the British government also attempted to shore up specific branches of the economy and to stimulate regional and sectoral development. The policy was thus targeted interventionism rather than dirigisme. The economy was provided with state support but was forced into the intended structural modernization. In this way the policy achieved in some respects the opposite of what it intended: monopolistic processes were strengthened rather than broken up, and obsolete structures were reinforced rather than overcome.

On the whole, British economic policy contributed little to the country's economic recovery, which began in the mid-1930s. At best, the monetary and currency reforms aided it a bit. The policy of targeted intervention in support of individual economic areas differed fundamentally from the global, countercyclical, and expansionist policy of the Swedish kind.

France. Large reserves of gold placed France initially in a relatively independent international position but seduced it into an attempt to retain the gold standard and thereby to maintain its exchange parity at a time when other countries sought to gain advantage in international trade through devaluation. Instead of devaluing or introducing exchange controls, the French government pursued between 1931 and 1936 the hopeless task of deflating the economy so that costs and prices would fall in line with the revalued or rather overvalued franc: interest rates were raised, money supply was limited, wages and salaries were reduced by 10 percent, wholesale prices were driven down by 25 percent, and the state budget was radically cut back, especially through reductions in pensions and civil service salaries. At the same time customs duties were further increased and impediments to trade intensified by import prohibitions and quotas. Minimum price levels, subsidies, production bans for foreign companies, and other kinds of interference with the market mechanism were as much a part of French economic policy as were measures for the easing of the labor market: married women were pressured out of paid employment, foreigners were sent home, and the age of retirement was lowered.

Despite these policies (as contemporary government circles believed) or because of these policies (as one would say today), the economic situation worsened. Bankruptcy hit not only small and medium-size enterprises, but also banks, large transport companies, and industrial concerns. The state saved those enterprises it regarded as of national importance and gained decisive influence through the takeover of share-holdings. A new kind of semi-publicly owned enterprise, the *société mixte*, emerged.

The failure of deflationary policy was certainly one reason for the success of the Popular Front in the parliamentary elections of 1936. The takeover of government by the Socialists and Communists led to a radical change of economic policy. Following the policies of the American New Deal and the Swedish example of countercyclical intervention, expansionary measures were now taken up: abandonment of the gold standard and the devaluation of the franc, wage raises of from 7 percent to 15 percent, public job creation programs, and the introduction of the forty-hour week and paid vacations. Agricultural incomes were supported through the assumption of a grain monopoly by a new state authority, the Wheat Board, charged with determining prices and purchasing eventual surpluses. In the industrial sector state-led cartels were organized. Specific acts of nationalization, affecting the railroads and parts of the aircraft and armaments industries, were undertaken primarily for political, rather than economic, reasons. These actions did lead to some amelioration, especially in the labor market, but far-reaching improvement was markedly absent. The new policy's time scale was too short to achieve much effect; in addition, the international situation showed signs of recession again in 1937-1938. The French economy, whose structure remained deficient in many areas despite the drive for modernization in the 1920s, could not be transformed in such a short time into a productive international competitor. This was the real problem; yet the deflationary, pro-cyclical policies pursued in the first half of the 1930s undoubtedly contributed to the duration of the Depression in France.

Belgium and the Netherlands. Belgium and the Netherlands reacted in a way similar to France. The retention of the gold standard and the associated overvaluation of the currency dictated deflationary and adaptive economic policies, yet monetary and credit policy was expansionary. The contradictions resulting from this combination were at least partly overcome by abandonment of the gold standard in 1935 and 1936 respectively. However, a genuinely expansionist policy did not follow, despite the participation of Social Democrats and Socialists in the respective governments. State influence in the economy was reinforced, though, and the beginnings of positive programs of job creation and regional economic development were detectable in the late 1930s.

Summary

Practically all European countries reacted to the world economic crisis by initially adopting the traditional classical liberal strategy: a policy of deflationary austerity. Stable currency and balanced budgets, reductions in prices and wages—these were the means to counter catastrophic drops in production and increasing unemployment. Only when political leaders and their economic advisors realized that this depression was no longer a normal economic downturn but a fundamental crisis threatening the entire capitalist system did they try new methods and instruments whose common characteristic was increased state intervention. Within this general picture two groups can be distinguished.

The first group comprises those strategies followed by authoritarian and dictatorial political systems. In Germany, and to a lesser extent in Italy, the response to the crisis was typified not by Keynesian-style countercyclical measures but rather by a relatively efficient forceful policy of rearmament and foreign economic expansion that stimulated economic recovery as a side effect. The crisis prompted the semi-fascist corporatist regimes of southeastern Europe to intensify their policy of developing a dissociative, autarkic industrialization. Their response also derived not from a short-term stabilization policy but rather from a long-term strategy of modernization.

The second group comprises those strategies developed within a liberal-democratic political framework. Sweden provided the classic example of Keynesian-style policy, in which the crisis was met by comprehensive countercyclical monetary and fiscal policies that could be revoked once the recovery was in progress. By contrast, Britain did not confront the crisis with macroeconomic measures but rather made use of limited state intervention in specific economic branches, sectors, and regions—in other words a sectoral and regional structural policy. France and the other countries of the Gold Bloc followed a third variant: a deflationary policy, which in fact deepened the existing crisis rather than countering it. These countries adhered longer than any others to the orthodox notions of currency stabilization, cutbacks, and restrictive monetary and fiscal policy. This changed only in the second half of the 1930s, when the social and political costs of the crisis could be supported no longer. The change from the classical liberal paradigm therefore had several variants, whose common denominator was a greater degree of state intervention—that is, a qualitatively new relation of politics and economics.

Imperialist Economics during the Second World War

Starting in 1939, the Germans succeeded in conquering a large part of Europe in a very short time. Including those countries that were not immediately occupied but were more or less dependent on Germany—Rumania, Bulgaria, Hungary, and to some extent Finland and Italy—by the autumn of 1942 virtually the whole of continental Europe was in German hands. Only Portugal, Spain, Switzerland, Sweden, and Turkey remained independent, although they adjusted their economies to German demand. The conquest and economic utilization of the different countries and regions of Europe was directly important not only for the conduct of the war, but also for National Socialist plans for the fundamental reorganization of European economy and society. A "Germanic world empire" was to be established under German leadership, based upon the economic foundation of the "greater European economy." In these plans the individual national economies played the role of reservoirs of raw materials and labor for the German economy, whose industrial core was delimited by the Germany of 1939 plus Alsace-Lorraine, Austria, and the Bohemian and Moravian Protectorate.

Although the German leadership never really succeeded in putting in place any components of this European New Order—time was too short—the occupied and dependent countries were integrated by a variety of devices into the system of the German war economy. The objective was to place at the service of the German war economy as much of the productive capacity of the European economies as possible—in the short term and ignoring long-term aims—to ease the burden on the Germany economy, which was not capable of bearing the economic load by itself. This led to general methods of exploitation that affected all countries in different degrees. There were also special methods of exploitation, for not all countries and regions were treated equally. Some national economies remained relatively independent and were integrated into the war economy by "voluntary compulsion." Other countries were ruthlessly pillaged and plundered by the Germans.

General Methods of Exploitation

1. From 1940 the Germans compelled occupied or dependent countries to organize their trade and payments one-sidedly in Germany's favor. Goods important for German war production were exported

from these countries without regard to the prevailing needs of their national economies. Exchange rates were also manipulated in favor of the Reichsmark. This pseudo-foreign trade brought about a reversal of trade. Whereas until 1940 a rising share of Germany's foreign trade had been conducted with southeastern Europe, it now shifted once more to western and northern Europe.

2. In the course of the war a central clearing system was created for all of Europe. Every country under German influence was forced to conclude a bilateral trade agreement with Germany. Equivalent values for the flow of trade were registered by clearing accounts, which were then mutually settled. Trade between countries was also conducted via the central clearing institution. This system was not a simple device for the clearing of mutual payments, however, for Germany both overvalued its own currency and depressed the export prices of other countries. In addition, all German occupation costs were booked to German credit in the clearing accounts and German clearing debts were entirely unlimited.

3. In all occupied countries occupation costs were charged, which constituted a not inconsiderable part of German war finance.

4. The use of foreign workers inside Greater Germany was another form of economic exploitation that affected nearly every national economy. Foreign workers were in part attracted on a voluntary basis, but for the most part they were forced laborers, fourteen million workers in all through the course of the war. In 1944 seven and a half million foreign workers toiled in the German war economy, 20 percent of the total work force.

Special Methods of Exploitation

Even before the outbreak of war, Germany officially annexed Austria (the Alpine and Danubian *Reichsgaue*) and the western half of Czechoslovakia (the Bohemian and Moravian Protectorate). These areas were henceforth regarded as organic parts of the Reich and its economy. This was not just a matter of decrees and ordinances; enterprises were systematically transferred into German ownership or came under German influence. Various methods were employed to achieve this. Jewish property was simply expropriated. The leading banks were merged into the German banking system. Major German concerns assumed large shareholdings in Austrian enterprises or merged with them. So-called management contracts were imposed, by means of which important Czech enterprises were virtually affiliated to German concerns. In all, around half of the industrial capital came under German influence.

The idea that the Austrian and Czech economies should become an integral part of the Germany economy was also reflected in state-directed investment policy. Industrial plants were founded specifically to supplement the German industrial structure: iron, steel, and aluminum works, chemical industries, machine construction, and so forth. Simultaneously, agricultural production was reduced. This also fitted into the National Socialist plans for the New Order, according to which the bulk of agricultural production was to be transferred to other regions of Europe. In sum, National Socialist economic policy aimed at making the Austrian and Czech economies serve the short-term ends of the German war economy, as well as at promoting in the long run their complete integration in the German economy.

The long-term plan for western Europe (France, Belgium, and the Netherlands) envisaged the following: in France the departments of Upper and Lower Rhine (Alsace) and Moselle (Lorraine) were annexed de facto and incorporated into the German Reich. The Wallonian areas of Belgium and the industrial centers of northern France were to be merged into a coal mining and industrial region, comparable with the Ruhr or Upper Silesia. Flemish Belgium and the Netherlands were, like the rest of France, to remain primarily agricultural.

Independent of these long-term plans, the occupation policy began in summer 1940, as previously in Poland, with a phase of "clearing out"—that is, the plundering of raw materials, goods, and means of production. By autumn these destructive methods were replaced by constructive ones, with orders shifted to use foreign productive capacity more efficiently. A functioning administrative apparatus, independent of military administration, was created to secure the orderly execution of specific economic controls, facilitate the settlement of contracts, and ensure that those trade and payments mechanisms introduced by Germany were not endangered by either financial or sociopolitical measures. The various German economic agencies, including the Wehrmacht, worked directly with the relevant ministries or participating businessmen. In this phase the different institutions had not yet been centralized, and there was no direct planning and management. This altered in 1942, when a closer integration with the German war economy became necessary. From early 1943 the French and Belgian economies were treated as part of Germany as far as production planning and management were concerned.

Although planning and management were applied to a lesser extent in these countries than in eastern Europe, they still required a degree of control over individual enterprises in strategic industries. Trustees were installed or supervision transferred to a similar German firm. In this way the independence of the enterprise was formally preserved, but the conduct of production was subjected to extensive supervision. Expropriation without compensation, as practiced in Poland or the Soviet Union, was rare. The German government supported the take-over of enterprises and capital participation by German enterprises only in branches important to the war. In general, however, industrial enterprises were left under the management of their original proprietors.

The policy of exploitation in northern Europe (Norway and Denmark) developed along lines similar to those in western Europe. Sweden was never occupied, nor was its economy ever fully integrated into the German war economy.

In Poland and the Soviet Union the war was not simply a war of political and economic conquest, but also an ideological war of extermination. Population and society were to be at least partly liquidated. Longer-term perspectives envisaging lasting occupation and colonization aimed at not only an economic reorganization of this area, but also a sociopolitical one. Many National Socialist leaders were convinced that only through the exploitation of this region's enormous resources could Germany compete successfully in the long term with the world's other great powers such as the United States. The practical policy of exploitation corresponded with the long-term objective. Enterprises important to the war effort were either directly taken over or placed under comprehensive control. A centralized system of planning and management ensured that production was properly organized to this end. Otherwise, systematic plundering was conducted with exceptional rigor. Robbery and exploitation reached a high point with the retreat of the army after the winter of 1941-42, during which a scorched earth policy was pursued. This meant deportation and murder of entire village populations, large-scale devastation, and confiscation or destruction of all agricultural and industrial productive resources.

The growing economic importance of southeastern Europe for the German Reich had become clear in the 1930s with the extension of trading relations. After 1939 the significance of this economic region as a supplier of agricultural and mineral raw materials to the German economy coincided both with the direct interests of the war economy as well as with the long-term prospect of the European New Order. But this did not apply to industrial production. Up to 1941 every effort to expand manufacturing industry in these countries was obstructed by the Germans; this behavior altered as German productive capacity reached its limits. From then on the production of goods important to the war effort was promoted.

The manner in which economic policy was applied to the allied states of Rumania, Bulgaria, and Hungary, on the one hand, and to occupied Greece and Yugoslavia, on the other, differed distinctly. The latter were occupied at the beginning of 1941 and plundered in the same way that Poland had been earlier and the Soviet Union would be a short time later. As far as its allies were concerned, Germany did not need to materially alter its policies. At the beginning of the war the existing close economic relationships had been made closer by a series of economic agreements that presented the opportunity of a further "peaceful occupation." German development projects and state development programs under German management endeavored to improve and expand the production of agricultural goods and raw materials. In industry the methods of overall direction ranged from direct management of enterprises by trustees to various forms of indirect supervision. In this way the economies of Germany's southeastern European allies served the German armaments industry without experiencing direct looting and plunder, although they did not fulfill many of the actual targets of the German arms planners.

Systems of Planning and Management
The different strategies of exploitation used by the Germans to place other European economies at the service of the German war economy do not describe the development of the economic system in Germany itself. Despite ever greater state intervention in the production process, up to 1939 Germany did not yet have a centrally planned economy. Not only were suitable instruments for planning and management absent, but also three rival organizations existed—the Four Year Plan, the Ministry of Economics, and the Military Armaments Office (renamed the Defense Economy and Armaments Office at the end of 1939)—whose competencies were by no means unambiguously delimited. This lack of proper definition of competence was in fact a central organizing principle of National Socialist rule; it prevented any potential rival to Hitler's supreme authority from consolidating a power base. Economic policy with respect to the war economy was at this time still preoccupied with providing the military goods for a series of lightning wars, or *Blitzkriege*. This strategy did not demand long-

term planning and management, but rather short-term concentration of available resources on the production of those military goods most necessary at the given moment.

The initiation of war brought changes. To supply the civilian population, an official rationing authority was established; its offices were tightly organized, and it was endowed with the powers to directly plan the output of particular sectors of production. In early 1940 the creation of the Ministry of Armaments and Munitions introduced a further planning authority charged with coordinating and rationalizing divergencies in production methods in the arms industry with respect to the use of raw materials, energy consumption, levels of equipment, quality, and delivery in order to reduce the overall costs of production. The new ministry did not achieve any notable standardization or concentration in manufacturing procedures and products, nor was manufacturing capacity extended. Contrary to what the rest of the world assumed, there was as little planning and management as there was mobilization of resources and reserves. The comparatively limited war effort in Germany itself was possible because of the consequential system of exploitation employed in the occupied countries. The collapse of the *Blitzkrieg* strategy in the winter of 1941–42 was a turning point, even though not until early 1943 and the declaration of total war were all economic means concentrated on the production of armaments.

Under Albert Speer the Ministry of Armaments and Munitions finally gained sufficient power, and finally was directed with the necessary degree of authority, to justify speaking of a centralized system of planning and supply within the broad framework of industrial self-management. Central planning and individual entrepreneurial initiatives were efficiently combined. Within macroeconomic guidelines and resource allocations assigned quarterly by a central planning agency led by Speer, producers' groups and committees were responsible for the organization and control of production in specific branches of the arms industry. These groups were always chaired by the managing directors of the relevant enterprises. This system was generally quite successful. The production of especially important goods was now centralized in a few large enterprises and organized along lines of mass production. But the allocation of labor and the procurement of raw materials continued to lie outside Speer's authority.

The examples of Britain and Italy demonstrate the similarity of the mechanisms employed in different countries in gearing up their economies for war production, a similarity that transcends the actual makeup of their respective political systems. Both countries—the one liberal-democratic, the other authoritarian-fascist—in principle employed the same planning and guiding instruments as did Germany. In Britain central direction did take longer to be introduced than in Germany. Even in early 1940 the British government was still using financial incentives for the changeover to war production. The central authority for the management of the economy remained the Treasury. In the course of the year a whole series of committees assumed decision-making power for production—the Food Policy Committee, the Economic Policy Committee, the Home Policy Committee, the Production Council—but not until early 1941 was the Lord President's Committee formed, with far-reaching powers over long-term production planning and management. Rationing and control of consumer goods were introduced; deployment of labor was indirectly managed.

The principal object of planning and direction, however, was the allocation of raw materials and means of production in the most important industrial branches. The geographical situation of Britain made state intervention relatively easy. A large part of the raw materials necessary for war production had to be imported, so the control of imports and shipping space was practically equivalent to control of the allocation of raw materials. The shift during 1942 from improvisation to a more efficient and rigorous system of rationing raw materials is mostly attributable to pressure from the United States, which insisted that the international supply of raw materials be managed more effectively. Within Britain industrial associations assumed control of the allocation of raw materials; in the case of non-imported raw materials and other supplies, control was taken over by the employers' associations of those industries that were the primary users of these materials. Such controls were introduced only when the supply of material involved became short. Rubber, for example, was not controlled up to April 1941 and was first rationed in 1942 by the appropriate control committee.

Various financial actions were also taken. Price controls were implemented directly by government agencies. Fiscal measures included a purchase tax to channel consumption and a profits tax to absorb war profits. Foreign exchange controls were also reintroduced. The raising of capital on the capital market was controlled by a Capital Issues Committee, which vetted and approved all stock issues.

Inadequate information was a particular problem in Britain; only during the war did comprehensive statistics on production become available. On the whole, however, developments in Britain were comparable with those in Germany, despite the differences in political systems and the associated prospects for transforming the economic system. At root, the same methods of planning and direction were used in Britain for redirection of the economy into war production, if somewhat later and without the brutal force applied in Germany. Britain also employed a mixture of state bureaucracy and economic self-management, transferring state powers to private interest groups and hence bringing about for the first time the efficient management of production under capitalist relations.

Summary
The imperialist policy of the Third Reich directly affected practically every country of continental Europe. The forms and methods of economic exploitation and also their long-term impact differed. Poland and the Soviet Union certainly suffered the worst. An orderly continuation of production was permitted only where products important to the war economy were concerned. The Germans treated Greece and Yugoslavia in a similar fashion. By contrast, in other northern, western, and southeastern European countries a system of production contacts and supply quotas, together with an appropriate managing bureaucracy, was introduced; the impact of this system varied from country to country, but it did permit a general continuation of production, though directed by the specific needs of the German war economy. The core of this system of exploitation, which included all of continental Europe, was for a long time not a rigorously managed centrally planned economy, but rather a system with the typical National Socialist characteristics of overlapping responsibilities between various authorities, improvisation, conflicting priorities, conflict of interest between the state bureaucracy and private management, and so on. Complete inclusion and efficient use of all resources arrived relatively late in the war—after 1942, when the military strategy of *Blitzkrieg* was no longer effective and the war economy had to adapt itself to a long-term war of attrition.

Reconstruction and New Beginnings after 1945

International Policy
After the Second World War memories of prewar times were generally negative in tone in contrast with the nostalgia that had prevailed after

the First World War. Most political leaders in the late 1940s recognized that insufficient international cooperation and protectionism had obstructed the reconstruction of the European economy after the First World War, intensified the Great Depression, and hindered the recovery of the 1930s. Outside Eastern Europe, the advantages of free foreign trade were generally accepted, and a liberal world economy was to form the basis for international, and hence also European, trade in goods and currencies. Opinions differed, of course, over the rate at which liberalization should be introduced. But cooperation, rather than conflict, was to set the tone of international politics. Moreover, the United States participated actively in the reconstruction of Western Europe in contrast to its obstructive policies in the wake of the First World War; the victorious allied powers also did not burden Germany with enormous reparations payments, but instead furthered its rapid integration into Europe as a whole. This situation applied to both Western and Eastern Europe. The Soviet Union no longer built up its economic system in isolation, as it had after the First World War, but rather drew in practically the whole of Eastern Europe. New forms of international cooperation thus emerged in the East as well as in the West.

American Assistance and Treaties on European Cooperation
The General Agreement on Tariffs and Trade (GATT) came into force on January 1, 1948, at the initiative of the United States. Although its terms and conditions were not so liberal as American free traders had wanted, it contributed during the 1950s to a worldwide dismantling of duties and import restrictions. American pressure for the rapid liberalization of international trade and currency dealing was not motivated merely by altruism. Unlike Europe, the United States had been strengthened by the Second World War; its productive capacity had been extended by the war, not destroyed. To expand further, the American economy more than ever needed world markets, which were to be secured by the "open door" strategy in foreign policy and by the promotion of liberalization in the international economy. Along with the humanitarian aspects of aid, then, the prospects of bigger and stronger markets played an important part in the decision to support European reconstruction. Moreover, the onset of the Cold War created the political conditions for close cooperation between the United States and Western Europe.

In this respect, the European Recovery Plan (ERP) announced in

1947 by General George C. Marshall, the American secretary of state, had an important political function. The object was to create stable social and political conditions in Western Europe through economic recovery and growth, posing an effective counterweight to the advance of Soviet Communism in Western Europe. The ERP, or Marshall Plan, was the most important part of American aid to Europe, which within just over a decade from the end of the war amounted to expenditures of $25 billion. The use made of this aid varied, but it was ultimately employed in all Western European countries in a manner corresponding to initial intentions: renewal of infrastructure, investment in key industries and the removal of bottlenecks in production, and the facilitation of private investment.

As soon as negotiations started in the summer of 1947 on the organizational structure for the centralized allocation of Marshall Plan assistance, basic differences of opinion between European nations on the form future European cooperation should take became apparent. Because of its global foreign policy oriented to the needs of the Commonwealth, Britain strove for a loose cooperation with no formal restrictions on freedom of action; France, on the other hand, proposed a strong supranational authority for the distribution of Marshall Plan funds, hoping to exercise its continental influence through this form of political integration. Whereas France, Italy, and the Benelux countries (who had formed a customs union in 1948) favored the formation of a European customs union, Britain and the Scandinavian countries rejected such a proposal. The Organization for European Economic Cooperation (OEEC), founded in April 1948 by sixteen Western European states, was merely a body that distributed Marshall Plan funds to individual countries. No real cooperation and agreement between the various national plans emerged. Nevertheless, the OEEC exercised significant influence over European economic integration, despite operating at the level of wide-ranging rather than detailed planning.

Treaties on European Economic Integration
The OEEC and its subordinate agency, the European Payments Union (EPU), marked only the beginning of further plans for European integration. In mid-1952 the treaty establishing the European Coal and Steel Community (ECSC) came into force, removing national control over the production of coal and steel in France, West Germany, Italy, and the Benelux countries, and placing control in the hands of a supranational authority. The leading idea behind this treaty was not, in

fact, economic cooperation and integration, but rather political security. Rising East-West tension raised the prospect of the integration of West Germany into Western Europe and eventual German rearmament. France sought in this treaty to strengthen the ties of the Federal Republic to the West as well as to effect a degree of control over the feared West German heavy industry. The supranational structure of the coal and steel community rendered British participation virtually impossible; this was also intentional on France's part. In addition, competitive economic interests deemed it advisable to gain some influence over West German coal and steel production. As far as West Germany was concerned, the treaty presented a further opportunity to be accepted as an equal political and economic partner.

The original objects of the ECSC were the orderly supply of the common market, the achievement of low prices, and the abolition of discrimination and subsidies. Moreover, the living and working conditions of the workers were to be improved. From the outset the ECSC considered itself a partial customs union, in which interstate traffic in the goods it administered should not be obstructed. Insofar as national rights of sovereignty had been transferred to a supranational institution, this form of cooperation transcended traditional bilateral or multilateral cooperation. This novel aspiration for a common economic and social policy—even if limited to one particular industrial sector—was the model for later attempts at integration.

The plans of the French foreign minister, Robert Schuman, on whose initiative the ECSC had been founded, went further. The ECSC was to be only the first step in the creation of a European economic community, which should in turn form the basis for the political unification of participant states in a European federation. On March 25, 1957, the ECSC countries signed the Treaty of Rome, which furthered the process of economic integration by establishing the European Economic Community (EEC) and the European Atomic Energy Community (EURATOM). The concrete objectives of the EEC treaty were:

1. Removal of duties and quantitative restriction in trade between member states, plus the creation of a common customs tariff and the adoption of a common trade policy with respect to non-member states (i.e., the creation of a customs union)
2. Liberalization of "invisible transactions"—movement of persons, services, capital, and payments
3. Abolition of existing restrictive trading practices and the hindering

of new ones; convergence of domestic legal and administrative provisions

4. Introduction of a common agricultural and transport policy
5. Coordination of economic policy, above all policies relating to demand management and employment, balance of payments, and the valuation of currency
6. Facilitation of adaptation to the conditions of the common market through the use of so-called exemption clauses, assistance funds, and an investment bank

The aim of creating a customs union and the coordination of national economic policies meant that, with the EEC, the stage of sectoral integration was left behind and the first step made towards general economic integration. The reasons why the six EEC countries rejected a general European free trade area demonstrate that the signing of the Treaty of Rome involved not simply economic but also political perspectives. A "hard" solution based upon a "small" Europe was intended to form the basis of an economically and politically united core that would possess sufficient substance, and radiate sufficient attractiveness, to draw in other European countries. The Rome treaty envisaged three phases of integration in all: in the first a customs union was to be created, in the second an economic union, and in the third a political union.

Consistent with its previous policies, as at the establishment of the ECSC, Britain did not seriously attempt to participate in the initiative taken by the six countries; instead Britain pursued within the framework of the OEEC a policy advocating general reduction in duties and the creation of a free trade area. This latter entity came into being in early 1960 as the European Free Trade Association (EFTA), including Britain, Norway, Sweden, Denmark, Austria, Switzerland, and Portugal. In contrast to the EEC, EFTA had very few supranational bodies, and they were endowed with very limited powers; neither a common external tariff structure nor a pretense to a common economic policy existed. EFTA envisaged solely the dismantling of duties and restrictions to trade in industrial goods between member states. Agreement was also reached on the removal of agricultural subsidies, complete residential freedom for the citizens of member states, the removal of fiscal duties and taxes, the prohibition of export duties with respect to member states, and the reduction of restrictive trading practices.

Britain did not merely decline to participate in the foundation of the EEC, but positively sought to prevent the EEC from coming into being. Political motives were decisive, as they were with other OEEC states. The implicit objectives of closer political integration and the limitation of national economic sovereignty written into the Treaty of Rome were regarded with scepticism or outright hostility. The idea that national rights could be transferred to a supranational organization, hence restricting the freedom of action for national economic and social policy, was for these countries out of the question at this time, largely because divergent economic structures were being created in individual countries.

American aid within the framework of the Marshall Plan was also offered to Eastern Europe, but under pressure from the Soviet Union these countries rejected the offer. So that these countries might have a body equivalent to the OEEC, a Council for Mutual Economic Assistance (CMEA or Comecon) was created on January 25, 1949, with the participation of the Soviet Union, Bulgaria, Hungary, Poland, Rumania, and Czechoslovakia. In 1949 Albania, and in 1950 East Germany, were added. The motives behind the foundation of Comecon were both political and economic. Among the explicit aims were the exchange of scientific information, the granting of mutual technical assistance, and support in the exchange of raw materials, foodstuffs, machinery, and armaments; but the precedence of implicit political objectives was never denied. As an instrument of economic cooperation and integration Comecon was at the start more or less inactive. The external economic relations of all member states were conducted primarily bilaterally and mainly with the Soviet Union. Attempts to harmonize the long-term development plans of member states via parallel trade agreements made little progress, since a centrally planned state monopoly over foreign trade was strictly maintained, and yet national development plans were set up without knowledge of trading agreements.

Not until the 1958 meeting of Comecon was the first attempt at international cooperation made. Principles governing price formation in Comecon intrabloc trade were announced. According to these arrangements, contracts should be arrived at bilaterally based upon the prevailing world price over an agreed reference period. Thus, Comecon represented initially a very loose association, which did not attain even the degree of cooperation that obtained in the OEEC. Nevertheless, it did demonstrate the beginnings of closer cooperation in the Eastern European countries.

National Policy

The national political situation after the Second World War differed greatly from that prevailing after the First. Reconstruction was not confined to the attempted restoration of prewar relations but was bound up with a new beginning. Even in ruling circles the interwar years were not regarded as a period worth restoring. The Great Depression had so shaken faith in the functional capacity of the existing capitalist system that changes seemed to be necessary. At the same time the 1930s had shown the degree to which, even in bourgeois democracies, liberal competitive capitalism could respond to state direction without incurring fundamental changes to the system.

Political constellations were roughly the same as those that had existed after the First World War. The left strove for partial or complete alteration of existing socioeconomic relations. Among the right there was a willingness to compromise—partly from improved insight, partly out of opportunistic motives, for the social dynamic pressed for change. This constellation existed in virtually all Western European countries, although a variety of politicoeconomic approaches developed, based on diverse political traditions, ideologies, and experiences.

In Eastern Europe the situation differed. The Soviet Union's assumption of power in this region left no room for free choice with regard to the future socioeconomic system. The adoption of the Soviet model of the centrally planned economy was simply decreed, effecting a complete break with the past.

The neoliberal approach. No other country in Europe sought to introduce a liberal economic order and economic policy in so systematic a manner as West Germany. Neoliberal theory developed a model that differed from the classical liberal model primarily in that the state, although allowing market forces freedom of action, created the overall conditions for the operation of the market and supervised the maintenance of competition. Direct state intervention in market processes with the objective of managing demand or countering unemployment was explicitly rejected. In German economic science this approach was called *Ordoliberalismus;* in the terminology of economic policy the slogan "social market economy" was used. That these terms embodied not only theoretical constructs but also practical economic policies became clear when the Allies ceded more responsibility and self-determination to the Germans.

The currency reform of summer 1948 was accompanied by a general reform of the economic system. The National Socialist system of planning and management, which had been retained after 1945, was now largely dissolved. With a few exceptions—foodstuffs, raw materials, housing,—the direction of production and consumption was transferred back to the market. Competition was promoted in various ways; the decision of the victorious allied powers to dissolve cartels and to disengage the relations between big banks and big industrial concerns, however, was primarily politically motivated. Not until 1957 did the Germans themselves pass a law against restrictive trade practices, and the difficulty of carrying out a policy to discourage concentration and encourage competition in a liberal democracy was illustrated not only by the law's inconsistencies, but also by the path followed from the first rigorous draft of the law in the late 1940s to its later, weaker formulation.

Property relations altered little; by contrast with some other states, no enterprises were nationalized. On the contrary, at the end of the 1950s, at a time when the concentration of property and income was once more well established, the federal government started to privatize its publicly owned companies.

Economic policy was also oriented to liberal principles. Monetary policy pursued the goal of stability, budgetary policy that of balance or surplus. Of course, deviations from the neoliberal model did occur. The Reconstruction Loan Corporation, founded in 1948 to administer Marshall Plan funds, followed an active investment policy in the distribution of its resources. Through a special program of loans, at the beginning of the 1950s the federal government redirected investment capital into key sectors whose weakness threatened to hinder reconstruction. Capital accumulation was generally encouraged by a deliberate policy of taxation and subsidy. Yet despite other specific economic actions, state interventionism remained generally limited.

The Christian Democratic–Liberal coalition government of the Federal Republic did, in fact, follow economic policies broadly in agreement with the neoliberal model in its first few years. The state created a framework within which the economy could move freely, and state intervention was reduced. That this policy sufficed to lead the West German economy into a phase of incomparable expansion can be attributed above all to the favorable basic economic framework; to the strength of the West German economy, which despite war and destruction remained internationally extremely competitive; and to the capacity and enthusiasm of the German population for reconstruction. International competitiveness also resulted among other things from the restrained wages policy of the trade unions, which provided broader political support for the policy of increasing output in these years.

The state interventionist approach. In France those forces seeking sociopolitical change were more powerful than in West Germany. The energy sector, large parts of banking and insurance, and various individual enterprises—Air France, the automakers Renault and Berliet, the armaments manufacturer Gnome & Rhône—were nationalized. Thereby the French state could claim in theory to control 20 percent of the capital of French industry. Apart from the alteration of property relations, postwar economic organization and policy were characterized primarily by a particular approach to planning (*planification*). The aim of the first two plans, which ran from 1947 to 1957, was to promote those economic branches important to reconstruction while pushing ahead with the modernization of the French economy.

Planification did not involve a centrally planned economic system. Already by the second plan the approach had shifted from an imperative plan based upon production quantities to an indicative plan based upon financial targets (see table 4.3). The planning instruments were credit allowances and impediments, tax breaks and penalities, acceptance of sureties and their refusal, subsidies, and so forth. More direct steering measures also existed: instructions to the state sector about investment, production, and hiring, credit quotas, providing building land at no cost or refusing building permits, and others. The state, by combining planning directives with the powers of intervention possessed by the finance ministry and the publicly owned banks, had particular influence in the financial sector, and this sector substantially determined the flow of investments. From the start the efficacy of French planning suffered from the absence of an effective planning bureaucracy. Ultimately, *planification* was structural planning, which left freedom of choice to the entrepreneur, but which so heavily influenced conditions surrounding the actual choices that the planning intentions of the state were worked into individual decisions.

The primary aim was to lay the foundations in the enterprises for future long-term balanced economic growth; the short-term guidance of demand was a less important objective. The original intention of guiding other aggregates of national income such as private consumption in addition to the volume and structure of investments remained unrealized, in part because the trade unions refused to cooperate. Thus, novel and far-reaching powers were transferred to the state, but at the same time it fell under the influence of economic interest groups, which decisively shaped policies on the numerous planning commissions. The actual development of French industry—rapid growth and increases in productivity, a high rate of investment—indicates that this policy was successful. Downturns in the business cycle could, however, be as little avoided here as in other countries.

Whereas France pursued primarily a long-term policy for growth and only secondarily a countercyclical policy, Britain gave the latter, Keynesian approach priority as a means of achieving full employment and promoting social welfare. Whether the changes in the ownership of means of production that also occurred in Britain were in line with Keynesian thinking is an open question. The Bank of England, electricity supply and distribution, gas, iron and steel, coal mining, railroads, and also for a few years road transport—these were all nationalized. The state became a large shareholder in a few large enterprises such as British Petroleum and Rolls-Royce. As in France, 20 percent of British industry passed in this fashion into the hands of the state—without, however, creating an effective interventionist instrument: state enterprises pursued relatively autonomous policies.

The extension of the social security system and a redistributive taxation system were certainly Keynesian in spirit and reinforced private demand. This was also true of monetary and fiscal policy. Disregarding the immediate postwar years, when the principal task was to effect a transition from an administratively controlled war economy to a liberal market economy, the purpose of monetary and fiscal policy was to dampen cyclical fluctuations and hence secure full employment and equilibrium in the balance of payments. Economic policy was organized around short-term countercyclical measures primarily designed to deal with crises. Longer-term priorities and targets, and hence a conception of longer-term planning, were not developed. Thus, Britain opted for a sociopolitically augmented Keynesian approach, which did not fully come to terms with the real problems of the British economy—obsolete production structures, run-down plant, and low productivity. Nonetheless, despite the weak economic growth of the 1950s, inflationary tendencies, and the difficult balance of payments situation, full employment was more or less achieved.

Italy presents yet another variant of postwar economic policy. The characteristic element of the Italian economic system was the high level of state ownership developed during the 1930s. The public sector was extended even further after the Second World War. Immediately after the war a part of the iron and steel industry, shipbuilding, and machine construction got into difficulties and had to be lent assistance through the Financial Fund for the Machine Industry (FIM), founded in 1947; such a step was tantamount to nationalization. In 1953 the National Hydrocarbon Agency (ENI) emerged to develop the energy sector, above all natural gas and mineral oil. These powerful state holding companies, which dominated a great part of the Italian economy, were managed independently of government but collaborated closely with the institutions of Italian economic planning. As in France, planning was characteristic of the postwar Italian economy. There were plans for regional and infrastructural improvement, special ten-year plans for the development of the railroads, schools, and universities, plans for assistance to regions with special problems, plans for the construction of workers' housing, and plans for the development of the iron and steel industry. The first national economic plan, extending from 1955 to 1964, was intended to contribute to the closing of the gap between north and south. These plans were less imperative than those in France, assuming the form of indicative projections. Efficient planning bureaucracies did not emerge (see table 4.3).

Here, and in the foundation of further more or less independent organizations, a tradition begun under the Fascist regime continued: whenever the traditional state bureaucracy failed to deal with specific programs, projects, and plans, new institutions were created. State planning was ultimately left to the large state holding companies, although these had to coordinate their own long-term investment strategy with the planning guidelines. Other continuities with Fascist economic policy persisted as well. Agrarian protectionism was not dismantled, nor were the barriers to internal migration removed. Wage negotiations remained centralized by the state, despite the reintroduction of autonomous collective negotiations between employers and employees. By contrast, monetary and fiscal policy was almost entirely liberal in character. The postwar Italian economic system was in general no longer corporatist; it was rather a liberal market economy with special features. The dominance of large publicly owned combines does not itself justify designating the Italian economy a state capitalist system, but neither was it a purely private capitalist system.

The cooperative interventionist approach. An entirely clear delimitation of this approach from the more customary state interventionism is not possible. Here, too, the aim was to provide greater guidance to market processes by installing elements of planning, direction, and social justice; private rights of disposal and freedom of action were restricted, and the domain of state intervention extended. Distinct from the state interventionist concept, however, was the aim of integrating social groups more closely into the process of economic and social opinion-formation and decision-making. Associations—that is, organized socioeconomic interest groups—should be jointly responsible for economic policy, thus effecting a balance of special interests and transferring responsibilities from the state. In this respect the approach had not only cooperative but also corporatist features. Conspicuously, this manner of building consensus in the formation of economic policy asserted itself in the smaller European countries such as Sweden, the Netherlands, Austria, and Belgium. Originally, the French model of *planification* and that of the British welfare state were also set up in this fashion; even the German neoliberals had considered reviving the corporatist tradition of the Reich Economic Council from the interwar Weimar Republic. Since these conceptions were never provided with a firm institutional basis in the larger states—in contrast to the smaller states—they become distorted, for state bureaucracy and employers' associations constituted a one-sided community of interest.

In Sweden the aims of full employment, social security, and economic justice dominated policy even more than in Britain. The point of departure for practically all economic policy was the labor market, characterized by centralized wage negotiations among highly organized and autonomous agencies. The aim of bringing about a more equitable distribution of income was additionally pursued through progressive social legislation and redistributive taxation and transfer policies. To secure full employment the labor market was tightly regulated and a countercyclical monetary and fiscal policy applied. A special instrument of economic management was the state-administered investment fund, which was supposed to direct investments according to macroeconomic criteria. Initially there was a great deal of scepticism concerning far-reaching prognoses or even longer-term planning. Considering that cooperatives and consumer associations, along with the employers' and employees' organizations, also had great influence, the Swedish politicoeconomic model can be seen as a form of Keynesianism augmented by social and corporatist elements.

The Dutch variant of centralized cooperative collaboration distinguished itself from the Swedish pattern in at least three ways: the state was more closely involved in wage negotiations; state controls over wages and prices required longer-term projections and planning; and, alongside full employment, stable prices and a balance of payments were important objectives of economic policy. Otherwise, the aim in the Netherlands was similarly to involve the various socioeconomic interest groups not only in the determination of wages and salaries, but also in wider economic decision-making processes; the core of Dutch economic policy, like the Swedish, was regulation of wages and the labor market.

Despite conditions peculiar to each country, economic systems developed in Belgium and Austria centered upon the independent co-operation of parties to the labor market, upon which basis state economic policy was then constructed. In these countries the wartime control and guidance system remained in place during the second half of the 1940s, and then was transformed into a liberal market economy. In Austria, where much of industry had been nationalized during the first postwar years, elements recalling the French model of *planification* emerged, without, however, being pursued further. The potential for guiding state industry was more like that of the Italian system, but combined with consensus-building mechanisms of a cooperative social partnership.

The centrally planned approach. The Eastern European states carried out a fundamental transformation of their economic systems. The central structural elements of capitalism were removed and replaced by centrally planned economies. In each country the process was different and took different amounts of time; ultimately, though, the Soviet model, right down to individual economic institutions and mechanisms, was imposed upon the Eastern European countries.

The central element of the state socialist planned economy is common or collective property. Very quickly—sometimes even before the seizure of power by the respective Communist party—a large part of industry was transferred into state, or "people's," property. Measured by the number of workers employed, by 1946, 82 percent of Yugoslavian industry was nationalized, and 84 percent of Polish industry. The transfer of property was delayed in Rumania and Bulgaria until 1948, but by the end of that year respectively 85 percent and 98 percent of industry was in the hands of the state; in Hungary the share had reached 83 percent by that time. In agricultural and artisanal production an additional form of group property was created—various types of cooperatives in which private property formally remained in place but individuals lost the right of enjoyment. The collectivization of agriculture began in 1948–1949, and in the majority of countries by the mid-1950s over 50 percent of the cultivated area had been removed from private ownership. Only in Poland was peasant resistance able to block collectivization, so that the private holding remained the dominant form of ownership; in place of state collective farms, the Polish state assumed the role previously played by the large landowners. Otherwise, private property in the means of production in agriculture, handicrafts, and trade was permitted only to a very limited degree.

Between 1948 and 1951 the organizational and institutional framework of a centrally planned economy developed in most Eastern European economies. The form, composition, extent, and utilization of production for a specified planning period were determined by a central administration. In this way a hierarchical economic administration on the Soviet model was created, according to the principles of a functionally differentiated organization. Two or three levels were usually created, the highest decision-makers being the leading party organs (Politburo and Central Committee) and the state (Council of Ministers). The State Planning Committee served the political leadership and at its highest level combined ministries with production functions (production principle), ministries with regional responsibilities (territorial principle), and central offices with special tasks, such as the Office for Prices and the Central Bank. The middle level of the planning administration was composed of the corresponding leading organizations of specific economic branches. Regional planning commissions or other state organizations followed at the regional level. Finally, at the lowest administrative level came the production units, which were in turn assigned to the corresponding mid-level organs. This structure has remained basically unaltered right up to the present.

The task of the various organs of economic administration at every level was to disaggregate planning targets into material and financial plan-instructions, which could then be transmitted to the respective areas of responsibility, right down to the level of the individual enterprise. Feedback, in the form of corrected and re-aggregated figures, passed back through the same informational channels to the highest level of economic administration. The State Planning Committee condensed the received data into variants of one- or five-year plans.

The monetary and financial system was likewise rigorously centralized. The transformation of the banking sector was generally completed by 1948. At the head came the central, or state, bank, which in conjunction with a number of specialized banks—savings banks, cooperative banks, foreign trade banks—was responsible for a plan using credits as performance incentives, and for supervision of the execution of the plan, as well as of the volume of cash in circulation. The state bank and its subordinate branch offices became executive and supervisory organs of state planning in that they supplied enterprises with the financing envisaged by the plan and also administered and audited firms' accounts. Transfers of money, therefore, served merely to guide the flow of goods in the fashion planned. The control of prices and wages was an additional important instrument of the centrally planned economy.

Even the substantive goals of economic policy for Eastern European countries were prescribed by the Soviet developmental model. The prime task in the 1950s was to lay the basis for autonomous industrialization, that is, to free the country from foreign dependency. An associated goal was to concentrate available resources on investment: accumulation was encouraged at the expense of consumption. A third central task was the development and extension of industry, especially heavy industry. Agriculture and consumer goods industries were correspondingly neglected. All of the countries followed this model and with its aid overcame the prevailing stagnation of Eastern European economies. Yet the adoption of centralized, accumulation-oriented economic planning systems created serious burdens: no regard was paid to national peculiarities such as the level of industrial development, the degree of foreign economic dependence, and politicoadministrative structures.

The economic self-management approach. In Yugoslavia, a new politicoeconomic system was conceived in 1946, which, as in other Eastern European countries, envisaged the centralized organization of state and economy on the Soviet pattern. Here, too, means of production were to a great extent nationalized and a planning bureaucracy developed. However, the failure to meet plan targets, gaps in the supply of foodstuffs, an inordinate bureaucracy, the political isolation consequent on exclusion from Cominform in 1948, and the resultant economic blockade by the remaining Eastern European countries were the major reasons why Yugoslavia very soon abandoned the centrally planned economic model and developed its own system. By 1950 the shift to a decentralized planning approach was underway. The so-called societal plans were merely overall guidelines within which individual enterprises could reach relatively independent decisions on purchasing, production, and sales. Monetary incentives and the distribution of goods through the market relaxed the original principles of central planning even further.

Nonetheless, the influence of the state in this first phase remained dominant. The state decided the amount of depreciation, determined the minimum level of capacity utilization, and planned and directed the extent and structure of capital investment. From its very beginnings, however, the Yugoslavian politicoeconomic model had the distinguishing feature of workers' self-management. The process of negotiation and decision-making at the enterprise level was to be democratized to include the workers. Success was modest. There was neither a spurt in economic development nor any further democratization. Just like the other Eastern European states, Yugoslavia in the 1950s struggled with the special problems of constructing a completely new economic system.

The syndicalist-fascist approach. The Spanish and Portuguese economic structures were extremely heterogeneous, characterized by wide discrepancies between the remnants of feudalism, subsistence agriculture, and an oligarchic stratum of industrial and financial magnates. Both countries were relatively untouched by the Second World War, after which they underwent neither politicoeconomic reconstruction nor a new beginning. Economic policy showed in fact considerable continuity. During the 1930s both Spain and Portugal had started to construct a corporatist-fascist system, characterized by a national syndicalist structure embodying the principles of unity, totality, and hierarchy. "Unity" meant the unification of employers and employees into a single organization; "totality" described the compulsory and exclusive character of the vertical syndicates of the different occupational estates; "hierarchy" indicated that the syndicates were run according to a strict chain of command. The syndicates had an instrumental character because they served as executors of state economic policy. In this regard the two countries differed somewhat; the corporatist structure in Portugal was at least intended to constitute a self-managing system free of the state, whereas the fascist corporations in Spain were conceived as direct political agents of state control.

The substantive economic policies followed by both states after the Second World War were characterized by isolationist, or even autarkic, tendencies on the external front and on the domestic front a mixture of state interventionism and liberal moderation. On the one hand, the state intervened with a scarcely comprehensible number of laws and decrees applicable to all areas of economic and social life; on the other hand, entrepreneurs and large landowners were given a free hand. A deliberate industrialization policy, initiated by Portugal in the 1930s and by Spain in the 1940s, was supposed to provide the infrastructural foundations of industrialization, remove sectoral and regional imbalances, and begin a process of import substitution. In Spain a publicly owned holding company, the National Institute of Industry (INI), acquired shares in important industrial enterprises and in this way pursued an active investment strategy. In Portugal the Development Fund, or later the Bank for Economic Development, sought to direct investment. At the same time, as in Spain, the state extended its industrial holdings. "Economic plans" looked after the medium-term perspective.

The pretension of fascist ideology to create an organic society and economy free of conflict was not realized. The reality of fascist power instead ensured that the enrichment of a few at the cost of many should be underwritten by an appropriate economic system. The pursuit of an industrialization strategy, which was supposed to spur on socioeconomic modernization, justifies describing both countries in the immediate postwar years as developmental dictatorships, but in neither case did the policy achieve a broadly based industrialization that would have brought about an improvement in general welfare. Only in the later 1950s and early 1960s did a genuine change in economic policy occur, when liberalization of external economic relations brought changes in domestic economic policy.

Economic Systems and Economic Development

Changes in politicoeconomic systems and the high postwar rates of economic growth were certainly related. In every country the state sought to improve the supply conditions of production and to stabilize demand. The question of whether any one of the approaches used proved to be especially effective can hardly be answered; but practically every country went through a period of extraordinarily favorable economic development, whether it had been heavily damaged during the war or not, and whether it was based on the model of a private market economy or that of a state planned economy. In this respect the connection between economic system and economic development should not be overrated. Favorable postwar conditions were certainly an important, if not the primary, cause for the economic growth of the following years. The adoption of particular politicoeconomic models by individual countries can be accounted for by varying historical experience, the contemporary constellation of political forces, and the development of productive forces. In contrast to the years after the

First World War, after the Second there was not merely economic reconstruction but a new beginning; moreover, the postwar reconstruction of the 1940s was followed not by stagnation but by a hitherto unknown economic expansion.

Reform and Convergence of Politicoeconomic Systems in the 1960s

International Policy

The worldwide (and hence also European) process of liberalization and integration that began after 1945 made great progress during the 1950s and 1960s. The GATT, originally conceived as a provisional measure, laid the foundations for a series of international rounds of trade negotiations, in which tariff and non-tariff barriers to trade between industrial nations were abolished.

Within the EEC the customs union foreseen by the Treaty of Rome was actually realized earlier than anticipated; by 1968 customs duties between the six founding members were entirely removed. Those countries that joined in 1973—Britain, Denmark, and the Irish Republic—had until 1977 to dismantle their previous duties. Quota restrictions also disappeared along with customs duties, although non-tariff restrictions to trade were not removed. Despite the continued existence of administrative and financial obstacles to the free movement of goods and capital, the foundation of the EEC began a process of increasing integration between the economies of the member states. The positive effect of this integration is disputed and in any case difficult to measure. But creation of the EEC did certainly provide an impulse to economic growth, since enterprises saw in the Common Market increased sales opportunities and adapted to the increased competition by adopting innovative methods of production and marketing. This positive effect was, however, diminished by the detachment of the EEC economies from those of non-member states, since the abolition of internal duties was accompanied by the erection of a common external tariff wall. The duties on foreign manufactured goods were not that high on average, but an effective redirecting of trade occurred nonetheless. In the late 1950s two thirds of the foreign trade of the six founding EEC states was conducted with non-member states; by the mid-1970s only one half. The integration of the EEC countries, however, has not markedly increased the "regionalization" of world trade, for the volume of trade between the EEC and third countries has risen considerably. Agricultural imports into the EEC were a contentious issue from the start; they have been subjected to high duties dictated by the organization of the EEC's agricultural market rather than to the low GATT tariffs as in the case of manufactured goods.

The realization of economic union proved to be more difficult, but progress was also made in this area. A common policy on competition was agreed to and implemented. Harmonization of fiscal policy was achieved by replacing the differing forms of indirect taxation with a uniform value-added tax. Technical norms, economic laws, and company law were standardized. Capital movements were liberalized as well as, in part at least, the provisioning of services. Despite this co-ordination in various areas, no concerted economic policy came about. The sole exception was agricultural policy. In other policy areas the individual governments were not prepared to surrender their national sovereignty—and this was especially the case with the intended political union. Despite the creation of numerous common administrative authorities, which materially contributed to the formation of a European identity, only the rudiments of a pan-European legislative and executive power emerged. The process of European integration remained stuck halfway to its goal.

The economic success of EFTA was limited. A degree of integration within the EFTA states arose from a modest intensification of trade within the free trade area, but the extent of intermeshing with EFTA was less than that between EFTA and the EEC. The foundation of the free trade area did not bring about the kind of growth that had occurred within the EEC, and the various member states of EFTA experienced quite different forms of development. After Britain and Denmark left EFTA in 1973, the EEC concluded a free trade agreement with the remainder of EFTA. Duties and quota restrictions for manufactured products in trade between EFTA and the EEC were dismantled in 1977.

The establishment of the EEC forced the pace of integration in Eastern Europe as well; by altering its statutes, Comecon attempted to transform itself into an eastern variant of the EEC. As in the EEC, the economic aims of Comecon can be reduced to the desire for increased prosperity. At the same time a step-by-step convergence in the socioeconomic performance of member states was to be achieved. Accelerated and stronger growth in intrabloc trade and the general strengthening of Comecon countries in world trade, and hence reinforcement of general defensive capacity, were further objectives. Differing conceptions for cooperation with Comecon emerged: the Soviet Union, along with Czechoslovakia, Bulgaria, and, to a lesser degree, East Germany, favored a centralized integrative concept; Rumania developed a concept based upon the autonomy of the nation-state; Poland opted for a functionalist-reformist path; and Hungary argued for a market-oriented approach. The Comprehensive Program for the Further Deepening and Fulfillment of Cooperation in Socialist Economic Integration of 1971 presented a mixture of these contradictory ideas but emphasized the principle of national sovereignty. Consequently, Comecon agencies had no real rights of disposal over property, no planning competence, no powers of decree, no means to set a budget, nor any judicial powers.

Since all rights within Comecon remained with the individual national governments—distinct from the EEC, where the European Commission had at least initiatory and executive functions—Comecon lacked the prerequisites for the exercise of independent economic policy. Despite the Principle of Sovereign Equality and Independence, the Soviet Union dominated economically and politically, on account of its abundant reserves of otherwise limited natural resources and its powers of military sanction. The progress toward integration was modest. Signs of a partial "internationalization" were visible only where agreement upon production priorities was possible. Individual countries concentrated on the production of particular goods, on which basis highly specialized trade (dubbed "cooperation") took place in raw materials and energy, foodstuffs, machines and machine parts, industrial mass commodities, and transport.

National Policy
Since the later 1950s, and particularly during the 1960s, a convergence took place between the various politicoeconomic approaches. Within Western Europe, those countries that had pursued longer-term economic planning shifted towards short-term countercyclical policy, and vice versa. Countries that had until that time mainly used fiscal instruments moved back to monetary measures, whereas those who had relied upon monetary policy adopted a more fiscal stance. The objectives of growth policy and economic management also converged. Even if actual priorities varied, practically all countries aimed at full employment, price stability, external economic equilibrium, moderate economic growth, and, with some reservations, a just distribution of income. Continuing differences stemmed from historical experience as

well as contemporary postwar problems. That West Germany assigned price stability such a high priority was unsurprising given that within the space of one generation its citizens had experienced one runaway and one suppressed hyperinflation. Countries such as Britain, on the other hand, whose principal problem in the interwar period had been a high level of unemployment, were inclined towards securing full employment before all else. Countries such as France, which had structural deficiencies, favored supply-oriented growth as an objective, achieved through policies intended to improve conditions for enterprises and the economic structure in general.

The convergence in the domain of longer-term economic planning meant, above all, that those countries originally without such planning now introduced its elements into their economic policies. West Germany moved hesitantly from regulative planning with expert advice and economic forecasting towards indicative planning with medium-term financial measures and global management with generalized economic guidelines (see table 4.3). In Britain, by contrast, a Conservative government initiated a planning model along the lines of French *planification* but without the imperative elements, complete with a planning office (National Economic Development Office), an economic and social council (National Economic Development Council), and branch committees (National Economic Development Committees). This model was upgraded by the 1964 Labour Government with a National Plan involving a ministry of planning, and in 1966 with an investment fund. Belgium also followed the French example, adopting the system of economic programming in the late 1950s. Italian economic planning gained a new central authority in 1962 with the formation of the National Commission for Economic Planning (CNPE) as well as the Interministerial Planning Committee (CIPE) in 1967.

Contrary phenomena accompanied this convergence of planning within the market economy. French *planification* shifted increasingly from imperative to indicative planning. Although the Dutch distanced themselves somewhat from econometric forecasting, in 1963 they introduced a plan for growth and investment that ran over several years. Here also the corporatist element was extended: in 1972 the Scientific Government Advisory Council was created as an overall coordinating council of specialists, and then in 1973 a Social and Cultural Planning Office was formed to bring more qualitative aspects of welfare into the planning technocracy. In other countries state influence over wages and income policy increased. At the same time in Sweden attempts

Table 4.3. Stages of Politicoeconomic Planning

Market as Independent Variable
(Domination of Market Trends)

	Prognosis: Demographic and economic statistics as basis for policy decisions; advisory committees of experts
Political planning "planning in policy" (regulative planning)	*Budgetary and administrative planning*: Domestic financial and procedural planning; organizational planning
	Regulatory structural planning: Negatively coordinated departmental planning, e.g., traffic, energy, and development planning
Planning policy "planning of policy" (indicative planning)	*Overall steering and planning of economic framework*: Anticipatory influencing of key economic indicators
	Active structural policy: Intersectorally coordinated public investment planning; regional development; planning of health and educational services
Societal planning "planning of society" (imperative planning)	*Detailed indicative planning*: Sector- and product-specific investment incentives
	Imperative planning: Direction of investment; administered prices, wages and salaries

Market as Dependent Variable
(Influencing of Market Trends)

Source: Roland Czada, "Planungspolitik," in *Pipers Wörterbuch zur Politik*, gen. ed. Dieter Nohlen, vol. 2: *Westliche Industriegesellschaften*, ed. Manfred G. Schmidt (Munich, 1983), p. 316.

were made to reinforce econometric forecasting, and the system of central wage negotiation increasingly proved ineffectual.

All these approaches to planning remained within the sphere of regulative and indicative planning and seldom reached the level of imperative planning. Within a macroeconomic planning framework that was ultimately little more than a medium-term projection of economic development, public authorities also pursued regional economic policy. They were, therefore, actually able to plan within those spheres for which they had responsibility—education, health, energy supply, traffic, and so forth. By contrast, only indirect methods, such as credit, sureties, subsidies, and tax relief, were available for the influencing of regional private investment.

The adoption of Keynesian demand management by those countries, initially following either a policy of long-term planning or a more liberal economic strategy, led to a convergence of policy instruments within demand management itself. In all countries this policy was based upon the manipulation of finance, money, currency, and income (see table 4.4). The convergence of economic policies was especially marked in the relation of monetary and fiscal policy. Thus, countries such as West Germany, Italy, and Belgium, which had in the 1950s primarily pursued monetary policy, went increasingly over to fiscal policy in the course of the 1960s. Britain, which had in the early postwar years relied upon fiscal policy, took the opposite route. The general outcome of all this was that in the course of the 1960s a hitherto neglected policy approach was increasingly applied: strong countercyclical demand management. Differences persisted, of course. If West Germany, Italy, and Switzerland placed a greater reliance on monetary policy, this reflected in some respects the heavily decentralized West German and Swiss financial systems and the low level of efficiency of the Italian; under such conditions rapid and coordinated alterations to the fiscal structure were not easily achieved. If Scandinavian countries, especially Sweden, and Britain emphasized financial policy, this was because greater opportunity for effective central intervention existed there.

Separating the countries of capitalist Western Europe according to the intensity with which they practiced demand management produces three broad groups. In Britain, Norway, Sweden, and to some extent Austria, interventionism was most marked; in France, Italy, and Belgium (and perhaps also Spain and Finland), it was less so; and West Germany, Switzerland, and the Netherlands pursued an explicitly liberal policy, although from the mid-1960s on the Germans and the Dutch also practiced economic management using fiscal instruments. If by "liberal economic system" is meant a financial policy strongly oriented to balanced budgets and a monetary policy whose primary objective is the stability of money value, and by "interventionist system" one that operated in a countercyclical manner in both policy spheres,

Table 4.4.   Instruments of Economic Management

Policy Area	Instruments
Fiscal Policy Agent: Government Goal: Stabilization of overall economic demand	State expenditure State income (taxes) Countercyclical reserves Investment incentives Depreciation provisions Subsidies

Monetary Policy
Agent: Central bank
Goal: Control of money supply and
    level of interest
	Minimum reserve policy
	Refinancing policy
	    Discount rate
	    Re-discount contingent
	    Lombard rate
	Open market policy

Currency Policy Agent: Central bank and government Goal: Secure external value of currency	Intervention in exchange market Foreign exchange controls Re- or devaluation of currency Swap arrangements

Incomes Policy
Agent: Workers' representatives,
    management, and government
Goal: Avoidance of destabilizing wage
    and salary settlements
	Government wage-price criteria
	    (concerted action)
	Wage and salary guidelines
	Wage and salary freezes

Source: Gerhard Willke, "Konjunkturpolitik," in *Pipers Wörterbuch zur Politik,* gen. ed. Dieter Nohlen, vol. 2: *Westliche Industriegesellschaften,* ed. Manfred G. Schmidt (Munich, 1983), p. 193.

then one can say that conservative-liberal governments favored the former, and social democratic governments the latter.

Those countries, such as West Germany and the Netherlands, that during the 1960s went from a liberal to an interventionist system tended to justify this step by using extremely complex models placing the formulation of fiscal policy in very close relation with forecasts of real economic development. Policy—and party politics—was not to have an entirely free hand. In the Netherlands the construct of the "structural budget deficit" was invented, in West Germany the "neutral budget." Countries such as Sweden and Britain, by contrast, had no need of theoretical justifications for budget deficits; rather the budget was very pragmatically adapted to the prevailing economic conditions.

In a series of countries the policy developments of these years—from reconstruction, to countercyclical demand management, to short-term crisis management, to longer-term structural policy aimed at the optimization of economic growth—reflected socioeconomic changes. Social and interventionist variants of liberal competitive capitalism that had been developed after the war seemed to prove themselves in the 1950s. Unprecedented economic growth and increases in general prosperity were the order of the day. The shift from a static countercyclical policy to a dynamic growth policy took place during the 1950s, since the need merely to overcome crises seemed to have passed, and attention moved to long-term stability and hence the planning and guidance of the process of economic growth. This meant, however, that the improvement of individual welfare no longer depended solely on the performance of the capitalist system. The social network had to be drawn tighter, the supply of public goods and services enlarged, and in general a juster distribution achieved. This had to happen because, on the one hand, the level of social expectations had risen, and, on the other, a highly developed economic system could less and less afford to leave the allocation of factors of production and goods to market forces. It was able to happen because of the absence of conflict between the profit interest and the extension of the social welfare state. Strong economic growth secured profits as well as the opportunity for redistribution.

No straightforward answer can be given to the question of whether the mixed economy of the postwar years was successful or not; and this goes for both long-term growth policy and the short-term policies associated with management of aggregate demand. In the long-term perspective—one must emphasize once more—the postwar European economies underwent an unprecedented phase of growth lasting a quarter of a century, a phase that was certainly related not only to the favorable conditions for postwar reconstruction but also to the new economic policies implemented. This period of growth ended at least temporarily in the late 1970s; in other words, the new economic order and policies could not secure stable economic growth in perpetuity.

To arrive at a judgement on the policies associated with the management of aggregate demand for countercyclical purposes is perhaps somewhat easier. Although a few instances exist in which Keynesianism was successfully employed to achieve stability, there are more cases in which it failed. In the majority of cases the measures were adopted at the wrong time and to the wrong degree, exacerbating given fluctuations instead of damping them. But it must be remembered that failure here is relative to the high expectation placed upon Keynesian policies in the 1960s: the creation of a dynamic European economy entirely free from crisis.

The disappointing results of Keynesian economics in Western Europe are due to a combination of inherent and exogenous elements. Fundamentally, an economic policy that seeks to direct the market process would seem to have objective limits because it attempts to immobilize the capitalist mechanism of reorganization through crisis and thus delays structural adaptive processes. The original Keynesian approach was oriented to aggregate economic behavior without regard to regional and sectoral differences; attempts to supplement this approach by planned structural policy have not been able to overcome this shortcoming. Hence Keynesian policy ultimately simply prolongs structural problems in the economy. The limitation of state policy to the macroeconomic level, with only an indirect influence on the expenditure and consumption of private enterprises and households through the use of incentives and restrictions, means that the microeconomic level, the level at which real decisions concerning the conduct of the production process are made, continues to be dominated by the market mechanism and private rights of disposal over the means of production.

Changes in politicoeconomic structures have also hampered the execution of Keynesian policies. The institutional framework within which Keynesianism was initially formulated and deployed in the 1930s and the 1940s has been transformed technologically, economically, and politically. Concentration and accumulation of economic power have weakened not only the mechanisms of the marketplace, but also the efficacy of state intervention in the economy. Technological production structures, which initially translated state-encouraged investment into increased employment, have altered into structures within which investment increasingly serves to bring about rationalization and thus to release labor and create unemployment. The postwar liberalization of international economic relations has also tended to undermine the functioning of Keynesianism by rendering domestic economic policy vulnerable to external influences beyond the control of individual governments. Finally, the financial resources immediately available for the manipulation of growth and demand are very limited in all Western European countries.

Although Keynesian policies were supposed to promote economic stability, they in fact became associated with economic instability. The combination of countercyclical demand management and long-term growth policy created an inflationary potential. Expansive monetary and fiscal policies were neutral with respect to this potential only if quickly followed by more restrictive policies; if such policies were instead put at the service of growth policy, then permanent or even cumulative budget deficits and a cheap money policy would lead to inflation, especially if, at the same time, full employment had been achieved with a consequent upward pressure on wages, and supplies of raw materials had become scarce with associated rises in costs. In the later 1960s and early 1970s such a situation indeed rose.

The altered economic situation brought modifications in the political system that further diminished the efficacy of countercyclical management of demand and supply. Social consensus broke down in the mid-1970s with the first signs of a serious economic crisis; political parties, entrepreneurs, and trade unions withdrew their cooperation; the "pact on growth" dissolved with the disappearance of growth. This divisiveness exacerbated inherent weaknesses in the policy framework, initially limiting its utility and ultimately rendering it inoperable. Although this breakdown in social consensus has not affected the technical diagnosis and prognosis of the economic situation upon which policy proposals are formulated, it has delayed and influenced the responses of economic policy. Between the pronouncement of a diagnosis and the deployment of policy instruments lies a phase of political discussion and decision-making, which must be kept as brief as possible in order for the chosen policies to be effective and appropriate. But this has become increasingly difficult to achieve as opinion on the objectives and relevant means of economic policy has become more contentious, for means and ends conflict with respect to the prime macroeconomic targets of price stability, full employment, balance of payments equilibrium, and economic growth.

The radical break with the previous form of economic organization in Eastern Europe, and the adoption of a model not fully developed even in the Soviet Union, necessarily led to substantial problems. The extreme centralization of the majority of the national economies up to Stalin's death in 1953 exacerbated the situation; the opportunity for independent decision on the part of subordinate authorities in the economic administration, in particular enterprises, was minimal. Bureaucratic paralysis and grave economic inefficiencies—sloppy planning, an obsession with pure quantity, unfulfilled plan targets, a poor supply situation, hypertrophied planning bureaucracies—were the results everywhere. By the mid-1950s cautious decentralization had been embarked upon together with greater emphasis on the production of consumer goods. The failures of this change led at the end of the 1950s to recentralization. Discussion of reform continued, however, and during the 1960s more far-reaching reforms were introduced. Until then the faults of the system had persisted, and in addition emergent shortages of natural resources and labor made a transition from extensive to intensive growth necessary. Purely quantitative increments of capital and labor, and the diversion of means of production from the consumer goods sector to that of producer goods had reached their limits. Growth had henceforth to be achieved by enhanced factor productivity through technical progress and the rational combination of factors; in other words, the system had to be more efficiently managed. The political problems of the 1950s—primarily in Poland and Hungary—certainly also contributed to a greater preparedness for reform.

Reforms in East Germany were relatively modest, embodied in the New Economic System of 1963 and the Economic System of Socialism of 1967. Here the sole concern was to organize the existing central planning system more efficiently. Planning authorities were reorganized; material plan-indicators were reduced in number and in part replaced by monetary ones; modern mathematical methods were applied to the formulation of plans; and planning directives were shifted to middle-level authorities. Such measures did not alter the fundamental principles of the central planning system. The Economic System of Socialism permitted enterprises to retain a portion of their output for investment and premium funds and to employ their resources more independently within the framework of planning guidelines over several years. An important part of the reforms concerned price formation; prices were first revamped to adapt to raised production costs and to facilitate the dismantlement of state price subsidies, and then they were generally reorganized in a more flexible manner. The extension of decision-making powers on the part of the enterprise was not, however, matched by sufficient flexibility in the still relatively rigid price system, despite the reforms; the result was disproportionality and instability in the economic system as a whole, leading to the abandonment of the new approach. Recentralization took place for the second time in the early 1970s.

Poland, Rumania, and Bulgaria likewise adhered strictly to central planning. Despite some alterations, the system remained unchanged in its basic structure and leading sectors.

The reforms described so far remained within the framework of the centrally planned economy; in other countries this framework was transgressed at least in part, in a real attempt to find a "third way" between the competitive market economy and the centrally planned economy. The socialist planned economy was no longer to be merely partially reformed but rather reconstructed from the bottom up as a socialist market economy. Three variants can be distinguished: the state-directed approach in Hungary, the participatory approach in Yugoslavia, and the intermediate route attempted by Czechoslovakia.

The introduction in 1968 of the New Economic Mechanism in Hungary represented a departure from the centrally planned economy and a transition to a market socialist approach with a considerable degree of state direction and control. The position and function of state property remained unchanged, despite the decentralization of planning and market coordination. The state—the Council of Ministers and the ministries—has since then chosen the enterprise's managing director, laid down the basic decisions on state productive capacity, and supervised the management of the enterprise. Individual enterprises, however, have been left relatively free to manage themelves on a profit-making basis. Discussion and decision-making are structured; self-management within the enterprise does not exist. Formal instructions or directives on the part of the state are rare, however, it being more usual to employ indirect measures. The state's five-year plan determines the growth and structure of national income; sets the dimensions of macroeconomic aggregates, such as consumption, investment, price levels, imports and exports; and formulates targets for each sector and branch. Five-year and one-year plans are implemented through economic regulators, that is, prices, wages and incomes, investment and credit, the exchange rate, and external trade, to name only the central instruments for indirect management. The Hungarian reform thus involved a combination of overall national economic planning, economic regulators, and a built-in market mechanism.

Yugoslavia's participatory conception of workers' self-management was a more open reform than those in other socialist countries. The transition from planned to market economy, with self-management and relative autonomy of enterprises, was a gradual one. The 1965 economic reforms ended this transitional period. The subsequent constitutional changes of 1968 and 1971 introduced the Basic Organization of United Labor, a new and extremely decentralized enterprise structure, which was endorsed by the new 1974 constitution and elaborated in greater detail. Two laws in 1976—Law on the Basic Elements of the System of Societal Planning and on the Yugoslavian Societal Plan, and the Law on Associated Labor—rounded off a reform process summarized by the slogans "decentralization," "democratization," and "de-statification." Yugoslavia thus continued along the path it had been following since the beginning of the 1950s. Non-state-owned economic units increasingly appeared alongside state authorities in economic discussion and decision-making. "Cooperation" was added to the market as the dominant mechanism in the economic process and to hierarchy as the dominant mode of determining state economic policy.

The Czechoslovakian economic reforms of 1967–1968, which were halted by the invasion of Warsaw Pact troops in the autumn of 1968, can be regarded as a third variant of the third approach, in which the form of decentralization adopted left the state less room for maneuver than in Hungary but more than in Yugoslavia. The important directive instruments retained by the state in this case were the distribution of income between enterprises, enterprise payments, prices, state revenues and expenditures, investment, credit, and other central economic regulators.

The overview of the various types of socialist economic systems given in table 4.5 subdivides them into two large groups: the centralized directive type and the decentralized parametric type. An overall comparison of the variations in economic system is rendered problematic by the complexity of the different structures, but the typification presented here provides a useful classification according to four central systemic elements: decision-making structure, guidance system, motivational basis, and developmental strategy. Apart from the Stalinist model originally introduced in the Eastern European economies (including Yugoslavia) after the war, the partially reformed economic systems that still dominate in the majority of Eastern European countries represent versions of the centralized directive type. Representing the decentralized parametric type is the New Economic Mechanism in Hungary, in which political decision-making processes—the leading role of the party and state organs, hierarchy at the level of the enterprise—still remain in place but in which market mechanisms play an important role in guidance and motivation within the framework of the planned economy. Next comes the system of market economy based

Table 4.5. Typology of Socialist Economic Systems and Their Variants

	Centralized Command System			Decentralized Parametric System		
	USSR (Stalinism)	China (Maoism)	East European COMECON countries[a] (Partial reforms)	Hungary	Yugoslavia	CSSR (Prague Spring, 1968)
Decision-maker	Party; economic planning bureaucracy; management	Party; councils of the "masses"	Party; economic planning bureaucracy; management	Party; economic planning bureaucracy; management	Party; workers' self-management	Party; collective organizations; management
Control system	Detailed directive indices; physical measurement of output	Directive indices; regional decentralization; physical measurement of output	Improved directive indices; monetary indicators and "levers"; free choice of workplace and consumer goods	Indicative planning; economic regulators; market mechanisms	Societal planning; state economic policy; market mechanisms	Indicative planning; economic regulators; market mechanisms

Motivation System	Ideological and material incentives coupled with plan targets	Ideological incentives	Predominantly material incentives coupled with plan targets	Contractually agreed efficiency wage; earnings incentives linked to profits	Wages dependent upon earnings of unit	Contractually agreed efficiency wage; earnings incentives linked to firm's gross income
Development strategy	Forced growth; accumulation-oriented	Dualistic strategy; autarky-oriented	Balanced growth; trade-oriented	Balanced growth; trade-oriented	Balanced growth; regional equalization; trade-oriented	Balanced growth; trade-oriented

Source: Jiri Kosta, *Wirtschaftssysteme des realen Sozialismus: Probleme und Alternativen* (Cologne, 1984), p. 185.
a Not including Hungary and Yugoslavia.

upon workers' self-management developed since the 1950s in Yugoslavia. The Czechoslovakian reform of 1968 survives only as a theoretical construct.

Convergence of Economic Systems

In view of the simultaneous adoption of planning elements to give stronger direction to the Western European market economies and the attempts in Eastern European centrally planned economies to effect a more efficient management by using market mechanisms, it is unsurprising that a debate over the potential convergence of the two economic systems emerged during the 1960s. Some analysts believed they could already detect a naturally emerging convergence. Various arguments supported this thesis: the autonomous dynamic of industrialization and the mutual interaction of both economic orders; sociological similarities such as the pursuit of progress and rational calculation, unlimited consumption and economic growth, social security and education; the rising level of concentration and organization in industrial economies and the resultant spread of large enterprises; and so forth. The systemic elements cited in favor of convergent tendencies were exceptionally heterogeneous, and showed a varying relevance to the system as a whole. In general, the convergence thesis suffered from the way in which its proponents quickly concluded from similar forms of production processes and techniques or similar structures in parts of the national economy that a systematic convergence was occurring. The rashness of the conclusion became quite evident in the course of the 1970s, for the two economic orders ceased to converge further.

Neoliberal and Market-Socialist Strategies since the 1970s

The economic situation altered considerably in the 1970s. The governments of European countries were confronted with problems that had occasionally appeared before but never on such a scale, among them a rising rate of inflation and unemployment; a stagnating national product and balance of payments disequilibria; growing budget deficits and unstable exchange rates; and disintegrative tendencies in the world market. Against this socioeconomic background a paradigmatic change in political economy took place. Up to the end of the 1960s and the early 1970s, Keynesianism was the dominant politicoeconomic approach in Western Europe. It sought to diminish cyclical fluctuations with a demand-oriented stabilization policy deploying global and indirect fiscal and monetary measures: incomes policy was employed to control the rise of wages and prices, and regulative and indicative planning was used to stablize the process of economic growth. During the 1970s, by contrast, variants of restrictive neoliberal monetary policies were taken up by many countries, accompanied by measures aimed at improving the efficient use of capital and labor in the national economy—so-called supply-side economics.

Before dealing more closely with such austerity programs, which entailed restrictions and rigorous cutbacks, a characteristic change in economic planning must be noted. The ambition of achieving overall economic management and planning in terms of key macroeconomic aggregates was given up in the 1970s. Instead, planning confined itself to specific, large-scale projects related to regional and structural development. In West Germany this shift was accompanied by intensive discussion of a targeted policy on technology and a growth policy related to particular economic branches. This was also the case in France, where the Seventh Plan for the years 1976–1980 reflected this change in priorities. In Britain the so-called Industrial Strategy—a conscious change of name from the completely unsuccessful National Economic Plan of 1965—sought to promote a limited number of investment initiatives.

Such examples could be extended. These measures and the associated concentrated promotion of large-scale technologies were supposed to stimulate the modernization of national economies. The combined interests of industry and the state were behind this changed approach to planning, since the market had not been effective in bringing about projects on the scale now envisaged. The amount of capital required and the returns were no longer calculable, and the level of profit and general profitability were uncertain. The state participated in the risk but left the return to private enterprises. Increasingly, the state also intervened in those cases where the external costs, that is, those costs borne not by the investor but by society at large, had greatly increased, such as investments endangering the environment. Private capitalist interests have traditionally taken no account of the environmental damage brought about by their production processes unless placed under some form of compulsion. Natural resources such as air, space, land, and water thus had to be subjected to ever greater protection.

Just as a detailing of the numerous variations of economic planning and Keynesianism was impossible above, so too is a recapitulation of all national variations of austerity policy. The central characteristic, however, was similar everywhere: a shift in objectives, giving priority to price stability and balance of payments equilibrium instead of to full employment and economic growth. To gain control over inflation, short-run administrative measures such as wage and price freezes were resorted to. More important, however, was the fundamental change in monetary and fiscal policy. Bank liquidity (free liquid reserves) was no longer an effective monetary indicator for the issuing banks; instead the amount of money supplied by the central banks was used (circulating cash plus liquid reserves). By using this more middle-range guideline for monetary policy, the money supply was adjusted to middle-range forecasts of economic growth rather than being related to a purely countercyclical fiscal policy. The efficacy of monetary policy was boosted by the adoption of floating exchange rates in the early 1970s, for hitherto the variability of international flows of money and capital associated with fixed exchange rates had repeatedly undermined national monetary policies. The Federal Republic of Germany led this shift to monetary policy; other countries were not so consistent in adopting it. But everywhere the tendency was the same: from a countercyclically oriented generous monetary policy to a medium-term restrictive policy of tight money.

A similar transformation occurred in fiscal policy. Here, too, policy shifted from a countercyclical and ultimately expansionary orientation to one emphasizing medium- or long-term restrictions. In every country austerity policy pursued budgetary "consolidation." Public spending was cut, especially spending on social programs; the supply of public goods and services was reduced; and revenues were increased at least partially through higher tax rates levied on private consumption and lower-income groups. The decisive macroeconomic dimension to be manipulated was no longer demand, but rather supply; this was another decisive characteristic of the new paradigm. Tax relief for private enterprises, monetary and other stimuli for investment, reduction of bureaucratic control of the economic system, and other measures were undertaken to improve the conditions of supply in the national economy.

Finally, the neoliberal-monetarist approach meant a withdrawal of the state from the economy. The state no longer had the task of regulating the economy by intervening directly but was to provide more comprehensive scope to the free play of market forces in order that the forces of supply and demand could cleanse the economy of weak, inefficient enterprises. Socioeconomically, the object was to free the western European market economies from "social ballast" and protect them from bureaucratic paralysis, lowering the internal and external costs of production and thereby improving the prospects for returns on capital investment. In general, this was intended to enhance the performance and productivity of the system and thus enable the national structures of production to adapt themselves more quickly to the competitive demands of a world economy, demands that had been sharpened by the business crisis.

The transition from planned Keynesianism to a neoliberal-monetarist policy of austerity did not occur simultaneously in every country. Those countries with marked corporatist political structures, such as Austria and the Scandinavian countries, departed from Keynesian policy relatively late. This was true also in West Germany, in which up to the beginning of the 1980s the Social Democrats and the liberal Free Democrats sought a middle path. In those countries in which the corporatist structures were either unworkable (as in Britain) or weakly developed (as in France or Italy), the shift in state economic policy took place rather earlier.

Leaving aside the paradigmatic shift embodied in the planning and management of war economies, the second change in the paradigm of capitalist political economy in twentieth-century Europe was brought about by the second world economic crisis in the century. The parallels between the two crises consist more in the strategies adopted to overcome them than in their causes and progress. In both cases the ultimate aim was to stabilize the currency and consolidate the budget with a help of a deflationary policy. In the early 1930s these aims led to a reduction in prices and a balanced budget; in the early 1980s they only reduced the rate of inflation and slowed the rise of new indebtedness. In both crises these strategies were supposed to bring about an improvement in the profitability of enterprises and hence enhance the competitiveness of national economies in the world market. Such policies can no longer be carried out so nationalistically as they were in the earlier crisis. This is preventd by the high level of real integration in the European and world economy as well as by a network of international institutions. Nonetheless, the policies adopted in the course of the second crisis of the late 1970s and early 1980s did have marked national and regional features.

If these new policies are judged in terms of their stated objectives of price stability, budgetary consolidation, improvement in the balance of payments, increased employment, and economic growth, then they had some success. Some countries managed to break the increasing trend in indebtedness; the balance of payments situation became healthier; and, above all, the rate of inflation fell. The objective of high employment, however, remained emphatically unachieved. Beginning in the early 1980s Western Europe experienced levels of unemployment unknown since the immediate postwar years. For a few years economic growth stagnated, but since the mid-1980s it has begun to recover once more. Ultimately, though, these policies of austerity were largely responsible for the fact that precisely those persons who were already in a fragile socioeconomic situation were hardest hit by the crisis and that among certain strata of the population a degree of poverty developed considered no longer possible in Western European social welfare states.

The 1970s also confronted the economies of Eastern Europe with new problems. National economic plans could not be fulfilled, despite the gradual reduction in norms. The real extent of the crisis became apparent only at the end of the 1970s and the beginning of the 1980s. All sectors of the economy came under the influence of crisis-related phenomena. Industrial production grew slowly, agriculture suffered from harvest failures, the infrastructure remained underdeveloped. Investment stagnated, real income sank, the supply of goods to the population worsened. In addition, considerable trade and payment deficits developed.

Just like capitalist Western Europe, state socialist Eastern Europe reacted by reforming economic policy, although these reforms were not so extensive as those of the 1960s. Instead, reform elements allowed to lapse in the early 1970s were once again taken up in the early 1980s. In Bulgaria a planning reform in industry executed in 1982 was in many respects similar to those measures adopted in 1980 in Czechoslovakia and East Germany emphasizing the principle of "self-management of enterprise resources." Targeted plan-indicators were reduced and constructed more efficiently; wages were made more dependent on productivity. The trend towards decentralization and the introduction of market mechanisms appeared to be greater in Bulgaria than in the other two economies. In Poland a further step was taken. The 1981 reform envisaged a combination of self-management, market coordination, and parametric guidance similar in many respects to the Hungarian model of a socialist market economy. Hungary itself—the only Comecon country that had adhered throughout the 1970s to a market-oriented reform of the original central planning system—embarked on a deliberate extension of its reformist model. Rumania announced in early 1978 the introduction of a New Economic Mechanism, but it was actually the country that adhered most strongly to the previous centralized system. In general, these new reform initiatives remained half-measures; the transition to a more effective decentralized system was not completed, and there are few signs it will be. Among other reasons, reforms in state socialist countries depend on the awareness and political will of the party leadership, in particular that in Moscow. In addition, overall reform is rendered difficult by the existing disproportionalities in the economic structure. But above all, economic reform automatically entails political reform, which very quickly reaches its limits in the state socialist system.

CHAPTER 5

Paths of Socioeconomic Development

To conclude this survey of the social and economic history of twentieth-century Europe, we shall take a second look at the development typologies of the major socioeconomic regions. In so doing we must pass over chronological and national differences to a greater degree than in the preceding chapters. To some extent we shall argue ideal-typically in order to highlight the characteristic developmental features.

Northern Europe

When one studies the history of the underdeveloped regions of northern, southern, and eastern Europe (past and present), the question arises almost automatically of how the Scandinavian countries managed so soon—in the first two decades of the twentieth century, with Finland somewhat later—to break out of their historical role as the suppliers of mineral, agricultural, and forest products to the highly developed states of western Europe and then transform themselves into mature industrial economies with a high level of social welfare. Their geographical position was not particularly favorable, their endowment in natural resources was not above average, and their limited populations also promised little in the way of developmental potential.

Yet these demographic relationships provided an important prerequisite for the progressive development of society and economy in this region. The northern European countries entered the later phases of the demographic transition relatively early; their natural population growth has been moderate throughout the entire twentieth century. Population pressure was additionally reduced up until the 1920s by large-scale emigration. Thus the supply of and demand for labor— the number of economically active persons and the number of jobs—were approximately equal. As a consequence of this equilibrium in the labor market the wage level was neither strongly depressed, as was the case in the overpopulated eastern and southern European countries, nor pushed upwards by labor shortages. Instead, the level of wages tended to rise steadily, which promoted the introduction of labor-saving technologies and created strong domestic consumer demand. Like several western European countries, however, the northern European countries, especially Sweden, also experienced a shortage of labor after the Second World War and covered the shortfall by importing foreign workers.

Social and political conditions also favored autonomous development. The Scandinavian societies were relatively open, without the strong class differences and profound differentiation of social strata that marked other European societies. The reasons for this were many: there were certain democratic traditions; the level of organization for the articulation and implementation of interests was extremely high; an economically and politically organized peasantry (cooperatives and peasant parties) and working class (trade unions and workers' parties) emerged relatively early as counterweights to industrialists and state bureaucracy. The Scandinavian societies were also ethnically and religiously homogenous. Apart from Finland, they were spared great population movements involving refugees and exiles. The educational system was exceptionally democratic and achieved relatively early a high level of education among the adult population. Emphasizing mass education with few privileges, it gave equal weight to classical-humanistic studies and technical training. The cultural and institutional dualism characteristic of other European countries did not develop here. The distribution of income and property did not differ greatly from that in other countries, but the differences between rich and poor were less marked and the general level of income—at least after the Second World War—was higher. The gap between town and country was overcome quite rapidly. The northern European societies were probably also less heterogeneous than other European societies because they neither were burdened with an existing or one-time colonial empire nor pursued expansionist foreign policies. The elites and privileges inevitably formed by such imperial ventures were thus absent, as were thinking and acting in terms of national grandeur and strong foreign policy. Social forces could concentrate rather on domestic development. In Norway, Danish colonial rule ended at the beginning of the nineteenth century and the subsequent Swedish dominance at the beginning of the twentieth; Finland achieved independence from Russia in 1917. This all contributed to the strengthening of social integration and stability, hindered far-reaching social upheavals, and furthered the spirit of compromise in political and other conflicts. At the same time the social conditions were laid for steady, autocentric economic expansion in the twentieth century.

Perhaps the most important economic prerequisite, the modernization of agriculture, was also present in the Scandinavian countries. Except for Finland, by the end of the nineteenth century they possessed a productive and consolidated agricultural sector, based on medium-size holdings and an innovative peasantry. Agriculture had reached a degree of productivity that enabled the release of labor and the production of sufficient quantities of foodstuffs for the growing urban industrial population, as well as the provision of agricultural raw materials for industrial processing. A further prerequisite for the transition from export-oriented economic growth to autonomous industrialization also existed: the Scandinavian economies succeeded relatively early in shifting from the production of unprocessed staples such as grain, wood, fish, and iron ore to the primary stages of processing, proceeding in the twentieth century to the export of finished and semi-finished goods. A third economic prerequisite, or rather a third reason, for the progressive path of Scandinavian development in the twentieth century was the chain reaction set off by the transformation of the structure of exports: the export-oriented sectors stimulated complementary stages of production and set in train at the end of the nineteenth century a broadly based industrialization that maintained its momentum in the twentieth. Compared with conditions in other peripheral regions, this industrial development was very favorable; it was also supported by the early buildup of a network of services and other infrastructural features. Leaving aside the regions of the far north, the Scandinavian countries thus had relatively early efficient domestic structures for trade, communications, transport, and money and credit.

More advanced development increased domestic demand for manufactured consumer and capital goods, a demand based upon intensive interaction between agriculture and industry. Particularly after the First World War, the level of domestic demand made it feasible to begin an import-substituting industrialization in both consumer and capital goods. The economic chain reaction included not only the complementary branches within the restricted export-oriented sphere of production but also the entire secondary sector. The dependence of the northern European countries on imported industrial goods thereby declined. At the same time industrial export production became more diversified, which led to internationally marketable consumer and capital goods as well as internationally recognized high technology in some areas.

As a result of this social and economic development, the Scandinavian countries created a particular socioeconomic policy model. Given the prevailing broad social consensus, social tensions led to the construction of a modern social welfare state during the interwar period—considerably earlier than in other European countries. The Great Depression brought about the completion of a transition from liberal policies to Keynesian state interventionism. This shift of paradigm in social and economic policy contributed further to social equilibrium. Among other things, the newly created employment opportunities led to increased female participation in the work force with corresponding emancipatory effects for sexual equality and the role of women in society. After the Second World War this social welfare–interventionist approach was further developed, and an autonomous Scandinavian policy model has persisted up to the present. Characteristic of these especially mature variants of the welfare state and Keynesianism were corporatist elements and strongly centralized processes of opinion-formation and decision-making. External policies oriented in principle to the world market were pursued, but they were not dogmatically laissez-faire. On the contrary, foreign economic policy served to promote domestic industrialization. Only after the Second World War did the northern European countries adopt an emphatically liberal position on trade, although they consciously maintained their independent position.

Southern and Southeastern Europe

The regional delimitation of this developmental path is not entirely correct: on the one hand, it only partially fits the industrialized areas of northern Italy; on the other hand, many of its characteristics also apply to Ireland, Poland, and Hungary. Chronologically, it pertains to the southeastern European countries up to the Second World War and the southern European countries up to the 1970s. These regions have until quite recently been, strictly speaking, underdeveloped and treated as peripheral economies. Unlike the northern European countries, these economies did not succeed in the first half of the century in overcoming their position at the socioeconomic periphery of industrial western Europe and were unable to attain an independent, autocentric industrialization of economy and society. What were the reasons for this continued backwardness?

Those relationships that affected northern European development so positively assumed in the countries of southern and southeastern Europe a form that hindered economic and social modernization: not until the 1950s and 1960s did these countries begin the demographic transition. The resultant high rate of natural population growth was matched by a shortfall in the supply of jobs attributable to stagnant economic development. Consequently, a serious disequilibrium between population growth, labor potential, and employment opportunities existed. Up to the 1930s pressure on the labor market was relieved somewhat by overseas emigration, but even so in the first half of the century countries in this region had an extremely low male labor force participation rate and the lowest female participation rate in all Europe. As a result the wage level in these countries was generally very low, and thus strong domestic demand could not develop.

The southern and southeastern European societies were still dominated by feudalistic elements at the beginning of the century; their social structures had scarcely changed over many years. The emergence of a new bourgeois financial and industrial elite, rather than bringing fundamental change, deepened the existing fissures in the traditional society by enlarging the already great disparities in income and wealth. Political relations were also backward; articulation of interests and participation remained underdeveloped. Attempts by the agrarian and urban lower classes to organize themselves were severely repressed by the ruling elites, sometimes with open force. Democratic institutions, insofar as they emerged at all, were permanently in danger of being corrupted through the one-sided exercise of self-interest. Political structures tended to foster old and new ruling alliances—above all of a corporatist-fascist form—that obstructed development. In the final analysis, they stabilized the traditional power structures instead of using the small potential for modernization through social integration. A colonial past and imperial ambition, as in Portugal, Spain, and Italy; expansionist foreign policy, as in Italy and with some reservations also in Poland, Yugoslavia, Bulgaria, Rumania, and even Greece; or revanchist thinking, as in Hungary—all these factors also reinforced the position of privileged elites and the traditional differences between classes and strata. In any event, nationalist ambitions were frequently used to counter demands for greater equality and liberality. The collapse of these foreign policy objectives contributed to the reform of social structures in eastern Europe after the Second World War (to be sure, overlaid by the revolutionary upheaval of the social orders) and in Spain, Portugal, and Greece since the 1960s.

Cultural poverty reinforced economic poverty. The educational level of the broad mass of the population was extremely low in the first half of the century, and the prospects of education scarcely improved. The educational system was not only backward but also sharply segregated into classical-humanist and practical-technical streams. A low level of qualification among the "human capital" meant low productivity of labor with negative effects on the process of economic growth. The deep sociocultural divide between town and country, which often first emerged in the twentieth century, also inhibited development, as did the tensions between ethnic, religious, and anticlerical groups existing in most countries. In general, the social integration and solidarity necessary to promote economic and social modernization were lacking.

At the end of the nineteenth century the bulk of the region's population was rural and lived off an agriculture whose structures had hardly changed at all over the centuries. The agrarian reforms of the nineteenth century frequently ended in counter-reforms and usually strengthened the power of the large landowners. The agrarian reforms of the first half of the twentieth century did change property relations, but they ultimately increased the spread of barely sustainable smallholdings. The discrepancy between inefficiently managed large estates and subsistence-based smallholdings was characteristic of eastern European agriculture up to the Second World War and of southern European agriculture up to the recent past. As a result, agricultural production either stagnated or, where it expanded, grew within the traditional institutional framework. Agrarian export products were only hesitantly subjected to refining and processing, if at all; they thus contributed few incentives for economic development. A domestic demand based on agricultural incomes did not emerge. In general, not only did agriculture not contribute to modernization, as was the case in northern Europe, it was in fact a serious barrier to development.

This was also true of services and infrastructure. In the north they both represented the advanced development and contributed positively to it; in the south and southeast they reflected the socioeconomic backwardness of the regions and constituted a further obstacle to progress. The structures of trade and communications were as underdeveloped at the end of the nineteenth century as those of transportation. They remained so for the first decades of the twentieth century and still today have not reached the western and northern European standards. The initial absence and the subsequent hesitant development of a functioning domestic money and capital market also hindered both the modernization of agriculture and industrialization.

Under these circumstances the potential for industrialization remained limited. Subsistence agriculture and sustained industrialization were hardly complementary. The industries that were nonetheless built up were not able to stimulate a chain reaction in related processing areas. A dualistic industrial and artisanal structure arose. A few relatively modern and potentially productive large enterprises emerged, but they were not integrated into a homogeneous industrial structure; rather they formed monopolized and cartellized enclaves—literally islands in a sea of handicraft and small-business activity. The industrial structure of these countries was characterized by sectoral and regional heterogeneity; only a few branches of industry were in any sense internationally competitive. Industrial exports were hence as little able as agricultural exports to stimulate a broadly based industrialization.

The political response to this backward, stagnating economic situation was the adoption of nationalistic modernization strategies based upon the existing trade relations. The import of cheap grain into Europe from overseas at the end of the nineteenth century threatened the agricultural economies of these countries. In reaction the states erected customs duties to preserve domestic agriculture. Industrial protectionism followed later. It laid the groundwork for a state-supported policy of industrialization through import substitution that was begun after the First World War. This policy tended, however, to support relatively unproductive and obsolete industries without any future in the marketplace. The investments thus made did little to promote a self-sustaining industrialization. The nationalization of a series of industrial concerns also tended to maintain existing structures rather than alter them. A policy of state bureaucratic interventionism based on liberal-capitalist foundations grew up, but it pursued no real concept of economic development. Moreover, the financial means available to interwar governments were limited. Interest payments on and the redemption of foreign debts constrained governments' freedom of action even more. The restrictive monetary and financial policies subsequently introduced further hindered economic development.

Such policies ultimately reflected the nationalist, corporatist, and fascist currents that found their appropriate political forms in dictatorial regimes. The alliance of a landed oligarchy, commercial and financial capitalists, and the state bureaucarcy had to be overcome if industrialization were to prevail against the pressure to remain a peripheral dependency. The various semi-fascist regimes in southeastern Europe, the Salazar regime in Portugal, the Franco regime in Spain, and the Fascist regime in Italy can be interpreted in this light. As socioeconomic modernization strategies, these "developmental dictatorships" failed. They had to fail, because the attempt to achieve economic modernization was not bound up with social and political renewal. Neither social relations nor the power structures of the old societies were significantly altered. In southeastern Europe it remained to the Communist dictatorships after the Second World War to abolish the old class structures and to carry out the breakthrough to an industrial economy and society. The model followed was the Stalinist centrally planned economy based on absolute economic self-sufficiency. In terms of development policy these regimes succeeded where the interwar ones had failed. In southern Europe fascism was ended first by the war and later by revolution and democratization. Here a liberal developmental model was adopted that consciously strove for closer association with western European integration.

Eastern Europe after 1945

The starting positions of the eastern European countries after 1945 were varied. The area that became East Germany and the Czech portion of Czechoslovakia were industrialized economic areas with corresponding social formations. In the southeast, agrarian social and economic structures still predominated. Poland and Hungary occupied a middle position. That these different countries then followed a common development path was determined by the seizure of power by Communist parties. The decisive difference with respect to the patterns of development in the non-communist West was that postwar society and economy were self-consciously and methodically reorganized according to an ideologically grounded development concept: the allocation of factors of production, the distribution of goods, and the stratification of social groups were determined no longer by the market but rather by a state bureaucracy that was the instrument of the Communist party.

Even demographic developments were strongly influenced. Apart from Czechoslovakia, East Germany, and Hungary, all other countries in eastern Europe continued to suffer from overpopulation even after the war. Through a rigorous promotion of birth control the various governments pushed forward the demographic transition, which was completed relatively rapidly during the 1950s and 1960s. The closed labor market without international migration, the loss of refugees, the forced pace of industrialization, and the exceptionally inefficient use of labor produced shortages of labor by the 1960s. This situation could not be ameliorated even by the rapid transfer of labor from agriculture, the increasing participation of women in the work force (the highest female participation rates in Europe), and an about-face in population policy, which began to encourage large families and births. Socioeconomic development was thereby divided into two distinct phases: an initial period of extensive growth and a subsequent period of intensive growth.

Social change was as revolutionary as demographic change. The old ruling structures, traditional differences between classes and strata, and elites and privileges were all rigorously abolished. No longer were birth and inheritance or income and property the decisive determinants of social mobility, but rather education and performance. Although new social distinctions did form, on the whole relatively egalitarian societies developed. This was expressed in a more equitable distribution of income and wealth, whose distributive mechanism, based on the political control of prices, wages, and consumer goods, functioned according to different principles than in the market economies of the West. Relatively quickly the Communist governments modernized and democratized their countries' backward educational systems: the still widespread illiteracy was reduced; higher education was in principle accessible to all; and the dualistic educational structure was abolished. Political socialization involved a permanent politicoideological agitation intended to create socialist consciousness and secure the socialist future. The communist systems did not acknowledge the right of democratic participation in the political and economic domain. On the contrary, the "dictatorship of the proletariat" and the principle of "democratic centralism" secured a monopoly of power for the Communist parties and within the parties themselves led to the concentration of power in the hands of a small number of cadres. Although undemocratic by bourgeois standards, such organization of political power was a constitutive element of the eastern European development path since it underwrote the rigid planning and guidance of the socioeconomic system. Generally, all eastern European states after 1945 followed the

Marxist-Leninist model of society. Yet in the course of its realization national characteristics emerged as political, social, and economic variations. The Yugoslavian social system deviated most strongly from the Soviet pattern, but the Hungarian, Polish, Rumanian, and East German systems also had distinguishing characteristics; thus one can argue that, although the eastern European states pursued a common goal of constructing a socialist society, they sought to reach it by differing paths.

The economic changes undertaken by the eastern European states after 1945 were also fundamental. Except in Poland, almost all agricultural land was expropriated. Large state and collective farms replaced private latifundia and smallholdings. Private ownership also became the exception in industry and handicrafts. A centrally planned economy emerged that directed all economic activity through a planning bureaucracy. Despite shortages of resources, each country—in accordance with the Soviet development model—built up its own heavy industry and its own producer goods sector. This was supposed to lay the foundation for an autocentric development that would overcome the structural weaknesses associated with peripheral capitalist economies. The extremely one-sided promotion of industry, especially of heavy industry, in the first phase of development led by no means to a balanced and homogeneous economic structure. It was carried out to the disadvantage of agriculture and the consumer goods sector. Nonetheless, the traditional inequities of the domestic market were successfully levelled, insofar as the market no longer satisfied the needs of the few at the cost of the many but rather supplied all with the basic, if admittedly modest, amenities of personal and public consumer goods. In this first phase the principal task was to break up the encrusted economic structures and to overcome stagnation. Quite consciously, therefore, extensive economic growth was pursued in order to eliminate the multitude of supply bottlenecks by means of sheer quantity of production.

In a second phase of development the transition from extensive to intensive economic growth occurred, and the still existing far-reaching structural imbalances were at least reduced, if not eliminated. Agriculture was promoted more strongly than hitherto; within industry the consumer goods sector gained in importance. The transition from extensive to intensive growth meant above all the alteration of production methods. The technique of quantity production was increasingly unable to meet demands for higher quality products and more efficient production processes. The growing shortages in the supply of labor forced the eastern European countries to rely more than before on technology as a factor of production. New technologies were increasingly used, although the technological spurt experienced by the Western economies since the second half of the 1970s did not appear very clearly at first. At any rate the relative inefficiency of these economies compared with the more developed capitalist states has not changed much.

In the initial phase at least, the Stalinist model of socioeconomic development was adopted without any regard to national peculiarities. The eastern European countries were more or less forced to rely on their own resources. Ties with the Soviet Union proved to have only limited positive effects for development. The decisive element was that external economic relations with the capitalist world market, from which the prerevolutionary economies had drawn some stimulus, suddenly no longer existed. Not only did foreign trade in principle play a subordinate role in the Soviet development model, but also the general economic backwardness of the eastern European economies meant that they could scarcely derive economic stimulus through mutual trade. Complete autonomy was thus at first another characteristic of the state socialist model of development. This changed in time. The attempt to achieve so-called socialist integration introduced in at least some areas of production an international division of labor. Relations with Western economies became more intense, and moves were made to re-integrate the individual national economies into the world market. Foreign trade was no longer to be merely a stopgap but was to actively stimulate the economy.

Domestically, the Stalinist development model meant a rigidly centralized control of the economy. All eastern European countries attempted to realize this model, and they all very quickly tried to reform it, because it proved highly inefficient. The ability of each country to carry out reforms varied, and no country managed to implement a fundamental structural change. The reforms undertaken, involving stronger market-oriented coordination and increased self-management and responsibility, were more often than not dismantled piecemeal or even suddenly revoked. In this context the model of development pursued by Yugoslavia should be recalled once again. Wherever reforms were pursued with some firmness, as in Hungary, the basic dilemma of the eastern European societal order became most evident: the lack of efficiency in the economic system requires reforms that, given the close interconnection of politics and economics, must have consequences for the entire society. If these reforms are not carried out, withdrawal of loyalty because of inadequate performance threatens. If they are carried out, then far-reaching political structural changes scarcely compatible with the general principles of state socialist societies become necessary.

Western Europe

To construct a common development path for western Europe is even more problematical than for the other regions. Not only are the individual differences between countries great, but also each country itself is heterogeneously structured. Moreover, Ireland, and in certain respects the Netherlands, do not fit the model; yet a number of the model's features are applicable to Czechoslovakia up to the Second World War.

The demographic transition began in western Europe in the second half of the nineteenth century and was by the 1920s—except for Ireland and the Netherlands—virtually completed. The supply of and demand for labor thus kept roughly in step, as was the case in northern Europe. Nonetheless, these countries suffered from high unemployment during the interwar period, and after the Second World War labor shortages, which had been episodic, became for almost two decades a chronic condition that was countered by the massive importation of foreign workers. The equilibrium of labor supply and demand over the century should not be permitted to conceal the large demographic fluctuations within western European populations, the result of wars, baby booms, and a sudden drop in the birthrate. At any rate the level of wages was never depressed by overpopulation for any length of time. In all western European countries except Ireland, a strong domestic demand developed, enabling an early transition to mass consumption.

In the course of the twentieth century differences between classes and strata in western European societies were markedly reduced. Social differentiation was shaped less and less by the status patterns of traditional society and increasingly by occupation and income. Material inequality in the distribution of income and wealth was also reduced, which is not to say that western European societies are no longer characterized by material inequality; relatively small differences in wages and salaries produce different living standards and life-styles, and hence social differentiation. This levelling of material inequality also contributed to enabling the western European countries to reach the stage of mass consumption rather early—either in the interwar period or shortly after the Second World War. This was an expression of the region's advanced economic development as well as itself a factor promoting that economic growth. The socioeconomic lead that western Europe held over the other European countries at the beginning of the twentieth century, and which it has been able to maintain up to the present except vis-à-vis the Scandinavian countries, was also a result of the relatively high educational level of its population. Genuine democratization did not occur, it is true, but an educational explosion after the Second World War aimed at providing the qualified labor necessary for economic expansion. As in the case of northern Europe, the western European societies benefited as well from the facts that they were not deeply divided along ethnic or religious lines, that the differences between town and country could be dismantled very early, and that the tertiarization of society took place without great conflict.

Western and northern Europe were the regions that during the whole of the twentieth century possessed variants of parliamentary democracy. (An exception that will not be discussed here was National Socialist Germany.) These long-standing democratic traditions were an advantage over the other European states. The liberal pluralism that characterized these political systems was based upon a high degree of interest articulation and mobilization. The various forms of political and economic participation were extended and expanded in the course of the century without fundamentally changing capitalist structures. In general, the socioeconomic developmental pattern of western Europe was marked by democratic, socially integrative elements, which also promoted economic development.

As in northern Europe, a close relationship between agricultural modernization and industrialization existed in western Europe, although there was a contrast between those countries and regions where agricultural modernization occurred earlier and those where it occurred later at an accelerated place. In general, western Europe was able very early on to develop agrarian structures that over a long period of time established the foundation not only for agrarian development but for industrial development as well. Even in the twentieth century western European agriculture provided the strongest impulses for modernization; it gave up the greatest number of workers to industry and achieved the highest levels of productivity as well as the most favorable production results.

Whereas in the other regions of Europe real industrialization began only at the end of the nineteenth century, it had started one hundred years earlier in some areas of western Europe; during the intervening period western Europe had supplied the rest of the world with industrial products. Even if individual western European countries followed different paths and were regionally quite dissimilar in structure, at the end of the nineteenth century western Europe was clearly the industrial heartland for the European continent, and ultimately of the world. Near the end of the twentieth century this is no longer the case. Those areas once on the periphery of the European world economy gained in economic strength and emancipated themselves; Japan rose to be one of the world's leading industrial nations, and other non-European countries also industrialized. Above all, at the beginning of the century the United States replaced western Europe as the industrial great power of the world. The characteristic economic elements of the western European development path should therefore be brought out not only with respect to the other regions of Europe but also with respect to non-European industrialized countries.

A lasting feature of the western European development path followed from its early industrial world dominance, namely a long phase in which the secondary sector was the most important employer in the work force. Only in western Europe did this phase last over half a century—from the early 1900s to the 1960s. In all non-European countries with a comparable level of development, the tertiary sector came immediately after the primary sector as the most important area of employment, and in those European regions that industrialized later the phase of industrial dominance was shorter and less pronounced. The "deindustrialization" of the occupational structure that began in the 1960s did lead to the service sector's becoming predominant in the economies of western Europe, but the differences with respect to economies elsewhere remained. Within the industrial sector, the delay in structural transformation is striking in comparison to the United States. Both regions had approximately the same industrial profile at the beginning of the century; in the United States this profile continued to change rapidly, whereas in western Europe a degree of structural rigidity set in during the interwar years that broke up only after the Second World War. Compared with North America one can thus speak of a degree of intersectoral over-industrialization and intrasectoral backwardness in western European industry.

At least some of the reasons for this contrast point to further peculiarities of the western European development path. From the nineteenth century on North America took the path of capital-intensive, laborsaving industrialization associated with rapid advances in productivity; western Europe followed the path of comparatively labor-intensive methods, with correspondingly slower rises in productivity. Whereas western Europe and the United States at the end of the nineteenth century had roughly equal levels of productivity, western Europe fell far behind in the first half of the twentieth century and was only partially able to recover its position after the Second World War. The fruitful circular relationship between the rapid growth of both production and productivity, which stimulates general economic and especially industrial structural change and brings about laborsaving industrialization, can be set in train and kept working only if a great deal of capital is invested. From the later nineteenth century to the Second World War not only was the rate of investment higher in the United States than in western Europe, but capital intensity also rose faster there. Only after the Second World War were the national economies of western Europe able to achieve higher rates of increase and catch up in part with the American economy. The lag in western European productivity is attributable, in part, to the lower rates of investment, for technical progress requires capital. The large technological gaps that developed between western Europe and the United States in the course of the twentieth century also emerged for the simple reason that in some areas western European industry was not so innovative as American industry. Thus, a further characteristic of the western European model of development, at least in the first half of the century, was a relatively low level of preparedness to innovate.

One cannot speak of an autonomous western European political path since no clear distinction can be drawn with respect to northern Europe. The development of corporative social welfare structures was not so pronounced as in Scandinavia, but here too an important element of social-oriented democracy was an interventionist social and economic policy, which assumed an ever greater role in shaping, guiding, and controlling the social and economic system. Although particularly strong interventionist episodes occurred during the two world wars, ultimately intervention increased more or less steadily throughout the century up to the 1970s. The objective of this state interventionism was to insert a degree of social security into the pure economism of the capitalist system, to ameliorate its functional deficiencies without diminishing the system's capability and productivity. On the one hand, the increased intervention of the state expressed the growing organizational complexity of highly industrialized economic systems whose capacity for self-regulation was declining; in some areas malfunctions were associated with such high costs that purely market regulation of economic decisions was out of the question. On the other hand, it expressed altered constellations of social power; the workers' movement and its political parties could push through reforms, and the ruling groups were forced to compromise.

In the 1970s the century's second world economic crisis was thus associated not only with a second paradigmatic shift in social and economic policy—from Keynesianism to austerity—but also with a shift in the social balance of power. External economic policy looked somewhat different. The traditional field of intervention in the later nineteenth century, tariff and trade policy, was expanded up until the Second World War, after which it was cut back—or, in other words, liberalized. Increased domestic economic management and liberal external economic policy became during the second half of the twentieth century further characteristics of western European development.

Postscript: Europe towards the End of the Twentieth Century

In January 1986, after eight years of negotiation, Spain and Portugal joined the EEC, thereby raising the Community's membership from ten to twelve countries and its population from 275 to 321 million. Under the stimulus of this new expansion, the Community's Council of Ministers concluded the Single European Act, which amended the original treaties to establish new priorities and to facilitate policy-making. The act, formally implemented in July 1987, reaffirmed the goal of a European Union but went beyond previous pious declarations of principle to provide a concrete program with an attached time limit. Article 8A stipulated that "the Community shall adopt measures with the aim of progressively establishing the internal market over a period expiring on 31 December 1992 . . . The internal market shall comprise an area without internal frontiers in which the free movement of goods, persons, services and capital is ensured . . . " Formal tariffs between the member countries of the EEC have not existed for some time, but inter-Community traffic is still inhibited by a thick web of red tape and national regulations. To achieve this ambitious goal of a single internal market, some three hundred non-tariff barriers presently in-hibiting free movement must be eliminated through harmonization or outright removal; these range from labelling and content requirements on consumer goods to levels of taxation—especially the level of value-added tax (VAT)—currency restrictions, and border police controls against illegal immigration and drug trafficking.

For the individual citizens of EEC countries, the creation of a truly free internal market could bring many tangible benefits. The virtual abolition of controls on internal borders of the Community should make personal travel between countries easier, faster, and cheaper. It should also result in a wider range of consumer goods at lower prices by reducing shipping charges through the elimination of costly waiting time for border clearances and by preventing the stoppage of foodstuffs and other goods at national borders on the spurious grounds that they do not meet specific national health, safety, or labelling standards. The full recognition of national diplomas will mean that qualified professionals could practice in any country of the Community with language being the only real barrier. The creation of a single market for financial services will enable citizens of member countries to open a bank account, contract a loan, or invest capital anywhere in the Community. Similarly, businesses will be able to expand more easily on a European-wide scale, in part because the member states have agreed to open large public contracts—those worth more than 5.5 million dollars—without prejudice to bidding by any company based within the Community. Finally, the harmonization of standards for broadcasting and telecommunications should not only promote cultural exchange and a greater sense of European cultural unity but also enable European high-tech developers to pool technical expertise and resources in order to compete more effectively with their giant American and Japanese rivals.

In spite of the scepticism of many observers and the strong opposition of the present British government to such controversial proposals as a European Central Bank and an eventual common European currency, the campaign for "l'Europe sans frontières" has been moving ahead steadily and has become a domestic political football in many countries, with rival political parties arguing over who can better prepare the country to meet the challenge of 1992. At its meeting in Hannover in June 1988 the Community's Council of Ministers declared that the agenda for 1992 was already one-third completed. The potential consequences of the creation of a single economic unit larger than either the United States or the Soviet Union are enormous for Europe and for the rest of the world. Fears that a "Fortress Europe" might restrict access to its market by surrounding itself with higher tariffs have been expressed in the United States, Japan, and the EFTA countries. Community leaders have denied this possibility and argue that, on the contrary, the projected integration will increase international trade overall by stimulating European economic growth. The achievement of the EEC's full internal market in 1992 could even lead to the dissolution of EFTA and thus end the thirty-year division of Western Europe into two trading areas. Both Austria and Norway have indicated that they would consider applying for full membership in the EEC in the near future, and Switzerland and Sweden are negotiating special associated relationships with the EEC.

No doubt, the large scale of internal free trade represented by 1992 will bring great opportunities to big business in general, especially to large European multinationals such as Olivetti, Philips, and Siemens. Whether and how soon the new internal market can overcome the mounting "Eurosclerosis" of the last decade—rigid labor and management practices, high social overhead costs, regional economic imbalances, and persistently high unemployment averaging 11 percent of the work force—remains unclear. And just how much real benefit the individual European will derive from the new mobility and European-wide competition is, of course, also unknown. The boundaries produced by cultural-linguistic differences as well as by the different national and regional paths of socioeconomic development outlined earlier cannot be easily overturned by a politically decreed unified market alone. On the other hand, long-term trends over the course of the twentieth century have generally encouraged the economic, and to a lesser degree the social, integration of Western Europe. To the extent that the European Community's project of a single European market in 1992 reflects and builds on these trends, it will succeed.

Foretelling future developments is a precarious undertaking for the historian in the best of circumstances. Predicting the course of change in Communist Europe is well-nigh impossible. But one thing is clear: the wasting malaise noted earlier in Eastern European economies and societies has continued into the second half of the 1980s. External indebtedness has risen further; production has fallen short of plan targets; inflation and unemployment have emerged openly; levels of productivity have fallen further behind those of capitalist Western Europe. Moreover, political unrest has mounted in several countries, setting off severe governmental crises in Poland and Yugoslavia in the second half of 1988. The economic remedies being prescribed have a familiar ring: reduction of central planning and increased use of market-oriented mechanisms in the socialist economy. As earlier, Hungary is playing the leading role in promoting this market socialism. Under new political leadership since May 1988, it has increased the number of products and services whose prices are determined by supply and demand, enlarged the scope of private enterprises, and even allowed the formation of independent trade unions. As before, the Hungarian remedy has not been adopted by all state socialist countries; the German

Democratic Republic, Czechoslovakia, and especially Rumania have rejected it as unnecessary and inappropriate.

In dramatic contrast to its attitude in the 1960s and 1970s, the Communist party of the Soviet Union has now itself taken up similar reform measures. The policies promoted by President Gorbachev and his supporters since achieving power in 1985 aim at a radical reorganization of the increasingly moribund Soviet economy by loosening the dictates of central economic planning, establishing market-oriented mechanisms, and increasing the individual responsibility of both managers and workers. Gorbachev's programmatic slogans of *glasnost* (openness) and *perestroika* (restructuring) have captured popular imagination in both West and East. Whether they will succeed in overcoming the social, economic, and political "mummification" that has gripped most of Eastern Europe since the late 1970s is still very much an open question.

Suggestions for Further Reading

The social and economic history of twentieth-century Europe is a vast subject and draws on research conducted in several disciplines, most notably history, economics, sociology, and political science. The following bibliography is intended as a selective introductory guide to the secondary literature on the topics and countries covered in the text. It focuses on general topical or national surveys in English but also includes some major works in German and French. For more specialized references the reader should consult the bibliographies of the relevant works. Periodical literature can be located by consulting *Historical Abstracts* (1952–), *International Political Science Abstracts* (1951–), *Sociological Abstracts* (1952–), *Journal of Economic Literature* (1963–), as well as the *Public Affairs Information Service Bulletin* (1915–). Convenient summaries of current events in individual countries are contained in the *Annual Register of World Events* (1758–), *Keesing's Contemporary Archives* (1931–), and the *Europa Year Book* (1959–); for current news the most consistently informative and readily available sources are *The Economist* (London), *The Times* (London), *The Financial Times* (London), *Le Monde* (Paris), and *The International Herald Tribune* (Paris). The basic socioeconomic statistics for European countries in the nineteenth and twentieth centuries are contained in Brian R. Mitchell, *European Historical Statistics, 1750–1975* (2nd ed., London: Macmillan, 1981); Peter Flora et al., *State, Economy, and Society in Western Europe, 1815–1975: A Data Handbook* (2 vols., Frankfurt: Campus Verlag, 1983–87); and Paul S. Shoup, *East European and Soviet Data Handbook* (New York: Praeger, 1981). These publications also list the most important national statistical series. In the course of the twentieth century, international organizations—such as the League of Nations, the International Labour Organization, the United Nations, the Organization for Economic Cooperation and Development, and the European Community—have assumed an ever larger role in the gathering, analyzing, and publishing of social and economic data and studies. Their publications have the advantage of multinational coverage and are usually more easily accessible than those issued by individual countries; specific citations of some of the most useful volumes and series can be found in the sources for the graphs and tables in this volume.

General

Aldcroft, Derek H. *From Versailles to Wall Street, 1919–1929*. History of the World Economy in the Twentieth Century, vol. 3. Berkeley: University of California Press, 1977.

———— *The European Economy, 1914–1980*. London: Croom Helm, 1982.

Archer, Margaret S., and Salvador Giner, eds. *Contemporary Europe: Class, Status and Power*. London: Weidenfeld and Nicolson, 1971.

———— *Contemporary Europe: Social Structures and Cultural Patterns*. London: Routledge and Kegan Paul, 1978.

Armstrong, Philip, Andrew Glyn, and John Harrison. *Capitalism since World War II: The Making and Breakup of the Great Boom*. London: Fontana, 1984.

Badham, R. J. *Theories of Industrial Society*. London: Routledge and Kegan Paul, 1986.

Barou, Yves, and Bernard Keizer. *Les grandes économies: Etats-Unis, Japon, Allemagne fédérale, France, Royaume-Uni, Italie*. Rev. ed. Paris: Seuil, 1988.

Berend, Iván T., and György Ránki. *The European Periphery and Industrialization, 1780–1914*. Translated by Eva Palmai. Studies in Modern Capitalism. Cambridge: Cambridge University Press, 1981.

Beyme, Klaus von. *Political Parties in Western Democracies*. Translated by Eileen Martin. New York: St. Martin's Press, 1985.

Boltho, Andrea, ed. *The European Economy: Growth and Crises*. Oxford: Oxford University Press, 1982.

Castles, Stephen. *Here for Good: Western Europe's New Ethnic Minorities*. London: Pluto Press, 1984.

Cipolla, Carlo M., ed. *The Fontana Economic History of Europe*. Vol. 5, *The Twentieth Century*. Vol. 6, *Contemporary Economies*. Glasgow: Collins, 1976.

Council of Europe. *Population Decline in Europe: Implications of a Declining or Stationary Population*. London: E. Arnold, 1978.

Flora, Peter, ed. *Growth to Limits: The Western European Welfare States since World War II*. 5 vols. Berlin–New York: Walter de Gruyter, 1986–88.

Flora, Peter, and Arnold J. Heidenheimer, eds. *The Development of Welfare States in Europe and America*. New Brunswick, N.J.: Transaction Books, 1981.

Graubard, Stephen R., ed. *A New Europe?* Boston: Little, Brown, 1964.

Guillaume, Pierre, and Patrick Delfaud. *Nouvelle histoire économique*. Vol. 2, *Le XXe siècle*. Paris: A. Colin, 1976.

Habakkuk, H. J., and M. Postan, gen. eds. *The Cambridge Economic History of Europe*. Vol. 6, *The Industrial Revolution and After: Incomes, Population and Technological Change*. Edited by H. J. Habakkuk and M. Postan. Cambridge: Cambridge University Press, 1966. Vol. 7, *The Industrial Economies: Capital, Labour, and Enterprise*. Edited by Peter Mathias and M. Postan. Cambridge: Cambridge University Press, 1978.

Hardach, Gerd. *The First World War, 1914–1919*. History of the World Economy in the Twentieth Century, vol. 2. Berkeley: University of California Press, 1977.

Hawke, Geoffrey R. *Economics for Historians*. Cambridge: Cambridge University Press, 1980.

Heath, Anthony. *Social Mobility*. Glasgow: Fontana, 1981.

Hohenberg, Paul M., and Lynn Hollen Lees. *The Making of Urban Europe, 1000–1950*. Harvard Studies in Urban History. Cambridge, Mass.: Harvard University Press, 1985.

Kaelble, Hartmut. *Auf dem Weg zu einer europäischen Gesellschaft: Eine Sozialgeschichte Westeuropas, 1880–1980*. Munich: C. H. Beck, 1987.

Kellenbenz, Hermann, gen. ed. *Handbuch der europäischen Wirtschafts- und Sozialgeschichte*. Vol. 5, *Europäische Wirtschafts- und Sozialgeschichte von der Mitte des 19. Jahrhunderts bis zum Ersten Weltkrieg*. Edited by Wolfram Fischer. Stuttgart: Klett-Cotta, 1985. Vol. 6, *Europäische Wirtschafts- und Sozialgeschichte vom Ersten Weltkrieg bis zur Gegenwart*. Edited by Wolfram Fischer. Stuttgart: Klett-Cotta, 1987.

Kenwood, A. G., and A. L. Lougheed. *The Growth of the International Economy, 1820–1980*. London: Allen and Unwin, 1983.

Kindleberger, Charles P. *A Financial History of Western Europe*. London: Allen and Unwin, 1984.

——— *The World in Depression, 1929–1939*. History of the World Economy in the Twentieth Century, vol. 4. Rev. and enl. ed. Berkeley: University of California Press, 1986.

Knox, Paul L. *The Geography of Western Europe: A Socio-Economic Survey*. London: Croom Helm, 1984.

Krejci, Jaroslav, and Viteslav Velimsky. *Ethnic and Political Nations in Europe*. London: Croom Helm, 1981.

Léon, Pierre, ed. *Histoire économique et sociale du monde*. Vol. 5, *Guerres et crise, 1914–1947*. Vol. 6, *Le second XXe siècle, 1947 à nos jours*. Paris: A. Colin, 1977.

Lupri, Eugen, ed. *The Changing Position of Women in Family and Society: A Cross-National Comparison*. Leiden: E. J. Brill, 1984.

Maddison, Angus. *Phases of Capitalist Development*. Oxford: Oxford University Press, 1982.

Milward, Alan S. *War, Economy and Society, 1939–1945*. History of the World

Economy in the Twentieth Century, vol. 5. Berkeley: University of California Press, 1977.

Milward, Alan S., and S. B. Saul. *The Development of the Economies of Continental Europe, 1850–1914*. London: Allen and Unwin, 1977.

Mitterauer, Michael, and Reinhard Sieder. *The European Family*. Translated by Karla Oosterveen and Manfred Hörzinger. Chicago: University of Chicago Press, 1982.

Pollard, Sidney. *Peaceful Conquest: The Industrialization of Europe, 1760–1970*. Oxford: Oxford University Press, 1981.

Rostow, Walt W. *The World Economy: History and Prospect*. Austin, Texas: University of Texas Press, 1978.

Salt, John, and Hugh Clout, eds. *Migration in Post-War Europe: Geographical Essays*. Oxford: Oxford University Press, 1976.

Senghaas, Dieter. *The European Experience: A Historical Critique of Development Theory*. Translated by K. H. Kimmig. Leamington Spa: Berg, 1985.

Shonfield, Andrew. *Modern Capitalism: The Changing Balance of Public and Private Power*. Oxford: Oxford University Press, 1969.

Smith, Gordon. *Politics in Western Europe*. 4th ed. London: Heinemann, 1984.

Stearns, Peter. *European Society in Upheaval: Social History since 1750*. 2nd ed. New York: Collier-Macmillan, 1975.

Strasser, Hermann, and Susan C. Randall. *An Introduction to Theories of Social Change*. London: Routledge and Kegan Paul, 1981.

Tilly, Charles, ed. *The Formation of National States in Western Europe*. Princeton: Princeton University Press, 1975.

Tipton, Frank B., and Robert Aldrich. *An Economic and Social History of Europe, 1890–1939*. Baltimore: Johns Hopkins University Press, 1987.

——— *An Economic and Social History of Europe from 1939 to the Present*. Baltimore: Johns Hopkins University Press, 1987.

Van der Wee, Herman. *Prosperity and Upheaval: The World Economy, 1945–1980*. History of the World Economy in the Twentieth Century, vol. 6. Berkeley: University of California Press, 1985.

Woodruff, William. *The Impact of Western Man: A Study of Europe's Role in the World Economy, 1750–1960*. London: Macmillan, 1966.

Northern Europe

Denmark

Johansen, Hans Christian. *The Danish Economy in the Twentieth Century*. London: Croom Helm, 1986.

Jones, W. Glyn. *Denmark: A Modern History*. London: Croom Helm, 1986.

Finland

Kiljunen, Kimmo. "Finland in the International Division of Labor," in *Underdeveloped Europe: Studies in Core-Periphery Relations*. ed. D. Seers, B. Schaffer, and M.-L. Kiljunen. Hassocks: Harvester, 1979.
Kirby, D. G. *Finland in the Twentieth Century: The History and an Interpretation*. London: C. Hurst, 1979.

Norway

Bergh, T., et al. *Growth and Development: The Norwegian Experience, 1830–1980*. Oslo: Universitetsforlaget, 1980.
Hodne, Fritz. *The Norwegian Economy, 1920–1980*. London: Croom Helm, 1983.
Ramsøy, Natalie R., ed. *Norwegian Society*. Bergen: Universitetsforlaget, 1974.
Selbyg, Arne. *Norway Today: An Introduction to Modern Norwegian Society*. Oslo: Norwegian University Press, 1986.

Sweden

Childs, Marquis. *Sweden: The Middle Way on Trial*. New Haven: Yale University Press, 1980.
Erikson, Robert, and Rune Åberg. *Welfare in Transition: Living Conditions in Sweden, 1968 to 1981*. Oxford: Oxford University Press, 1986.
Himmelstrand, Ulf, et al. *Beyond Welfare Capitalism: Issues, Actors and Forces in Societal Change*. London: Heinemann, 1981.
Koblik, Steven, ed. *Sweden's Development from Poverty to Affluence, 1750–1970*. Translated by Joanne Johnson. Minneapolis: University of Minnesota Press, 1975.

Southern Europe

Greece

Freris, A. F. *The Greek Economy in the Twentieth Century*. London: Croom Helm, 1986.
McNeill, William H. *The Metamorphosis of Modern Greece since World War II*. Chicago: University of Chicago Press, 1978.
Mouzelis, Nicos. *Modern Greece: Facets of Underdevelopment*. London: Routledge and Kegan Paul, 1978.

Italy

Acquaviva, Sabino, and M. Santuccio. *Social Structure in Italy: Crisis of a System.* Translated by Colin Hamer. London: M. Robertson, 1976.

Hildebrand, George H. *Growth and Structure in the Economy of Modern Italy.* Cambridge, Mass.: Harvard University Press, 1965.

King, Russell. *The Industrial Geography of Italy.* New York: St. Martin's Press, 1985.

Pinto, Diana, ed. *Contemporary Italian Sociology: A Reader.* Cambridge: Cambridge University Press, 1981.

Rusconi, Gian Enrico, and Sergio Scamuzzi. "Italy Today: An Eccentric Society." *Current Sociology,* 29:1 (1981).

Portugal

Baklanoff, Eric N. *The Economic Transformation of Spain and Portugal.* New York: Praeger, 1978.

Mayer, Jean. "Regional Development in Portugal (1929–1977): An Assessment," in *Disparities in Economic Development since the Industrial Revolution,* ed. P. Bairoch and M. Lévy-Leboyer. London: Weidenfeld and Nicolson, 1981.

Robinson, Richard. *Contemporary Portugal.* London: Allen and Unwin, 1979.

Spain

Carr, Raymond, and Juan Pablo Fusi. *Spain: Dictatorship to Democracy.* 2nd ed. London: Allen and Unwin, 1981.

Harrison, Joseph. *The Spanish Economy in the Twentieth Century.* London: Croom Helm, 1985.

Lieberman, Sima. *The Contemporary Spanish Economy: An Historical Perspective.* London: Allen and Unwin, 1982.

Eastern Europe

General

Berend, Iván T., and György Ránki. *Economic Development in East-Central Europe in the Nineteenth and Twentieth Centuries.* New York: Columbia University Press, 1974.

Beyme, Klaus von. *Economy and Politics within Socialist Systems: A Comparison and Developmental Approach.* Translated by Barbara Evans and Eva Kahn-Sinrich. New York: Praeger, 1982.

Conner, Walter D. *Socialism, Politics, and Equality: Hierarchy and Change in*

Eastern Europe and the USSR. New York: Columbia University Press, 1979.

Drewnowski, J., ed. *The Crisis in East European Economies: The Spread of the Polish Disease*. London: Croom Helm, 1983.

Jackson, Marvin R., and John R. Lampe. *Balkan Economic History, 1550–1950*. Bloomington: Indiana University Press, 1982.

Kaser, Michael C., and E. A. Radice, eds. *The Economic History of Eastern Europe, 1919–1975*. Vol. 1, *Economic Structure and Performance between the Two Wars*. Vol. 2, *Interwar Policy, the War, and Reconstruction*. Vol. 3, *Institutional Change within a Planned Economy*. Oxford: Clarendon Press, 1986–87.

Kende, Pierre, and Zdenek Strmiska, eds. *Egalité et inégalités en Europe de l'Est*. Paris: Fondation Nationale des Sciences Politiques, 1984.

Lavigne, Marie. *Les économies socialistes soviétique et européennes*. 3rd ed. Paris: A. Colin, 1983.

Lovenduski, Joni, and Jean Woodall. *Politics and Society in Eastern Europe*. Bloomington: Indiana University Press, 1987.

Matejko, Alexander. *Social Change and Stratification in Eastern Europe*. New York: Praeger, 1974.

Rugg, Dean S. *Eastern Europe*. London: London University Press, 1985.

Smith, Alan H. *The Planned Economies of Eastern Europe*. London: Croom Helm, 1983.

Albania

Pano, Nicholas C. *Albania: Politics, Economy and Society*. London: F. Pinter, 1984.

Schnytzer, Adi. *Stalinist Economic Strategy in Practice: The Case of Albania*. Oxford: Oxford University Press, 1982.

Bulgaria

Dobrin, Bogoslav. *Bulgarian Economic Development since World War II*. New York: Praeger, 1973.

Feiwel, George. *Growth and Reforms in Centrally Planned Economies: Lessons of the Bulgarian Experience*. New York: Praeger, 1977.

Lampe, John H. *The Bulgarian Economy in the Twentieth Century*. London: Croom Helm, 1985.

Czechoslovakia

Kosta, Jiri. *Abriss der sozialökonomischen Entwicklung der Tschechoslowakei, 1945–1977*. Frankfurt: Suhrkamp, 1978.

Krejci, Jiri. *Social Change and Stratification in Postwar Czechoslovakia.* London: Macmillan, 1972.

Mamatey, Victor S. and Radomir Luza, eds. *A History of the Czechoslovak Republic, 1918–1948.* Princeton: Princeton University Press, 1973.

Stevens, John N. *Czechoslovakia at the Crossroads: The Economic Development of Communism in Postwar Czechoslovakia.* Boulder, Colo.: Westview, 1985.

German Democratic Republic

Childs, David. *The GDR: Moscow's German Ally.* London: Allen and Unwin, 1983.

———, ed. *Honecker's Germany.* London: Allen and Unwin, 1985.

Deutsches Institut für Wirtschaftsforschung Berlin. *Handbuch DDR-Wirtschaft.* 4th ed. Hamburg: Rowohlt, 1984.

Edwards, G. E. *GDR: Society and Social Institutions.* London: Macmillan, 1985.

Legters, Lyman H., ed. *The German Democratic Republic: A Developed Socialist Society.* Boulder, Colo.: Westview, 1978.

Hungary

Berend, Iván T., and György Ránki. *The Hungarian Economy in the Twentieth Century.* London: Croom Helm, 1985.

Ferge, Zsuzsa. *A Society in the Making: Hungarian Social and Societal Policy, 1945–75.* White Plains, N.Y.: M. E. Sharpe, 1979.

Heinrich, H. G. *Hungary: Politics, Economics and Society.* London: F. Pinter, 1986.

Janos, Andrew C. *The Politics of Backwardness in Hungary, 1825–1945.* Princeton: Princeton University Press, 1981.

Poland

Landau, Zbigniew, and Jerzy Tomaszewski. *The Polish Economy in the Twentieth Century.* Translated by Wojciech Roszkowski. London: Croom Helm, 1985.

Lane, David, and George Kolankiewicz, eds. *Social Groups in Polish Society.* London: Macmillan, 1973.

Leslie, R. F., ed. *The History of Poland since 1863.* Cambridge: Cambridge University Press, 1980.

Rumania

Gilberg, Trond. *Modernization in Rumania since World War II.* New York: Praeger, 1975.

Jowett, Kenneth, ed. *Social Change in Rumania, 1860–1940: A Debate on Development in a European Nation.* Berkeley: University of California Press, 1978.

Tsantes, Andras C., and Roy Pepper. *Rumania: The Industrialization of an Agrarian Economy under Socialist Planning.* Baltimore: Johns Hopkins University Press, 1979.

Turnock, David. *The Romanian Economy in the Twentieth Century.* London: Croom Helm, 1986.

Soviet Union

Kerblay, Basile. *Modern Soviet Society.* Translated by Rupert Sawyer. New York: Pantheon, 1983.

Littlejohn, Gary. *A Sociology of the Soviet Union.* New York: St. Martin's Press, 1984.

Munting, Roger. *The Economic Development of the USSR.* London: Croom Helm, 1983.

Nove, Alec. *The Soviet Economic System.* 3rd ed. London: Allen and Unwin, 1986.

Yugoslavia

Banac, Ivo. *The National Question in Yugoslavia: Origins, History, Politics.* Ithaca, N.Y.: Cornell University Press, 1984.

Jambrek, Peter. *Development and Social Change in Yugoslavia: Crises and Perspectives of Building a Nation.* Lexington, Mass.: D. C. Heath, 1975.

Prout, Christopher. *Market Socialism in Yugoslavia.* Oxford: Oxford University Press, 1985.

Singleton, Fred, and Bernhard Carter. *The Economy of Yugoslavia.* London: Croom Helm, 1983.

Western Europe

Austria

Arndt, Sven W. *The Political Economy of Austria.* Washington, D.C.: American Enterprise Institute, 1982.

Butschek, Felix. *Die österreichische Wirtschaft im 20. Jahrhundert.* Stuttgart: G. Fischer, 1985.

Fischer-Kowalski, Marina, and Josef Bucek, eds. *Lebensverhältnisse in Österreich: Klassen und Schichten im Sozialstaat.* Frankfurt: Campus, 1982.

Steiner, Kurt, ed. *Modern Austria.* Palo Alto, Calif.: Society for the Promotion of Science and Scholarship, 1981.

Belgium

Bartier, John, et al. *Histoire de la Belgique contemporaine, 1914–1970*. Brussels: Renaissance du Livre, 1975.
Baudhuin, Fernand. *Histoire économique de la Belgique, 1914–1968*. 3 vols. Brussels: E. Bruylant, 1946–70.
Riley, Raymond. *Belgium*. Folkestone, England: Dawson, 1976.

Federal Republic of Germany

Balfour, Michael. *West Germany: A Contemporary History*. New York: St. Martin's Press, 1982.
Childs, David, and Jeffrey Johnson. *West Germany: Politics and Society*. Rev. ed. London: Croom Helm, 1981.
Conze, Werner, and M. R. Lepsius, eds. *Sozialgeschichte der Bundesrepublik Deutschland: Beiträge zum Kontinuitätsproblem*. Stuttgart: Klett-Cotta, 1983.
Dahrendorf, Ralf. *Society and Democracy in Germany*. New York: Doubleday, 1966.
Hardach, Karl. *The Political Economy of Germany in the Twentieth Century*. Berkeley: University of California Press, 1980.
Krejci, Jiri. *Social Structure in Divided Germany*. London: Croom Helm, 1976.
Smith, Eric Owen. *The West German Economy*. London: Croom Helm, 1983.

France

Braudel, Fernand, and Ernest Labrousse, eds. *Histoire économique et sociale de la France*. Vol. 4, *L'ère industrielle (années 1880–années 1970)*. 3 parts. Paris: Presses Universitaires de France. 1979–83.
Caron, François. *An Economic History of Modern France*. Translated by Barbara Bray. New York: Columbia University Press, 1979.
Casanova, Jean-Claude, and Maurice Lévy-Leboyer, eds. *Histoire économique de la France, 1880–1980*. Paris: Presses Universitaires de France, 1987.
Haley, David. *Contemporary France: Politics and Society since 1945*. 2nd ed. London: Routledge and Kegan Paul, 1984.
Hough, John R. *The French Economy*. London: Croom Helm, 1982.
Lequin, Yves, ed. *Histoire des Francais XIXe–XXe siècles*. 3 vols. Paris: A. Colin, 1983–84.

Great Britain

Halsey, A. H. *Change in British Society*. 3rd ed. Oxford: Oxford University Press, 1986.

Marwick, Arthur. *British Society since 1945*. Harmondsworth, England: Penguin Books, 1982.

Matthews, R. C. O., C. H. Feinstein, and J. C. Odling-Smee. *British Economic Growth, 1856–1973*. Stanford: Stanford University Press, 1982.

Noble, Trevor. *Structure and Change in Modern Britain*. London: Batsford, 1981.

Pollard, Sidney. *The Development of the British Economy, 1914–1982*. 3rd ed. London: E. Arnold, 1983.

Royle, Edward. *Modern Britain: A Social History, 1750–1985*. London: E. Arnold, 1987.

Stevenson, John. *British Society, 1914–45*. Harmondsworth, England: Penguin Books, 1984.

Ireland

Brown, Terence. *Ireland: A Social and Cultural History, 1922–1985*. Glasgow: Collins, 1985.

Kennedy, Kieran A. *Economic Growth in Ireland: The Experience since 1947*. Dublin: Gill and Macmillan, 1975.

Meenan, James. *The Irish Economy since 1922*. Liverpool: Liverpool University Press, 1971.

Peillon, Michel. *Contemporary Irish Society: An Introduction*. Dublin: Gill and Macmillan, 1982.

Netherlands

Goudsblom, Johan. *Dutch Society*. New York: Random House, 1967.

Griffiths, R. T., ed. *The Economy and Politics of the Netherlands since 1945*. The Hague: M. Nijhoff, 1980.

Vries, Johan de. *The Netherlands Economy in the Twentieth Century, 1900–1970*. Assen: Van Gorcum, 1978.

Switzerland

Bergier, Jean-François. *Histoire économique de la Suisse*. Paris: A. Colin, 1983.

Luck, J. Murray, ed. *Modern Switzerland*. Palo Alto, Calif.: Society for the Promotion of Science and Scholarship, 1977.

Index